THE PENGUIN FILM REVIEW

11

THE PENGUIN
FILM REVIEW
1946-1949

Editorial Board: R. K. Neilson Baxter
Roger Manvell *and* H. H. Wollenberg

Executive Editor: Roger Manvell

A reprint with an introduction
and index by Roger Manvell

Volume II

ROWMAN AND LITTLEFIELD
TOTOWA, NEW JERSEY

THE PENGUIN FILM REVIEW
first published in nine parts between
1946 and 1949 by
Penguin Books Limited
Harmondsworth Middlesex England

This edition published in the United States 1978 in two volumes by
Rowman and Littlefield
81 Adams Drive,
Totowa, New Jersey

ISBN 0–8476–6029–x

Printed in England by The Scolar Press Limited
Ilkley, Yorkshire LS29 8JP

THE PENGUIN
FILM
REVIEW

6

CONTRIBUTORS INCLUDE
Thorold Dickinson – Lotte H. Eisner
Elizabeth M. Harris – Cecil Hepworth – Roger Manvell
Guy Morgan – Andrew Miller Jones

ONE SHILLING AND SIXPENCE

THE PENGUIN
FILM REVIEW

Editorial Board : R. K. Neilson Baxter
Roger Manvell *and* H. H. Wollenberg
Executive Editor : Roger Manvell

6

PENGUIN BOOKS

LONDON *and* NEW YORK

1948

First Published April, 1948

PENGUIN BOOKS LIMITED

Harmondsworth, Middlesex, England

MADE AND PRINTED IN GREAT BRITAIN

by Hazell, Watson & Viney, Ltd.

London and Aylesbury

CONTENTS

★

EDITORIAL   *p.* 7

CRITICAL SURVEY   Matthew Norgate   11

CASH DOWN AND NO CREDIT
                                Guy Morgan   15

TYPE-CASTING SCREEN-WRITERS
                                Martin Field   29

THOSE WERE THE DAYS   Cecil Hepworth   33

ROUND THE WORLD'S STUDIOS
                            H. H. Wollenberg   40

TELEVISION AND CINEMA
                        Andrew Miller Jones   45

THE GERMAN FILMS OF FRITZ LANG
                            Lotte H. Eisner   53

INDIAN SPRING   Thorold Dickinson   62

THE NATIVE FILMS OF MEXICO
                        Maria Rosa Oliver   73

THE FUNCTION OF THE SPECIALISED CINEMA
                        Elizabeth M. Harris   80

WHO ARE THOSE TECHNICIANS?
                            John Shearman   87

BRITISH FILM MUSIC   John Huntley   91

6 CONTENTS

DIALOGUE FOR STAGE AND SCREEN
Clifford Leech *p.* 97

ACTORS OF THE SOVIET CINEMA
Catherine de la Roche 104

THE POETRY OF THE FILM   Roger Manvell 111

STATISTICS   H. H. Wollenberg 125

BOOKS ABOUT FILMS
Reviews edited by R. K. Neilson Baxter 126

EDITORIAL

*

FOR a good many months now the Cinema has provided front-page news for the Press and subjects for lively discussion in Parliament and in public. There is, for instance, the new British Quota Act; there are the dollar-saving taxation measures; there is the United Nations World Trade Charter, with its clause referring to national film quotas, claiming equal access for films of all nations under conditions of *strictly commercial competition* to all the theatres of all other nations after permitting national quotas of screen-time for the protection of native films.

It all sums up to a rather complex and intricate subject, and controversial advocates of the various and frequently opposing interests have been wrangling hard and have brought their cases before the public. It all indicates that the Cinema obviously has reached a cross-roads. It appears that the real issue behind all those problems boils down to the one fundamental question: is film to be regarded, in the first instance, as a commercial or as a cultural product? Should film come within the sphere of trade and business, or should film, on principle, rank with the other media of art, information, and entertainment, and be handled accordingly? Mankind has to decide which way to turn. Not business interests, but the inestimable influence of the Cinema upon human society and civilisation – to the good or to the bad – should, we feel, be the determining factor in shaping policy and development.

It is therefore encouraging that certain trends have lately been in evidence of a cultural as against a commercial approach in the international scene. They deserve recognition and support. There is, for instance, in the specialised field of documentary, the emergence of a world union. There is the movement towards a world federation of cine-technicians, a movement in which Great Britain plays a distinguished part through the Association of Cine-Technicians. It provides, among other tasks, for an exchange of the creative forces in film-making from one country to another. And then there are the expanding and meritorious activities of UNESCO. By mentioning UNESCO, the fundamental issue in question becomes even clearer. Should matters of the Cinema primarily come under the jurisdiction of UNITO (the United Nations International Trade Organisation) or in the province of UNESCO (the United Nations Educational, Scientific and Cultural Organisation)? In other words, should they be regarded internationally as a subject of trade policy or of cultural policy? We unequivocally take the latter viewpoint.

Responsible people all over the world have become more and more aware of this situation, mainly in Europe, in Latin America, and even in the United States, where the film industrialists, using all their considerable means of influence, are the real champions of the business approach as the guiding international principle.

The power and prosperity of the American film industry are due primarily to its being organised on a free-trade market of 120 million.

If other countries earnestly wish to safeguard their film production as a cultural responsibility, they, too, will have to think of putting their production efforts on an economically firm and large foundation. Here we think, in the first instance, of the countries of Europe among which a common film policy could be devised; perhaps, to begin with, between the Western European states connected with the Marshall plan, but with a resolute view to future expansion. This way an area of 200 million people could be secured for the showing of their national film products. The unhealthy conditions of a more or less permanent crisis in almost all film-producing countries could thus be overcome. The future of their creative forces would be secure if such an area for the exploitation of their products could be organised.

By creating a union in film economics, the conditions for cultural progress in the various national production efforts would be created. A cultural film policy could be evolved.

For this purpose a plan should be set into operation by a system of co-production and film exchange, so that resources, studio facilities, talent, manpower, and screen-time could be harnessed for the greatest advantage of the combined film efforts of those nations. Their dependence on Hollywood supplies could be lessened to a considerable degree. Their production standards could be developed on the basis of a large and secure market. Production costs could be adapted to its potentialities, and even film finance could be co-ordinated.

In Britain, those responsible should turn their eyes to these opportunities.

FORTHCOMING

Among the articles in Penguin Film Review VII will be some personal notes by Arletty called *Strictly Entre Nous*, an article by Harold Salemson on Capra, Catherine de la Roche on the new cult of realism, Clement Cave on a new policy for newsreels, Charles Crichton (director of *Hue and Cry*) on children in films, and articles on the Marx Brothers by Richard Rowland, and on *Monsieur Verdoux* by Roger Manvell. We have been asked by Inter-State Films, Ltd, to point out that the dubbing of the Mexican *Maria Candelaria* referred to in E. Harris's article in our last issue on the Palestinian cinema was American and not English.

Penguin Film Review can be supplied on subscription at the rate of seven shillings for four successive issues, post free. Orders, accompanied by remittance, can be placed either with your usual bookseller or with the publishers direct (Penguin Books Ltd., Harmondsworth, Middlesex).

CRITICAL SURVEY

MATTHEW NORGATE

*

IT is the business of a moving picture to move. In the early days this primary function was fulfilled simply by doing on the screen those things which cannot be done on the stage, and trick photography vied with continual change of scene to attract a public to the new form of dramatic entertainment. In time trick photography gave birth to the cameraman's technique, the ability to shoot a scene in the most effective way, whether the camera conspired to deceive the eye of the spectator or merely guided his attention where it was demanded by each individual shot in its relation to the whole film. Trick photography as an attraction in itself was soon played out, but the need for continual change of scene has persisted, though the present-day mobility of the camera means that a single shot can stay on the screen longer than it could without becoming tedious.

A major milestone in this technical evolution was of course the invention of the tracking shot, and in no film was its use more notable than in *The Blue Angel*. It was used here most sparingly; if my memory, aided by the film's recent revival at the Everyman, is accurate, it was used just twice. Once half-way through the film, when Jannings had just been sacked from his professorship for his association with the cabaret singer, and the camera slowly receded from him as he sat at his desk, wallowing in despair; and again at the end when, down and out, he had made his way back to his old haunts, and sat once more at the desk no longer his, to die. The effect of this second shot depended of course upon one's recollection of the earlier one, and the reprise provided the most perfectly dramatic moment

11

of the film, appealing to the emotions through the eye, and doing it as it could be done in no other medium.

What happens to-day? I submit that the coinage is debased, that cameramen have become so expert, so far advanced from the stage at which they harped endlessly on camera angles, that the movement – and placing – of the camera tends to defeat its own ends, and the most uncritical spectator is forced to become conscious of the camera instead of being cajoled into forgetting its very existence. Who but could pause to wonder how on earth the whirlpool sequence in *I Know Where I'm Going* was done? Who could escape a wholly adventitious nervousness when watching Burgess Meredith tottering at the top of the fire-escape in *Mine Own Executioner*, solicitous not only for the safety of the actor (rather than the character the actor was playing – another fly in the ointment of technical bravura) but also for that of the camera crew thus forced into one's consciousness? By all means don't let us become static, but let us use the cameraman's skill without exploiting it.

But this is only one kind of movement. The cinema must also move with the times, and in Britain this means that we must regain our prestige of the war years, both as to quality and quantity of output. With American imports drying up, and a new quota act on the way, we have suddenly much more screen time to fill; and we have given the native filmgoer a taste for better pictures of which we are now in danger of starving him. We spent a quarter of a million on *Anna Karenina* (so it is said) and heaven knows what on *An Ideal Husband*. No harm in that if our less ambitious productions are worthy; but many of them are not. 'You can't photograph a man's mind', a certain producer is on record as having said; you can, of course, and you *must*. Critics have inveighed against the cult of violence in films from both sides of the Atlantic, and rightly so. But if violence, for which an appetite has been created, is to go, it must be replaced by something else if the box-office is not to suffer, and the answer to that is films like *Crossfire* and *Hue* and Cry and Take My Life, which did not cost the earth to make and in which violence is incidental and legitimate and not the be-all and end-all of an industry determined to play safe and get its money back because others got theirs the same way.

I should have liked to get through this article without mentioning finance, which is not a critic's business. But Mr Rank's announcement that his major productions cost him a loss of £2,000,000 over five or six years cannot go unnoticed, especially when one remembers that one of these was Cæsar and Cleopatra, which displaced from his war-time studios something like six unmade films that might have turned the loss into something more like a profit. One is accustomed to point to the French cinema as a lesson in economy to the film financiers, but in France the cinema scene is at present a sorry one. Quality is largely sustained, and extravagance is still kept down, but thanks to an agreement signed by M. Blum and Mr Byrnes soon after the liberation, the production of feature films has dropped in quantity by over thirty per cent since 1946 and France's cinemas are now flooded by American films at the expense of the French film industry. No wonder that there is a clamour in France for a revision of the Blum-Byrnes agreement and for more Government support. So the lesson we must now learn from France is that the home product must be fostered, and for that we can never expect such an opportunity as awaits us to-day if we will but grasp it. That opportunity lies both with our Government and our film industry.

The cinema is always dying and always being reborn. The latest renascence is in Italy, if one may so far generalise from the three fine Italian films shown recently in London – Open City, To Live in Peace and Shoe Shine. Each of these has the vigour and the integrity of the work of true artists, expressing the spirit of a country free at last, making full use of material so to speak on the directors' doorstep, imbuing every studio shot (except at the end of Shoe Shine) with that feeling of absolute actuality which the latter-day British cinema seems to find so hard to achieve. Here, in a sense, Hollywood manages better than we do, but that is because we have been taught for so long and so consistently to look upon America as the sort of place Hollywood, except on rare truth-telling occasions, has shown us. This, however, puts a premium upon truth of character as distinct from truth of atmosphere, and Hollywood tends less and less to face æsthetic facts.

If Hollywood has imposed upon its customers an atmospheric convention, Wardour Street tries on a new convention in every third film, by which I mean that, having relatively little world market, our producers seem to think it unnecessary to adopt any but an opportunist policy in such matters. So Miss Lockwood goes on playing wicked ladies, Mr Granger gets fat parts because they're fat parts, Dennis Price is killed off in the third reel. Dump them down anywhere you like, but they still look and sound the same, whether they're gipsies or farmers or thugs or ladies and gentlemen. To hell with atmosphere, we've got to cut down on something else besides scripts; where does atmosphere get you, anyway?

But I am not altogether gloomy. I think British films have been acted better lately, and I have noticed no deterioration in American acting, though now and then one detects a hint of despair among the more intelligent players. And it seems reasonable, if stars must be fabricated, to promote Jean Simmons and Kieron Moore, both of whom have now proved that they are not directors' dummies. The only Hollywood star, old or new, who has made me sit up and take notice lately was Chaplin, whose own performance in *Monsieur Verdoux* was in such marked contrast to his 'traditional' direction. As a director, his methods seem to have changed little since his early days; as an actor, they don't need to. If only Charlie would come off it, and let the underdog be championed by implication once more, and pension off the technicians on the Chaplin lot, then what a film we might see. But in *Verdoux* heaven knows he didn't overwork his cameraman.

CASH DOWN
AND NO CREDIT

THE CONTRIBUTION OF SCREEN-WRITERS
TO FILM PRODUCTION

GUY MORGAN

*

As Honorary Secretary of the Screen-writers' Association, I recently organised a Screen-writers' Questionnaire with a view to charting for the first time a little-known and recently developed literary territory that is popularly believed by those outside it to be an exclusive Eldorado.

Copies of the Questionnaire were sent to 160 full members of the Association, whose statutory qualification for membership is to have received at least two writing credits on feature films.

The project was a shot in the dark. On the one hand, writers, being by disposition occupational individualists, are notoriously averse to form-filling; on the other hand, as a class they might be expected to be articulate in the expression of their complaints and their anathemas.

The results were as anticipated. Fifty completed forms were returned, and proved relatively valueless statistically, but colourful and explicit (in some cases to several additional pages of forceful typescript), on the problems, pitfalls, and perversions of their craft.

If this article, which is a summary of their views, seems unduly querulous, it is not because screen-writers habitually view themselves as the Cæsar's wife of film production, but because they were specifically invited to list the factors adverse to successful screen-writing.

The fact that only fifty replies were received was not in itself surprising; this number probably represents the total of writers actively engaged at any time in writing British films. For the personnel of screen-writing is made up of a comparatively small core of experienced regulars, swollen by migratory workers from the professions of novelist, dramatist, radio-writer, journalist, and producer's wife.

As I am dealing mainly in this article with the opinions of screen-writers more experienced than myself, it would be as well to define, as far as is statistically possible, the class from whom the symposium is drawn.

Of the fifty screen-writers who replied, twenty-seven described themselves as whole-time screen-writers, twenty-three as part-time screen-writers. Forty-three of them were also engaged in other literary work during the year, in the following over-lapping categories : writing plays (30), writing novels (22), writing for radio (5), journalism (5).

During 1946, forty-three were actively engaged in writing feature films, four in writing short films, and three did not write at all. Of those writing, twenty-six were employed under full-time contract, and twenty-one on individual assignments which provided an average of four months' employment during the year.

Between them they had earned screen credits for 134 original screen stories, 515 screen plays or adaptations, and 159 short films, during an average of twelve years spent writing for the screen. Thus the unanimity with which they voice their grievances carries the authority of experience and merits close examination by all those who have the power of remedy.

This unanimity was most marked in the replies to the most leading question : 'What, in your opinion, are the practices of current film production that present the greatest obstacle to successful screen-writing, or most adversely affect the prestige of screen-writers?'

The replies fell under eight general headings:

(1) The lack of publicity or reference by critics to the writer of a film (21).

(2) The employment of too many writers on one script (20).

(3) The unlimited dictation by producer, director, etc., in the writing of a script, and subsequent alterations without the writer's knowledge or consent (16).

(4) Lack of encouragement for original screen stories; preference for adaptations of successes in other media (10).

(5) Lack of clear run-through with a production; absence of the writer from the floor during shooting (9).

(6) Lack of sufficient liaison between writer and director (9).

(7) The habit of calling in well-known writers of other media irrespective of whether they are experienced in film technique (8).

(8) Lack of recognised training for screen-writers (7).

I propose to deal with each general heading in turn (though the majority are interrelated), in the hope that a discussion of these topics may give the layman, the would-be screen-writer, and even some producers, a better understanding of the problems that every screen-writer has to face.

1. 'Screen play by Uncle Tom Cobbleigh and All' – Who cares?

It is ironic that the screen-writer's greatest grievance should be, not against the technical manhandlers of his script, but against fellow writers – the critics.

The film critics' habitual lack of mention or assessment of the screen-writer's part in film production is held by the majority of screen-writers to be the greatest single limiting factor to the proper function of their craft.

It is not such a small matter as might at first appear; it is a segment of a vicious circle.

Because the critics give little or no credit to the writing of a film, the producer sees no point in publicising the writer, arguing that the public do not care. In his paid publicity the producer gives the impression that his stars, his director, and he himself are responsible for any success achieved by the film. The critics, impressed and uninformed, consequently disregard the writer. As a result, the writer lacks the prestige and authority in film production to protect the integrity of his own work, which in many respects is more fundamental than the work of star, director, editor, or producer.

This may seem a sweeping claim, but in screen-writing, as in every other form of literary effort, 'in the beginning was the word'; for all the coloured wrappings of star personalities, costly production, catch-penny advertising, block-booking, and theatre ownership, the profits ultimately depend on honest artistic endeavour, and the basic commodity peddled is one individual's perception of truth.

There is a limited number of directors who can be counted on to make a good film out of a good script; there is a larger number of directors who can make an indifferent film out of a good script; but there are few if any directors who can make a good film out of a bad script. In fact, it is doubtful if all the directing, acting, editing, and producing in the world can make a good film if the writing is bad. Everyone knows this to be true of stage plays, but few seem to appreciate that it is also true of films.

Here is how a screen-writer, who is also a producer and who should therefore be in a position to see both sides of the fence, states the case:

'The writer's experience is that he is regarded as a necessary evil rather than as the maker of the blue-print from which the film is to be made, and without which nothing in a studio can even commence. The only exceptions to this rule are the playwrights and novelists with big names who are employed to write a script, and who, with remarkably few exceptions, are without the technical knowledge to do so.

'The consequence of this is that the actual script-writer is without prestige in the eyes of directors and producers, whose opinions, as first readers of the writer's work, become at once the opinion of the entire production machine. Except in his contract, the writer is discounted as a contributor to the final result. The classic example of this is to be found in the case of the recently exhibited film, *Odd Man Out*. I cannot claim to have read all the critiques of this film, but in the many I did read, all of which appeared in the national Press, in not one single instance was the script-writer mentioned; in one only did I find a reference to the writer of the novel (F. L. Green) or to the screen-writer who collaborated in translating it to the screen (R. C. Sherriff). The point here being made is that the script – the shooting script – was entirely forgotten as an item of importance.

'There is only one channel through which the prestige of the writer can be enhanced – that of the critics. It surely is remarkable that, even when the writer receives a solo credit for an original story and screen play, he is rarely mentioned in critiques. Until the critics realise the importance of his contribution to the film, his prestige will never be established. At the moment, generally speaking, he has none at all.

'There is only one way in which the writer can achieve personal recognition, and that is by becoming a writer-director, and when he does this, he is still forgotten as a writer: the script is again ignored.'

This complaint is not limited to screen-writers on this side of the Atlantic. It has been the basis of a long-standing feud between Hollywood screen-writers and New York critics, the most telling salvo in which was fired from Hollywood recently when they published a review of the novel *For Whom the Bell Tolls* as it might have been written by a New York film critic.

After praising by name the publisher, the printer, the compositor, the binder, and the proof-reader ('Joe Guggenheimer has turned in his best job to date, except for a misplaced comma on page fifty-eight'), it ended with a special tribute to the paper manufacturer 'whose wise choice of plain white for the paper did so much to offset the somewhat gloomy nature of the material'. There was no mention of the Author.

If this seems exaggerated, I could quote from many current film reviews, and practically from any written by the film critic of *The Times*. Take, for instance, his review of *Hue and Cry*, an original story and screen play by a single screen-writer (T. E. B. Clarke), who worked in close and equal collaboration with the director throughout production.

The Times critic wrote:

... the industry has a new director (and there are few of them) who has something to say and knows precisely how to tell it. The story he has to tell is a good one ... The story is simple enough, though he gives it all the painstaking and lively detail that a good adventure story should have. Scene after scene is brilliantly composed, with the dialogue always giving bite to what is merely conventional in the situation ...

There was no mention of a writer ever having been involved.

There is an historical reason for the lowly position occupied by the writer in film production. The writer came comparatively late into films. In the early days films were shot 'off the cuff' by the director, and scripts were no more than bald, uninspired lists of technical instructions following a crude dramatic formula of build-up and suspense. Little or no attempt was made to achieve visual interpretation of the subject in literary form ahead of shooting.

At first secretaries were all that were needed to record what was improvised in a day's shooting: writers were brought in later to help the director put down what *he* wanted. The tradition of the screen-writer being no more than a literary amanuensis still persists.

It is interesting to note that one Hollywood commentator recently attributed the improvement in British films to the 'British film industry's discovery of the writer'.

The Screen-writers' Association has long fought for greater publicity for the screen-writer, and has made a small initial step towards this end by obtaining the agreement of producers that writers' names shall always be used in paid studio advertising wherever the director's name is used, but it lies principally in the hands of the critics to redress the balance. I was a critic myself for five years, and I am just as much to blame.

Not all critics, however, ignore the fact that there can be no film without a script: for, as another screen-writer testifies, 'there is a pronounced tendency (both in the studio and the Press) to give all the credit for a good film to the producer and director, and all the blame for a bad film to the screen-writer'.

A familiar retort of critics is that authorship of screen plays is so often shared by so many writers and adapters that space alone forbids their mention and multiplicity of contribution confuses the credit. This leads to the second most frequent grievance:

2. *Too Many Cooks, or 'Hooray for a Fresh Mind!'*

There is a strange belief of many producers and directors that one writer can take over and improve another writer's story and characterisations with the facility of a plumber called in to finish off another plumber's work.

How often have screen-writers heard that favourite production knell – 'I think we should have a fresh mind on this'? It is the formula of mistrust by the non-creative producer in the creative writer he employs; the 'relay theory' of writing films, based on the assumption that Shaw, Coward, Shakespeare, Pinero, Molière, Uncle Tom Cobbleigh, Mrs Tom Cobbleigh and all, would inevitably write a greater screen play in collaboration or in relays than any one of them would have been capable of writing by himself; the pathetic belief that 'The Last Supper' would have been better if painted by nine artists, and that two people write better than one, and a football team better than two.

There is no doubt that this practice destroys any identity of style in the writing of a picture and is chiefly responsible for the disparity in the prestige enjoyed by the playwright and by the screen-writer. It has a pernicious effect on writers themselves, as each new writer assigned to the subject inevitably feels he must justify his contract by the extent of the alterations he makes.

The Screen-writers' Association has made considerable progress towards checking this evil by limiting the number of writers who may receive credit for a screen play to two, except in cases where a third writer's contribution amounts to 33 per cent of the script, and then only by mutual agreement between the three writers concerned.

3. 'Let's have an aria and an earthquake.'

The unlimited power of producers, directors, and other departments of the production machine to alter a writer's work, in many cases without consulting him, is a natural consequence of the writer's lack of prestige. No playwright suffers from the same disability.

When the screen-writer's script leaves his typewriter it usually passes into the hands of a conference, and it is the screen-writer's common experience that he finds himself on the outside of a circle, consisting of producer, director, casting director, art director, costing expert, production manager, and circuit-booker, with less say in the future of his story than any of them.

Though presumably the casting and set-designing are based on what he has written in his script, his opinion is rarely sought, and he finds himself as powerless to avert either an aria, an earthquake, or a happy ending, as he would be in real life. The survival of his original conception under such circumtances is as great as the miracle of St. Sebastian, who was pierced by a thousand arrows and survived.

It is simple for a writer to say that the scenes he wrote were beautiful and other people messed them up beyond recognition. There must be many times when a writer feels glad that he personally did not have the job of realising in production the scenes he wrote. He can, however, reasonably claim that it is part of his function to have some say in the making of a picture he writes, and that the practice of taking his script, switching him to a new assignment, turning his pages over to other writers, and making the film without consultation with any of them, is an outrageous dichotomy of an author's relationship to his own work.

The Screen-writers' Association believes that some system of payment of the screen-writer by royalties, giving him a share in the success or failure of the film he writes, would perhaps do more than anything to increase his say in film production.

4. *'No wonder British films are so good these days. Look at the screen-writers they've got : William Shakespeare and Charles Dickens.'* – American paper.

A writer-producer writes: 'As a producer I have found that little extra kudos is derived from making an original screen story, and that from a prestige point of view it is in fact more profitable to adapt classics to the screen. This is a dismal state of affairs, since the film future *ought* to depend for its life-blood on original creative writing direct for the screen.'

While British studios, as at present, are practically all producing only a few first-features per year, their preference in choice of subject-matter is heavily for the safety of the successful novel or play, with pre-sold audience appeal and publicity value, than for the risk of original material conceived in terms of the medium. Ready-made subjects from other media have to be re-orientated for filming, are often basically unsuitable, and much creative energy is wasted in their adaptation.

There is a persistent tendency to treat Screen and Stage as similar arts simply because they share the common ground of telling a story through visual dramatic action. They are, however, as completely different in technique and final artistic achievement as painting and sculpture, or music and dancing, and the hope of both lies in their divorce.

I paraphrase from a recent article by the stage and film producer, Rouben Mamoulian: To the two elements of the Stage – performance and audience – the Screen brings a third and most important element: the camera, which is itself both creator and ideal spectator.

While both mediums are basically emotional, the Stage, with its physical restrictions, its slower and steadier tempo, is better qualified to handle complicated ideas and thoughts, while the Screen is superbly equipped to deal with action and visual imagery of both everyday life and imaginative make-believe. Add to this the fact that a film, to be successful, must appeal to millions, while a play makes good even if it satisfies a select group of thousands, and that feelings can unite more people than can thoughts and intellectual premises.

The wide practice of transferring Stage plays to the Screen generally results in films that are inferior to the plays. This happens because while the intellectual texture of the play has been condensed and emaciated, no added emotional or visual values have been brought in to compensate. A play is a good play because it has been specifically written to fulfil the requirements of the stage. The better the play the more difficult it is to transfer to the Screen. Its essential architecture defeats the effective use of the camera. To use the camera for photographing a play is to play a piano with one finger.

The Screen has its own language and should write in it, and not depend on translations.

5. *'The Writer's place is at his typewriter.'*

This prevalent theory, which excludes the writer from other phases of production, is being killed slowly, and its demise has been speeded by the recent successes of writer-director and writer-producer combinations.

The argument for a greater share in production by the writer has been forcibly put by Jay Richard Kennedy, a Hollywood writer-producer, in an article in *The Screen Writer*.

He says: 'It is simple common-sense that the writer, and no-one but the writer, conceived and incubated an idea. He gave birth to it, raised it, visualised scenes designed to express this idea and created characters concerning whom, it is hoped, he developed certain passions. No matter what changes may take place from paper to film, no matter what valid additions or deletions may come about as a result of "kicking the material around", no matter how many re-writes take place, something has remained in that author as a result of this experience which, if he is still on his feet, gives him a lasting perspective regarding the scenes and characters that supplies him with knowledge concerning the dramaturgical pitfalls in the story, and instinct as to where, when, and how violence can be done to the story, characters, and scene design. This is part of his contribution which is not in the script.

'The studio has paid for it and then denies itself the opportunity of benefiting from it. His right to contribute some of the judgment born of the experience of writing the story must not depend on the common-sense or self-interest of the producer, but must be inherent in the terms of his employment. The playwright enjoys this status. To a more limited extent so does the novelist.

'Only by actual participation in daily shooting can the screenwriter learn the limitations of his art and how to overcome them'.

6. Writer and Director.

This has been dealt with in part above. It should be added that it is not enough that some studios have the intelligence to realise that the director and producer must work closely with the writer. So long as a fundamental difference in authority persists, when disagreement becomes basic, producer and director more often work on the writer, rather than with him, and if expedient, they work around him.

If, on the other hand, a writer wishes to devote himself exclusively to writing, then, in the best interests of the industry, he should not be penalised for this by being the lowliest participant in the decision-making end of film production.

The screen-writer seldom becomes a director solely for the sake of increased income. If he is a good enough writer, he can get this by writing, which as a form of occupation is more agreeable and less wearisome. Writers become directors because they find it is the only way they can ensure that their original conceptions reach the screen, and it is significant that the emergence of the writer-producer and writer-director in Britain coincides with the improvement in quality of British films.

Perhaps the ideal relationship in an essential partnership would be for the director to act as producer while the writer writes, and for the writer to act as producer while the director directs.

7. *The Big-name Theory.*

There is a prevalent belief in film production that a famous name in another literary medium must automatically make a good screen-writer and can therefore be called in to give advice over the head of a less famous but more experienced screen-writer. What perhaps is more dangerous to the industry is the complementary attitude of famous literary names who finance their more serious work by churning out film treatments which they frankly regard as a chore.

The shortage of writers trained in film production, and the great number of writers who regard training as unnecessary, raises perhaps the most serious question of all:

8. *'How can I learn to become a Screen-writer?'*

This is the question a secretary of the Screen-writers' Association must be prepared to answer most frequently, and it is the question that he finds most difficult.

The majority of the small band of experienced screen-writers in this country were trained in the Scenario Departments that existed before the war at B.I.P., Gaumont-British, Gainsborough, London Films, Ealing, and Warners at Teddington. It may be added that half a dozen or more leading screen-writers in Hollywood graduated from the same schools, as well as our leading writer-directors and writer-producers.

Of late these departments have been reduced in numbers. During the war years only two such departments existed, and these on a very small scale. The central scenario department started by the Rank Organisation has recently been disbanded.

To-day most of the major producing companies have no Scenario Departments and rely for screen plays upon writers who have been trained in the last decade.

We cannot hope to expand the industry on any considerable scale until we can call upon at least three times as many efficient screen-writers as we can to-day, and as an absolute necessity every Production Company of any size should have a Scenario Department, the principal object of which should be to train writers from other literary fields in the technique of screen-writing and to encourage them to work exclusively, or mainly at any rate, for the screen, even though such departments are, at the beginning, costly to maintain.

Another factor, which itself is dependent on an increase in the number of screen-writers, is the necessity for making more and quicker pictures with the existing facilities in this country.

At present the British film industry is out of balance, making mainly high-budget A-pictures. On such pictures few producers can afford to take the risk of a new writer or even of an original screen story.

In Hollywood the industry is firmly bedded down on the steady flow of a vast majority of B-pictures. The B-picture is the training-ground of talent, the forcing-ground of new ideas, the chance to experiment.

Many fear that cheaper and quicker pictures may mean a surrender of quality and a return to the bad old days of 'quickie' production, but against this the writer is the first line of defence, and if the cutting down of film budgets means fewer writers on the same script, one of our aims at least will be achieved.

The Screen-writers' Association does what it can, through its large Associate Membership, to train new writers by lectures, competitions, discussions, and visits to studios, but it can do no more than provide a potential source of new writers unless the studios actively co-operate.

In glancing through this formidable catalogue of complaints, I must admit that I am inclined to side with the reply of one screen-writer to the question, 'What are the practices of current film production that present the greatest obstacle to successful screen-writing, or most adversely affect the prestige of screen-writers?'

He wrote, succinctly – 'Bad screen-writing'.

TYPE-CASTING
SCREEN-WRITERS

MARTIN FIELD

★

THE Hollywood 'film industry', like the steel, auto, meat pack-
ing, or oil industries, prides itself on its efficient operation. A
familiar 'efficiency' is the casting of actors according to type:
hero, *ingénue*, villain, villainess, and so on. What is less well
known is that Hollywood exercises similar efficiency with regard
to screen-writers, who are cast according to type, just like actors.

When a film producer is casting a picture, he consults the
Players' Directory, which lists all the professional actors, complete with photographs and motion-picture credits. In this way,
the producer can line up his cast pretty quickly. The categories
are neat and time-saving: women, divided into Leading Women,
Ingénues, and Characters and Comediennes; men, divided into
similar categories; and children.

There is no Writers' Directory for a film producer to consult,
but there is a compilation of film-writing credits which can be
explored in the search for a suitable screen-writer. And, of course,
writers' agents are always ready to give the producer a sales talk
on their clients' particular abilities.

Type-casting of writers can be divided into two general kinds:
first, there is type-casting according to the content, or kind, of
story to be written, and second, there is type-casting according
to the form, or structure, of the screen play to be written.

Type-casting according to content means that certain writers
are typed as being good only for certain kinds of films, such as
Western, mystery, comedy, or musical. For example, before Alan
Le May became a screen-writer he wrote such novels about the

West as *Painted Ponies, Gunsight Trail, The Smoky Years,* and *Empire For a Lady.* When Mr Le May became a screen-writer, he 'naturally' was assigned to write such Western films as *Northwest Mounted Police, San Antonio, Cheyenne,* and others.

Examples of similar 'typewriter casting' are almost as numerous as the number of screen-writers working in Hollywood. Valentine Davies wrote a whimsical original story about a man who was convinced he was Santa Claus. The film version, *Miracle on 34th Street,* was a great success. Director-Producer Frank Capra had long owned Eric Knight's fanciful tale about a man who could fly, *The Flying Yorkshireman.* Hoping that Mr Davies could give to *The Flying Yorkshireman* the same successful 'touch' of whimsy that distinguished *Miracle,* Mr Capra 'cast' Mr Davies for work on *Yorkshireman.*

Millen Brand wrote his successful novel, *The Outward Room,* some years ago. Metro-Goldwyn-Mayer bought the film rights to Mr Brand's novel, and that, apparently, was the end of Mr Brand's contact with the film industry. But then, last year, Twentieth-Century-Fox purchased *The Snake Pit,* a best-selling novel by Mary Jane Ward. As was *The Outward Room, The Snake Pit* was about a girl who had been in an insane asylum. Who was the logical man for Twentieth-Century-Fox to hire to adapt *The Snake Pit* to the screen? Correct. Mr Brand was yanked out of his Pennsylvania farm for the job.

Last year Albert Maltz was assigned to write the screen play of *The Robe,* a novel of Christ's time. At first sight, this would seem not to be type-casting at all, since Mr Maltz's reputation was based on his flair for realistic, modern screen plays. However, further examination of Mr Maltz's qualities as a writer bears out the fact that his assignment to *The Robe* was not, so to speak, out of his writing character. In certain scenes of the grim war films, *Destination Tokyo* and *Pride of the Marines,* Mr Maltz displayed high spiritual and humanistic qualities; there was a concern with man, an idealism, that is seldom evinced on the screen. This deep perception of human values was vitally necessary in the screen play of a film of faith like *The Robe*. The selection of Mr Maltz as the screen-writer was not, then, the departure from accustomed writer-casting that it seemed to be.

Mr Brand and Mr Maltz represent the kind of type-casting which seems to be all right. You may well ask, Then why isn't it all right for the producers to type-cast in all cases? The answer is that, in the majority of cases, further thought uncovers a major flaw in the system of type-casting. For instance, the man who writes one musical comedy after another is bound, after a while, to use similar devices in all his scripts. And in the case of the writer who constantly turns out mysteries, usually the same kind of sleuth is on the trail of the same kind of criminal for much the same reasons. In short, type-casting of writers produces a great many clichés and stereotypes in the screen play and, inevitably, in the finished film.

Also, worth-while writing contributions to the screen can be held back because of type-casting writers, as in the case of Preston Sturges. For quite some years Mr Sturges had a reputation in Hollywood as a dependable screen-writer who could be called on for a good job on such dramas as *Diamond Jim, Port of Seven Seas, The Power and the Glory* and *If I Were King*. Forgotten or overlooked or ignored was the fact that Mr Sturges had first come to fame as the author of a hit comedy play, *Strictly Dishonorable*. However much Mr Sturges wanted to write the kind of satiric comedy for which he felt best suited, he was not given the opportunity until with the additional authority of a director he wrote and directed *The Great McGinty*.

So much for type-casting of writers according to the kind of story, or content. The other general kind of type-casting to which writers are subject is that according to the form, or structure, of the story. Before a story reaches the screen, it goes from original story form (if it isn't a novel or play) to treatment or adaptation, and then to screen play (which can be divided almost endlessly into First Finished Screen Play, Polished Screen Play, Third Final Finished Screen Play, and, perhaps, Final Shooting Script).

Writers who have developed reputations for turning out good original stories written directly for the screen find it difficult to get screen play-writing assignments because producers have them typed as original story-writers. The same thinking applies to another classification, that of 'adapters'. When a novel or play is bought by a movie company, it must first be adapted before its screen play can be written. Certain writers have acquired reputations as adapters because they are ingenious about consolidating several minor characters into one character or telescoping scenes for more effective screen purposes. Topping the list of Hollywood writers in both prestige and pay are the dialogue and script polishers, who go to work after a screen play is finished and give the dialogue and plot situations 'touches' and 'twists' which make for a brighter, less hackneyed film.

So we see how the final screen play takes shape, like an automobile on an assembly line, from the screen original to the adaptation to the screen play, to the final polish job. What is the effect of this 'efficiency'? Many writers are far from happy about it. Just as actors object to being typed, so do writers. Most of them want a chance to prove their versatility instead of being strait-jacketed under a stereotyped group heading.

Every now and then Hollywood cries that its writers are sterile and incapable of 'original' or 'fresh' writing. Usually the people who lament the loudest about this state of affairs are the selfsame producers who constantly type writers and thereby keep them in the same monotonous, uncreative writing rut.

In fact, some writers darkly suspect that this pattern of dividing the work on pictures among several writers may be part of a producers' plan for minimising the individual importance of writers. The producers can only reply that motion-picture production is an 'industry' and type-casting of writers is the most efficient way of doing things. And who are writers to criticise? After all, the Chicago meat-packing industry can only claim that it 'uses everything but the squeal'. Since the advent of sound, the film industry has been doing much better than that.

FRITZ LANG'S GERMAN FILMS

1 and 2. 'Destiny' (1921). With Bernard Goetzke as Death and Lil Dagover and Walther Janssen as the lovers.

3 to 6. 'Siegfried' (1923). With Paul Richter as Siegfried, Hans von Schlettov

as Hagen and Margarete Schoen as Kriemhild.

7 to 10. 'Metropolis' (1926). With Brigitte Helm as Maria, Gustav Fröhlich

as Erik and Rudolph Klein-Rogge as Rotwang.

11 to 14. 'M' (1932). With Peter Lorre as the child murderer. (Stills 1 to 14

by courtesy of the Cinémathèque Française, Paris.)

NEW CONTINENTAL
FILMS IN BRITAIN

15. 'Copie Conforme' (Monsieur Alibi). A French film directed by Jean Dreville, with Louis Jouvet. (Stills 15 to 21 by courtesy of the Academy Cinema, London.)

16 and 17. 'La Bataille du Rail' (French). Directed by René Clement. Won Grand Prix International at Cannes Festival 1946 for best production of any nation.

18 and 19. 'Enrico IV' (Italian). Directed by Giorgio Pastina from Piran-
dello's play; with Osvaldo Valenti as Enrico di Nolli.

20 and 21. 'Crime and Punishment' (Swedish). Directed by Hampe Faust-man; with himself as Raskolnikov.

CHAPLIN'S 'MONSIEUR VERDOUX'

22 to 25. 'Monsieur Verdoux.' Scripted and directed by Charles Chaplin, with Mady Correll as Mme Verdoux (22), Martha Raye as Annabella

Bonheur (23), Margaret Hoffmann as Lydia Floray (24) and Marilyn Nash
as The Girl (25).

B.B.C. TELEVISION AT ALEXANDRA PALACE

26. 'Martine' (Jean-Jacques Bernard). Produced by Harold Clayton; with William Bridges and Victoria Hopper.

27. 'Fanny's First Play' (Bernard Shaw). Produced by Stephen Harrison; with George de Warfaz.

28. 'Mourning becomes Electra' (Eugene O'Neill). Produced by Royston Morley; with Basil Langton and Marjorie Mars.

29. 'Death of a Rat' (Jan de Hartog). Produced by George More O'Ferrall; with André Morell, Pamela Brown and Frederick Richter.

30 and 31. 'At Home Abroad: Denmark.' A documentary programme produced by Andrew Miller-Jones.

THOSE WERE THE DAYS

REMINISCENCES BY A PIONEER OF THE EARLIEST DAYS
OF CINEMATOGRAPHY

CECIL HEPWORTH

★

WHEN one wants to talk about the early days of film-making it is extremely difficult to know where to begin. You know so much already about present-day methods; about producers, directors, actors and actresses, camera-men, art directors, technicians, electricians, musicians, cutting-room experts and continuity girls, that it is practically impossible for you to visualise a time when not one of these people existed. And yet we made films – of a sort. Crude they were in the extreme, but we like to think that their halting steps led gradually to better things and pointed in the end to that near perfection which is your heritage to-day.

I think I must begin with the Royal Polytechnic Institution in London's Upper Regent Street. If that were in existence now, it would be about 120 years old, but I am thinking of some sixty-five years ago, when it was to me, and to thousands of other small boys, the place of our utter delight. For gathered under that one roof were examples of all the latest scientific achievements of the day. There was a model electric railway with trains that ran all by themselves, and alongside that railway were a couple of Wheels of Life, Zoetropes, which gave movement to drawings of living figures. There was a famous automaton which walked a tight rope along the whole length of the great hall – I never found out how that was done. There was a monster induction coil giving a spark which they said would kill a horse, and a huge frictional electricity machine from which, turning it slowly, you could draw miniature lightning into your small and rather scared knuckles. And then for sixpence you could take your seat with a dozen other small boys in the big Diving Bell and be completely submerged, with your feet dangling just above the surface of the water which the contained air was pressing down. I have heard it said (with complete disregard of the truth) that the band played particularly loudly while the diving bell was going down, so as to smother the screams of the drowning people inside!

In the optical theatre, which was a notable part of the old Polytechnic, all that was known of magic-lantern projection was demonstrated to the full, and in its operating-room, which, I remember, ran the whole width of the theatre, some twelve or more lanterns were installed, many of them using hand-painted slides, not photographs, of various sizes up to ten inches in diameter. Beale's Choreutoscope was shown here frequently (an early form of very crude Living Pictures), and there were many other optical devices of great popular appeal. In this theatre there were daily lectures, mildly instructional but always entertaining, by such men as B. J. Malden, my own father T. C. Hepworth and Professor Pepper. Here the famous 'Pepper's Ghost' was born, also the very clever ghost illusion invented by J. J. Walker, the organ builder. Indeed, the very air about that spot is filled with ghosts for those whose memories will carry back so far. I am told that on the day the old Polytechnic was closed for ever, I was found, a very forlorn little boy, lying on the stone steps before the closed front door, weeping my heart out.

Who can doubt that if the old Polytechnic had lived it would have been the very place to have welcomed and honoured the new art-science which was destined, though no one knew it then, to be the greatest medium for education and entertainment the world has ever known? It seems almost like a sensate act of fate that when a clever Frenchman was searching London for a suitable hall in which to exhibit his new invention of Living Photographs, he should have drifted to one built on that very spot and set up his apparatus there.

The name of that Frenchman was Louis Lumière: the date, 20 Feb., 1896.

That was the date of the first public showing of films in this country. Without counting some earlier, very brave, but not successful attempts; without counting many inventors' pipe-dreams which never came to birth, that was, so to speak, the official birthday of the cinematograph here.

I am not going to attempt to delve into the actual history of cinematography, partly because the history of an invention is, for most people, very dry and uninteresting; partly because I don't myself know much about it – it is so largely a matter of vague rumour and conflicting memories – and partly because the real interest starts with the showing upon a screen in a public assembly. But it is not to be supposed that Lumière is to have the whole credit, or anything like it. The courage of the early experi-menters, even the pipe-dreamers who only conceived but went no further, all contributed something – and who knows that it wasn't important? – to that notable birthday.

Me? I had no share in it. There was nothing of courage in what I did. It was always just a lark for me. Even now, after fifty years of it, what little I do is still something of a lark! I was suckled on amyl acetate and reared on celluloid.

Did I say the beginners were very crude? Here is an example of it. The stage was a back garden at Walton-on-Thames. The scenery was three flats painted by me. It represented the side wall of a little house with a practicable window. I (the only actor), as a burglar with a black beard, climbed in at the window (scene 1) and climbed out again with the swag (scene 3). Then the three flats were turned round, for the interior of the same house was painted thereon, and the burglar was seen inside (scene 2). It was, I think, the first time that a 'story' had been produced in separate scenes. The drawback was that in the middle scene the burglar was clean-shaven, for in the excitement of changing the scenery I had entirely forgotten to put on my beard. We held a little inquest on it afterwards and decided that it wasn't sufficiently important to warrant a re-take, and though we sold many copies we never had a complaint!

There were only two or three of us in the little company at Walton, and we did everything ourselves. First we thought of a story; then we painted the scenery if it wasn't all open air, as it usually was. Then we acted and photographed it, the one who was not acting turning the handle. Then we developed and printed it, and took it out to our fair-ground customers – there were no 'Electric Palaces' in those days, not even converted shops. After that we reassembled and put our heads together to think of another story.

Story pictures were only part of our output. For instance, I photographed Queen Victoria's visit to Dublin, and that was No. 96 in our catalogue!

A very great deal of what would now be called News-Reel material was made by the little company from Walton and helped to swell our catalogue, and in among it we made trick pictures, comics, dramas (rather small ones at first), and almost every kind of film you could think of. And while we were gradually building up from the crudity of the first fifty-footers (showing-time, fifty seconds) to bigger, better, and more worth-while pictures, other people were feeling their way from the circus tent, through the village hall, the converted shop, and the glaring 'Electric Palace' towards the comfort and magnificence of the modern picture theatre. I had a tiny share in that movement too, for before I even dreamed of making pictures myself I bought a terrible mechanism for a guinea, fitted it on to a limelight lantern and, with half a dozen throw-out forty-foot films of R.W. Paul's and about a hundred lantern slides of my own, I toured the country and gave an hour and a half's entertainment in church rooms, mechanics' institutes, and the like. It took some little ingenuity to make those six miserable little films fill out the time. I showed them, repeated them, showed them backwards, showed them again and argued with the people in them or stopped them in peculiarly awkward attitudes. Anyway, I got away with it and had many repeat engagements, building up the repertoire with the money I earned.

I thank the special providence who looks after amateurs and fools for the fact that I never had an accident, for my little machine was set up on a borrowed table in the middle of the audience, and there were no safety precautions of any kind.

Once, when I had progressed to the dignity of many more films, joined together and wound upon a spool, I was showing from the very front of the gallery in a chapel of some kind, turning the handle for the films and talking through my hat – well, lecturing, between whiles. About the middle of the show the take-up spool fell off its spindle and dived into the audience below, unwinding as it went. I had to haul the film in hand over hand talking all the time. Meanwhile, a terribly anxious man, the friend who had engaged me, kept calling in a loud whisper: 'Tell Cecil not to strike a match. Tell Cecil not to strike a match.' A boy from downstairs brought me my empty spool with a sad tale of an irate gentleman immediately beneath me who had two lovely tram-lines cut on his bald head by the edges of my spool.

My brief mention a moment ago of R.W. Paul and his basket of throw-out films will have suggested to you that there were other film-makers before I started. ... Indeed, I was by no means the first, although I was among the early ones. It is a strange coincidence, and one which must be carefully noted by historians, that Paul actually showed in London some films of his own make on the same day that Lumière gave his first exhibition at the Polytechnic. But Paul's show was a private one and, besides, as he freely admitted to me, his pictures were not as good or as steady as those of the Frenchman.

The question of steadiness is important. It is, of course, chiefly a matter of the accuracy of the perforations down the edges of the film by which it is drawn through the mechanism. Lumière used one pair of holes per frame. Moreover, he used the same pair for taking, printing, and projecting, and it mattered very little, therefore, whether the holes were very really accurately spaced. Paul and the other Englishmen used the four-hole perforation inherited from Edison, and most of the early English films were dreadfully unsteady. It showed up alarmingly on 'scenics' – rivers and hills, and so on. It was said at the time that thus the Scriptures were fulfilled and the mountains skipped about like young rams.

One of my cherished possessions is an early film of Paul's of the Race for the Derby in 1896 – Persimmon's Derby. It is interesting rather than good. The last time I used it in public an old showman who had been in the audience came up to me afterwards and pointed out, what I hadn't noticed, that all the policemen in the picture were wearing beards. I asked him how it was that he seemed to know more about the picture than I did myself, though I had shown it so often. And then the old rascal unblushingly admitted that he had shown it not only for the Derby of 1896, which it really was, but for eight succeeding Derbys afterwards.

Many strange things happened in those early days, and sometimes one had to think pretty quickly to meet an unexpected situation. I was giving my lecture once in a large hall built underneath a chapel. My apparatus was set up as usual in the heart of the audience, and while I was waiting beside it for the hour to strike when I was to begin, the dear old parson came and sat down beside me. He said he was quite sure that my entertainment was everything that it ought to be, but he knew I would understand that, as shepherd of his little flock, it was his duty to make doubly certain and would I let him see my list of pictures. So I handed him the list and watched him mentally ticking off each item until he came to the pick of the whole bunch, a hand-coloured film of Loie Fuller in her famous serpentine dance. He said at once that he could not allow that – a vulgar music-hall actress. I said rather indignantly that there was nothing vulgar about it; that it was indeed a really beautiful and artistic production, but he was adamant and insisted that it must be omitted. Then I had to begin. Apart from my reluctance to leave out my best picture, I was faced with the practical difficulty of how to do it. For this was the last picture but one on the spool. There was no earthly means of getting rid of it except by running it through in darkness, and I didn't think the little flock would stand for that. Then, just as I came to the danger-point, I had a sudden brainwave. I announced the film as 'Salome Dancing before Herod'. Everyone was delighted. Especially the parson. He said in his nice little speech afterwards that he thought it was a particularly happy idea to introduce a little touch of Bible history into an otherwise wholly secular entertainment.

And he added that he had no idea that the cheenimartograph had been invented so long!

ROUND THE WORLD'S STUDIOS

H. H. WOLLENBERG

★

CURRENT production on the whole is characterised by what can justly be called the New Realism. It is the specific style of post-war production, certainly in European studios. As in British films, where it sprang up from documentary influences, we meet it in the representative films of Italy (starting with *Open City, Paisa, Sciuscià*, etc.), France (where its tradition goes far back to the early films of Renoir and Pagnol of fifteen years ago), the Scandinavian and other smaller countries; we also meet it in the revived German production. And we meet it in the new Russian production which, after its stressing of historical and patriotic films during the war, has now turned to realistic films on post-war problems and reconstruction.

The many international film festivals, official and unofficial, held during the second half of 1947, offered opportunities of viewing representative films of a good many nations. A survey proves distinctly that the New Realism is the common denominator of the vast variety of subjects and of the natural differentiations in technique and purpose. There are definite indications that this continues to be the dominant note in most European studios. The preference for certain realistic subjects, connected mainly with war, liberation, underground, may have changed, as was bound to happen. Significant is it that, among other themes, the classics of literature and drama have once again become a fairly frequent choice within current production schedules. Dostoyevsky's *Brothers Karamazov*, Tolstoy's *Kreutzer Sonata* (Italy), Victor Hugo's *Ruy Blas*, Stendhal's *La Char-*

treuse de Parme (France, the latter being made in Rome), Cervantes's *Don Quixote* and Lope de Vega's *Fuente Ovejuna* (Spain) are a few examples, just as are the British productions of *Hamlet, Oliver Twist, Anna Karenina,* and quite a few others.

No doubt one of the reasons is the consideration of exports; a drama or novel of world fame, from the producer's point of view, makes for international appeal. However, the style of films, as of any other piece of art, does not depend on the subject as such, but is determined by its makers. It is the treatment that counts. In its great majority, the present generation of film artists and technicians, first of all directors, stands for the New Realism. The persons representative of the evolution are creative artists such as Alessandro Blasetti, Frank Capra, Marcel Carné, Alberto Cavalcanti, Charles Chaplin, René Clair, Jean Cocteau, Carl Theodor Dreyer, Julien Duvivier, S. M. Eisenstein, Jacques Feyder, John Ford, Howard Hawks, Alfred Hitchcock, Gerhard Lamprecht, Fritz Lang, Ernst Lubitsch, Lewis Milestone, G. W. Pabst, Vsevolod Pudovkin, Jean Renoir, Robert Siodmak, King Vidor, and William Wyler. This list of pioneers, given in alphabetical order, is by no means complete. Since 1940, the following names have been added: the French Jacques Becker, René Clément, and Henri Georges Clouzot; the Czech Jiri Weiss; the Italian Alberto Lattuada, Roberto Rossellini, and Vittorio de Sica; the American Preston Sturges, Orson Welles, Elia Kazan, and Billy Wilder; the Mexican Emilio Fernandez; the Swedish Alf Sjöberg and Arne Sucksdorff; the German Helmut Käutner and Wolfgang Staudte. However, it must be said that British studios are second to none as regards the rise of fresh directing talent, led by Laurence Olivier, Carol Reed, and David Lean.

*

As far as quality is concerned, the names of young European directors indicate the significant standard achieved in the sign of the New Realism; a standard which obviously compares well, to say the least, with that of the world's largest production centre,

Hollywood. This is the more remarkable as, in the economic field, things look less encouraging in Europe. It should be realised that in most European countries the studios have been and are working under the conditions of and against an almost constant crisis. France is probably the most obvious example. The balance sheet of French film production, as placed before an Inter-ministerial Commission, showed a deficit estimated at no less than 1,000 million francs in 1947. Nothing is more significant than René Clair's return to the United States for an indefinite period (with Jean Renoir to follow), after his triumph with his Paris production, *Le Silence est d'Or*. The French Government, conscious of the importance of the film industry, goes on with regulations and reorganisations in its endeavour to help its pro-ducers, but, as René Clair put it, 'placing a ceiling on admission prices does not put a ceiling on production costs'. Anyhow, al-though the effect of the difficulties is noticeable in a certain drop in the number of films as against last year's output, the schedule of subjects in production is promising, and so are the artistic ambition and the resourcefulness active in France's studios.

As for smaller countries, let us turn to Denmark as an example of the difficulties faced by their producers. Denmark's contribu-tion to the evolution of screen art right from its beginnings has been invaluable, and her post-war efforts, though small in num-bers, have upheld the tradition. Reports from Copenhagen some time ago emphasised that Danish production was facing dim prospects since the return of American film imports. The vast supply of American pictures caused the exhibitors to change their programmes more frequently, and the screen time available for national productions had been decreasing rapidly. Conse-quently they disappeared too swiftly from the theatre pro-grammes, and trade circles estimate that they were frequently seen by only one-third of their potential audience. The increas-ing dollar shortage, however, at last forced the Government to take action, and imports were drastically cut down.

The development in Denmark (similar to those in other

countries) clearly shows the evil that is at the root of the crisis. We know the symptoms only too well from our own experience in Britain, if we only decide to be honest about it: (1) mass imports of films, the production costs of which have been recovered in their home market; (2) films not nearly fully exploited in the cinemas, a fact most detrimental to home production; (3) at the same time a steady rise of home production costs under the influence of Hollywood's fantastic expenditure.

An analysis from the producer's point of view of the position in Britain can be found in R. J. Minney's book, *Talking of Films*. We are in this article not concerned with discussing the book as such, but Mr Minney's conclusion that British film costs must come within the scope of home-market finance adds point to our argument. Himself a producer, he states: 'It is exceedingly difficult now, if not actually impossible, for an independent producer to make a picture'.

Here, really, is Europe's present problem with regard to film production. Incidentally, it is also the problem of the national film effort in Latin-American countries, quite especially Mexico. Here the Credito Cinematografico Mexicano (the State-controlled film bank) has set a ceiling of about 80,000 dollars on production costs per feature film, as compared with current production budgets of about 120,000 dollars.

Naturally, things are different in those countries where, as in Czechoslovakia, the State has taken over the film industry. As far as production is concerned, the organs of the State are in a position to control production costs, including such items as star salaries. On the distribution and exhibition end, the monopoly is able to regulate imports in a way which makes the financial basis for home production secure, while the minimum requirements of the cinema programmes are supplemented by imports. The steady progress of film-making in Prague and the noteworthy efforts in countries such as Poland are probably due to that system.

*

If, in spite of vast financial difficulties which, of course, have to be viewed against the general background of European economics, European post-war film production has made headway artistically, the explanation is undoubtedly the New Realism. Its approach, its style, corresponds with contemporary atmosphere. There are indications of a revolution in audience tastes progressing gradually. The trend is confirmed by recent developments in Hollywood, with its finger always on the pulse of the public. It appears to be a distinct departure from its tradition and an adjustment to the New Realism when Hollywood producers, incidentally following the example set by their British colleagues, start to send their units to other countries for exteriors. Location trips to Europe, Africa, Canada, and South America have been scheduled by all the major companies. The purpose, no doubt, is to secure more authentic backgrounds, a more realistic atmosphere for their pictures.

Herewith connected, a certain change in subjects is noticeable. As the result of an inquiry made by the *Film Daily* with 372 American Press and radio critics, the trade paper made the following comment: 'Hollywood's weakness as it is confronted with increasing competition from British studios is to be found in the types of stories it selects for transfer to the screen'.

This seems a clear hint of the trend which I described as the New Realism. At the same time it shows that even the most extravagant sums spent on screen rights are not the essence of success in film-making. No doubt, a certain financial minimum is indispensable to assure the requisite technical standards. Beyond this, however, quality cannot be bought. This is the most encouraging conclusion drawn from international film-making in its present phase.

TELEVISION AND CINEMA

ANDREW MILLER JONES

*

THE B.B.C. Television service has been in effective existence for four years. It is hardly to be expected that during so short a time a new art form should have crystallised. It will be some years before television has reached the perfection of broadcasting or the film as a means of expression. The reason for this is chiefly post-war economics. Pre-war equipment, though capable of great improvement as a result of subsequent scientific research, is still being used, and this fact, together with the limitations of studio space and other accommodation, prevents the possibilities of the medium from being fully developed. Yet, though it is too early to dogmatise about television, sufficient progress has been made in spite of difficulties to justify an appraisal of its achievements and to speculate on its potentialities.

A comparison between television and film is inevitable. In the first place both reach their audience by means of two-dimensional moving pictures. The television screen is smaller than the cinema screen, but so is its audience, and the viewer sitting four or five feet from his receiver finds the picture relatively the same size as in the cinema. Each medium employs a flexible camera which enables the director or producer to select points of emphasis. The conventions established in the cinema of cutting from shot to shot during a piece of continuous action, of mixing to establish a lapse of time for change of place, and of fading as a means of punctuation, apply equally in television. The subtlety of acting rendered possible by close-up technique is a common requirement of both media. Finally, the magical disregard of natural laws, made possible in film by trick camera work, is a device which can be used in television to a limited

45

extent, though achieved by other means. But here the resemblance between cinema and television comes to an end.

The cinema presents to its audience excerpts from past time, and the audience knows it. News-reels are the obvious example of this. However soon they are shown after the events they record have taken place, they are only of historic interest and the drama has gone out of them. Television, on the other hand, through its Outside Broadcast units, brings the news back alive. It enables its viewers in their homes to share the excitement and the sense of being present at great occasions with those actually present on the spot. Thus one of the most important attributes of television is Immediacy. Immediacy is an equally important factor in the effectiveness of studio productions and presentations. In this, television has something in common with the theatre, which has a power that the cinema can never have. To see a record of something which has happened and to witness something which is palpably occurring before your very eyes are two entirely different matters. It is the difference between belief and make-believe. To have seen Part One of *Mourning becomes Electra* on the television screen was to be moved as never in the cinema. It was to know what the Greeks meant by tragedy purging through pity and terror. I think my point will become clearer if a comparison is made between a live sound broadcast and one known to have been recorded. Except in broadcasts of actualities, it is illogical to make a distinction between a first-time broadcast and a recorded repeat, and yet every Itma fan knows that the Thursday broadcast and its repeat at the week-end are not the same thing. The difference is psychological, but none the less real for that, and the sense of being fobbed off with something second-hand is even more acute when a programme is broadcast for the first time in recorded form. A barrier, that is not only of technical processes, has been erected between those taking part and the audience. On the one hand, the stimulation of rising to the occasion is absent, and on the other the thrill of knowing that the performance is taking place at the instant of listening for each listener's individual benefit and capable of being judged on its merits is replaced by an expected mechanical perfection. All this is doubly true of television. Actors have admitted that they prefer the television camera to the ciné camera because they perform before a live audience, who are known to be there though unheard and unseen. Moreover, the actors are able to give a more individual and homogeneous rendering of their parts in television, where they begin at the beginning and can develop a characterisation through to the end, than in the film studio, where they are little more than puppets obedient to the wishes of the director who may require Romeo to die first and woo his Juliet afterwards. This is the fundamental difference between television and film-making.

For those who have had no experience of television it might be as well to give a brief account of what is entailed in putting on a production. Whatever it may be, play, feature, illustrated talk or variety, the producer must know, before he starts rehearsal, the distance, angle, and length of every shot, and he must see that his script observes the unities of time and place. This is not so important as in the theatre. It is possible to show a character in a succession of different settings, but not more quickly than the actor can cover the physical distance on the studio floor between them. And unless film is specially taken and inserted into live sequences, there are limitations to the kind of scenes which can be portrayed. This device is favoured by some producers, but personally I feel that it is not good television, except to evoke atmosphere. It calls attention to television's limitations and invites comparison with the cinema on its own ground, while at the same time sacrificing the advantages of immediacy already discussed. The script having been turned into a camera continuity, the sets having been worked out in conjunction with the design department and the lighting engineers, and the cast chosen, the producer, who has exercised control in each of these processes, begins rehearsal. For a play there will be approximately ten days without cameras or scenery, and from three to six hours with cameras in the studio. Not until the studio rehearsal do the cameramen have the opportunity to rehearse their all-important part. But they will have had an opportunity of studying the scale plans giving camera plot and set layout. This is the blue-print of a production, and a copy is issued to each technician concerned. In charge on the studio floor is the Studio Manager, who marshals the actors by means of hand signals and directs the scene attendants and property men, who often perform silent miracles of scene-shifting while the studio is on the air. The Studio Manager, like the cameramen and sound staff, receives instructions through headphones connected to the producer's talk-back in the control gallery which lies behind a sound-proof window set high on one wall of the studio. In front of the producer's desk are two screens, one showing the picture being transmitted and the other the opening set-up of the next camera to be used. In this way the engineers are able to adjust a shot electrically before it is put on the air, and the producer can ensure that each shot is matched with the one which precedes it. Any camera, apart from the one being used for transmission, may be called for by the producer on the preview channel by giving instructions to the vision mixer. The appropriate camera having been satisfactorily lined up on preview, the producer will indicate to the vision mixer, seated close behind him and thus able to take both visual and verbal cues, when he wishes to go over to it. The mixer is able to produce cuts, mixes, or fades by manipulating controls on her panel as required. When it is realised that there may be anything from sixty to 120 camera changes in an orthodox production of an hour-and-a-half play, it will be obvious that a high standard of concentration and teamwork is required on the part of producer, vision mixer, and cameramen; for though the camera continuity will indicate the points at which a change of camera is required, the actual moment of change is a matter which cannot be decided in advance. Also in the control gallery are the sound engineer and gramophone operator. Their jobs, while no less vital, re-

quire less moment-to-moment control on the part of the producer.

Though orthodox productions follow film technique in cutting from long-shot to mid-shot to close-up, continuous action
brings it own complications. It is impossible to cut in successive
shots from a long shot to a closer one in the same vertical plane,
since the nearer camera would be in the field of view of the one
farther away. This makes it necessary to arrange the movements
of the actors so that they present themselves for a close-up to a
camera set up outside the field of view of the preceding camera.
Fig. 1 shows the long-shot and Fig. 2 the succeeding closer shot:

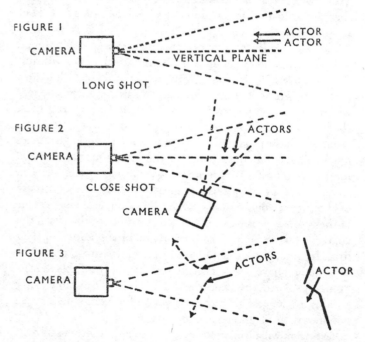

FIGURE 1

CAMERA

VERTICAL PLANE

ACTOR
ACTOR

LONG SHOT

FIGURE 2

CAMERA

ACTORS

CLOSE SHOT

CAMERA

FIGURE 3

CAMERA

ACTORS

ACTOR

I have stressed the phrase orthodox production, since a new
method has recently been developed which is loosely known as

one-camera technique. This was formerly a term of abuse at Alexandra Palace applied to those producers recruited from the theatre who produced as if for the stage and set up a camera in place of the audience. If they tracked and panned their camera, this was the greatest concession they made to the medium. The new technique is quite different. It consists of producing the actors for the camera to a much greater degree than is the normal practice. If the camera opens on a long-shot, the movements of the actors are so arranged that when the action calls for close-up emphasis the actors are in the right position. If, as in Fig. 3, actors are in close-up and it is necessary to show the entrance of a third through a door at the rear, 'business' will be arranged so that the close-up actors will move out of the camera's field of view to allow the door to be seen.

This is an elementary example, but by working out a script on this principle, and by careful advance rehearsals combined with camera movement, it is possible to present a play requiring three successive sets with three cameras and two camera changes without dispensing with the advantages of varying lengths of shot and without loss of pace. The great virtue of this method is that most of the producer's work can be done before the camera rehearsal, and, in consequence of the less complicated studio routine, a smoother and more polished production is likely to result. There are situations, of course, in which the slavish use of one camera would be dull – where, for example, no movement of the actors is possible as in a scene at a dinner-table when the characters speak in quick succession and brief glimpses of their listeners' reactions are required. So far the plays presented by the new method have been especially suitable for the display of the producer's virtuosity, but the results have been sufficiently striking to suggest that the accepted film technique may be modified with advantage in television.

Television will ultimately develop into an art form in its own right capable of being judged by its own standards of criticism, as the cinema and the theatre are. And, when it is more widespread, it will become in the dramatic field as much a rival, but no more, of the cinema and the theatre as they are of one another. But as a medium for the expression of ideas, and as a social force, it will have no rival. Certainly not in the documentary and instructional side of film-making, which might well become an adjunct to television. The specialised film which bears a message depends for its audience on non-theatrical distribution, and this means that it is shown to those who are already half converted. Television, like broadcasting, of which it is in some respects a development, goes into the home, and its audience consists, not of hundreds or thousands who have met for a common purpose, but of individuals multiplied thousands of times over, who will represent, when television is universal, every shade of opinion and every kind of social and educational background. Such an audience require quite a different approach from a film audience. The oratorical style of some newsreels and of the March of Time would be quite out of place on the television screen, where intimacy is the keynote.

The fact that television goes into the home and can count on a large audience determines not only the manner but the matter of the non-entertainment side of its programmes – using the term 'entertainment' in its narrowest sense. It means that a comparatively large number of viewers can be expected for programmes of limited appeal and that this audience can be increased by beguiling the casual viewer into looking at an item which he might not ordinarily have gone out of his way to see. In this way the general standard of taste can be raised. Particularly is this to be hoped for in the visual arts to which the average Englishman is notoriously insensible. The standard of architecture in our towns is appallingly low, the design in everyday things, with few exceptions, conventional and derivative rather than fitted to purpose and arising out of the materials of which articles are made. At first sight, insensitivity to good design might seem to be lamentable but unimportant – but, in fact, its effect is to make life drabber than it need be and, in these days when exports are all-important, it will lose us markets. By way of excuse, manufacturers of mass-produced goods will point out that demand conditions supply. I believe that one of the responsibilities of television is to raise the standard of the demand. Public taste in the aural arts has improved beyond all expectation as a result of twenty-five years of broadcasting. It is not too much to hope that television will have the same effect for the visual arts.

THE GERMAN FILMS
OF FRITZ LANG

SOME IMPRESSIONS BY LOTTE H. EISNER

*

In a few hundred feet every film of quality reveals the style of its director. The films of Fritz Lang, whether they were shot in Germany, France, or America, maintain a certain style even where new national influences or the pattern of another epoch can be detected. The style of Fritz Lang, although intensely personal, derives from his early contact with Germany, where he, a Viennese, first worked, and from the art form of the period – expressionism.

*

The post-war atmosphere in the Germany of 1919 to 1926 was a most curious one. It is perhaps impossible for other countries to understand the frenzied search for new formulas, the passionate desire to establish a new dogma. After Germany's so-called revolution (which in reality was limited to the intellectual bourgeoisie), German artists and writers saw as the only solution possible the expressionistic style which Stanislavsky's and Meyerhold's Soviet theatre was revealing to them in a more influential manner than a small isolated group of painters and sculptors working in Berlin and Munich before the war had done. Expressionism was making *tabula rasa* of all previous artistic principles; besides, as an entirely abstract style it was already very near the native doctrine of art based upon intellectualism rather than upon a conception of form perceived entirely through the senses.

But it was not easy for the punctilious German minds to get rid of their pre-war ideology, their 'Weltanschauung'. Their

53

mentality had not yet recovered from its megalomaniac imperialistic dreams and from the shock of defeat. Disillusioned, the German intellectuals who would not and could not resign themselves to hard, plain reality, clung to their old reputation as a 'people of poets and thinkers', and endeavoured to take refuge in a sort of subconscious world full of anguish, unrest, and a vague remorse, obsessed by the memory of a glorious past. Everything became mysterious to those who had nothing to lose, and believed they possessed at least the treasures of mysticism; impenetrable mist seemed to cover the objects of a real world that had slipped out of their grasp.

This longing for chiaroscuro (as it were) found its ideal means of expression in film art. Here they were able to evolve in a visual but unreal manner phantoms created by their perturbed minds. In this unstable period, where all market values were soon to crash, Germany seemed impregnated by an overwhelming sense of fatalism which was transformed into a violent art. The cruel gods of Valhalla, the ghosts of Eichendorff's romantic poetry, E. T. A. Hoffmann's demoniac fantasy, and Freud's psychoanalysis were all mixed together. They tortured themselves as they were soon going to torture others. They found a temporary escape in films formed in their own image, films of horror, death, and nightmare. This feeling gave a sort of glamour to the films of directors like Robert Wiene and Richard Oswald, who, once they had to abandon the expressionist style, revealed themselves as very mediocre. If expressionistic art succeeded in stimulating second-rate directors, what did films of this style become in the hands of a born creator like Lang?

Before Wiene shot *The Cabinet of Dr Caligari* the subject was offered to Fritz Lang. It is useless to conjecture how this film would have turned out under his direction. When two years later he shot *Destiny*, it was, like *Caligari*, a film of expressionist atmosphere. But while the fantastically distorted settings of *Caligari* resulted in an intentionally flat and linear pattern, Lang's architectural sense overcame the more purely graphic style of the original expressionists. His small medieval town somewhere in Germany is, in spite of its fantasy, more real than the one the somnambulist Cesare haunts owing to the subtle use of light which creates a sense of architectural depth.

A German critic once pointed out the preponderant part light plays in the *mise en scène* of his countrymen; he called this method 'light as a dramatic factor'. German directors liked to use spotlights placed lower than the settings to be lit in order to create curiously unreal contrasts and extraordinary shadows; they accentuate angles in order to exaggerate their sharp outlines. For Lang, however, light is a means of emphasising the form and structure of his settings. Yet the basic idea of light as a means of obtaining dramatic effect is at its best in *Metropolis*, when the mad inventor's torch chases Maria until she is caught in a circle of light out of which there seems to be no escape. (The intermittent light of an electric advertisement-sign obsessing the sick brain of the cashier-murderer in *Scarlet Street* has a similar effect.)

Light also helps Lang to create atmosphere in an almost impressionist manner; through luminous, transparent reflections he creates a kind of counterpoint between the lighting and the settings. Sometimes he chooses natural sources of lighting; in *Liliom*, for instance, he tried on the set for more than one hour to capture the vision of flickering lights from a turning merry-go-round reflected on a greyish wall. For the search in the brushwood in *M* enormous spotlights were pointed on to shrubs which had previously been sprinkled with water in order to show a kaleidoscope of gleaming drops. Lang remembered this experience – for nothing gets lost in the evolution of his intelligent technique. It reappears in his American films. In *The Woman in the Window* the involuntary murderer, bent under the load of his victim, searches his way through a similar thicket. The vampire in *M* stops at a shop-window where glittering knives are reflected and where the child's frail form is soon to appear. The same technique reappears in the vision of *The Woman in the*

Window, where headlights slide an instant over the glass surfaces of the shop-front and the portrait, until the fatal silhouette of the living woman appears on this same surface.

In all the American films of Lang reflections of light are used to create associations. Puddles on the pavement at night when the lamps of invisible cars are glittering seem to forebode unrest and tragedy. Instead of showing in *The Woman in the Window* a direct scene to promote the catastrophe, the action is reflected from the polished surface of a mirror.

The play of shadows, this counterpart of light, is often used in German films for its ornamental value as well as for its psychological effects. When in *Metropolis* during an accident corpses are carried away, Lang only shows the gigantic shadows of the bearers framing the actor Fröhlich, the only visible witness. Shadows create much of the thrilling and melodramatic atmosphere of *The Spy*. In *Scarlet Street* the legs of the man who has hanged himself cast a dark shadow on the wall for a moment just to mark the suicide as something casual. More impressive still is the murderer's shadow in *M*, cast this time on a poster promising a reward for his capture. Here the dramatic effect seems the result of natural circumstances; the shadow soars like a dark bird of prey over the little girl, unaware of its sinister warning.

It is strange to realise that the same art directors, Warm and Röhrig, designed the sets for *Caligari* and for *Destiny*. They forced their ideas upon Wiene, whereas they submitted to Lang's authority. There is an absolute contrast, for instance, between the hallucinations of the winding staircase hanging in the void of *Caligari's* abstract world and the firmly designed structure of the narrow steps leading straight up to the House of Death.

For Lang, architecture, like light, becomes a 'dramatic factor', but this does not mean that Lang was in complete bondage to expressionism. He only makes use of this style for his psychological or his decorative purposes, for example when he wants to express the soulless, anonymous force of the masses in *Metro-*

polis or to stress the mysterious elements in *The Spy* or *Mabuse*. The gigantic settings of the *Nibelungen Saga* contain no trace of expressionism: the huge, barbaric frescoes in this film derive their style from the original legend itself. Remembering his stay in New York, Lang tried for *Metropolis* to adapt the sky-scrapers to the macrocosm of his city of the future. But here the characters had not the stature and force of ancient German heroes and were crushed; only the masses of the workers were able to match this.

Critics have sometimes blamed Lang for constructing his vast-scale exteriors in the studio or on the studio lot with a huge amount of plaster, stucco, and canvas. Yet the artificial forest of *Siegfried* breathes life; sunbeams weave across the dense trees and a radiant haze floats between their heavy trunks. A painting by the Swiss artist, Arnold Boecklin, inspired this vision like other scenes of the *Nibelungen Saga*, and also the Island of Death in *Destiny*. If here paintings come to life on the screen, we could, vice versa, halt the Nibelungen film any moment and find ourselves in front of a well-balanced, self-contained, and static picture.

From the static symmetry of the *Nibelungen Saga* a slow rhythm emanates, inexorable like the fatality of the ancient legend. This rhythm becomes dynamic in the mass movements of *Metropolis*. Lang, an indefatigable observer, had seen Max Reinhardt directing groups of extras on the stage. The decorative grouping of actors in the Nibelungen film betrays some resemblance to Reinhardt's modernised classical style. Lang has also observed a crowd arranged as a dark, compact, amorphous mass, from whose nucleus at rhythmical intervals chorus leaders rise as in Greek dramas. This technique suited his slave-workmen in *Metropolis*, dressed in timeless garments, with bent heads, stooping shoulders, and absence of spirit. Their *marche funèbre*, continuous, monotonous, anticipates Hitler's march in the future towards the charnel-house.

Lang's workmen of the underground city are automata,

their arms the spokes of a gigantic wheel. But, apart from these robots, Lang likes to group his actors into a definite geometrical frame. In the *Nibelungen Saga* the human body often seemed a decorative element in the settings; for instance, the endless row of warriors, faceless with their helmet vizors down, all leaning motionless on their shields in the same attitude. Such ornamental grouping gains life only when, behind these figures, the passing of a royal procession is shown – a moment of great cinematic animation because the shields seem at the same time to hinder the view. In *Metropolis*, grouped figures become more and more an element of the architecture itself, arranged in a triangle or a half-circle.

This geometrical stylisation, the last vestige of expressionistic æstheticism, never gives way to a mere mechanical routine. Lang's crowds, although 'architecturalised', remain full of life, like the cluster of children in the inundation sequence flocking around Maria on the last island of concrete which the floods have not yet covered. This pyramid of their imploring arms is more eloquent than the cleverly regulated scramble of greedy hands outstretched towards the false Maria in the gala-cabaret scene. Here the movement is confirmed in a triangle, just as is the threatening movement of the workmen rushing to kill the robot. This crystallising of groups in various geometric forms finds its culmination where it becomes an integral part of the action, as, for example, in the scene where the workmen advance to a centre on radial lines, moved by the same collective revolutionary will that turns them into human beings.

*

M marked a new phase in Lang's career, and that not merely because it was his first dialogue film. The preceding films, *Woman in the Moon* (a sort of fantastic sequel to *Metropolis*) and *The Spy* (a variation of the first *Mabuse*), seem merely casual experiments. Nevertheless, *The Spy*, in its manner of mixing reality with an imaginary underworld, is a prelude to *M*. A comparison between the tribunal scene in *M*, where thieves judge a murderer, with the workmen's assembly in *Metropolis* to hear Maria speak of the dawn of a happier world, marks Lang's evolution: his crowd has ceased to be a neutral and anonymous mass in the old expressionist manner.

But the experience of expressionism had been of value for Lang. While the habit of employing his actors like pawns on an imaginary chess-board had given him an extraordinary capacity for making the best use of space, he was now no longer restrained by artificial stylisation. The shot of a wide, deserted asphalt area seen from above, where men stand barring the way for the murderer, is derived from the action itself. Thus the synthesis of a personal artistic conception and the natural development of the dramatic plot is a complete one. The mere relating of facts is replaced by visual impressions: an untouched plate, a vacant chair, the terrible void of an empty staircase, are convincing forecasts of tragedy impressively created by the exact counterpoint by *montage* with the sound effects. Or the only indication that the dreaded murder has been committed is the little victim's ball, which has rolled out of the thicket – a visual commentary more eloquent than any scream from the child could have been. Lang, however, had already acquired a command of the use of sound: the song so dismally dreary in the mouths of playing children, floating in their shrill voices across the courtyards of the slums; the mother's call for the missing child ebbing away in the sickening hollowness of the staircase; some jerky measures of Grieg's troll-melody whistled again and again as a sinister *leitmotiv* whenever the pervert appears, there are instances of sound used in a purely cinematic way. Finally, the sharp, hard knocking of the shut-in murderer trying to open a locked door, a sound that instead of freeing him betrays his presence, or his gasp like an out-hunted beast in the attic, have a vigour which only this early period of experiment could produce.

*

The German speculative mentality likes to make films based on a well-planned theory. Lang's screen plays, at least those made in Germany, can be analysed as 'films à thèse'. Owing to Germany's unstable period of anxiety, a number of Lang's scripts and films deal with personified death and a destiny that has nothing in common with the sophisticated Destin which Carné and Prévert try to introduce into *Les Portes de la Nuit*. Germany's uneasiness and moral aimlessness created likewise Nietzsche's superman-type (seen in a film, *Spiders*, of 1919, the two *Mabuse* films and *The Spy*) or the anti-social megalomaniac and sadist type in *M*, which both led to Hitler. On the other hand, Lang seeks to raise the issue of justice for the pursued (even in connection with his pervert in *M*) in preference for these outlaws beyond official jurisdiction. He often shows the inexorability of fate and the irresponsibility of mankind. It is not mere chance that two of his recent American films, *Woman in the Window* and *Scarlet Street*, seem just variations of the same theme of human bondage; no less than four of Lang's early screen plays of 1919 show a man led to destruction by the fatal vamp.

*

Is Lang's film of the *Nibelungen Saga* really, as is sometimes presumed, a prelude to fascist racial theories? Its subject as well as its style is developed from the same Germany in which moral and economic conditions pointed ahead to Nazism. But the contrast between the fair hero and the dark villain, derived from a Northern legend, is far away from that insipid 'Gentlemen prefer blondes' attitude which *L'Éternel Retour* strives to instil in such an eagerly collaborative way. This blond versus black theory is by no means the quintessence of the ancient Tristan and Isolde theme. Thomas Mann, the great German author, speaks in his novel, *Tonio Kröger*, of that longing for blond hair and blue eyes by which the darker type is obsessed. Perhaps Lang found in shooting his *Nibelungen Saga* a kind of solution to a latent nostalgia from which he was able to free himself in America with his films directed against racial frenzy, just as he rid himself of a certain German sentimentality in his screen plays by leaving his collaborator, Thea von Harbou, behind in Nazi Germany. Lang is himself only half German: his mother was a Jewess. For, if some scenes in his silent films seem out of date to-day because of their naïveté or conventionalism, this must have been Thea von Harbou's and the Ufa's contribution to an uncongenial partership. Thus, in *Metropolis*, the artificial reconciliation of the workmen with their indifferent master, the easygoing, trivial slogan of 'the heart which has to be mediator between the directing brain and the toiling hands' contrasts deeply with Lang's revelation of social injustice as manifested in *You Only Live Once*, the most dynamic of his American films.

Anyway, Lang has so far not been free to follow entirely his own artistic ideals. He is now independent, working with his own company, for which he is financially responsible. Will he remain in a position to make his films without compromising? The tone of *Scarlet Street* (notwithstanding the moralising end caused by the censorship code) is much closer to artistic and ethical non-conformity than the more conventional *Woman in the Window*.

INDIAN SPRING

THOROLD DICKINSON

*

Thorold Dickinson spent the first three months of 1946 in India surveying on behalf of the Rank Organisation the possibilities of feature film production on location in that country. In the following article, amongst other things, he gives his reasons for postponing the project.

*

OUR plan was to sample as much of Indian life as air travel, and some sense of proportion, would allow in fourteen weeks. Our quest was twofold. First, for a film story strong enough to hold apathetic Western audiences but sympathetic enough not to hurt Eastern susceptibilities. And, secondly, to forecast the real state of working conditions for a foreign film unit.

Cairo was our first night's stop. At dawn we left for the Persian Gulf. Prophetically we flew into stormy weather as we headed for Asia. We lunched R.A.F. style at Shaibeh airport near Basra, surrounded by bitter, hopeless, homesick Air Force personnel. Outside the mess-shed were miles and miles and bloody miles of sticky mud to the horizon, under grey, heavy skies. Within, hot, greasy food served out of chipped handleless china at long tables and, to read, nothing but tattered out-of-date magazines and cheap fiction. Broken chairs, squalor. For King and Country. Oh God, oh Araby. This is the Forces' programme.

After Karachi, eastwards again across the Sind Desert. And flying into India on this route we saw a dramatic sight. From south horizon to north horizon there is a straight border line. On one side of this ruled border, ridge upon ridge as on a seashore from which the tide has run out, lie the desert sands, the windblown waves running east to west. On the other side, closely cultivated land – the opposite picture to all one had heard of drought and starving millions. This contrasting image is symbolic of India's real problem. Rich earth if there is water; desert if there is no irrigation. The farmed land is a victory for the years of labour of British engineers, their Indian colleagues, and the stoical Indian farmers. At that line capital investment and practical irrigation problems have been held by the water-less sand.

The peasants take advantage of every foot of watered land. A mosaic of cultivated patches huddled around countless vil-lages. Is it possible that so many communities living in mud huts can exist cramped together on so comparatively little arable land? Of 400 million Indians only one-tenth live in towns; the rest share 700,000 villages sited wherever water allows. And water is tragically scarce in the months of hot weather before the monsoon wind brings the rain. Dust hangs in the air, filter-ing the sunlight. Dust, stirred up by a sudden wind or by running animals or a hasty motor-car, can hang as thick as Hollywood's idea of a London fog. Dust and water opposing each other are the real combatants in India. To their conflict all other divisions must sometime each year give place.

Calcutta – 5 p.m. Sunday afternoon. Over-travelled, we bumped wearily through a 'suburb' of Calcutta of nightmare poverty. How to convey the heavy, illiterate, acquiescence-through-hunger of thousands upon thousands of people who own nothing material in this world but their sari or their loin-cloth. Tiny dusty fires in gutters, tattered sheds like bookshelves with a family on each shelf, and the overflow of humanity lying on the roadside just staring. Calcutta's population was doubled between 1940 and 1946. Its resources could not shelter all who came seeking the better livelihood that war offers to workers in the cities. In Calcutta we, too, at first could find no shelter, but were eventually lodged in an Indian hotel, where rooms are made ready for guests only after their arrival with their own servants and personal furniture, including bedding. In a crowded seven days in this city of beggars and big business, meeting lively intellectuals and visiting film studios, we went out to the studio of Jamini Roy, who twenty-five years ago was a sensitive painter, but who now allows his work to be exploited in mass copies by student pupils. In this artist of great personal charm and serenity there seemed to be a strange psychological confusion. Unable to talk Hindustani, we could not begin to resolve the problem.

The physical discomfort and mental depression of fourteen anti-rabic injections (a bite from a dog in the Calcutta hotel, chained to its nervous master's door) may have aggravated my antipathy to New Delhi, that appalling red-sandstone gesture to imperialism. Arriving at the Government guest house, we learnt that all spare bedding had been shipped to Singapore and guests were expected to travel their own, Indian fashion. Although late at night, I taxied to several total Indian strangers to whom we had the most formal letters of introduction – but who generously lent us blankets as if it were a nightly custom – and assembled enough covering to keep us only shivering slightly against the chilly January night. The plains of Northern India have ideal weather for five months of the year. Warm, rainless days, often frosty nights, but nobody tells you that before you go there.

The Most Important Person, who had invited us to visit India, lunched us admirably and suggested that we should plan a colour film embracing the last 2,000 years of Indian history. With only one life within our grasp, we countered with other proposals, and although disappointed he gave us practical assistance and smoothed our way on the many occasions on which we had to ask his staff for help.

One of the three or four compensations in New Delhi was our meeting with Sir William Stampe and his Indian colleagues. A Sunday morning, spent within a small aeroplane flying over the

BRITISH FILM PRODUCTION

32 to 36. 'Anna Karenina' (London Film Production). Directed by Julien Duvivier; with Ralph Richardson as Karenin (32), Vivien Leigh as Anna Karenina and Kieron Moore as Vronsky.

37 and 38. 'Snowbound' (Gainsborough). Directed by David MacDonald; with Marcel Dalio (37), Dennis Price, Robert Newton, Guy Middleton and Stanley Holloway.

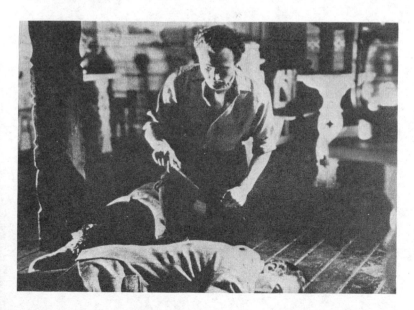

39 and 40. 'Rescue' (Gainsborough). Directed by Ken Annakin; with Phyllis Calvert, James Donald, Margot Grahame and Francis L. Sullivan.

41 and 42. 'Against the Wind' (Ealing). Directed by Charles Crichton; with John Slater, Gordon Jackson and Robert Beatty.

43 and 44. 'The World is Rich' (C.O.I.). Produced and directed by Paul Rotha. A starving boy in India and food demonstrators in the Ruhr.

45 to 50. 'Oliver Twist' (Cineguild). Directed by David Lean; with Robert Newton, Francis L. Sullivan, Alec Guinness, Kay Walsh and Mary Clare.

50. Josephine Stuart as Oliver Twist's mother.

51 to 55. 'Hamlet' (Two Cities). Directed by Laurence Olivier; with himself as Hamlet, Eileen Herlie as the Queen, Basil Sidney as the King, Jean Simmons as Ophelia, Felix Aylmer as Polonius and Terence Morgan as Laertes.

54 and 55. The King and Laertes.

United Provinces examining his scheme of irrigation by tube wells, became romantic and exciting when a running commentary at first hand of the history of his struggles and setbacks accompanied our flight over the fruitful farming land below. On another day outside Delhi, Sir William's Indian colleague showed us in detail some of these same villages and farms which depend for their survival on each measured drop of water from tube wells where they exist, but more often from the ancient wells that have watered farms there for centuries. Farms so small we should call them allotments. Farmers with primitive equipment and, where no new wells exist, only their circling bullocks turning the creaking wheels at ancient well-heads, heaving and tipping the leather buckets which pour the water into the narrow, raised channels.

India is stiff with material for stories of all types and subjects. But communal differences and the problem of Pakistan, even in 1946, vetoed a large proportion of dramatic opportunities. European and American audiences, apathetic about India, would have to be won by tension and conflict far greater than is necessary in subjects closer to their own lives. Yet conflicts like these are, to put it mildly, tabu among Indians and would provoke active opposition to a film unit working on location.

And, indeed, we found a physical obstacle to our project – the unrest which has spread to the violence of autumn 1947. This atmosphere of deep disquiet was more disturbing to us than any previous experience during war or peace. In Calcutta we had seen homesick G.I.s in their thousands holding resentful mass meetings against their prolonged exile in Asia. The multitudinous Press throughout India, a Press largely with a very different attitude to the conveying of news than is customary in the West, was resentful of the courts-martial which were passing judgment on the ringleaders of the Indian National Army. That the scene of the trial was the Red Fort in Delhi, site of the overthrow of the last Moghul Emperor during the Indian Mutiny, only aggravated misunderstandings and grievances.

The I.N.A. trials, the unrest among the American G.I.s spreading to the British forces, affected in turn the Naval and Air Forces of India.

These forces are recruited from some of the most intelligent and well-educated families in India. Of India's 400 million inhabitants only about 50 million can read and write, and the percentage from among these of young men equipped to master the intricacies of modern sea and air armaments, and to be articulate and responsible when in authority, is comparatively not large. The disaffection, then, which arose at this time in India did not originate in mob hysteria, but in the frustration of educated young men in the lower officer groups who held no hope of promotion to higher rank under foreign domination. Or so it appeared to us. Our conclusions seem to have astonished some people, who still regard the people of India as a vast mob rather than as a host of individuals.

Motoring into the Western Ghats to visit an irrigation dam some ninety miles out of Bombay a few days after our arrival there, we met a British troop train and two large military road convoys making for the city. A week later the grievances among the young recruits in the naval training-school at Bombay flared up into open mutiny which spread among twenty ships in the harbour and, during its suppression by Indian police and British parachute troops, inflamed the civilian population and led to thousands of casualties.

During our first days in Bombay, main centre of Indian film production, our project was well received by the English-speaking film players who looked forward to showing their talents for the first time on foreign screens. Intelligent and far-sighted Indians shared this opinion. They wanted the real India sympathetically treated in a film for international audiences. Indian film producers, on the other hand, feared that the use of more finance and of more advanced technique than they could afford would show up their own less ambitious film production to less advantage. We met their objections by arguing that our film was to be made in English and would therefore not compete with theirs in their own markets and their many languages.

Although we spent our time almost exclusively with Indians during the whole fourteen weeks of our tour, it was in Bombay in our fourth week that we first experienced that delicate give-and-take of spontaneous friendship with a number of Indians which, on looking back, makes the many difficulties and dis-comforts of the journey well worth their momentary nuisance value.

The embarrassments caused by the mutiny cut right across our researches in Bombay. One Tuesday morning Indian naval ratings began demonstrating in the streets, shops were closed, transport left the streets. It became hard to keep any engage-ment. Everything European – a name on a building, the wearing of a tie round one's collar, or the flying of a flag other than Con-gress, Moslem League, or Communist – was an invitation for trouble. And by trouble, I mean TROUBLE. I took a taxi, never a reliable form of transport and now rare. As we were crossing a main thoroughfare I saw several hundred naval demonstrators coming towards us headed by a lorry loaded with young men shouting slogans. In the middle of the crossing my taxi broke down. On its bonnet, I was horrified to see, a small Union Jack fluttered. The demonstrators were within a few yards. The taxi driver miraculously started the engine again, we jerked our way into a side street. For the moment that was that.

Next morning I tried to cross the same street on foot. More crowds and greater excitement than the day before. An elderly Parsee, in his curious uniform of knee-length cotton jacket but-toned to the neck and his American-cloth formalised turban, ran at me and beat me on the chest with his hands. 'Go, go', he shouted. 'You bring trouble. Hide. They're burning the English in the square along there. Go back, for God's sake.' I went back. People were running. Every shop was shuttered, every door locked. I tried to enter the friendly cinema where the Rank films were being shown, but that too was locked up. I edged round the square to see what was really going on. The crowd was excited, but no one was being burnt. That was perhaps happening somewhere else.

On the Thursday I heard bursts from automatic weapons fired at mutineers inside the barracks. Civilians joined in the demonstrations. Rioting began to spread through the city.

On Friday a Moslem friend took me to a morning performance of a Congress propaganda play, *Dewar*, purporting to show how the British divided India to rule her. I was the only European in a crowded and demonstrative audience. We divided the intervals between calling upon the players back-stage, who were courteous and communicative, and watching the well-laundered crowds in the street outside attacking the Indian police and burning a British military lorry. Most remarkable of the sights was a column of men, led by one who was brandishing the three flags of Congress, Moslem League, and the Communists on the same pole for the first time in history. I was safe in the theatre, for the tradition of personal hospitality is as strong in India as anywhere on earth. The rioting was directed not at known individuals but at the representatives of a hostile idea. As one of the latter I found great difficulty in returning to my hotel. I went part of the way hidden in the back of an old cab. We were held up for a time by convoys of armoured cars and lorries filled with armed troops covered in protective netting, while a bomber and a squadron of fighters demonstrated overhead. The cabby became frightened. We left him and walked against a tide of men and women fleeing from the business section of the city in which we were staying.

From this date all military traffic appeared to be under orders to travel through the crowded city at not less than fifty miles an hour, so that I began to wonder who was trying to provoke whom to achieve what.

Our Indian friends behaved nobly. My wife was ill with food poisoning, another of the trials of a tropical climate. Our friends acted as bodyguards, messengers, and entertainers in turn, and

not for a moment were we allowed to feel unwelcome. Our two
or three rebuffs in India came from those to whom we were impersonal representatives of a hated domination.

This week of nightmare reached its climax with bodies lying
unburied in the streets, where a curfew failed to prevent 200,000
Indians sleeping nightly on the pavements for lack of accommodation. Twenty silent ships in mutiny lay in the harbour with
guns trained on the shore, guns that were never fired. And in the
air-conditioned restaurant of the hotel, within sight of the ships,
Europeans and Indians danced the week-end away with a sang-
froid indistinguishable from indifference. On the same harbour
front boats from the silent mutineers crept to the quays at night
and were loaded with food from the tables of the diners on the
terraces of the rich clubs. The diners were helping to carry the
precious consignments to the dinghies. A film in itself, but who
would let us make it?

A week later we found the unrest had spread to Madras. The
withdrawal of British and American forces had led to increased
unemployment and drought had shortened the rations. Two
days before our arrival a European civil servant had fired a revolver into a crowd which surrounded his car and had killed an
Indian boy of fourteen. I asked a Brahmin to send me the Press
cuttings of the public inquiry. 'There will be no public inquiry,'
he said resentfully. He proved to be right. In this part of Southern
India, where coolies do much of the work which in Northern
India is done by bullocks, this surprises nobody.

Bombay and Madras could hardly show a greater contrast,
though both are large cities. Bombay, cosmopolitan-Indian,
sophisticated. Vulgar architecture, vivacious city life. Madras,
solid, pleasant, colonial architecture, an atmosphere of a community with deep roots, bookshops full of closely argued
scholarly studies. India, at all times leisurely, is here like a college
close. (Lahore, outside its walled city, was also leisurely, but in
the manner of the fashionable well-to-do.)

From Madras we visited a famine area. A seventeen-mile-long

reservoir was dry. Peasants had dug holes in the bottom, and their bullocks licked the salt mud in them, cattle that like to stand in deep water through the heat of the day. The peasants drank from a well so rancid as to turn the stomach and pitifully tried to gather a maize crop which crumbled to dust in the hand. The heat, even in early March, was appalling. On our way back to Madras we entered Conjeeveram, one of the seven sacred cities of the Hindus. We had letters to the keepers of two of its thousand and eight temples. Tension; police in the streets; shops shuttered; popular resentment at our car. We saw the two magnificent temples, fed the elephants, were garlanded, and gave alms. On our way back to the Madras road we turned into a wide main thoroughfare which was entirely blocked by a riot outside a grain-shop. A cloud of dust hung above hundreds of white-clad yelling peasants, lathis were being brandished and blows struck. Our Indian driver kept his head, turned the car in almost its own length and drove us safely away. Four Indian policemen were beaten to death in that incident. Rioters had a short system with foreign cars at that time; they were known to bar the doors to keep the occupants from escaping, to open the tank and set fire to the petrol.

Experiences like these coloured one's appreciation of the opportunities for research. Yet we think we learnt something of Indian history, the contrasting architectures of Hindu in the South and Moghul in the North, the beauty and intricacy of Hindu music and dancing. We felt the passionate, complex, variable temperature of the Indian character. We saw Benares, the city whose life springs from the Hindu religion in all its manifestations, and enjoyed the settings and liveliness of traditional romanticism in the Indian state of Jaipur. It might be that our meetings with the emotional outbursts of the Indian mob were coincidental and not to be set too seriously against our chances of smooth working in India.

We happened to return to New Delhi on the day of the Victory Parade. The procession and the fireworks in the avenue before the Viceroy's House in New Delhi were offset by the rioting in Old Delhi. The victory decorations were torn down and burnt, the military procession was diverted from even entering the old city, and the flames from the town hall in Old Delhi competed with the gaiety of the fireworks in the night sky above the new city.

The last disquieting episode we experienced was on our way to the Kulu Valley to the east of the Punjab. Our train stopped at Amritsar long enough for the passengers to eat at the station restaurant, and an Army officer took his revolver from his luggage before leaving the train for his meal. He told us one was a fool to go unarmed to dine in that town.

The Kulu Valley, some twelve miles long, lies north to south in the southern slopes of the Himalayas. The people, in a stronghold difficult to reach even in these days, are handsome and smiling and not very hardworking. Their climate, eighty degrees in summer with two or three weeks of snow in the winter, is such that, as we were told, you drop a seed on to the ground and it grows. This valley of 70,000 people is Hindu to a man. There are three hundred known gods and goddesses, who all have their fiestas, and dancing and the sound of music and drums beating distantly are part of the air one breathes. These man-made gaieties flourish against an embroidered background: the rush of mountain streams from the snow-capped hills, the blue sky reflected in the water on the terraced rice-fields, the stylised wooden houses of great charm built on the steep slopes of the valley. And when we were there, the cherry and the pear in full bloom above the wild tulips in the spring grass. 'If there be Paradise upon earth, it is here, it is here, it is here.'

There are countless stories in folk-lore and local history full of fire and colour and violence (some of which are denied point-blank by the inhabitants but are corroborated by Indian District Commissioners), but naked and unashamed they would never pass a Western censor.

We returned to New Delhi to report our findings just as the

Cabinet Mission were settling down to discussion, and it was agreed to delay any decision to work in India until the autumn of 1946. By then it was time to delay further. There are three contrasting subjects I want to make which would cover much of what we saw and learnt. But active history-in-the-making is at the moment too tragic and too dangerous to allow one to take thirty or more technicians to the East and be sure to bring 'em back alive. Indian film production has been almost at a standstill for the last eighteen months. There could be no sympathy for the European who would rush in where even the Indian fears to tread.

THE NATIVE FILMS
OF MEXICO

MARIA ROSA OLIVER

*

MEXICO has in its very nature a great photogenic asset: in its indescribable translucid atmosphere, landscape, architecture, and men harmonise. Under the sun, the white-washed walls of its buildings, the carved stones of its pre-Columbian ruins, the tiled domes of its baroque churches and the huge straw hats of its people, stand out against deep skies or silver-edged heavy ink-blue clouds. Even its plants, such as the piked magüey and the flat circular-leaved nopal, are clean-cut and neat to the eye: light and shadow play on them as on the high cheekbones and full-lipped mouths of the Mexican faces.

It did not take long for nearby Hollywood to discover the plastic quality of the neighbour country, but, Tantalus-like, it could only look at it; not use it. There are several reasons for this, among them the will of the Mexicans to have a moving-picture industry of their own, and the fact that Hollywood could not reproduce in its studios Mexico's historical background or the Mexican way of living, without distorting or falsifying them. Mexico's history is a long sequence of sufferings, territorial mutilations, and revolts against foreign intrusion and exploitation; the good man in Mexico is not rewarded with material success, and drama in his life has generally not a happy ending.

On the other hand, compared with Hollywood, Mexico's film industry is poor, and as transportation and equipment to shoot scenes in the open are expensive, it cannot profit as it should from its natural advantages. Great sums are needed in order to show on the screen 'the wind that swept Mexico' a quarter of a

73

century ago, the agrarian revolution which its great fresco painters have fixed on the walls of the public buildings. Nevertheless, the folk-lore is so colourful and characteristic in the Aztec land that merely by reproducing it in the sets, a picture with both interest and charm can be created.

It was natural, therefore, that films with local colour and nothing else were not only done, but overdone. Their songs soon became popular throughout the American continent, specially those of *Allá en el Rancho Grande* (Over There on the Big Ranch), in which Tito Guizar, Mexico's first actor-singer, sang the song that gives the title to the picture. One after another, films with an excess of serenades, silver-embroidered tight trousers, immaculate white felt *sombreros,* easily drawn guns, dancing and drinking, were shown on every Latin-American screen.

The Mexicans at first, and their neighbours to the south later, soon got tired of this rather cheap and folk-lorish display. As a consequence, fewer and fewer of this kind of picture were released, and these were generally second- or third-rate musical comedies. The pendulum swung in the opposite direction: 'serious' pictures, based – just as in the competitive Argentine production – on European novels and happening in a sort of no-man's land, were filmed in Mexico's studios.

This drift towards the parlour or bedroom plays only satisfies the not too cultured audiences. The public, used to the best North American and European pictures, cannot fail to react against the lack of style obvious in this sort of film: our countries, young as independent nations, have not yet achieved that traditional style of living that lends a certain charm even to the most conventional European drawing-room comedies. Furthermore, as most of our good actors come from the poorer classes, they act stiltedly in this kind of social milieu. And finally, nowadays, in this part of America as elsewhere, in order to interest alert audiences the individual problem portrayed must be made a part of the collective one.

But as Mexico's artists, writers, producers, directors, and actors came to feel the power of their land and understand its spirit, they recognised their shortcomings and searched for a solution to enable them to express with artistic and poetic sense Mexico as it really is. The Mexican film industry has already released several fine pictures of this kind, the first of which was filmed ten years ago, under the title of *The Night of the Mayas*, filmed in Yucatan under the direction of Pancho Cabrera with Arturo de Cordova as leading actor. Then, with a script by the poet Xavier de Villaurrutia, Julio Bracho directed *Crepusculo* (Dusk), and the director Emilio Fernandez, assisted by the cameraman Gabriel Figueroa, made four films based on scripts by the well-known novelist Mauricio Magdaleno: *Bougainvillia*, *Las Abandonadas* (The Abandoned Ones), *Flor Silvestre* (Wild Flower), and *Maria Candelaria*, all of them starring Dolores del Río. With the same actress, and also with a script by Mauricio Magdaleno, the director Roberto Gabaldon filmed the rather melodramatic picture *La Otra* (The Other One), while Emilio Fernandez, this time with María Felix as star, directed *Enamorada* (In Love), based on a script by Iñigo de Martino, with Gabriel Figueroa's assistance. María Felix acted also as leading lady in *La Mujer de Todos* (Everybody's Woman), directed by Julio Bracho. Among these productions we can also mention two not based on Mexican scripts: *La Carreta* (The Chariot), directed by Roberto Gabaldón, based on the novel of the Spaniard Blanco Ibañez, with Roberto Soler as leading man, and *Doña Barbara*, based on the novel of the Venezuelan Romulo Gallegos, who himself carried out the adaptation. This was directed by Fernando de Fuentes and had María Felix as star. Not all of these pictures have the same artistic quality; but we will speak later about three of them which are of undoubted merit.

Meanwhile the folk-lorish sentimental musical comedies went on being released as before. In these productions, Jorge Negrete, Mexico's film-star idol, towers over the colourfully clad extras who surround him, and, like Frank Sinatra in the States, makes women swoon with his songs. He is the embodiment of the 'he-man', the bad boy who wins his girl with tears and by knowing when to use his revolver, which is far too often.

But just as in the United States one could not classify Chaplin's pictures into any definite category, so in Mexico one must classify apart Cantinflas' films. Undoubtedly Cantinflas (Mario Moreno) has given to the Spanish-speaking part of the New World the first generic popular type-actor it has ever had. Without reverting to the broad-brimmed Mexican hat or the multi-coloured plaid (serape), he has popularised throughout the continent Mexico's loafing street-boy, and he emphasises in such a profoundly comic way the psychological Latin-American traits that no matter of what social standing or country we may be, we recognise ourselves in him. By attitudes that show him full of surprise, by a certain slowness in his gestures and a furtive dreaminess in his eyes, he conveys to us that part of ourselves which goes on as a daydream in our subconscious. And lacking as we do a conventional language in which to express that chaotic subconscious brooding, Cantinflas has created a special crazy talk: he brings together the most absurd and nonsensical terms, and in his harangues, monologues, and explanations, overwhelms the audience as the Marx Brothers do with their acting. The Mexican comedian uses this rhetorical flow in a way so true to reality that this style of speech has come to be denoted in contemporary idiom by the verb *cantinflear*.

As Romeo in a burlesque of Shakespeare's play, as D'Artagnan in *The Three Musketeers*, as amateur bullfighter in *Nor Blood Nor Sand*, as shrewd loafer in *That's the Detail*, as policeman in *The Unknown Soldier*, as bell-boy and tango-dancer in *Grand Hotel*, as newspaper-seller and soldier of the last war in *One Day in Hell*, as cobbler and trapeze artiste in *The Circus*, as janitor and spiritualist medium in *I Am a Fugitive*, Cantinflas works into the atmosphere of the picture the essence of the baggy-trousered tramp that he always impersonates. The scripts and direction in the Cantinflas pictures are far below the level of his talent: his producers, or maybe he himself, seem to rely wholly on the strength of his personality, in this way running the risk of wasting one of the most genial comic actors of our time.

Cantinflas' more recent productions, as well as all the first-rate Mexican pictures, are shot at the Churubusco Studios. Situated in the outskirts of Mexico City, these enormous, red-bricked, modern studios can compete with the best of Hollywood. Churubusco Studios promote their own productions and rent floor-space to other film companies. Half of Churubusco Studios' shares belong to R.K.O., and the other half to Don Emilio Carrega, owner of Mexico's most important broadcasting station.

The annual production of Mexican films is around sixty films, the number released by only one of Hollywood's studios. Class A films (super-productions) cost in Mexico an average of 1,000,000 Mexican pesos; Class B, 600,000 Mexican pesos, and Class C, 300,000. At Mexico's current rate of exchange its pictures cost three or four times less than those of Hollywood. Taking into account the cost of production and the quantity of films released annually, the percentage of good-quality and artistic films made in Mexico is to its advantage.

Competitors in Latin-America's film market, Mexico and Argentina have begun to exchange actors, many of them popular also on the stage. The public, provided that a picture is spoken in Spanish, does not discriminate about its origin. Through the screen the Mexican accent has become popular in Argentina, and an Argentine accent in Mexico, whilst both are liked in the rest of Latin-America.

Three Mexican pictures, already mentioned, have transcended lately the limits of the Spanish-speaking countries. All three of them were directed by Emilio Fernandez (known in Mexico as 'el Indio Fernandez'), a man of extraordinary artistic intuition and a talent for crowd grouping and crowd movements that places him in the line of his country's great mural painters. But in these pictures it is difficult to separate Fernandez' achievements from those of his cameraman, Daniel Figueroa, who, as no one else till now, has the gift of conveying photographically the sense of eternity in Mexico's architecture and the frailty of the human body beside it. The excellent teamwork in these pictures is completed by the scripts of Mauricio Magdaleno on which they are based, and by the actors with an extraordinary sense of national character who play in them.

The first of these productions to be released was *Flor Silvestre* (Wild Flower), based on an episode that occurs during the first agrarian revolts in 1909, when bandits join the revolt of the Indian peasants in order to loot, rob, and rape. It is the touching story of a young half-Indian couple drawn into the revolutionary turmoil. The crudity and cruelty of certain scenes are almost unbearable for foreign audiences, but are nevertheless the peak moments of a theme carried out with great artistic and historical integrity. Dolores del Río plays the young wife and mother in such a natural way that it is difficult to imagine that she is not herself a real Indian peasant-woman. Barefooted, wrapped in the plain rebozo, her strange, extremely dignified loveliness stands out in all its beauty. Pedro Armendariz, to-day Mexico's most promising young actor, plays as her leading man. Broad-shouldered, with high cheekbones, slanting Indian eyes and clear-cut features, he has the indifferent, aloof air that matches Dolores del Río's graceful dignity and is part of the unusual charm of the Mexican people.

Maria Candelaria, filmed by the same director, the same cameraman and leading actors, is a dramatic love story that happens in the village of flowery Xochimilco, among people still primitive in their collective reactions and extremely sensitive in their individual feeling. Fernandez has given the whole picture a slow rhythm in keeping with the atmosphere that envelops the sleepy waters of Xochimilco's streams, where everything seems to be in suspense till an unexpected event breaks the slow tempo of the flower- and fruit-gatherers' quiet existence: wild passion bursts out then like a hurricane and destroys the happiness and the lives of the two lovers. Certain scenes in this production are among the most beautiful that have ever been filmed, and undoubtedly it would be difficult to find actors more close to the spirit of their earth than Dolores del Río and Pedro Armendariz are in this deeply poetical picture.

Enamorada, with a script by Iñigo de Martino, Fernandez as director, and Figueroa as cameraman, features the beautiful María Felix in the rôle of an aristocratic provincial girl who, after insulting and ill-treating the young revolutionary General (Pedro Armendariz), who has occupied with his troops the town in which she lives, ends by falling in love with him. The romance could not be more simple, but each episode happens in a spot that emphasises Mexico's natural or architectural beauties. The background gives authenticity to every situation, gesture, or word. It does not matter that the plot reminds you of *The Taming of the Shrew*, nor that at the end you recall the last scene of *Morocco*, since every archway, street, plaza, church-tower, church-ceiling, altar, or panorama, tells you of a civilisation that persists in the emotions of the people that have inherited it.

That is what Mexican pictures will show to the world: a country where two traditions have blended and live in the feeling, work and art of its people.

Buenos Aires, September 1947

THE FUNCTION OF THE
SPECIALISED CINEMA

ELIZABETH M. HARRIS

★

A SPECIALISED cinema is frequently thought of as one which shows films of an origin other than British or American. While this is partly correct, it does not define what *kind* of film is, or should be, shown in such theatres. There is no inherent reason why French, Russian and other foreign films should be any different in quality from the average British or American film. Yet, even if their artistic merits were no greater than those of the average English-speaking film, the specialised cinema would still serve a valuable purpose – that of acquainting the British cinema-goer with life, not necessarily as it is lived, but at any rate as it is seen by film-makers in the various countries of the world.

But this, though important, is not the chief point. As a matter of fact the quality of the average film shown at a specialised theatre is usually considerably higher than that of the average film in the ordinary cinema. The reason is not far to seek, so far as foreign films are concerned. The number of specialised cinemas is small, and they are therefore in a position to pick and choose among foreign films and to exhibit only the best of them in this country. Of course, foreign producers are by nature neither more nor less artistically inclined than, say, their Hollywood counterparts. They are, however, confronted by the fact that Hollywood has a virtual monopoly of the ordinary commercial film, and can produce this type of picture more glamorously and more attractively than they will ever be able to do. In addition, producers in the smaller countries have only a small home market in which to recover their costs. They are therefore compelled to keep these comparatively low, and instead to exercise greater ingenuity in both subject and presentation. To capture foreign markets, as they do not possess either the resources or stars of Hollywood, they must depend on the production of films which are qualitatively above the general run. In plain words, quality is a very *paying* proposition for them. They do not, of course, always succeed in this aim, but it is surprising how many fine films, fresh in subject-matter and treatment, have been produced of recent years in some of the smaller countries (e.g. from Switzerland *Marie Louise* and *The Last Chance* – each film the only one produced in its year – *Frenzy* from Sweden, and *Day of Wrath* and *Red Meadows* from Denmark). If one considers that the number of films produced each year in these countries is very small, the percentage of good films among them augurs well for the future development of the international film.

Specialised cinemas, however, do not show only foreign films. A considerable number of first-rate British and American films have had their premier showing in such theatres. Some have been short documentary films – a type of film, it may be said in passing, which has always been of considerable importance for the development of the whole of film art – which were thought too advanced or not of sufficient interest for their audiences by the big circuits. Others have been films like *The Forgotten Village* which, partly because of their subject-matter and treatment, but largely also because of their unusual length (somewhere between a short and a feature), could not obtain a premier showing in an ordinary cinema. Lastly, there are cases like that of *Strange Incident* – by general consensus of critical opinion one of the outstanding American films of the last decade. This film was first shown almost stealthily, without the least attempt being made to draw public attention to it. A London specialised theatre immediately recognised the extraordinary sincerity and artistic quality of the film, booked it, and gave it its first press showing and publicity in this country. The same remarks apply to feature-length documentary films like *Children on Trial*. Many of these films, shorts, semi-feature and feature-length films, which had all been regarded, at first, as unsuitable by ordinary commercial exhibitors, have later had bookings up and down the country as a result of their first run at a specialised theatre.

We have therefore several countries (and their number is steadily increasing) producing each year a certain number of films of a sufficiently high quality to merit the attention of anyone seriously interested in the cinema. On the other hand, there is no doubt that there exist in this country large potential audiences who are, or would be, willing to support a film purely on its artistic merits, without the attraction of well-known stars or the knowledge that the film cost several hundred thousand pounds to produce. This audience, knowing that film is essentially a visual medium, would not even be deterred by the fact that the dialogue is in a foreign language and has therefore to be made comprehensible with the admittedly not always completely satisfactory aid of English subtitles.

The obstacle between supply and demand is the vast, centralised structure of the commercial exhibitors' circuits, which have, so far, only on the rarest occasions taken the risk of showing foreign (i.e. non-English-speaking) films in their cinemas. When therefore the cinema lost its universal character with the advent of the sound film and the consequent Babylonian confusion of tongues, the need arose for a new instrument which would safeguard the international character of the film as an art under the changed conditions. This instrument is the specialised cinema.

The function of the specialised cinema, like that of every other cinema or commercial enterprise, is to make a profit. The difference between it and the commercial cinema proper lies in the way in which it tries to achieve this aim. The main object of the commercial cinema is to maximise its box-office receipts, and it does so by exhibiting the ordinary run of English-speaking films, which have been specially produced with this purpose in mind. This does not mean that all these films must necessarily be bad. What it does mean is that the overwhelming majority are made on the theory of the lowest common denominator, i.e. to whomever else they may appeal, they must not be above the head of the most ignorant spectator with the least-trained taste. All this points to the fact that the commercial cinema does not regard the present level of popular taste as, so to speak, a base from which to build upwards towards something better, but as a given and unalterable datum to be exploited for the purpose of maximising box-office receipts.

The position of the specialised cinema is radically different. Apart from the fact that the films it shows are foreign (a fact which, by itself, would only attract an extremely small number of people), its sole *raison d'être* is that its programmes are usually of a better quality than those of the commercial cinema. Its audience is a specialised audience which visits the cinema almost exclusively because of this difference in quality, and if a programme does not come up to expectations, it will simply stay away. In contrast therefore to the commercial cinema, artistic quality is a definite box-office necessity for the specialised house.

It would, however, be an over-simplification merely to say that, while the commercial cinema exploits the bad taste of the culturally under-privileged, the specialised cinema exploits the good taste of the privileged minority. It must not be forgotten that the present audience of the specialised cinema was largely created by the specialised cinemas themselves – a task which required, and still requires, cinema owners and company directors who must not only be good enough business men to be prepared to create their own market (always a most risky undertaking), but men to whom artistic quality and the education of public taste must appear more important objects than mere box-office receipts. Otherwise they would probably never have entered this field, and had certainly best stay out of it. In this creation of a high-class audience, the specialised cinemas have had the constant and valuable support of the film societies, which have given showings of films of outstanding artistic value in districts where for various reasons it is impossible to maintain a specialised cinema. Film societies, however, are not an ideal: they are a creation of necessity, pioneer efforts whose objects are necessarily limited. The exhibition and appreciation of works of art in closed groups can never be a completely satisfactory state of affairs – art has too important a function in the life of the community for its enjoyment to be restricted to small circles of connoisseurs. The idea to be aimed at is the showing of these films in the same cinemas and on the same terms as ordinary films, and in the struggle for this aim the specialised cinema is a farther – at the moment the farthest – development of the work of the film societies. This means that there does not exist any real competition or conflict of aim between them. Both are instruments in the fight for the same objectives, and each possesses its different and distinct function. It is, however, clear that where a specialised cinema exists, the functions of a film society are, of necessity, considerably diminished. Furthermore, it is not altogether desirable that film societies all over the country should, as happens with increasing frequency, show greater interest in the big successes of the London specialised cinemas than in the many other films which for one reason or another have not achieved such popularity. Such booking of 'London successes', whether for prestige reasons or for the purpose of increasing membership, must ultimately lead to a commercialisation of the film societies, which would be in complete opposition to the ideals which they were founded to serve.

Finally, just as in the bigger towns film societies must give way to specialised cinemas, so perhaps in time to come the latter, its aims achieved, will be swallowed up by the ordinary cinema. But that, at the moment, is looking a long way ahead.

To sum up the situation of the specialised cinema, we must return to what was said above about the commercial cinema, and make a few corrections. Film, like any other art, cannot simply be divided into mass-production without artistic value on the one hand and a restricted but artistically valuable minority movement on the other. Nor can it be regarded as an unconnected collection of good, bad and mediocre films, each produced without relation to what went before or will come afterwards. The art of the film is an organic whole, and whatever is done, every new idea or experiment – whether it appears first in a documentary film about the family life of the bee and whether it is produced in England or in Timbuctoo – is likely, sooner or later, to influence film-makers in every corner of the globe. Improvements in art are mostly made by small groups, or even single individuals, who have no great name to recommend them and only modest means to carry out their intentions. So long, however, as there exist channels through which they can bring their work to the attention of the general public and of their co-workers in the field, the way is open towards the development and improvement of the technique of their art and the education of public taste. The recent renaissance of the British cinema, which cannot be explained without reference to the documentary movement of the thirties and the devoted and often little-recognised work of a comparatively small group of directors and producers, provides clear support for this thesis. The peculiar strategic importance of the specialised cinema resides in the fact that it is not simply a place where good films in foreign languages are shown, but that it is the *only* channel through which creative and experimental work in the field of international film art is brought before the general public. It thereby performs a possibly slow, but certainly constant and cumulative work of improving public taste with regard to *all* films which come before it, and thus enables the commercial film-producer to take for granted a rising level of public taste. This in turn may serve to diminish his fear of financial failure through too great a devotion to art and neglect of the lowest common denominator.

It must not be thought that the frequent vulgarity, tasteless-ness and insincerity of the ordinary commercial film is alto-gether due to ill-will and ignorance on the part of its makers. The artistic and technical talent and resources available in, say, Hollywood are great enough to produce each year dozens of films of a quality as high as anything that is shown at a film society or a specialised theatre. What holds them back is a great sensitiveness – a sensitiveness to the smallest fluctuations in box-office receipts. More than all manifestos, books or critical admonitions, it is the financial success of artistically first-rate films in specialised cinemas which will convince the commercial film-world that there exists no law of nature which makes tripe or 'kitsch' more profitable than serious art, and that it may just be possible that people will appreciate and pay for a good thing if it is offered to them. That is the language of the box-office – a language widely and thoroughly understood. To use this language in the cause of the film as an art may not be the least important function of the specialised cinema.

WHO ARE THOSE
TECHNICIANS?

JOHN SHEARMAN

*

AT the beginning or end of every film there is a screenful of names – the technical credits.

As far as most of the lay Press and B.B.C. critics are concerned, these technicians might have no real existence at all; this recital of their names might be merely a rather odd conventional device to make the customers listen to some pompous music and settle themselves in their seats before being plunged into the excitements of Sequence One, Scene One, SLOW FADE IN DAY EXTERIOR (Stock Shot), The Grand Canal, Venice – or whatever.

Most of the critics write about three aspects of films only – acting, story, and situations. To read them you would think they all subscribed to the Agateian heresy – 'Put that box down over there and turn the handle whilst the cast acts'.

Now, of course, films will always tend to have a story – usually the same old one; of course films will tend to use actors and actresses; of course they will have situations. But films are not only acting and story and situation – they are films. Novels have story; the stage has actors and situations and story, yet it is quite easy to distinguish one from the other, and still easier to distinguish either of them from film. Each bears, as it were, a distinguishing mark; each medium has its own characteristic technique. The technique is the distinguishing mark.

In a film the complicated, heartbreaking, fascinating business of direction, set-designing, photography, sound recording, editing, and dubbing is performed by a fairly large number of technicians whose work is not merely a series of mechanical operations carried out according to pre-ordained rules. It is in no way comparable to the factory production of, say, standard parts for motor-cars. Each step is an individual's unique work, bearing the impress of his mind – or at any rate it ought to be.

A young actor gives a brilliantly sinister performance in to-morrow's West End release – fine; the reviews will tell us of it. But did a young operator achieve some brilliantly sinister camera movements; did an almost anonymous man in a cutting-room assault the nerves with a brilliant piece of sound and picture cutting; did a recordist get, with infinite pains, a piece of track – music, effects, or dialogue – possessing that haunting quality which makes you more aware of everything you hear for a week afterwards? … maybe they did, but it is rare indeed for the critics to say so. Equally, a bad performance or a banal plot will get its slating, while a bad bit of technique will pass unnoticed.

It is probable that the critics are in fact aware of film technique going on as a confused noise in the background. Now and again, in a muddled sort of way, it crops up in their writings. The director nearly always gets a bracket to himself, and there may be a *faute de mieux* line to the effect that he handled the story (or the cast) 'briskly'. The camera, too, crops up occasionally, 'allowing us a brief glimpse of' something or other, or 'dwelling lovingly on' something shapely – usually mountains, but some-times legs.

Sound hardly ever gets a mention, except that now and again a well-deserved half-brick is heaved at the score for being too loud and too long. Editing is a suspect branch of technique. The critics are apparently not aware that editing has taken place un-less they see a couple of hundred feet of ultra-fast cutting or a confusion of superimposes. When they do see this sort of thing they reckon it must be *montage*, which nowadays is the unmen-tionable word (it has a long-haired, greenery-yallery, phoney-æsthetic connotation), so they pass it by in disgusted silence.

The art department sometimes gets a grudged word for some 'true to life' or 'lavish' settings, though usually these are vaguely ascribed to the director or the cameraman. Few critics try (for instance) to distinguish between the art director's and the cameraman's contributions to the final result – the lit set.

In short, about half the creative work in a film is virtually ignored, which means that the other half (story, acting, and situations) inevitably gets an over-emphasis.

Does this matter? The short view is that the critics are writing for next week's cash customers who only want to know what the film is about and who plays in it. Even so, it can be argued that if the customer is entitled to critical pointers about, say, story, he is equally entitled to pointers about technique. If it is good for him to know that the plot is hackneyed, will he not be a still better man for knowing that the cutting is sloppy and the photography conventional to the point of boredom? And when the rare winner comes along, will he not appreciate it the more if his cinematic mentor hints at the technical achievement which has enhanced the genius of the story and the fineness of the acting?

On the long view, assuming that film is an art and that informed art criticism is important, it seems a pity that half the art should arouse no criticism; neither blame, praise, nor constructive suggestion. It is as if all painters were criticised solely on what they chose to depict – a portrait of a saint or a social reformer having automatically more merit than a portrait of a sinner or a spiv; a landscape with honest labourers being considered a better work than a landscape with idle lovers, irrespective of the painting.

If criticism is concerned with raising the standards of the art, if critics want to make a positive contribution to films, then they ought to be willing to notice film technique as well as acting technique and story technique. They are doing a first-class job now in making people critically aware of the content of films. Because of their efforts fewer and fewer people go to the pictures in a purely escapist mood. Audiences are beginning to want and enjoy better screen stories; they are beginning to *think* in the luxurious hypnotic dark of the cinemas. As a result, film-makers are encouraged to make films about subjects which demand and deserve thought. The next critical step is to make the audiences aware of film technique as well. If they were so conscious, we might get some real advances in technique – for technicians are at present devoting more and more time and energy to giving the pictures a highly polished surface which is admirable – admirable and *dull*. Almost every film to-day is technically competent – competent and nothing else. Portrayal has become entirely subservient to the thing portrayed: the frightening rattle of the conveyor belt is faintly heard to-day around the studios and cutting-rooms.

Critical recognition, whether it be attack or admiration, of the work of the film technician can help to bring technique back to its proper importance in film-making.

BRITISH FILM MUSIC

JOHN HUNTLEY

*

'My argument is that in the last resort film music should be judged solely as music – that is to say, by the ears alone, and the question of its value depends on whether it can stand up to this test.' – ARTHUR BLISS.

WITH the recording of some forty minutes' music for Laurence Olivier's production of Shakespeare's *Hamlet*, Dr William Walton is in the news again. The Oldham composer, an undergraduate of Christ Church College, Oxford, entered the film world in 1935 with music for the Elizabeth Bergner film, *Escape Me Never*. The score suffered for being one of those 'rush jobs' which are still all too frequent in studio circles. A year later came music for *As You Like It*, but this was not a very happy example of screen Shakespeare; both the film and its music have now been forgotten. 1939 marked the next step, with the Redgrave-Bergner picture, *Stolen Life*; the story was highly emotional and Walton's music just kept the sentiment within bounds.

These three films were experimental for the composer. The scoring was on the whole adequate but uninspired. Pascal's *Major Barbara* (1941), however, was an entirely different matter. For the first time there was the desire to see the film three or four times with a minimum of one viewing devoted to the sound track. In *Next of Kin* (1942), one exclusive music viewing was called for, and this facility was conveniently provided for in the Services by compulsory Security shows in barracks and camps all over the country; the picture was perfectly enjoyable, even at a sixth screening, on account of some delightful orchestration by Walton in the stirring battle scenes and a grand passage provided for a music-hall strip-tease act. *The Foreman Went to France* and *Went The Day Well?* (1942) were less interesting musically, though there is a fine section in *The Foreman* for the refugee sequence. Leslie Howard's *First of the Few* (also in 1942) is fitted with a superb score; the fugue for the Spitfire construction sequence left one listening to the music almost – but not quite – at the first time through.

Henry V has two main features: the aptness of the music and the completely integral nature of the scoring in relation to the dialogue. The H.M.V. company have issued a set of four records (C.3583-86) presenting the main speeches and music sequences. From Olivier's viewpoint it was a mistake for him to play all the parts himself; for such an artist this error is unforgivable. From the music angle these records are indeed a rare treat in noting down such a magnificent account of a motion picture. Side One opens with the flute roulade that accompanies the shot of the Globe Theatre handbill floating in the breeze. A flourish on trumpets introduces the panoramic view of London in 1600, complete with a choir singing plain-chant. As the flag of the theatre is raised to the sound of a trumpet, the interior of the Globe is seen with all the bustle and excitement prior to the commencement of the Chronicle of King Henry Fifth.

Side Two introduces the complete solution to the problem of how to combine music and dialogue without loss to the power of either mode of expression. As Chorus gives the invitation 'On your imaginary forces work', the music has a decorative moment to assist the mind of the beholder. Then a short tremulous section links the first Chorus speech to the King's exhortation 'Once more into the breach', following through the cry of 'England and St. George!' with a stirring theme to conclude with a brief moment from the Siege of Harfleur in which the music rides jointly with Shakespeare's lines. The scenes of the night before Agincourt are mostly played in silence (sides 3 and 4), but as Chorus outlines the setting ('Now conjecture of a time'), the music, perfectly balanced and controlled, comments discreetly on the sentinels, stead threatening stead, the armourers 'accomplishing the night, closing rivets up', and the sound of the crowing cocks. The famous speech 'Upon the King' and its overture are spoken with only an occasional horn announcing the passage of the dark hours of night.

The Battle of Agincourt is represented in the recording by the 'St Crispin's Day' pronouncement (side 5), which leads into the battle music itself. First the preparations of the troops are heard and a statement of the charge theme. French horns are used for the tucket which ushers the arrival of Mountjoy, the French herald. Side 6 is devoted entirely to the music. The French mount in their armour, a toast is drunk, the drums roll, the trumpets sound, and the charge is on. To the thunder of hooves, the long line of French cavalry gradually increase their speed from a canter to a full gallop until the very music itself is galloping alongside them. King Henry, meanwhile, is preparing to receive the onslaught; arrows are ready, the bows are taut, stakes are sharpened and stuck in the ground. The sword is raised aloft, motionless. When the French are almost on top of them, the sword falls and the archers let loose a great volley of arrows, zinging through the air in a never-to-be-forgotten sound. As the missiles fall among the horses there are many casualties. By now the opposing forces have come to grips and furious hand-to-hand fighting breaks out (side 7). The day belongs to King Harry and his men; this time there is no triumphal tucket as the French herald approaches to announce 'The day is yours'.

The scene changes suddenly to the French court as the Duke of Burgundy laments on the ruin of war-torn France to the accompaniment of strings and woodwind. The final Chorus speech follows (side 8), leading into a madrigal as the theatre flag is lowered. The floating handbill returns with its flute passage and the credit titles of the production unfold to the sound of the Agincourt Song. The final credit reads: 'Music by William Walton. Conducted by Muir Mathieson. Played by the London Symphony Orchestra'. The gramophone records were made by the Philharmonia Orchestra, conducted by the composer, in the H.M.V. Studios at Abbey Road, St John's Wood. It is to be hoped that a similar souvenir of *Hamlet* will be issued by the Gramophone Company following the outstanding success of these most enterprising and enjoyable discs.

Among the musical forms created by the cinema is the tabloid concerto. In cases where the story calls for the performance of serious music within the structure of the plot, there are two possibilities. First, extracts may be taken from symphonies and concertos of the concert-hall repertoire; *The Seventh Veil* is a perfect example, with its quotations from Grieg and Rachmaninoff. The alternative is to compose special miniature works on classical lines, designed to suit the specialised requirements of the film which, by its very nature, cannot allow the action to be held up for thirty or forty minutes for the performance of a full-scale work. A British composer, Jack Beaver, claims to have produced the first tabloid concerto, which can be heard in *The Case of the Frightened Lady* (1940). Charles Williams has also made experiments in this direction, notably in *The Night Has Eyes*, and most recently in *While I Live*, featuring piano tracks by Lady Betty Humby-Beecham, while Addinsell's *Warsaw Concerto* (Columbia D.X.1062) crystallised the style and perpetuated it for all time. Although the title Concerto is often dropped, the principle recurs in Hubert Bath's 'Cornish Rhapsody' (Columbia D.X.1171) and in Edward Ward's concerto, 'Lullaby of the Bells', from the American film *The Phantom of the Opera* (Decca F.8460). 'A Voice in the Night' from *Wanted for Murder*, by Spolianski (1946), and the American 'Spellbound Concerto', by Miklos Rozsa (both on Columbia D.X.1264), are fine examples of the gentle art of tabloid. Arthur Bliss went a stage farther in *Men of Two Worlds* (1946); his 'Baraza' is a miniature, rather than a distillation, complete in form with three distinct movements and piano cadenza (Decca K.1174).

For the Bette-Davis – Claude-Rains film *Deception*, Warner Brothers' staff composer, Erich Wolfgang Korngold, has produced a tabloid 'cello concerto. The story is just another variation on the old triangle theme, with Claude Rains as the com-

poser and Paul Henreid as the 'cellist; excerpts are heard from
Haydn's 'Cello Concerto, Beethoven's Appassionata Sonata
(first movement), Chopin's Prelude in E Major, and Beethoven's
Seventh Symphony (second movement). The 'cello sound track
is recorded by some unnamed woman 'cellist in the Hollywood
studio orchestra, under the musical direction of Leo F. Forbstein.
The synchronisation is excellent, with Henreid using the right
fingers at the right time and sliding when he is supposed to slide.
The specially composed ' cello work starts off at the beginning
and jumps to what would be the last movement; Korngold is so
pleased with the tabloid that he is going to write in the missing
parts and turn it into a full-scale work.   With a name like Wolfgang Korngold, a musical career was the only possibility and
this fifty-year-old Austrian-born composer was producing opera
in Vienna and the United States by the age of sixteen. He has
been writing for the films for many years and periodically an-
nounces his intention of leaving them for good in order to take
up other forms of composition. Within a few weeks, however,
he is back in Hollywood on his next picture. In 1936 he won an
Academy Award for his music in *Anthony Adverse*, and in 1938
he carried off another Oscar for his work in *The Adventures of
Robin Hood*. Korngold's thematic material has often left much
to be desired, but his orchestration for the microphone is always
carefully calculated to suit the requirements of the studio recording theatre. In *The Sea Hawk* there were some fine moments;
for example, for scenes in a swamp, a thin melody on muted
brass accompanied by cymbals, Chinese blocks, timpani, and
tambourine. Other scores of note include *Green Pastures,
Juarez, King's Row*, and *Elizabeth and Essex*.

How long is this 'Phoney Lives of the Composers' series going
to last? Having chopped up Chopin, ripped up Rimsky-Korsa-
kov, pickled Paganini, and chockered Tchaikovsky, the film
world is now preparing onslaughts on Moussorgsky (complete
with Bare Mountain Ballet), Bach, and Elgar; Brahms, Schu-
mann, and Liszt were, of course, all suitably wrapped up and

tucked away at one fell swoop in 'Song of Love' some time ago. If this pace goes on, the amount of turning-in-graves is liable to produce major changes in the surface of the earth.

YOUR GRAMOPHONE RECORD LIBRARY

Items of interest not previously reviewed in this column

1. Alexander Nevsky – Cantata (Serge Prokofiev).
Ten sides of music from the famous Soviet film; very dull in parts, but brightened by a few great moments, notably the 'Song of Alexander Nevsky' and the woodwind passage allocated to the villains of the piece.
Recorded by the Philadelphia Orchestra, conducted by Eugene Ormandy; with the Westminster Choir (conductor: John Finley Williamson).

Columbia L.X.977-981.

2. A Young Person's Guide to the Orchestra (Benjamin Britten).
Outstanding set of records based on the Crown Film Unit documentary production, *Instruments of the Orchestra*. A treat for young and old alike.
Recorded by the Liverpool Philharmonic Orchestra, conducted by Sir Malcolm Sargent.

Columbia D.X.1307-09.

3. Incidental music from *The Loves of Joanna Godden* (Ralph Vaughan Williams).
Very episodic but interesting collection of themes from the Ealing Studios film.
Recorded by the Philharmonia Orchestra, conducted by Ernest Irving.

Columbia D.X.1377.

4. Two scenes from *Duel in the Sun* (Dmitri Tiomkin).
Uninspired and uninteresting. Even the recording is technically not up to the usual standard of the Boston Orchestra.
Recorded by the Boston Promenade Orchestra, conducted by Arthur Fiedler.

H.M.V. B.9556.

DIALOGUE FOR STAGE
AND SCREEN

CLIFFORD LEECH

★

DRYDEN'S *Essay of Dramatic Poesy* has something to say about stage dialogue. It was in the period of rhymed heroic drama, and Dryden was anxious to defend his own use of rhyme in the theatre. Adversaries had alleged that no one in the audience would believe that the characters could spontaneously deliver themselves in couplets, either in long series or with the couplet divided between two characters. Dryden's reply was simple: of course the spectators did not believe that rhyming was unpremeditated, they recognised it as artifice and rejoiced in it the more. The pleasure they experienced was the pleasure which comes from the recognition of a pattern skilfully achieved, as one delights in the obviously planned movements of a dance.

Rhyme is not suitable for every kind of stage play, or for every kind of poem, but Dryden's principle concerning stage dialogue gives us an important clue to understanding what is right for the theatre. A play is a kind of ceremonial to which, with part of our mind, we respond as to a civic pageant or religious ritual. The actors are our spokesmen, going through largely traditional roles and working out a story that follows a recognisable plan. The Greeks and the medieval mystery players were in no doubt about this: not only was the manner of their speech highly formalised in verse-structure, but the stories they used were from traditional lore and were invariable in their main outline. Post-Renaissance drama has acquired a narrative interest which to some extent differentiates modern from classical and medieval plays: with one part of his mind, the spectator is curious or anxious about what is going to happen on the stage, but at the same time he knows from the beginning the main course of the play's events; he knows that the hero and villain of a melodrama will get their alleged deserts, that somehow Hamlet and Othello will be destroyed, that Jack will have his Jill again. The tone of the play is made apparent in the opening; the characters, how-ever individualised, occupy traditional positions in their rela-tions with each other; and complete surprise has no place in the dramatic scheme of things. Only in times of theatrical degenera-tion, whether in Beaumont and Fletcher tragi-comedy or in inter-war crime plays, do we find the playwright setting out to deceive the audience and to twist the plot in a way that we could not have anticipated. But even then the audience gets to know the tricks of the trade, to work on the slightest hint as to the turn events will take, so that a kind of pattern, albeit reluc-tantly, emerges.

This ceremonial character in a stage play makes a patterned form of speech inevitable for the best work. It may not be in rhyme, or even verse, but we need in the theatre exactly that sense of premeditation in the words used that Dryden recognised as conditioning the audience's reaction to rhyme. The Greeks used iambics for the non-choral parts of their tragi-comedies because that metre was the nearest to the rhythm of actual speech and yet recognisably metre. The Elizabethans found blank verse similarly appropriate, though they heightened the effect of pattern by occasional passages in rhyme, especially at the end of a scene or to point a character's departure from the stage. The best comedy of the Restoration was written in a prose that cultivated the grace and precision that the fashionable world aspired to but halted behind in the transactions of daily life. In the period of mediocrity that followed, there was still no pretence that the characters on the stage spoke in the fashion of real people: they had a stage dialect, with set forms of speech for the expression of love, hatred, remorse, patriotism, and the other few emotions that they were called upon to show. Only in the 'naturalistic' drama of the late nineteenth and early twentieth centuries was there a desire to make characters in a play as nearly as possible replicas, in speech and action, of the men and women outside the theatre.

This naturalistic drama, from Robertson to Galsworthy, was bound up with the dramatic exposition of social problems: it was not doctrinaire, but questioning; it was divorced from ceremonial pattern because there was no form of ritual act which playwrights and spectators could conscientiously take part in. It was a product of a growing scepticism concerning the rights and wrongs of human behaviour. In intention it was documentary.

The difficulty was that the playhouse was the home of ritual, not of documentary exposition. The shape and size and style of the building, the bright lights, the corporeal presence of the actors, their raised voices, their conventional groupings and movements – all these things had grown out of a tradition of dramatic ceremonial. Documentary could not flourish until the cinema came.

The nineteenth-century theatre put the players securely behind the proscenium arch, allowing the apron to fall into disuse and aiming at the illusion that the audience could see through the fourth wall of a room. But the naturalistic method remained highly conventionalised because the theatre cannot present people speaking and behaving as in real life: they would not be heard, could not be sufficiently differentiated from one another on the stage. The fourth-wall technique was a fumbling for the cinema, as was the documentary purpose of the problem play.

In the cinema we are not corporeally present with the actors, who may be dead or an ocean and a continent away. They may not even speak our language, they cannot respond to our enthusiasm, they never address themselves to us, they do not have to orientate themselves in relation to a row of footlights, for the camera can go amongst them and choose its angle of vision at the director's will. Only in the cinema is 'real life' dialogue possible and right. Only there does the obviously premeditated speech jar. When we hear stage dialogue in a film – whether good stage dialogue as in *Pygmalion*, or competent as in *Spectre of the Rose*, or flat-footed as in *The Philadelphia Story* – we are conscious of dissatisfaction, of an inherent inappropriateness: the epigrams, the patterned responses, the set speeches need the ceremonial ambience of the playhouse and the living presence of the player. It was a revelation of the nature of cinema when we heard the speech of actuality in *The Magnificent Ambersons*, with the accents, the idioms which we recognise from extra-theatrical experience as the common vehicle of human utterance.

The stage play is a staccato thing, jumping from scene to scene and using set speeches, songs, high points of action and dialogue, building up to them and then deliberately relaxing tension. The basis of cinema is continuity, with its moments of emphasis more completely integrated within the general, quasi-musical structure. Its speech may be rhetorical, when it shows people who under the impact of a powerful stimulus inevitably express their feelings in rhetorical terms – in a court scene, for example, or in a moment of aspiration or denouncement. But always the speech of film characters will be the raw material, taken directly from observation of actuality, which the director will use for the shaping of his sound-pattern: as his visual pattern will emerge from his assembling of the visual images of actuality that he must also reproduce for photographing. A set speech in the cinema is as jarring as a manifest studio-street or an unconvincing piece of back-projection. An epigram which cannot be accepted as spontaneous is as intrusive as a studio orchestra suddenly invoked for the accompaniment of a song.

This is not to say, of course, that the microphone and the camera are to be exclusively used for the recording of natural phenomena. The film-maker has to fashion his material, but he must avoid the appearance of artifice. The rough jesting of the underworld, the fine speech which sporadically can come to instant birth, the formless ramblings of everyday talk – these are parts of the stream of articulate utterance which he must endeavour to reproduce and work into his structure. He may, too, use speech to suggest the stream of consciousness which exists in perpetual counterpoint to the stream of utterance. Writing in *Close Up* in June 1933, Eisenstein saw that the internal monologue of James Joyce was a vehicle of expression available for the cinema, but it requires great skill in the handling; we must get the impression of the actual sequence of thoughts, feelings, reminiscences, not of a theatrical soliloquy. The set forms of blank-verse articulation, as in Shakespeare, or of O'Neill's literary prose in *Strange Interlude*, demand a ceremonial ambience. Just as the cinema does not lose a documentary character when it presents a sequence of dream images, so it is free to give articulation to the stream of unexpressed consciousness, provided that we are truly made to feel that the character's mind is being laid bare for us. This is, of course, in the highest degree difficult, and often to-day we get theatrical soliloquies in the cinema. A way round the difficulty was found in *Brief Encounter*, where the wife's musings are given formalised literary expression with the excuse that she is imagining how she might actually tell her story to her husband. This device would become threadbare with frequent use.

There is non-documentary cinema in cartoons, puppet- and silhouette-films, works of sheer fantasy (from *Caligari* onwards), musical comedies, and the like. In all of these the dialogue will be as remote from actuality as in the playhouse. But, like the occasional screen versions of Shakespeare, such films are off the high road of development, sometimes providing valuable explorations into film-method but without the spirit of sceptical inquiry that is inherent in documentary. *Henry V* owed some of its success to its war-time appearance: it was easier then than it would normally be to arouse a feeling of ritual union in a cinema audience. That it was a *tour de force*, however splendid, may become more apparent when Olivier's *Hamlet* is on view.

The film-maker whose work moves along the high road (Duvivier, Carné, Welles, Lang, Ford, Reed, Lean, at their best and most characteristic) is not a propagandist but a passionately interested observer, a man with a point of view but no panacea, prejudices but no firm faith. The documentary with a patent message, like *The Way We Live* or *The Great Promise,* is as theatrical as *Cæsar and Cleopatra* or *The Barber of Seville,* and far more specious. For this reason the use of choric commentary is dangerous: it can be discreet and effective, a valuably explicit statement of what is implicit in the document itself, as in *The River, A Song of Ceylon, The Magnificent Ambersons*; it can use patterned speech which is recognisable as such, it can in fact be as sharply distinguished from the language of the film's characters as the choric passages of Greek tragedy were from the dialogue; but it must not do more than point the statements of the film; it must never preach, or work itself up; it must never attempt to impose a ritual pattern on the film's documentation.

It follows that neither the stage-play nor the platform-speech can serve as a model for film dialogue or commentary. The writing of dialogue for the screen needs a peculiar skill – a power of aural observation, an ability to reproduce from what is observed the thing appropriate to the filmic structure, and a power to recognise the significant spontaneous utterance. We need a special fineness in film language as in the visual image, and that fineness will come from selection of the right material as well as from skill in its reproduction. Pagnol, aided by Raimu, gained much of his strength from the way in which a natural eloquence invested his main character's utterance in *La Fille du Puisatier.* It was an eloquence which welled up from the earth, not working towards a series of argumentative points or sallies of wit, but flowing on as part of the continuing stream of human utterance. On a grander scale there was the interplay of diverse voices in *Les Enfants du Paradis.* That film, despite its historical setting, was within the documentary kind, for its more heightened speeches came naturally and acceptably from people of the theatre: the vocal extravagances were convincing in their peculiar context of playhouses and adjoining streets. And when one gets in the cinema that feeling of conviction, one seems brought into direct contact with new experience. In part one recognises what one sees, and feels the reproduction to be correct; in part one is given the film-maker's eyes and ears and selective will. But that will never happen if the language or the visual picture is manifestly formalised.

ACTORS OF THE SOVIET CINEMA

CATHERINE DE LA ROCHE

*

THE Soviet Union is rich in actors. Already in pre-revolutionary times the Russian theatre had established some of the magnificent acting traditions for which it is internationally famous. During the five-year plans the theatre, cinema, and amateur dramatic work developed enormously, attaining the widest possible popularity in both urban and rural districts. Much talent was discovered among the peoples of the various national republics, and, also, a particular appreciation and fondness of histrionic art, which has become one of the most vital branches of the country's cultural life. They love a fine performance in the Soviet Union, and they go to extraordinary trouble, even in the hardest circumstances, to put on a good show and to attend it. The theatre, and especially the cinema, have become people's arts in a real sense. As part of their work, actors keep in close personal contact with different sections of the community and with public affairs. When the best among them are honoured by the title 'People's Artist' (more colloquially translated 'national artist'), this is no conventional courtesy, but, rather, an apt designation of the artist's quality.

This active contact between artists and society is, of course, the foundation of socialist realism (discussed by S. Burov in *Penguin Film Review*, No. 4). Its broad principles, however, give scope for a variety of styles, and the greatest actors of the Soviet cinema, who began their careers working in diverse highly individual schools of acting – theatres,. academies of drama, film institutes, film directors' permanent units, etc. –

have played a leading part in broadening the cinema's range and developing new techniques.

The most important influence has been the Moscow Art Theatre, many of whose actors have occasionally appeared in films. Some of its principles are as valid in cinema as on the stage: expression from within, not mere mimicry; understanding of a character's development, his hidden motives, his relationships with other personages, an understanding so thorough as to enable the actor 'to bring to his portrayal the character's past life': 'starting with *oneself* in acting', that is, using the material inherent in the actor's individuality, instead of striving after traits that are alien to him; above all, an untiring search for a full expression of truth instead of a naturalistic imitation of it. Even some of the Moscow Art Theatre's technique in preparatory work proved applicable in cinema, especially practice in partnership between actors and in creating a homogeneous 'ensemble'. Finally, this theatre's profoundly realistic style, which allows of no exaggeration, was akin to the kind of realism demanded by the movie camera. It is a style deriving largely from the character of the people drawn to and accepted into the Moscow Art Theatre. Its actors have temperament: they are chosen for this quality, which is considered as important as talent, intelligence, sensibility, or physique, and in consequence their acting is a process of controlling passions rather than inducing them. Hence the 'inner' force so characteristic of their style and, indeed, of all the first-class Soviet actors.

Among the first to adapt successfully the principles of the Moscow Art Theatre in a film was the cast of 7 *Daring People* (1937), including Tamara Makarova, Oleg Zhakov, and Peter Aleinikov, all of whom belong exclusively to the cinema. Their task was to impersonate average citizens working in the Arctic and to reveal the heroism, joys, and sorrows of routine work. They created a controlled, sincere, and perfectly unified style, while developing their own personalities. This achievement was attributed in part to intensive research by the actors themselves and to rehearsing. Directed by Sergei Gerasimov, who is famed for his handling of actors, this picture was the turning-point in the careers of the three famous actors mentioned, just as his latest film, *The Young Guards*, promises to be the making of the State Film Institute undergraduates appearing in it. *The Young Guards* was the first picture to be 'rehearsed' with resounding success at the recently instituted Film Actors' Theatre. As mentioned in one of my previous articles, stage versions of film scripts are publicly performed here by the cast of the future film in order to give them the same opportunities of developing and correcting their portrayals as are enjoyed by stage actors.

Makarova, who enjoys enormous popularity, has appeared in all Gerasimov's films and in many others. Except in *Masquerade* and *Stone Flower*, she has mostly impersonated typical young women of the present day – a peasant girl in *New Teacher*, a housewife in *The Vow*. She has a melodious speaking voice and a peculiar gift for catching the lilt and 'folk-lore' harmony of the Russian language. Never afraid of seeming ordinary, she has a serene way of making the very ordinariness of some of her characters both eloquent and moving. Her latest part is in a children's film called *First-Form Pupil*.

There are few actors who have made as many pictures as Zhakov. His versatility is quite remarkable: an heroic army commander in *We from Kronstadt*, the reactionary academician in *Baltic Deputy*, a traitor in *Great Citizen*, the charming old doctor in *Song of Abai*. Zhakov plays heroes and villains, young men and old, becoming completely transformed in each of his roles, though he seldom uses make-up. At the same time he has a very individual, restrained style of his own. He has recently scored a new success as a young doctor who makes a grave mistake in his work in *In the Name of Life*.

Elena Kuzmina is also an actress who works entirely in films. Already in her early pictures she revealed a peculiar ability for making a contrast in her physical appearance according to her state of mind: she would make herself look quite plain as an idle or unhappy girl, then suddenly become transfigured and beautiful as a result of inspiring thoughts or emotions. In *Girl 217*, where she played a girl sold in slavery to a Nazi family, she used her gift for the reverse process: a charming young girl became transformed into a hard, embittered old woman. Passionately interested in current affairs, Kuzmina hopes to participate in a film exposing the surviving influences of Fascism.

The actors who have created the classic portrayals of the Soviet cinema are in most cases associated with the theatre. Boris Babochkin, for instance, came into films from the Academic Theatre of Drama. His impersonation of Chapaev established a tradition in the treatment of biographical roles. Babochkin had little physical resemblance to Chapaev, hero of the Civil War, nor did he aim at an exact likeness. Instead, he sought to reveal Chapaev's mental and emotional characteristics, concentrating on the traits that were most typical not only of him but also of other partisan leaders of the epoch. It was one of the first so-called 'composite' characters, representing specific human qualities shared by others. At the same time the portrayal was so individual and so true that even Chapaev's relatives recognised it as such. Since then Babochkin has acted in many films, but in his own opinion he has never done as well as in *Chapaev*. During the war he became a director, and in this capacity he has made two successful films, starring in both, *Native Fields* and the recently completed *Destroyer Neistovy*.

The aged professor in *Baltic Deputy*, so brilliantly impersonated by Nikolai Cherkassov when he was only thirty-two, was even more of a 'composite' character than Chapaev, for, though partly founded on the biography of Academician Timiryasev, the portrayal represented the progressive minority among scientists during the Revolution. Cherkassov is not only one of the most talented artists of our time, he is a virtuoso who has done most things in the show world. Starting as an eccentric theatrical actor, clown, dancer, mime, and acrobat, he had a taste for everything difficult and, for a time, avoided drama because he thought it looked easy. When he did take up dramatic acting in theatre and films, he put all the enthusiasm of his passionate nature into the job. He proved himself an actor of as much intellectual as emotional power, capable of playing any character in any style. The improbable casting of a young man like himself in the part of the old professor was a result of his own initiative and unabashed campaigning – he had fallen in love with the character. Since then he has impersonated the degenerate prince in *Peter I,* Maxim Gorki in *Lenin in 1918,* and given a superb stylised interpretation of the complex character of Ivan the Terrible. He continues working in the theatre, is deputy to the Supreme Soviet, a fiery political orator and a man of broad culture, brilliant wit, and driving energy. Despite his fame and achievements, he appears in bit parts when invited, though there's no danger of his being missed in them! In the new film, *In the Name of Life,* he appeared for a few memorable moments as a watchman. He has a bigger part as a film director in Alexandrov's new musical comedy, *Spring,* appearing without make-up, and, as usual, earning the praise of the critics.

One of the biggest new acting successes is Boris Chirkov's in the name part of *Glinka,* the life-story of the great nineteenth-century Russian composer. Chirkov started acting in an amateur dramatic circle, then in a Leningrad theatre. He won a particular kind of popularity and fame before the war as Maxim in the 'Maxim Trilogy'. These full-length serial films told a fictitious story about a labourer who became a minister, yet Chirkov invested his role with so much charm, humour, and warmth, that 'Maxim' became a sort of national figure. These pictures, incidentally, were another example of good results obtained through intensive rehearsing before production. And so was *New Teacher* in which Chirkov played the name part with great insight.

In the middle 1930's, on the strength of the experience gained in making several successful historical and biographical films, the Soviet cinema began to produce pictures with actors imper sonating Lenin and Stalin. In the case of national figures who are so widely known, the actors were, of course, chosen as much for their physique as for their talent, and, with the aid of make-up, the resemblances achieved were remarkable. The late Boris Shchukin of the Vakhtangov Theatre (a subsidiary of the Moscow Art Theatre) was the most successful in portraying Lenin. In *Lenin in October* and *Lenin in 1918*, he gave sustained and convincing performances which had depth and were much more than mere imitations. Michael Gelovani, actor of the Georgian theatre and, like Stalin, a Georgian, has impersonated Stalin in several pictures, the best and longest performance being the one in *The Vow*. Since then he has played the same role in two new films about the war, *Last Days of Berlin* and *The Third Blow*, and in *Light Over Russia*, the story of Lenin's plan for the electrification of the Soviet Union. In this picture N. Kolesnikov, an actor of the Omsk theatre, is making his début in the part of Lenin.

Many of the finest performances have been created in historical films. General Kutuzov, for instance, was brilliantly impersonated in the film of that name by Alexei Diki, a celebrated theatrical producer and actor in his fifties, who made his film début in this part. It was a reinterpretation in the light of present-day knowledge of the general's role in history and of his character, for which Diki had prepared himself by a profound study of the subject. He has remained in films, scoring an even greater success in the name part of Pudovkin's *Admiral Nakhimov*. Evgeni Samoilov, famous for his portrayal of Shchors, the Ukrainian hero of the Civil War, gives another fine historical impersonation as Lieutenant Burunov in *Admiral Nakhimov*.

Lyubov Orlova is the most famous musical-comedy star. Starting in the Nemirovich Danchenko Theatre, she has appeared in all Alexandrov's musicals including *Volga-Volga* and *Bright Path*. Gay, spontaneous, and very talented, she has played a leading part in evolving an optimistic, satirical style of comedy, with the wit directed against something silly or unpraiseworthy and never ridiculing honest folk or ideas. She has recently won new laurels for her double role in *Spring*.

Among the up and coming younger actors the most promising seem to be Lyudmila Tselikovskaya, who started in the Vakhtangov Theatre, then starred in *Spring Song* and played Ivan's young wife in *Ivan the Terrible*; Galina Vodyanitskaya, graduate of the State Film Institute, who gave a moving impersonation in the name part of Zoya, the eighteen-year-old partisan girl hanged by the Nazis; and Vladimir Druzhnikov, of the Moscow Art Theatre, who played the illegitimate son in *Innocent though Guilty*, the leading role in *Stone Flower* and who has since appeared in *Glinka* and a new colour musical, *Tales of Siberia*.

The work of all these actors, and of many more who are equally distinguished, is purposeful, always experimental, and, as far as possible, co-ordinated as between studios and theatres, so as to give each of them a chance to widen his range.

THE POETRY
OF THE FILM

ROGER MANVELL

*

THE film is a new art form depending for its existence upon a
mechanical invention. This apparatus of cinema was not suffi-
cently developed for public use before the last decade of the nineteenth century. In its brief fifty years as a popular medium for
entertainment the mechanics of cinema have undergone considerable modification, each variation implying new and more
complicated æsthetic powers for the artist to develop. The silent
film was consolidating its æsthetic when sound became of commercial importance for its exploitation with the public. Tinted
stock and the various colour processes (from the British Kinema-
colour of 1908 to Technicolor, Kodachrome, and Agfacolor to-
day) have offered æsthetic advantages over the black-and-white
image which have as yet scarcely been developed. Side-tracked
and held back by the ever-present need to serve the commercial
demands of the production companies and of the largest audience the world can muster, it is easy to understand how the
artists of cinema are only now proving to the discriminating
public that their medium has a right to be considered as seriously
as the other fine arts which are concerned with narrative and
exposition.

It is at once the cinema's advantage and disadvantage that it
commands a public of 235,000,000 a week. It holds popular attention on a scale unknown to any other narrative art form.
But at the present level of public education, the degree of discrimination which has produced the finest examples of psychological writing in the novel and the drama or of emotional ex-

111

pression in poetry, is not to be found in this wide international audience which kills time casually at the cinema and asks no more than the regular star-parade and the display of colour, action, and excitement in the simple stereotypes of the Hollywood picture. While these demands may be more fundamentally healthy than many critics care to admit, they lead to conventions of story and character which defeat their own ends until commercial cinema is bogged down in its own success and lives on the display of the physical beauty and personalities of the stars.

This situation must not lead to the neglect of the film as an art form, any more than the recognition of the novel as a sensitive medium of human expression must be denied because the bulk of narrative-writing is pulp. Poetry, from the point of view of most people, is nothing but the rhyming ballad which accompanies the dance-number or the slick limerick in the cloakroom.

The film in its fifty years has had the services of more distinguished artists and actors than the theatre. Many men and women who would otherwise have been the poets of the twentieth century have found their medium of expression in the motion picture. To them is due our right to speak of the poetry of the cinema, whether we find it in the *avant-garde* movement of France or whether we look for it more widely in a number of films made by Soviet Russia, by Germany before Hitler, by the smaller industries of Sweden and Czechoslovakia, or by America, France, and more recently by Britain.

*

The use of the word 'poetry' is always ambiguous, even when applied solely to the literary medium. To use it of the film is to imply that the motion picture is capable of moments of intense emotional concentration as well as prolonged periods of narrative and character presentation which are rich in human understanding and illuminate the experience of life. It implies that the medium is flexible and eloquent under the control of the artist, and that it offers him resources of expression which will win his devotion and excite his genius. It implies also that these resources are not available in the same form in the other narrative arts, and that the film becomes a speciality and the film artist a specialist. It implies that the film is not a mere substitute for the drama or the novel, but an art with its own peculiar properties to arouse the æsthetic susceptibilities of artist and audience.

Certain qualities it possesses are at once obvious and have frequently been discussed. While the novel is a narrative form dependent on the descriptive imagination of a writer working for the single reader, the film narrates by means of a series of photographed images representing the chain of physical action and showing the development of the characters by means of actors and dialogue. Whereas the novelist can narrate, if he wishes, through dialogue and the indirect description of action, his special powers (as shown, for example, by Proust and Joyce) lie in the analysis of his characters' motivation, since he has direct access to their minds and himself creates their emotional structure. The dramatist's skill lies ultimately in his power over dialogue as an expression of character, and over the pace and timing of his narrative in terms of the scene divisions of his play; he, too, depends on the actor to convey his meaning to an audience group, held together in the common communion of the theatre. The personal relation of actor to audience is of the greatest moment in the live theatre: he is there to establish through his individual presence the experience of the drama. This link is not achieved in the same way in the cinema, where only the image of the actor is present. In the star-parade of commercial film the audience is much more concerned to identify its own human desires and dreams with the experiences portrayed by the actor. Since the actor is not there in his own person, the fact of his distinction from the audience itself, from its secret vanity, its desire for fame and personal success, is less apparent. This was possibly first observed over twenty-five years ago by

D. H. Lawrence,* and has become a commonplace of criticism to-day, as well as a factor of great importance in the assessment of the social influence of the cinema.

The film owes its power to the mobility of its images combined with the selective use of sound, and its æsthetic derives from this. Its poetry lies in the richest use of these potentialities by the artist, as the power of literary poetry derives from the potentialities of words used in the service of emotional experience.

*

The æsthetic of the silent cinema lay in the development of mobile composition in the photographic images for the purpose of the vivid communication of human action. The lack of sound was a great drawback, and the use of interspersed titles was a hindrance to the development of the visual action. In the great examples of silent cinema the titles played very little part and were only used where absolutely necessary to clarify the visual action. A few films were made with no titles at all.

The mobile composition of the silent film was twofold: first, the selection of the movement to be shown in the individual image; second, the relationship and the timing of the flow of the images as a group. The possibilities of the silent screen were first demonstrated maturely in D. W. Griffith's *Intolerance* (1916), which followed his important, though less striking film, *The Birth of a Nation* (1915). It may be said that the great sets of Babylon were grandiose and vulgar, and that the actors made their characters into miming automata; these same sets and these same actors without the film-poet D. W. Griffith might have produced only a tawdry spectacle. Yet the attack on Babylon in the finale of the film, interspersed as it is with three other actions reaching their parallel climax in different periods of history, becomes a *tour de force* in the grand style, with a rhythm built up to a crescendo in which image beats on image with an impact which has a terrible significance of its own, a

* *The Lost Girl*, Martin Secker, pp. 129–31.

visual experience which reiterates through the very nature of the film medium itself the terror of intolerance in the lives of men and in the demonstration of history. For this reason it is famous in its own right and exercised great influence on the more subtle and more profound work which was to follow it in the decade of the twenties.

Poetry derives much of its life-blood from imagery. By means of juxtaposed comparisons, observation becomes more acute and experience is clarified and enriched.

> The fog comes
> on little cat feet.
> It sits looking
> over harbor and city
> on silent haunches
> and then moves on. *

The purpose of Griffith – for that matter the same had he been a descriptive writer – was served if he enabled the spectator to share directly and vividly in the experience of the fall of Babylon. The poet begins to take the place of the reporter when the emotion of imaginative participation is induced, and the spectator becomes personally involved in the action through his imagination. The highest levels of poetry are not attempted here, but it is at this point that they may well begin. The spectator watches: the emotional values of the spectacle are sensed and the imagination catches fire. Wordsworth's sonnet written on Westminster Bridge in London is the evocation of such emotion. So Griffith, directing the flow of our attention, says: 'Look here at this, and this, now this. You see, now, as I select, what you shall see, how it was, how I feel about it. This great wall, the men who fall from it, is it not like the hill of Golgotha, the streets of the massacre of St Bartholomew, the platform of the American gallows? The juxtaposition is of the simplest, each enriching the significance

* *Fog*: a complete poem by Carl Sandburg, as visual in its impression as a film image.

of the other. The medium of cinema, like that of poetry, derives its strength from the comparison of images, the swift relation of ideas through the juxtaposition of human actions.

The Russian cinema of Pudovkin and Eisenstein derived its technique from Griffith. They, too, were concerned with ideas symbolised by the details of human action and the mobile visual world. The massacre on the Odessa steps in the famous sequence from Eisenstein's *The Battleship Potemkin* (1925) is the development of this same technique, the selection of images and the rhythm of their presentation so that certain ideas, certain emotions, shall be induced in the audience. The chaos of movement of the scattering crowds contrasted with the sharp and static shadows of the lines of steps; the precision of the movements of the soldiers, photographed in every detail; the organised, cold cruelty of massacre; the moments of action selected for individual treatment, the mother and her dead son, the nurse whose wounded body pushes the child's perambulator down the steps, the movement of the perambulator as it tips over, sharply linked to the movement of the sabre which cuts open a woman's face. Here the crowded multitude of detail is organised for emotional and ideological effect. It is the film used emotionally for the interpretation of history. The extraordinary sense of rhythm and the telling selection of spectator viewpoint (camera set-up and camera-angle) are seen once more in the procession of prayer for rain in Eisenstein's *The General Line* (1929), where the peasants bow before the sacred image to a rhythm which increases with their religious ecstasy and culminates in a passion of movement (movement of bodies and movement artificially created by the cutting of the photographic shots) as the banners wave and the men and women beat their breasts in a frenzy of supplication.

In Germany the impression of the macabre was evoked by the design and lighting of the film set and the selection of especially photogenic actors. This culminated in the films in which Emil Jannings appeared, such as *Vaudeville* (1925), *Faust* (1926), and the early sound film, *The Blue Angel* (1930); and in the films of Fritz Lang, who used fantastic sets in *Destiny* (1921) and created the curious spectacle of *Metropolis* (1926). In most of these films the artists turned away from actuality. Whereas most directors in the cinema and the average members of their audience prefer a surface resemblance to reality in a photographic medium, it had been demonstrated from the earliest trick films of such pioneers as the Frenchman Georges Méliès that the camera's reputation for truth could be exploited to increase audience-credulity in the fantastic. The superimposed image is the nearest approach to a ghostly actuality, far more effective than the lighting tricks of a mechanised stage. The creation of the atmosphere of otherworldliness, severed from banal trickeries, was the peculiar power of the early post-war German cinema and of the *avant-garde* who turned to the psychological fantasy and to surrealism in their attempt to free the cinema from the representation of superficial reality. The peculiar quality of *The Cabinet of Doctor Caligari* (Wiene, 1919) lies not in a sense of rhythm but in the curious beauty of the two-dimensional images of photographed theatrical sets designed in the expressionistic style, and in the evocation of a macabre mad world by the mimetic movements of the actors. The film could have been unbearably impressive had the full powers of the cinema been used; as it is, it remains one which has as much charm as it has horror.

It was during the silent period that the cinema went a stage farther than the use of sympathetic sets and lighting to emphasise the mood of situation and character. In films like *Secrets of the Soul* (Pabst, 1926) and *The Ghost that Never Returns* (Mikhail Romm, 1929), images were invented which went beyond the representation of actuality in an endeavour to interpret the sequence of thought and emotion. In *The Ghost that Never Returns* the prisoner awaiting release on parole now sits, now paces in his cell, and his mind, excited by the thought of reunion with his family and fellow-workers, seems to conjure his father, his wife, and his comrades into the narrow cage while he moves about in concentrated thought, until eventually he breaks up and falls on his bed weeping, when instantaneously a dual image of him is seen, the one collapsed, the other bent against the wall of the cell. Later, when the time for release seems to him to have arrived, a steady crescendo of views of him rushing to look for the warder through the cell bars build up into a climax of agitation. In such scenes as these the director, as the responsible creative artist, has to depend on the degree of concentrated acting he can obtain from the actor. However flexible his use of the multitude of shots he makes with the camera, he needs the details of intense facial and bodily acting which only the imaginative and skilful actor can offer. This was especially true of Mme. Falconnetti's performance in Karl Dreyer's film made in France, *La Passion de Jeanne d'Arc* (1928), where the intense suffering of her face haunts the long series of close-shots which make up so much of this poetic, deeply personal film. The mood of the tragedy is constructed out of the portraits of remarkable, almost symbolic faces and the careful use of images of instruments of torture with other objects whose associative values collectively made the film a strong emotional experience which can never be wholly forgotten.

The *avant-garde* movement used the simple association image to create subjective mood in the poetic manner: *Brumes d'Automne* (Kirsanoff, 1928) used the wet autumn leaves slowly dropping into water as the background for the tragedy of a woman who commits suicide after her lover deserts her, just as Pudovkin in *Mother* used the reiterated image of the ice-flow on a river breaking against the bridge parapets to symbolise the defeat of the workers' procession before the Tsarist horsemen. But in *The Seashell and the Clergyman* (Germaine Dulac, 1927) the imagery goes beyond simple association and becomes part of the action itself after the manner of dream-narrative. The scheme of Freudian symbolism became a means of creating an imagist film movement which constructed its narrative in psychological terms: the work of Bunuel was psychological in this imagist sense, and the subtle beauty of the late Jean Vigo's *Zéro de Conduite* (1933) and *L'Atalante* (1934) was much influenced by this imagery, and was the highest expression of it in films which remain among the most moving yet created. Neither should films like Jean Epstein's *Fall of the House of Usher* (1928) be forgotten; they were not profound, but by means of a series of flowing, evocative, superimposed fantasy-pictures they created the atmosphere of the macabre and horrible, and demonstrated the visual flexibility of the film medium and its hypnotic power.

*

The coming of sound undoubtedly led to an expansion of the expressive potentialities of the film. Speech allowed the introduction of dialogue and commentary (eliminating the hindrances which written titles had always brought to the visual action of the silent cinema); natural sound greatly increased the impression of actuality in a medium which ranged so easily over the surface of the earth with all its noises; music enabled the mood and atmosphere of a film to be emphasised and controlled. In the sphere of commercial exploitation the cinema made use of the novelty of sound by completely subjecting the medium to it. Films were made which were little but talking or singing, visually unexciting, cutting from one speaker to the next merely to keep pace with the flow of theatrical dialogue.

The artists were not satisfied. Clair in France, King Vidor and Milestone in America, Hitchcock in Britain, and Pabst in Germany were among those first few who demonstrated that sound was of the greatest importance as a part of the whole of film expression, but should not be used as its master. Sound could act in counterpoint to the visual image, giving it a significance it could never achieve alone. The well-known repetition of 'knife' in *Blackmail* (Hitchcock, 1929), the use of train-noises during the fight in *Sous les Toits de Paris* (Clair, 1929), the use of tapping during the last rescue sequences in *Kameradschaft* (Pabst,

1932), the subjection of speech to cutting in *The Front Page* (Milestone, 1931), and the use of natural sounds to underline the emotional values of the situation during the swamp sequence in *Hallelujah* (Vidor, 1930) began to show that sound must be interknit with the visual image in an art where the primary attention of the audience is always given to the picture. For the degree of potential hold over the spectator is much higher for sight than for sound, for the sight experience is a direct recognition of people and things in motion seen enlarged on a screen in a darkened hall, whereas sound has to be received aurally, recognised, and understood, thus requiring greater effort and concentration.

It is a commonplace of artistic practice that the realisation of the limitations of an art is an important part of the technique of its use. The field for experiment is narrow in the commercial cinema, but even there a few directors were able to handle sound imaginatively. It soon emerged as a general principle that all branches of sound (speech, natural sound, and music) should be used with economy, and that the occasional complete silence could itself have tremendous effect. Imagery could also be introduced in the sound-track. One of the earliest Russian films, *The Road to Life* (Nikolai Ekk, 1931), expressed the sorrow of a crowd by the dying fall of escaping steam as a railway engine drew to a standstill, whilst Pudovkin, in *Deserter* (1933), allowed the cars of the somnolent capitalists to be police-controlled to waltz music. The work of the composer of music for films became recognised as more than the provision of suitable background harmonies: the music could become an integral part of the complete experience of the situation, as the music of Walter Leigh for Basil Wright's *Song of Ceylon* (1935) or Prokofiev's for Eisenstein's *Alexander Nevski* (1938), or the scores of Georges Auric and Maurice Jaubert for Clair's early musical films became an interpretation of the essential quality of those sequences which had musical accompaniment.

*

The poetry of cinema grew more complicated and more rich. The response of sight to sound and sound to sight seemed to present ever wider opportunities which artists like Pudovkin, Eisenstein, Cavalcanti, Clair, Lang, Vigo, Rotha, and Asquith used with increasing insight, and often with increasing simplicity. Experimentalists like Orson Welles produced a new kind of film rhetoric, a Walt Whitman or Carl Sandburg style in the medium of cinema, a style which thwarted every stereotype of commercial entertainment and astonished and irritated the general public. No more acceptable were *The Grapes of Wrath* (John Ford, 1940), *The Oxbow Incident* * (William Wellman, 1943), and *The Forgotten Village* (John Steinbeck and Herbert Kline, 1944). These films are all remarkable expressions of the American artistic idiom, even though one was made in Mexico with all the sympathy and sentiment of American feeling for simplicity of life. They rise frequently from the higher levels of emotional narrative to the degree of poetry itself. For poetry recognises the essential value of a human word and gesture in time of pain or joy and reveals it with no more emphasis than a just sense of timing. Again and again this happens, as for instance when the mother burns her letters before the destruction of her home in *The Grapes of Wrath*, when the men listen to the last letter written to his wife by the innocent farmer they have lynched in *The Oxbow Incident*, or when the camera moves gently from the dancing of the village peasants at a child's funeral to the still fatalistic, sorrowing face of the mother, her acceptance overlaid with sadness. These moments are selected by the poetic eye, which watches always for the instant that epitomises the whole.

The French cinema has given evidence of the most consistent emotional maturity during the period of the sound film. Organised though it is on a strictly commercial basis, it has none the less produced a large number of distinguished pictures. The creative cinema of Germany was destroyed by Hitler, that of America by the need to please continuously the demands of an

* Retitled in Britain: *Strange Incident*.

international audience of a low quality, not necessarily of intelligence, but of emotional understanding. Apart from documentary, British cinema has only achieved a consistently high standard in very recent years. The quality of French cinema suffered a temporary set-back during the years of Occupation, but the more distinguished French directors had previously shown their observation to be unique, though many of their best films have given dialogue an over-prominant place.

French cinema is remarkable for its humanism, and depends almost as much on the fine quality of its chief actors as upon the imagination of its leading directors. The films of the late Jean Vigo were unique for their poetic treatment. *Zéro de Conduite* contains images and incidents of superb fantasy to present the problems and emotions of boys in an ugly boarding-school. *L'Atalante* is constantly released from the restraints of actuality to emphasise by imagery the experiences of its chief characters. The achievement of other directors has been mainly in a realistic style, presenting French life with authenticity and understanding, heightened only by the intensity of the emotions revealed in the stories and the acting required by them. These films seem to epitomise the spirit of pre-war France as faithfully as the plays of Tchehov epitomised that of pre-revolutionary Russia. They have the poetry of realism because they emphasise always the human values of every situation, tragic, tense, grave or gay. Such films as *La Femme du Boulanger, Le Jour se lève, Le Fin du Jour, La Grande Illusion*, and *Les Infants du Paradis* illustrate this treatment. There is no over-emphasis, no rhetoric, only a fine balance of direction, scripting, and acting. It is rare to have the emphatically designed conclusion that Malraux gives to *Espoir* (1939), which, in its triumphant use of crowd movement, individual portraiture, the procession of wounded men and Honegger's music, is the nearest approach of French cinema to the symphonic structure of the Russians. More typical is the understatement of *Crime et Châtiment* (Chenal, 1935), where the treatment is classical Greek in its endeavour to keep physical violence off the screen and show only emotional violence, or the famous end of *La Bête Humaine* (Jean Renoir, 1938), where the train, deserted at full speed by its mad driver, is left to a fate in the spectator's imagination.

Only recently, during and since the war, has British cinema, other than documentary, begun to show a similar balance and maturity. This, too, is the work of a few directors only whose sense of their art survived the chaos and uncertainty of the commercial cinema before the war, or who have developed since. The experience of the war years produced a stillness of the spirit which emerges in such films as *The Way to the Stars* and *Brief Encounter*. The emotions associated with heroism in action or in suffering were successfully understood in films like *San Demetrio London*, *Nine Men*, *The Silent Village*, *The Gentle Sex*, *We Dive at Dawn*, *Millions Like Us*, *The Captive Heart*, *Western Approaches*, and *The True Glory*. Though these films may not be thought of as poetic in treatment, there are moments in all of them when the prosaic aspects of human relationships in a common service are transcended, and the illumination of life by a finer emotional quality is revealed as clearly as in the more distinguished work of the war poets.

*

The film is young, without a tradition in its own right to give it the dignity and status which are at the disposal of the other arts, should they be needed to guide the developing artist in the fulfilment of his task. As a medium it is of the greatest technical complexity, and the film-director has to be a master of a number of specialities if he is not to fail in one or other of the branches of cinematic technique. He is like a man required to play several instruments at once. He has to control an army of technicians who, however skilled they may be in their own particular departments, may not understand the unity of art he is seeking to achieve with their indispensable help. He must be a sensitive judge and critic of dialogue, acting, set design, motion photography, and music. All these forces he must subdue to the one purpose: the creation of a series of impressions which in the end will illuminate the imagination of the spectator. The difficulties of the director are indeed endless, but his overriding problem remains – the need to produce for audiences large enough to cover the great cost of film production. His work, in so far as it is successful, becomes part of a great movement to bring maturity of emotional perception and understanding to large numbers of people who, too frequently, are unwilling to meet the artist half-way. This is both the dilemma and the supreme opportunity of the poet of the cinema.

(Reprinted by the courtesy of the Grey Walls Press from their Miscellany, *New Road*.)

STATISTICS

H. H. WOLLENBERG

★

In the *Board of Trade Journal* the results were published of a report made by the Social Survey from information collected by interviews conducted during March and October 1946. Thirty-two per cent of the population go to the cinema at least once a week, spending £100 million each year at the box-office. They are subdivided into two principal groups: housewives and the 'higher-paid sections of the working class'. Two-thirds of regular film-goers 'shop' for their films according to these Government fact-finding statistics.

As for age-groups, the following details on cinema attendances are given:

	Age			
	0-4	5-9	10-16	16 and over
Once a week or more .	13 %	49 %	65 %	32 %
Less regularly . .	9	27	31	41
Do not go now: never	77	24	5	27
Samples . . .	231	248	265	3,137

Further details of adult attendances are shown in the following table:

	Age					
	16-19	20-29	30-39	40-49	50-59	60
Once a week or more .	69 %	57 %	35 %	28 %	22 %	11 %
Less than once a week .	28	34	46	52	43	28
Not now or never .	2	9	19	20	35	61
Samples . . .	116	537	692	685	508	596

Sixty-five per cent of Britain's school-children see films once a week or more.

BOOKS ABOUT FILMS

Edited by R. K. NEILSON BAXTER

*

To complete our survey of Western European critical writing
(France in Issue 3; Switzerland in Issue 4), Moura Wolpert
now contributes some views on recent Italian publications:

*After some thirty years of, to say the least, mediocre film
production, Italy has once again emerged as an important contributor to film technique, and the few examples of her revived
production we have seen have shown us that new creative
forces are at work which cannot be lightly dismissed. Unfortunately, however, the first books about film to have reached
us from Italy do not tell of new developments or new talent,
but review the work of old masters instead.*

*Editoriale Domas, Milan, have published the first seven in
their series of books on famous films. Each contains some 120
stills, neither well chosen nor well reproduced, and printed in
chronological order with short captions explaining the action
or dialogue; in other words, the story of the film in pictures.
Each volume further contains either a biographical note on the
director or a short criticism of the film – or both, as well as an
index of the director's other works. The series includes No. 1,
La Kermesse Héroïque (Jacques Feyder), compiled and introduced by Aldo Buzzi; No. 2, La Passion de Jeanne d'Arc (Carl
Theodor Dreyer), by Guido Guerrasio; No. 3, Alba Tragica
(Le Jour se Lève – Marcel Carné), by Glauco Viazzi – there is
something to be said for this volume, for even if we cannot see
the original film any more, we can at least console ourselves a
little with these stills! No. 4 contains two comedies with Larry
Semon, known in Italy as Ridolini, Ridolini e la Collana della*

Suocera (*Ridolini and his Mother-in-Law's Necklace*) and Ridolini, Esploratore (*Ridolini the Explorer*), compiled by Aldo Buzzi. No. 5 is Il Bandito della Casbah (Pepé le Moko – *Julien Duvivier*), by Glauco Viazzi; No. 6, Le Million (*René Clair*), by Bianca Lattuada; and in No. 7 Aldo Buzzi once again 'reviews' two Max Linder comedies: Sept Ans de Malheur and Io e il Leone (*I and the Lion*). Except for zealous fans and collectors, these books are of no great value to the more serious-minded student of the cinema.

Aldo Buzzi is the editor of a series entitled Biblioteca Cinematografica, published by Poligono Società Editrice, Milan, 1945. The first of these volumes, Entr'acte, *is an elaborately set out and detailed survey of individual shots in this early René Clair film. In a short preface, Glauco Viazzi discusses the work of René Clair, and then goes on to describe each shot in detail – whether long, medium, or close-up, composition and contents, giving the number of frames and the length of time the shot is held on the screen. He has selected his stills with obvious care and imagination, though here again reproduction leaves much to be desired.*

No. 2 in the series deals with Joris Ivens' Zuiderzee in much the same manner. Corrado Terzi has here undertaken the explanation, but going into greater detail than Glauco Viazzi in Entr'acte. *Apart from a very short note on Ivens and his films, he includes an interesting appreciation of Zuiderzee, in which he concerns himself particularly with rhythm and montage, but treating it not so much from the artistic as the technical point of view.*

Because of their technical nature, these two books will probably be of little interest to the general reader, but might be of some help to the amateur and student cinematographer.

Another series of books published under the title Biblioteca Cinematografica (Poligono Società Editrice, Milan, 1945), and edited by Glauco Viazzi, *is more general in character. In Volume I,* Umanità di Stroheim, *Ugo Casiraghi sets out to* show the 'humanity of Stroheim and other wise men', in a collection of articles. They are short, informative, critical appreciations of Stroheim's work as an actor and director, of Carl Dreyer's Vampire, White Nights of St. Petersburg, by Grigori Roshal and Vera Sroyeva, and the works of G. W. Pabst, Victor Sjöström, and Julien Duvivier. In a chapter entitled 'Hitchcock and Forst: two interpretations of "Rebecca" ', Casiraghi compares the treatment by Hitchcock and Willy Forst of a similar subject. The book is well illustrated with a selection of stills not often seen in books published in this country. Though Signor Casiraghi is by no means very profound or original in what he has to say, this book is nevertheless worth reading as an example of how the new Italy assesses the established masters of the cinema.

No. 2 of the series is Ragionamenti sulla Scenografia, by Baldo Bandini and Glauco Viazzi. It is an extremely well planned and thought-out treatise on set design and set construction, covering a variety of subjects from 'the æsthetic birth of the film' to 'poetry in set design', music, architecture, and includes a short history of set design for the cinema. It is a readable work on a subject of which little has so far been written (or published in this country, at any rate), and for that reason alone it deserves translation. It is copiously illustrated with stills, as well as designs and diagrams, though here again better paper and better reproduction would have achieved a far more satisfying result.

The last of these new Italian books is No. 4 in the same series, René Clair, by Glauco Viazzi. So much has already been said and written about René Clair that it is no easy task to say something very startling or original. It is obvious that the author is here writing about his hero. As a film director, he ranks Clair far above any of his countrymen; above all, however, he looks upon him as a pure artist who has achieved true greatness in his medium, the film. This book is a serious critical analysis which should find grateful readers in this country.

THE PENGUIN
FILM
REVIEW

7

CONTRIBUTORS INCLUDE

Arletty – Charles Crichton
Rachael Low – John Maddison – Roger Manvell
Ivor Montagu – Catherine de la Roche
Josef Somlo

ONE SHILLING AND SIXPENCE

THE PENGUIN FILM REVIEW

7

THE PENGUIN
FILM REVIEW

Editorial Board : R. K. Neilson Baxter
Roger Manvell *and* H. H. Wollenberg
Executive Editor : Roger Manvell

7

PENGUIN BOOKS

LONDON

1948

First Published September, 1948

PENGUIN BOOKS LIMITED

Harmondsworth, Middlesex, England

MADE AND PRINTED IN GREAT BRITAIN

by Hazell, Watson & Viney, Ltd.

Aylesbury and London

CONTENTS

★

EDITORIAL 7

SERGEI EISENSTEIN   Ivor Montagu 10

STRICTLY ENTRE NOUS   Arletty 17

MR CAPRA'S SHORT CUTS TO UTOPIA 25
Harold J. Salemson

THE MASK OF REALISM 35
Catherine de la Roche

CHILDREN AND FANTASY 44
Charles Crichton

NEWSREELS MUST FIND A NEW POLICY 50
G. Clement Cave

THE FIRST GENERATION OF THE CINEMA 55
Josef Somlo

ERNST LUBITSCH   H. H. Wollenberg 61

AMERICAN CLASSIC : THE MARX 68
BROTHERS   Richard Rowland

MONSIEUR VERDOUX   Roger Manvell   77

THE STRUCTURE OF THE BRITISH FILM   83
    INDUSTRY   R. K. Neilson Baxter

ROUND THE WORLD'S STUDIOS   91
                    H. H. Wollenberg

FILMS FOR INTERNATIONAL UNDER-   96
    STANDING: THE UNESCO STORY
                    Ernest Borneman

THE IMPLICATIONS BEHIND THE SOCIAL
    SURVEY   107
                    Rachael Low

HOLLYWOOD'S 1948 LINE-UP   113
                    Max Knepper

THE SCIENTIFIC FILM   117
                    John Maddison

BOOKS ABOUT FILMS   125
                Edited by R. K. Neilson Baxter

ILLUSTRATED SECTION
                Compiled by Roger Manvell

EDITORIAL

*

CREATIVE writing about the film is like creative writing about music and painting; few of the best exponents of film-making prove to be good at examining in words the fundamentals of the art they demonstrate so well in celluloid. Few great composers or great painters have also been great critics and students of their art. The energy of ear and eye, apt in judgment after years of practice and experience, cannot easily be matched by the equally difficult and different process of explanation in words. Only the experienced writer possesses the necessary facility.

Reviewing films is not the same as film criticism, though it may lead to it. A man may review films all his life and yet know little more than whether the films of the week are likely to prove good or bad entertainment for his readers. He performs within these limits an important service, but it is not criticism in the sense meant by Aristotle or Coleridge. It does not deal with the principles behind an artist's achievement in his art. It does not inspire the artist with a new conception of the powers of his medium. The great critic is a man who, like Coleridge, uncovers, if only for occasional moments, the resources of inspiration, and gives the poet the benefit of discovery in his art. All poets may write greatly without the assistance of the critic's theoretical discoveries, but few poets do not gain strength from the knowledge of such writings.

Criticism can be of many kinds. It can be historical, studying the evolution of an art through the generations of its practitioners. It can be social, revealing the link between creative work and the environment from which it was derived, and the nature of the effect such creative work has had upon those influenced by it. It can be technical, analysing craftsmanship and form. Or it can be æsthetic, showing the new kind of beauty revealed by the

7

art, and its relationship to the general conception of beauty deriving from the philosophical system of the writer.

Compared with poetry (which as an art has probably received the profoundest treatment by critical writers, seeing that it is in itself a medium of words) the film has scarcely begun to exist either as an art or as a source of critical contemplation. It exists, after fifty years of rapid development both in technique and content, comparatively speaking in the age of Marlowe, and certainly not yet in the age of Shakespeare. It is as rough, as crude, as eloquent, as vital, as entertaining as Marlowe's plays, though it occasionally possesses subtleties of feeling which went unrecorded in that fierce age before Shakespeare himself came to give them unique expression. Distinction of critical writing can, we suppose, only follow hard upon a genuine and sustained period of creative achievement, though in the sphere of theory alone there is little doubt that the future writer already possesses sufficient data to trace more completely the potentialities of film art than any critic has so far attempted to do, except in a very few cases such as Arnheim or the late Sergei Eisenstein.

The difficulty for the theorist lies in the comparative lack of opportunity for experiment and the great expense of work in the sound-film medium. Experiment has too often to be imagined on paper rather than experienced in practice. That is why the unusual film is received with so much enthusiasm by the critic and student, an enthusiasm often exaggerated beyond the real merits of the film. The need is now for professional scholarship in the film, divorced (for certain periods of the student's career at any rate) from the need to earn a living from the commercial practice of film-craft. The film-critic, as things are now, has too often to invent his own bread-and-butter principles and muddle along with a few out-worn critical platitudes about composition, movement, editing and synchronisation. The film-makers themselves are often either too busy to think beyond the picture in hand, or else sunk in the groove of a standardised technique which has proved itself satisfactory enough for telling stories to habitual patrons. The rewards of popular film-making are notoriously good, though it should be remembered that in Shakespeare's time the wealth and popularity he achieved did not stop him writing continuously for some twenty years the most extraordinary plays the theatre has ever known.

We need now the benefit of the results arrived at through the combined forces of the professional student of the cinema working closely with the kind of film-maker who is excited by his art into extraordinary achievement. Each will inspire the other in the general evolution of the medium in which both believe. In whatever way the professional student of the cinema serves or assists his creative colleague, whether through historical, social, technical or æsthetic research, he will do so only by virtue of his independent position as a thinker and his sense of the purposes and principles which have guided the finest critical writing upon the older arts. It is to be hoped that the Universities and other educational foundations will assist in the organisation of motion-picture studies on this level, assisting the creative artist and elucidating the true merit and significance of his work.

FORTHCOMING

AMONG the articles planned for Issue VIII of PENGUIN FILM REVIEW are *The Animated Film* by John Halas, *The American Reaction to British Films* by F. del Giudice, *Hamlet* by Roger Manvell, *Position of the French Cinema* by Georges Auriol, and articles by David Rawnsley, Ronald Neame, and Catherine de la Roche.

SERGEI EISENSTEIN

(1898–1948)

IVOR MONTAGU

*

S. M. EISENSTEIN died suddenly on February 10th, 1948. He was found by his colleagues next morning sitting at his desk in his library. An unfinished thesis on colour and three-dimensional film was before him, and beside it lay open the Marxist classics on which it was his custom to draw for illustrative quotation in his philosophical work.

Sergei Mikhailovitch died comparatively early. He was only fifty. When he directed *Battleship Potemkin*, he was no more than twenty-seven. He was born in Riga, of Jewish descent. At the time of the Revolution he was a nineteen-year-old architecture student. In Moscow, the student became associated with the Theatre of the Red Army, a show of topical vaudeville skits in which the young Kazak, G. V. Alexandrov – assistant director on *Potemkin* and raised to co-director credit on the next two pictures – performed as acrobat. Eduard Kasimirovich Tisse, son of a Swedish sea-captain, literally farthest-sighted human being and most wonderful exterior cameraman in the world, was making news reels. The three young men got together on Eisenstein's first film *Strike*, and stayed together a long time.

In 1925 came *Potemkin*. It lasts only fifty minutes, but it is doubtful whether any other film has ever made such a noise in the world or ever will. *Potemkin* was originally conceived as an episode, perhaps only a single reel, in the epic *1905*. It outgrew its scenario. This film is itself a most perfect example of a creation in which the creative process continued alive long after

scripting and through every stage of realisation. Even the exquisite mist shots were *ex tempore*, Tisse making immortal art
of what to many another photographic expert would have
seemed merely a prohibitive calamity.

Then came the *General Line* (shown in U. S. S. R. as *The
Old and the New*). Its theme was the struggle for collectivisa-
tion of agriculture. It took three years to make. When it was
finished, the Political Bureau of the C. P. S. U. saw it, and
Eisenstein often told me of the deep impression Stalin's sagacity
left with him. So long had passed that new aspects had assumed
importance in the solution of the problem, and an extra reel
was added.

But meanwhile, in 1927, Eisenstein had made a superb,
magnificent squib, *October* (called abroad *Ten Days That
Shook the World*). Work on the farm film was interrupted, and
the Revolution picture, which had to be ready for the Tenth Anniversary of the Revolution, was rushed through in a few weeks
of days and nights, the three doping themselves to stay awake.
Pudovkin made a Festival film too, *The End of St Petersburg*.
'I bombarded the Winter Palace from the *Aurora*,' says Pudovkin, 'while Eisenstein bombarded it from the Fortress of St
Peter and Paul. One night I knocked away part of the balus-
trading of the roof, and was scared I might get into trouble, but,
luckily enough, that same night, Sergei Mikhailovitch broke
two hundred windows in private bedrooms.' Those were the
days!

After the *General Line*, Eisenstein, Alexandrov and Tisse set
out for the West. Abroad, sound-film was coming in. At home,
the Five-Year Plan, wherein quantitative expansion was planned rather than large-scale qualitative change. So with a bless-
ing, twenty-five dollars each and a year's leave, the young men
were released upon the world their films had shaken. After
adventures in France and Switzerland and London lectures by
Eisenstein to classes organised by the Film Society, the three
followed me to Hollywood with a Paramount contract. We set

up house with an esoteric she-cook, half Negro, quarter Red Indian and quarter Irish. There is no space for one-hundredth of our tales: our comradeship with Charlie; the Academy meeting at which Hollywood heard, for the first time, from Eisenstein what a close-up is really *for*; the party where the journalist asked Eisenstein: 'Do people ever laugh in the Soviet Union?' and S. M. E. replied: 'They will, when I tell them about this party'; the conference at which Goldwyn told us (he really did) how much he admired *Potemkin* and could Eisenstein do him something on the same lines, but a *leetle* cheaper, for Ronald Colman?

S. M. E.'s first plan – a contemporary American story set in a house of glass – wouldn't jell. None of us, nor any of the American writers working with us, could get going on it. Out of *Sutter's Gold* we were manœuvred by internal studio politics. Then *An American Tragedy*. We knew it was impossible for *us*. But the choice was forced. The Dreier classic was impossible for *us* because its theme is that not the murderer but his environment (in this case the shape and moral values of American society itself) is responsible for the murder. Perhaps others could have burked such a theme; let those who saw the version Hollywood eventually turned out judge this point. But where our consciences reside we were short of elastic. A campaign of vilification of us as *Red Dogs* had been growing in Hollywood ever since S. M. E.'s arrival. It was taken up by a Congressman named Fish just as our script was completed. One day (before it was read, maybe), it was acclaimed as the greatest ever written for the studio, the next it was read and we were out on our ears. I verily believe that before the Paramount moguls read that theme in all the mighty power of Eisenstein's script they had not even had any idea what the subject was about. To them it had been – just another well-known story property.

Then Eisenstein had a choice of a film in Japan or a film in Mexico with Upton Sinclair's help. I will not reopen old sores. Suffice it that in my view neither S. M. E. nor Sinclair – though each blamed the other – was really at fault in what happened. The disaster was inevitable. But what must have been a masterpiece was taken away to be finished by other hands.

Back in U. S. S. R., S. M. E. was heartbroken, and for long confined himself to lecturing in the film college. Grisha Alexandrov diverted to an independent career as director of comedy musicals. A Soviet Film Jubilee, with top honours for almost everyone else and a reported dictum of Stalin ('I'm damned if the old rascal gets anything until he wakes up and does some creative work again') shook him into activity. There followed the abortive *Bezhin Meadow*, twice started and twice stopped, culminating in the grand assault of the Central Committee of the C. P. S. U. on Eisenstein as a formalist, egotist and what have you, and every word of it just, as spoken of S. M. E. in his mood of that time.

He was 'punished' with a long holiday in one of the most exquisite spots of the whole U. S. S. R., choice of his next subject, with the greatest Soviet composer as musician, the co-director of the finest Soviet sound-film as coadjutor and unlimited resources for the film, which was the simple, unprofound, but flowing and lovely pageant opera *Alexander Nevsky*. Then the war. In the first weeks he used his knowledge of England to help with adapting M. O. I. films for the Soviet audiences. Then he went to Central Asia and produced the first part of his monumental *Ivan the Terrible*. The finishing of the second part coincided with a stroke. After a slow recovery in the Kremlin hospital, he learned that the film had been listed, with two others, as giving a false impression of history (its historicity was, in fact, only a bit better than Shakespeare's). A long and serious talk with Stalin followed, and S. M. E. was engaged in recasting Part 2 and preparing a Part 3 when he died.

Eisenstein was a man of vast erudition. He not only read but could write and lecture in French, German, Spanish, English, as well as Russian. He read voraciously. He marked marginally everything he read, from novels to sociology, with film notes.

He acquired so many books, his flat was so full of them piled on the floor and piled so high, that if he wanted to consult one he had to go out and buy another copy, as search for it at home was useless. He was constantly drawing – caricatures of his interlocutors, fanciful figures, sometimes naughty ones, but also, exactly and imaginatively, what he wanted either to film or to explain. A pupil who heard him and whose imagination was not nourished for ever must be a dull one. Those who listened to his London lectures include almost every young English director, of a certain generation, who has since proved himself.

Eisenstein's great and peculiar theoretical contribution lies in the application of Dialectical Materialism to æsthetics, the theory of novel creation by conflicts. To state it in simplest terms: in art as in nature the interaction of a and b do not make $a + b$ or even $a\,b$, but c. He followed and traced out this process through countless phases of film-making and of artistic creation in other fields, and showed the construction of artistic effects following the same dialectical laws as process in nature. He first derived these ideas from a study of editing, but recognised – following his combat over the formalism of *Bezhin Meadow* – that in doing so he had assigned a hypertrophied significance to editing, and that when he sought the application of the same principles in every creative phase, not only in the inter-shot creation, but in the intra-shot, in the composition of the single frame, in the construction of the narrative and in the shaping of the actor's performance as well, the content was immensely strengthened and enriched.

But the theoretical achievement is inseparable from the practical. In twenty-three years – from 1925 to 1948 – S. M. E. completed only five films, but each is a masterpiece – not, certainly, a universal masterpiece in the sense in which a work by Shakespeare or the great humanist novelists is universal, but each picturising with epic majesty what was perhaps *the* vital contemporary aspect of experience for the Soviet people at that time: *Potemkin*, revolt against oppression; *October*, the triumph of the people; *General Line*, the achievement of the agrarian revolution; *Nevsky*, patriotic defence against external aggression; *Ivan*, the consolidation of the threatened State. If none of its successors created in the world outside quite the earth-rending impact attained by the first – which lifted the cinema in one stroke out of the realm of passive entertainment or subjective self-expression and minor æsthetics to the rôle of direct agent in the world's affairs – this was perhaps due to the fact that none of the themes of the successors embodied quite the same universality of appeal. Each contains passages of expression so vivid and complete that they will inevitably be admired and studied and imitated so long as the medium of the cinema seeks similar effects by similar technical means.

Of some of the wider and profounder influences, it is necessary to say a few words.

First is the use of real material as an ingredient in realistic effect. Through *Drifters* this became essential to the whole school of English documentary. It is interesting to note that Eisenstein came from theatre to films through his search for realism. He first tried, of course unsuccessfully, to produce *Strike* as a play in a real factory (instead of a theatre). The cinema was clearly the next logical step. Of course, the use of real material in settings has always been implicit in the cinematic method; Eisenstein developed editing to enable him to use 'non-actors' as characters, in contradistinction to Pudovkin, who used actors edited in the same way as non-actors. (There are no professional actors in any but the last two films, i.e. the talking films.)

The second influence is the usage of rhythms to produce tensions and excitements. Of course, simple rhythms of subject alternation (the condemned in contrast with the galloping pardon) have been used ever since Griffith, but Eisenstein developed rhythms based on subtle visual forms, or, more properly speaking, temporal visual forms, which produced a response in some degree independent of the spectator's sympathy for the content. His irresistible success in this respect (attested of course by the banning of his films in so many countries) was not achieved by any mechanical formula, but by an encyclopædic study of human anthropology and psychology (supplemented by sociology), including a specialisation in the ecstasies of the saints – and an artist's sensitivity to every effective facet of the pieces of film enjoyed.

The third influence is the exploration of the philosophical byways of editing: (a) *dialectical*, there are whole passages of the *General Line* (e.g. the separator scene, with the milk – water – numbers transition; the marriage of the bull and the cow, with the growth in age and size of the bull, and the hand-tinted fireworks) where Eisenstein employs the transformation of quantity into quality (and its reverse) for his effects; and (b) *ideological*, e.g. the 'Gods' sequence in *October*, with its annihilation by caricature of the misuse of religion in the name of counter-revolution; the 'Kerensky peacock' sequence in the same film, which says more indelibly almost everything explicit in *Fame is the Spur*.

Other important influences are the compositional relationship of music and movement (*Nevsky*), of subtle movements and speech intonation (*Ivan*). Books can and will be written on Eisenstein's work in all these fields, but, much more, films for ever will reflect it.

That massive brow, those twinkling eyes, that brilliant intellect and restless energy are now no more. But the fame that he won for the Soviet cinema and the impress of his tools on the thought and method of world cinema are alike indelible. The inspiration engendered by his works has become a treasured part of the progressive culture of the peoples. The doctors told him not to work hard. So his Soviet colleagues have written an epitaph for him: he died at his post.

STRICTLY ENTRE NOUS

ARLETTY

★

I KNOW very well that many people who saw me in *Fric-Frac* and *Hôtel du Nord* believe that I am as much a Parisienne as the Eiffel Tower. But, in fact, I was born at Courbevoie of parents who came from Puy-de-Dôme: my father was from Ayat and my mother from Lac de Tazenat. This is the district which Maupassant took for the setting of his story *Mont-Oriol*, and I was given the name of his heroine – Arlette. So that was how I began life, born Arlette Bathiat, at 33 rue de Paris, Courbevoie.

My father was a miner at Saint-Éloi-les-Mines. He was a wonderful person and a very skilled worker. I admired and loved him very much, and can still remember his strength and his gentle face, but I lost him in 1916.

If you expect me to tell you how I played at being a great actress when I was a child I am afraid that you are going to be disappointed. Oh yes, I know that many stars will tell you how they loved to dress themselves in their mothers' and grandmothers' old clothes in the attic and play at being the marquise or the Queen of Fairyland. But I never did. I played at nurses and hospitals instead. Everybody knows that you do not have to go very far to hear women talking about their operations and what a time they had when their youngest was born. I took in all that, and decided to set up my own hospital, laying my dolls in line and covering them with a sheet. Then I made my rounds, looking at the numbered ticket which I had attached to each one.

'And how are you this morning, Number 24? I think we shall have to operate on you. Oh no, there is nothing to be afraid of, my good woman, up you get. And Number 10, you are looking a lot better to-day. We shall soon have you up and about. What?

You've still got a pain? Down to the theatre with you, another operation will soon put you right.'

And so on, until in the end my dolls were cut to rags and my mother scolded me, saying that I was a wicked girl and God would punish me. I never believed that, because all the doctors and nurses seemed to get by all right. I think my mother found my pastime a little morbid!

I was never a marvel at school. The only subjects which I liked were history and arithmetic. It is well known in France that the Auvergnats have good heads for figures, so I could not very well go wrong in maths. I often made parodies of poems which we had to learn, and I remember one which went something like this:

> My father is a miner, my mother patches clothes;
> Being the daughter of these two, I'm twice stony broke.

When I began to work for a living, it was in an office as a shorthand-typist. Without boasting, I was good at the job, and can still remember most of my shorthand. In 1916, after being in several offices, I went to work in the office of Briand who, at that time, held office as Keeper of the Seals. Later, when my father died, I went to work in the Darracq armament factory, where I made shells.

On the suggestion of a friend, who gave me all the necessary tips, I became a mannequin. I liked this much better than being a typist; I saw more of life for one thing, and very few women find it disagreeable to wear pretty clothes and be admired. At first I worked in the smaller fashion houses, and then I went to Paul Poiret at the time when he was one of the most fashionable designers. The next step in my career was as artist's model, and I was soon enjoying a success as one of the pin-up girls of the moment. I still had no idea of making the theatre my profession – I used to go there a lot as a spectator, and my favourite at the time was Ève Lavallière, whom I have never ceased to admire for her personality.

When I was a kid of five or six, I went to see La Goulue ('The

Glutton'). I should explain to English readers that La Goulue had been one of the great figures in the Paris entertainment world for many decades. She used to appear at the Moulin-Rouge in the old days, complete with her cage full of lions. The walls of this cage were covered with a painting by Toulouse-Lautrec of three of her lions and La Goulue herself. This picture was found some time later, cut into fragments, but it has since been patched together again and is now in the Albi Museum.

But to return to my meeting with La Goulue. At the time when I saw her she was at the end of her career, dressed like a market woman in a blue apron, with her an old sick lion. There was a current joke that the lion's roars were really made by a gramophone record played at the back of the cage. I was there with a crowd of mischievous urchins of my own age. To show off in front of them I bawled at La Goulue, 'Your old lions have got false teeth!' Her hand shot through the bars and grabbed the hem of my dress. 'You'll soon see about that', she shouted in a fury. I started to yell blue murder, thinking she was going to drag me into the cage and throw me to the lion. I pulled away with all my might, but as I hadn't any knickers on and my dress was hoisted up around my waist, the joke was turned against me. I got away and made off amidst the hoots of my pals. I recalled this incident to La Goulue some years later and she was very amused. She had not forgotten it either.

Eventually I entered the theatre through an introduction by somebody who had known me as a model. He said one day, 'Would you like to act?' Almost without thinking I replied, as I often do, '*Pourquoi pas* – why not?' My first appearance on the stage would amuse you. I sang 'Tipperary', accompanied by the pianist Estéban.

I will not go into all the details of the parts I played. It went the usual way, sometimes good and sometimes not so good. I sang, I danced, now I played in a farce, now in a tragedy, some of my rôles I liked and others I was not very keen on. But I had made the theatre my career by this time and I had to stick to it.

You must not think that I wanted to get out, because I was mostly happy, and anyway I have the kind of philosophy which makes the most of all situations and I never expect fortune to throw gifts into my lap. Some of you who remember the Paris theatre between the wars may have seen *Le cochon qui sommeille* or *Plus ça change*, with Raimu and Spinelly. If your memory is very good, you may even remember me.

Until I played in *Hôtel du Nord* I took only small parts in films. In one film, *Les Perles de la Couronne* – a Sacha Guitry picture – I played the Queen of Abyssinia and nobody could say that I was blacker than I was painted! When the critics reviewed the film they christened me 'the black pearl'. I had a real python for a partner in some scenes. That might well have been disturbing had it not been for the snake-charmer who was sporting enough to hang around when the scenes were being shot – just to see that it did not take a sudden dislike to me.

I remember an amusing incident during the making of one of the early films in which I took part – *La Garçonne*. I did not as yet know a lot about the film business and everything interested me tremendously. When I was not wanted on the set, I used to sit quietly in a corner and take in everything going on around me. Once, when I was doing this, I noticed that a man sitting nearby was watching me. Strictly I had no business to be there, as it was a scene in which I did not appear – it was a retake of one of Suzy Solidor's scenes. It occurred to me that I should say something before he told me to clear off, so I ventured, in a small voice, the profound observation, 'It's amusing, all this, isn't it?'

He gave me a quizzical look and said, 'Well, you know, when you have commanded 40,000 men on the plain of Jena as I have done, it surprises you even more'.

I went off to find Jean de Limur, the producer, to learn more about this queer individual. When I asked him, he looked at me a little reprovingly, 'That's Napoleon'. Then I was convinced that everybody in films was crazy. It was not until later that I discovered that the odd person was Robert Dieudonné, famous for his part as Napoleon in the days of the silent films. He was Napoleon again, playing opposite me in *Madame Sans-Gêne*.

I cannot remember at the moment all the things in which I appeared at that time, but there was the film *La Chaleur du Sein*, with Michel Simon, Dorziat, Jeanne Lion and Jean Paquis; the operetta *O mon bel inconnu*, by Sacha Guitry and Reynaldo Hahn. Koval and Simone Simon also appeared in that. There were many other plays, including *Azor*, *La Danseuse Éperdue*, *Mon Gosse de Père*, *Le Bonheur*, *Mesdames* and *Fric-Frac*. I played in both the play and the film of *Fric-Frac*, and I remember an amusing incident which occurred one night just before the curtain went up.

In the play Michel and I rode on to the stage on a tandem. This particular evening I was not feeling so good, and I felt above all in need of an encouraging word from somebody. I should explain that at the time Michel himself was very depressed by the loss of Zaza, a tame monkey of great intelligence but considerable ugliness. She was a mixture of orang-outang and chimpanzee, and used to eat at the same table as Michel, dressed in woman's clothes (Zaza – not Michel). I asked him how I looked, hoping for a kind word from him. Michel stared at me for a moment, and then, just as our call came and we mounted the tandem, he turned to me and said in a heart-broken voice, 'Oh, how you remind me of Zaza!' As we rode out on to the stage I forgot about my depression in the effort to choke back my laughter.

I must admit that *Hôtel du Nord*, with which I really started my major parts in films, is one of my favourite parts of all time. When I was in London one week-end at the end of 1947, Roland Gant told me that this film is still shown from time to time in the cinemas exhibiting French films. He showed me a circular issued by the Hampstead Everyman Theatre, which said of *Hôtel du Nord*: 'Whenever we think of the French cinema, we think, rightly or wrongly, of this film'. That is a very pleasant thing to have said about a film which I enjoyed making, and it is gratifying and flattering to know that there is a public in England which still enjoys it.

The following year, that is to say in 1939, I was in my next Marcel Carné film – *Le Jour se Lève*. A personal point – if I had gained something of a reputation for undressing in *Hôtel du Nord* by the manipulation of the zip-fastener on my dress, I went even farther in *Le Jour se Lève* where, for several seconds, I was entirely nude. In speaking of this film I should like to say how heartening it has been to read in the British Press of the protests against the destruction of this film by Hollywood in order that an American imitation – *The Long Night* – might be circulated without fear of challenge. Although I am naturally sad when I hear of the disappearance of something in which I took part, please believe that it is the principle of the action to which I object. Taken to its logical conclusion, it would mean the destruction of the Mona Lisa because a painter thinks he could create a smile with more box-office appeal or likely to take the eye of the tooth-paste advertiser, or the burning of every copy of *Romeo and Juliet* in order that everybody might be forced to see the brilliant new version, complete with close-up kiss and celestial choir in the happy ending. I think that this is the opinion of most people who protested against the *Le Jour se Lève* affair. It was very interesting to read the excellent article by Simon Harcourt-Smith in *Picture Post* on this subject and the comparison between the two films.

Shortly before the war I made *Tempête sur Paris* with Annie Ducaux and Eric von Stroheim, and *La Femme que j'ai le plus aimée* with Noël-Noël, whose *La Cage aux Rossignols* you have apparently liked so much in England. In that film – *La Femme que j'ai le plus aimée* – I had my dog 'B flat' with me.

One of the films in which I enjoyed acting most was *Circonstances Atténuantes*, directed by Jean Boyer. Those of you who have seen it will remember how gay it was. There was Michel Simon as the judge, notorious for the severity of his sentences, becoming the leader of a gang of light-hearted and light-fingered crooks, whose respect he earned by the dexterity with which he burgled his own house and stole his wife's hideous ornaments. I can still remember what fun I had as The Panther, trying again and again to pocket the judge's cigarette-case. And there was the final scene where everything ends well, the crooks converted to honesty, the judge and his wife happier and more human, all of us singing the theme-song 'Comme de bien entendu'. In these days of enormous expenditure and long periods on location, etc., it is worth remembering that this film – a success – was made in only two weeks.

During the war I made only three films, *Madame Sans-Gêne*, *Les Visiteurs du Soir* and *Les Enfants du Paradis*. Perhaps I shall one day return to my first love – the theatre, to such a favourite rôle as that of Mrs Chevely in Wilde's *The Ideal Husband*. I like a change now and then, and I am convinced that one cannot repeat with success something rare. For example, *Les Visiteurs du Soir* was something very special both as a film and also for me because of the part I played. But it is ridiculous to attempt something of the same kind again. That goes for *Les Enfants du Paradis* as well, of course. This is also a film with a difference, and by being different it was a success and cannot and should not be copied.

I believe that every picture, as a work of art (and it is worthless if it is not approached as such), should be a shaped and complete entity like a jewel, polished and well-set. The performance of the artists in full understanding of the author's intention is the pure gold of the jewel's setting. Nowadays, with the high perfection which film-technique has attained and the genius of the producers and directors, both artists and author are greatly assisted – the artist by the aid of colour, background music, etc., in his interpretation of the author's intention; the author, on the other hand, knows that those aids are there to call upon when he needs them to heighten an effect, to strengthen an emotional appeal.

To me, as an actress, it is complete understanding and sincere interpretation of the rôle one plays which is most important. One must be natural and sincere and *feel* what one is portraying. But is not that the most important thing in life as well? When I am no longer sincere, when I no longer say what I think, when I can no longer respond to feeling – then I shall surely be dead. In the same way I believe in eternal love – the kind of love shown in *Les Visiteurs du Soir*, where the hearts of the lovers continue to beat after they are turned to stone. And if it is not true, where is the value of life? One may suffer more, but one is a real being. I think it was Herbert Spencer who wrote 'Life is a comedy for those who think and a tragedy for those who feel'.

In the arts I think I am most moved by poetry, but I also adore music. I have never had training in musical appreciation, so all my reactions are completely instinctive. Most of all I like Beethoven, Bach and Mozart, and particularly such religious music as Mozart's *Requiem*. Amongst contemporary composers I am most attracted by the work of Ravel. In painting and sculpture I prefer the work of Michelangelo, Leonardo da Vinci and Rodin. I suppose I should say that I really prefer sculpture to painting, despite my admiration for van Gogh, Cézanne and their contemporaries. One of my favourite pastimes is sketching.

But I have written more than enough about my past, my likes and dislikes. My plans for the future I prefer to leave to the future. Perhaps I shall continue to make films, perhaps I shall go back more and more to the theatre. Again, I may travel, for although I adore Paris, I would also love to travel all over the world. I like to come to London now and then, but I am afraid that one day a taxi will run over me, because I always look to the left instead of to the right when crossing the street. I like London – maybe I shall make films in England one day – *pourquoi pas?*

(*Translated by Roland Gant.*)

MR CAPRA'S SHORT CUTS
TO UTOPIA

HAROLD J. SALEMSON

*

> Mr Capra goes to town,
> Does a job and does it brown;
> Company with young Jefferson Smith,
> Mr Capra goes to town.

THAT was the lyric of a song entitled,appropriately enough, *Mr Capra Goes to Town*, and introduced in an early edition of that lively revue, *Meet the People*, which was born in Hollywood at Christmas of 1939. The song was dropped after Capra's *Mr Smith Goes to Washington* had lost the first blush of its newness, but the tribute to Frank Capra's eager energy, his enthusiasm, his thoroughness and his entirely (if, perhaps, unconsciously) pro-democratic genius, has lived on.

In fact, throughout the world, the name of Capra is quickly recognised as that of one of Hollywood's outstanding film creators. And this is as it should be, not merely because of the box-office success of his pictures, or the studio publicity around his name, but because of the fact that he is one of the few directors in Hollywood's increasingly mechanised film-production set-up who can be held clearly and consistently responsible for his work.

Capra, along with a handful of other Hollywood producer-directors, does not merely execute subjects which the studio heads assign to him. He is responsible for the selection and development of his scenarios, and for their ultimate realisation. In a word, he is a true 'film author'.

In this, it will be argued, he is not unique. The names of Welles, Sturges, Wyler, Brackett and Wilder, Vidor, Mamoulian and numerous others will be brought up.

Yet, none of these actually compares to Capra in the overall body of work produced. Welles in almost all his films, Sturges and Wyler in a few, have no doubt exceeded Capra's achievements. But Welles has been at it too short a time, as has Sturges, and Wyler has not been on his own long enough (his earlier films were run-of-the-mill) nor does his body of work reflect the personality or consistency of Capra's. Brackett and Wilder have not yet reached above more-than-average Hollywood proficiency, and Vidor seems to have lost his early touch; while Mamoulian has never fulfilled the exciting promises of his first pictures.

Fritz Lang, in his cycle of German films and again in the several films he did on crime and the concept of guilt in Hollywood, made major contributions. But the entire collection of his work, again, does not have the weight of Capra's.

What, then, makes Capra stand apart from the rest?

His achievement of nearly twenty years has been consistent. It is impregnated with a peculiar, personal approach. There is a main, central theme running through his work that is as permanent as Marcel Proust's concern with the conception of time and remembrance.

Capra has spent the better part of a lifetime in a quest for Utopia – or, more precisely, in a quest for short cuts to Utopia. The fact that he happened to express himself in the motion-picture form, one which could at the same time bring him a very considerable fortune, is perhaps only coincidental – while perhaps a major contributing factor to his having developed as he did.

The burden of Capra's work can be rapidly summed up as follows: there is a great deal wrong with the contemporary world. The solution to what is wrong, however, is not a revolutionary one. We are overlooking something. If we could just discover what that something is, and restore it to its proper place in our society, all the wrongs would right themselves, and we would head for the smooth sailing which our social organisation is alleged to be able to provide, and yet somehow fails to do.

The trouble is, that each new 'something' that is proposed proves to be as insufficient as the preceding 'somethings', and Capra goes on to look for a new panacea. In the course of his search, he has provided some of the best film entertainment ever, and millions the world over have been only too happy to accompany him from one false lead to another.

How did Capra get that way?

The son of a miserably poor Italian family from Palermo, established in Los Angeles, Frank sold newspapers as a tot to add to the family's income. Through industry and luck, and two years of toil after graduation from high school, he was able to save enough to finance his college education. Because of his small size at sixteen, he was able to get a job with the Western Pipe and Steel Company crawling inside pipes to inspect them. This furnished his tuition fees and expenses for his first year at the California Institute of Technology.

A brilliant student, and editor of the college magazine, he won a $500 scholarship, which he devoted to a tour of the States to study artistic and musical manifestations in various cities and college centres. His study of engineering was obviously already taking a back seat to the creative cultural interests evidenced by his magazine editorship.

The arts and letters had by now completely outdistanced his interest in engineering, and Gower Gulch's independent producers soon found an eager young graduate engineer hounding them for film assignments. His break came with *Screen Snapshots*, at Columbia. Next job: gagman for Our Gang comedies; then, gagman for Harry Langdon at Mack Sennett's.

Capra finally became a full-fledged director with the Harry Langdon feature comedies, *Tramp, Tramp, Tramp, Long Pants* and *The Strong Man*. That his technical training at Caltech had stood him in good stead is attested to by the fact that these remain to-day, after twenty and more years, as models of their type in the cinema archives of the world.

But Harry Langdon decided to direct himself, and Capra was again unemployed. He made a picture called *For the Love of Mike* with an unknown actress named Claudette Colbert. And both wished it had never been. Capra went back to writing gags for Sennett.

Finally, becoming a contract director at Columbia, Capra made such pictures as *The Certain Thing, So This is Love*, and a number of others before hitting the top in box-office popularity with *Submarine, The Power of the Press, The Younger Generation,* and other hits which led the late great Harry Alan Potamkin to dub him with that immortal tag, 'The gem of Columbia's ocean'.

This was the early 'thirties. The Depression had just hit. Roosevelt was President. And Capra, the immigrant starveling of twenty years before, was a well-heeled Hollywood director, now well enough entrenched to be able to command both his own salary and his own subjects for films. From here on, a strange chemistry within the man was to account for a series of increasingly socially-significant films, yet increasingly idealistic and panacea-seeking, increasingly 'escapist', in fact.

That Capra was, and remains, aware of social evils and wrongs, there can be no doubt. The subject-matter of his great films testifies to one of the keenest social consciences in film history. That he sensed and senses the need for drastic reform is evidenced by his choice of collaborators. His writers, his advisers, his associate producers have almost invariably been selected by him from among Hollywood's most progressive individuals. These spoke the language he understood: their fight for equality, justice, democracy, was his own goal in life.

But the Cinderella-boy who had made good, the immigrant ragazzo up from poverty to Hollywood's fabulous luxuries, could not bring himself to share the views of some of his collaborators. Socialism? Communism? Reorganisation of society from the roots up? Hardly. This was the right type of society: had he not achieved an unheard-of success in it? Capra was, and is, essentially a Conservative.

Damon Runyon's heart-warming story of *Apple Annie* furnished Capra with the first clear expression of what was to become his own peculiar contribution to the thinking of our time. It became *Lady for a Day* on the screen. Some of his previous films had had a similar sympathetic, human feeling, to the extent that he had been able to inject it into subjects that were not entirely of his choosing. Now, for the first time, he was on his own: he could present a first outline of what can be called Capraism. Human goodness, human charity, the understanding and warmth of fellow-beings against the harsh realities of apple-selling on the street corners of an unemployment-ridden society. The success of the film proved that there could be no doubt that Capra had the 'common touch'. He spoke to the people in a language they understood and with which, so far as it went, they agreed whole-heartedly.

It Happened One Night, perhaps the finest comedy ever filmed by anyone but Chaplin, contributed its note of condemnation of snobbery and the smug unfeeling stupidities of the rich. *Broadway Bill*, for all that it might appear a diversion from the main quest, was nevertheless a pæan to honesty and humanity.

With *Mr Deeds Goes to Town*, however, Capra settled down to the forthright expression of his credo. By this time, the Depression was well advanced. No one doubted very much that there were many things woefully wrong with the world. It is easy to imagine the conferences that must have gone on between Capra and his writers. The latter, without any doubt, must have proposed solutions to the story much more basic and revolutionary than the version that was ultimately released. But Capra was the master, and he had the 'touch'.

The same adaptability, the same driving urge, the same devotion to a set of principles which knew how to make the best of a bad bargain and adapt themselves to the realities of a tough world – these qualities were now to prevail and allow him to make films as progressive, as socially significant as possible within the existing framework of the film industry, and yet not offend anyone, not incur the slightest suspicion of leftism or revolutionary tendencies.

Mr Deeds, after all, within its hilariously told story, uncovered much of the plight of the people of that day, and proposed that the goodness of inspired rich landowners, returning property to the people, would solve the inequities of distribution in a profit-system society. Of the underlying causes which brought about the people's plight, not a word. That is not Capra's concern: he is strictly a reformer, not a revolutionary. His background may not have made that the only development he could take, but his work is evidence that his formation by this time brooked no other type of solution.

With *Lost Horizon*, the quest took a more escapist turn. The relationship to contemporary life was less direct. Nevertheless, in prologue and epilogue, and strewn through the dialogue, it was there. But now the solution was Shangri-la: no longer a reform that would make a Utopia in our own society, but a materialised Utopia high in the Himalayas, where goodness exists alone, and immortality is its reward.

It may be said here that these subjects were not his; that *Lost Horizon* was Hilton's rather than Capra's. The fact that others may have thought along parallel lines does not detract from the originality or consistency of Capra's drive. It was he who selected the subject for filming, who shot it as it was shot – and he seized upon it because it fitted in with his constant search for subjects, whether original or already done in another medium, which could serve as vehicles for the unswerving Capra message.

With *Meet John Doe*, there was a return to reality and the closest approach to a revolutionary film that Capra ever made. Here it was the common man's need for a leader, along with the earlier return to the land of *Mr Deeds*, which became the solution that would be the short cut to Utopia. Honesty and courage in leading the people in terms they understood, that was the formula.

Because of the unchanging reticence to call things by name, to make clear the revolutionary implications, *John Doe* brought Capra under severe attack from the Left for what appeared objectively as a pro-Fascist call for a Man on a White Horse. The interpretation was doubtless unfounded, but not nearly so unfounded as the recent allegation by columnist Hedda Hopper, at the time of the Un-American Activities Committee's investigation into Hollywood, that *Meet John Doe* was a prime example of Communist propaganda on the screen. Nothing could be farther from the truth. If anything, because of his refusal to face up to a revolutionary solution to society's troubles, and his eagerness to find a short cut to happiness, Capra might some day be prey to the phony plan of a Fascist demagogue – much more quickly, at any rate, than he is likely to accept any radical Socialist proposal.

You Can't Take It With You gave him a chance to express his familiar homily in less controversial terms. If only people would realise that money isn't happiness, the film said; if only the mad scramble for earthly possessions could be ended.

Mr Smith Goes to Washington was to be Capra's most completely democratic and honest picture of all. Credit for this, perhaps, must go in part to the increasing influence over the film of Capra's then-regular scenarist Sidney Buchman. No finer pæan of praise has ever been sung to democracy in any form more engaging. All the positive elements are there: honesty, equality, devotion to the democratic tradition, understanding of the significance and achievements of Abraham Lincoln, Thomas Jefferson and others.

And how do we pay tribute to this free legacy of ours? By electing honest men to the corrupt halls of Congress – and by extension to the parliaments of the world. Men of good will can solve all of our troubles, without violence, without bloodshed.

All too true. But once again there is not a profound word of what makes the other lawmakers corrupt, of why the general run of politicians are dishonest and thereby put honesty in Jeff Smith at such a premium. Capra offers a panacea which treats the symptom of the illness, but not the source of infection.

Just before the war, Capra made one more film, *Arsenic and Old Lace*, which is a diversion from his straight line of inquiry. Perhaps because he made this for another company, where he was given or felt he could afford to take less latitude than at Columbia, where he ran the show; perhaps just because he wanted to relax and exercise only his comedy talents; whatever the reason, of all his mature efforts, *Arsenic* was to be the only one which reflected no social criticism to speak of, and consequently called forth no presentation of a cardinal virtue which could end the evil.

His experience in World War II was to prove further that his concern with what was wrong with the world was not fortuitous. As Commanding Officer of the Signal Corps Photographic Centre and later as Assistant Chief of the Army Pictorial Service, Capra made outstanding contributions to the library of training and informational films which were to form the body of the American fighting man's understanding of Fascism and why we fought it. The very fact that Capra had never appeared sufficiently to have understood this before the war indicates perhaps that his great quality was that of an executive rather than a theorist: just as he turned out his civilian pictures by working with politically- and socially-aware scenarists whose radical solutions he restrained, so was his choice of strongly anti-Fascist collaborators largely responsible for the quality of his service films. But only the warm-hearted humanity, as well as the technical proficiency, of Capra himself could in the final analysis have accounted for such films as *The Battle of Britain*, *The Battle of Russia*, *The Battle of China*, the *Why We Fight* series, *Know Your Ally Britain*, *The Negro Soldier* or *San Pietro*.

When ex-Lieutenant-Colonel Capra returned to civilian life,

ARLETTY

1 to 3. Photographs by Teddy Piaz (Paris) and Germaine Kanova (London).

NEW SWEDISH FILMS

4 and 5. 'Rallare.' (Svensk Filmindustri.) A film of railway building.
Director: Arne Mattsson; featuring Victor Sjöstrom.

5. 'Rallare.'

6. 'I am with You.' (S.F.) A religious film made partly in Africa.

PAUL DELVAUX

7 and 8. Stills from a Belgian film made by Henri Storck on the theme of a number of Delvaux's paintings.

LUBITSCH'S EARLY FILMS

9. 'Köhlhiesel's Daughter.' With Henny Porten and Emil Jannings.

10. 'Carmen' (1918). With Pola Negri.

11. 'The Mountain Cat' (1921). With Pola Negri.

12. 'Madame Dubarry' (1918). With Pola Negri.

CROSSFIRE—AN IMPORTANT

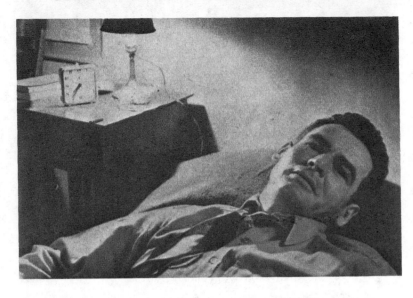

13 to 18. A film on racial intolerance, produced by Adrian Scott, directed by Edward Dmytryk, screen play by John Paxton.

13 and 14. Robert Ryan as Montgomery. 15 and 16. Robert Ryan with Steve Brodie as Floyd.

17. Robert Young as the detective Finlay with Gloria Grahame as the dancer Ginny.

18. Montgomery in the final scene of attempted escape.

NEW SOVIET FILMS

19 and 20. 'Young Guard.' Directed by Sergei Gerasimov. A film of Komsomol resistance during the occupation of Krasno-Don.

21 to 24. 'Education of the Senses.' Directed by Mark Donskoi. Donskoi

once more achieves success in the direction of children in this story of three generations of young people.

25 and 26. 'Cinderella.' Directed by K. Kasheverova and A. Shapiro, with the character actress Ranevskaya centred in each still.

27. 'Ballerina.' Directed by A. Ivanovsky.

28. 'In the Name of Life.' Directed by Zarchi and Helfitz; with Nicolai Cherkassov as a door-keeper.

29 and 30. 'Spring.' Directed by Alexandrov; with Lyubov Orlova and Nicolai Cherkassov. A musical comedy about film-making.

as a partner in Liberty Films, now one of Hollywood's top independent producers, his first film proved conclusively that Capraism had not changed. *It's a Wonderful Life* combines, perhaps, several of the panaceas of his early pictures, but the level of the attack remains the same. Money isn't everything: goodness and understanding must prevail. People must trust and help each other. And don't wish you were dead, because, if you but have the strength of character and purity of vision to see it, all is for the best in the best of all possible worlds – or, at least, it will be when the Good People get together and give evil its just desert.

Strangely enough, in a post-war period where such a message would appear to be more needed than ever before, the film was a dud. Capra appeared no longer to be in tune with the public as he had so unerringly been before the war. Artistically, the film showed little or no advance over his earlier achievements; at the box-office, an equally important factor in Capra's code, it showed definite retrogression.

Capra's next is to be *State of the Union*, the Lindsay-Crouse play which will afford him in essence the same type of vehicle as *Mr Smith Goes to Washington*. Within the framework of a rollicking comedy, which presents a tremendous technical problem through the need to keep it topical in a period of fast moving political change (it is to be released during 1948's Presidential election campaign), Capra again has a character whose justification for existence is the injection of amateur honesty into a political world of professional corruption. The director's good will and lack of partisanship may best be reflected by the casting, which includes Katharine Hepburn alongside of Adolphe Menjou, the two stars who have, rightly or wrongly, come more than any other two to be identified in the public mind with the political Left and Right, respectively, in Hollywood.

State of the Union will offer, even better no doubt than *It's a Wonderful Life*, a ground for comparison of the post-war Capra to the great director of the earlier period. Will the film in any way deepen the understanding exhibited in *Mr Smith*? Whether it does or does not, will it reach the consciousness of the average movie-goer as each pre-war Capra film did and as *It's a Wonderful Life* most certainly did not?

In a word, it will give us the answer to the big question which must appear of prime importance to all thoughtful critics and movie-goers: Is Capraism dead, or can it still develop along with the temper of the times and continue to retain public attention through its diversified presentations of virtue as the ultimate answer to what ails this world of ours?

Whatever the answer, and whatever the consequent future for Frank Capra as a maker of films, the past body of his work will remain for the student of films as the most consistent and original contribution by any commercial film producer, one that places his name technically alongside those of Chaplin, Griffith and the other masters, and intellectually on a level with the names of the same Chaplin, Welles, Wyler, and the great European directors who have made the film the tremendous vehicle for ideas which it is. None, with the exception once more of Chaplin, has contributed a more consistent work of art to screen history; and, despite Capra's personal shortcomings (or because of them), none has given a more significant personal imprint to the work he has produced.

THE MASK OF REALISM

CATHERINE DE LA ROCHE

*

DESPITE all that is written about the realism attained by the fictional film of Britain and other European countries, despite the fascinating analyses coming from America – Siegfried Kracauer's, Parker Tyler's – which are based on the premise that motion pictures reflect the dominant spirit of the times, I believe the view that the cinema is a phenomenon, rather than an interpreter, of the age which produced it is as valid as ever. At any rate, people like myself, who have had to make selections of pictures typifying a nation's way of life for exhibition in other countries, have special cause to hold this view with some feeling. For up to now the cinema's representation of contemporary life has been wildly unbalanced and fortuitous. If some aspects of reality have been portrayed, they are outnumbered by omissions and evasions, half-truths and distortions.

You only have to compare film lists with some elementary facts of life to see how great the discrepancies are. Take the pictures of most immediate general interest in this country, for instance – the British and American films shown here in the post-war period (two and a half years at the time of writing). There were no British films devoted to contemporary rural life (have you seen a *modern* English country house in films, by the way?), and yet one-fifth of our population lives in the country, and a revolution is taking place in farming, attended by immensely exciting changes in human relationships and values. In America over two-fifths of the people live on the land, and they are involved in vast migrations resulting from the redistribution of man-power. How often is their drama interpreted in film? Examples can be multiplied if you glance at figures showing

35

the occupations, ages, incomes and social conditions of populations, or scan the diaries of recent years giving the main events and records of national (which means human) achievements and failures. It becomes apparent that some of the truly typical features of present history have never been dramatised, while incidental and comparatively exceptional subjects get repeated attention. And if, as is often the case, it is the less articulate sections of society that are overlooked, this does not mean that they are the least dynamic or creative, or that their share in shaping life is the least important and colourful.

*

But what of the themes the cinema *has* made its own? The lists I mentioned are headed by crime films: 48 per cent of the imported American total, composed of 31 per cent melodramas, thrillers, etc., plus 17 per cent Westerns, and 28 per cent of the British output. Without the Westerns and other period pictures, crime stories are still the largest single category among modern subjects. Despite the sad increase in crime, the proportion of murderers in our midst isn't as formidable as that!

Now if these miles of celluloid reflected the social and psychological realities special to our epoch which cause tragedy, if the lives of the various characters had been integrated with their particular environment, the cinema would have shed light on at least one (the worst) aspect of present history. But this rarely happens. Instead, the exploitation for profit of 'crime that doesn't pay' has become the most efficient 'line' in the industry. As a result of accumulated production experience, the external realism in any noteworthy crime film is near-perfect. Even the fashionable psychological introspections are often impressive, until you notice how expertly non-committal the treatment is. Each case, it would seem, is an isolated case, suggesting no solution, pointing no moral. A maze of incidental motivations takes the place of a deeper analysis of the origins of crime. You are drawn into the familiar, apparently natural atmosphere of evil and neurosis, learning nothing except for the equivocal implication that crime is a flourishing part of existence, though the law always wins.

An outstanding example of the British spiv cycle, *They Made Me a Fugitive*, though uncompromisingly realistic in characterisation and atmosphere, gave no idea what induces men to become spivs, or what might provide a counter-attraction for them. *Possessed* was representative of the stereotyped film version of psychoanalysis, though, as the melodrama of a possessive woman possessed by her own amorous frustrations, it was excellent. Pictures of this kind, surrounding their tragic prima-donnas with solicitude and luxury, tend to glamorise insanity and encourage self-contemplation. They only show the psychiatrist's unfailing patience, giving no idea of the enormously wide range of tactics, including shock tactics, called for in the conscientious practitioner's work, and ignoring the tough, agonising side of psychoanalysis, which does not encourage self-indulgence or egocentricity in the patient.

With love appearing in practically all films, it might have been expected that the cinema would evolve this eternal theme a stage farther and bring it up to date. Yet it is precisely in the treatment of love that the cinema has adhered most tenaciously to the emptiest stereotypes of the literature and drama of the past. Because so many films are based on the money-making factors of star-boosting, sumptuous décor and happy endings, pretty women have to be presented in 'advantageous' situations, surrounded by adulation, and men appear as amorous figures, neither sex having any apparent interests other than romance. Old-fashioned formulæ in modern dress are quite good enough for this.

But only new patterns and combinations, seldom attempted, can depict the new realities. Our epoch has produced probably the most fundamental changes in the relationship between men and women ever known, changes which have not yet attained stability and which are still conflicting with the more long-standing traditions of the past. The emancipation of women, the advance of science, economic and international stresses have presented men and women with a new set of choices and responsibilities, freedoms and restrictions, which affect their attitudes to each other, to marriage and to parenthood. New ethics are in the making. Every day we encounter the drama and complexity of it all: the woman who wants it both ways, expecting protection from the men with whom she now competes in politics, professions and (on unequal terms) in industry; the man who wants it both ways, expecting to be served by the wife who shares the fatigue and hazards of bread-winning; the manifold conflicts arising from professional rivalries, the vexed question of status, opposing convictions and, by no means least, money, which usually determines whether marriage is possible, whether having a family is possible.

Except in a few films like *The Searching Wind* or *The Years Between*, points such as these are assiduously avoided. Instead, the American cinema, perhaps with a motive, has evolved the stock situation in which a woman with brains enough to run a profession lacks what it takes to get a man. Otherwise there's the success story of the beauty in show business and occasional glimpses of the career woman already on top. How she got there, how men and women are sorting out their respective functions in life, we hardly ever see.

In Britain the situation is particularly complex owing to the disparity in the numbers of men and women, which has been increasing since the last century. Now, with over 5 million more women than men, the relation is roughly 5 to 4, and the disproportion is heaviest precisely in the marriageable age-groups. Inevitably this accentuates the question of the relative values of both sexes. In some spheres the preponderance of women may put them in a leading position, but mostly it works the other way. In many jobs, where women compete *against* men, it means cheaper rates and subordination; in private life, where women compete *for* men, it means fewer chances of marriage.

Thus, while women have won new rights and a measure of equality in society, in the question of marriage they are seriously restricted, and it is the men who have the choice and greater freedom, if only because there are fewer of them.

The social and psychological implications are enormous. Marked attitudes have evolved among both men and women in their approaches to each other: there's a special point in that measuring of one another's strength at first encounters; many reversals of rôles; a sharpened awareness of who calls the tune and why; particular motives for compassion and sacrifice. Even in the best movies the characters seem to be oblivious of all this. And in the average picture, as we know, the heroine usually has a choice of men. Producers plug this situation on the assumption that it provides an illusion of wish fulfilment for the largest section of their audiences, the women. Perhaps they will realise one day that, for audiences who have this wish, it can be singularly irritating to see the problems of its fulfilment underrated, while for those who have not, this stock situation can be exceedingly boring.

*

While omitting some topics and standardising a narrow approach to others, the cinema has evolved a set of subsidiary themes, or patterns in undertone, which recur in films on the most diverse subjects. Often they reflect attitudes not openly professed and, in consequence, it may sometimes be hard to establish whose attitudes they are and to what extent they represent existing trends. Some, no doubt, do represent popular myths and dreams, but in the final analysis, every film reflects the choice, judgment and taste of its makers – no portrayal of life can be impersonal.

Most of these patterns are used to advocate a perpetuation of the *status quo*, and they have become so familiar that you hardly recognise them for what they are. In the American film there is the set of variations centred round the ideal of freedom of opportunity, at least for the few, to gain unrestricted wealth: the millionaire is characterised either as a charming eccentric, a harmless, charitable old dear, or a hardened business man whose fundamental kindliness is easily brought out by some invigorating and ennobling encounter with the poor; success stories imply that the sky's the limit for him who has what it takes to reach the top; at the same time the common man's lot is not bettered, his station in life is a fixture, the poor are always with us. Among the scores of films illustrating one or several of these points were *It Happened on 5th Avenue*, *Love and Learn* and, not surprisingly, *The Bishop's Wife*, sent as a prestige piece for the Royal Command Performance. Then there is the pattern of the hero rising all the way to success, only to return thankfully to his starting-point after having seen the dangers of high life: the rich also have their troubles, there are advantages in a modest existence.

The general idea behind these and other motifs (some contradicting each other, some dating from biblical times) is that the interests of rich and poor can well be accommodated within the existing social order. The common man's dreams of money and a bit of kudos are fostered, even a measure of satire on the abuses of big business (as in *The Hucksters*, say) is tolerated as a safety valve through which he can blow off steam. But the big money maker is never the enemy. On the other hand, there can be virtue in poverty. Always attention is deflected from anything that might suggest change: this would counteract illusions of dream-fulfilment and threaten the interests of big business. Occasionally these deep-rooted conventions are respected, even in the few films expressing the opposite view, perhaps as a condition for getting them made at all. The exposures in *The Best Years of our Lives*, for instance, were partially cancelled out or obscured by the stereotype solutions in the incidentals of the plot.

There are counterparts of these patterns in the British cinema. The series of films with West End titles, such as *Piccadilly Incident* or *The Courtneys of Curzon Street*, gives a romanticised view of an aristocracy which is essentially benevolent to the lower orders. *I Know Where I'm Going* used two familiar but contradictory motifs in the same story with perplexing results: money, it implied, is not a thing to covet, but the beautiful life that a goodish amount of it can buy is. Perhaps the film did at least indicate *what* to go for!

But tendentious stereotypes are not typical of the British cinema, which is more prone to use its consummate skill in ignoring or by-passing leading points than to harp on them. Of late, however, its own tendency has been in another direction. It has excelled, even in unpretentious productions like *It Always Rains on Sunday*, in capturing the living atmosphere of localities and showing human beings in whom you can believe implicitly, though you may not learn much about them. These films are vital, moving, but, for all their unquestionable integrity and insight, they are stories developed in vacuo, detached from the wider issues of the day; nor were they meant to be anything else.

Odd Man Out, deservedly renowned for its superb artistry, was a *tour de force* of both skilful evasion and detachment within the strikingly life-like environment of a Northern Irish city in post-war times. It shows how a man kills and dies in the name of a cause, how various citizens reveal themselves through their reactions to him and his deed, but it dexterously conceals the aims and identity of the cause. The human motives are thus obscured, their link with present history severed. And when, at the end, the drama reaches out towards the higher plane of universal truth, it fails to attain it: if the particular can be a valid basis from which to proceed towards the general, evasion cannot serve as a foundation for anything save confusion.

*

It often seems, I know, that the range covered by the cinema is wide indeed, what with memories of tropical forests and snowy mountains, rich homes and poor ones, history, classics, tragedy, farce, musicals and what have you – all seen on the screen. And, no doubt, a good deal of truth has been revealed in fragments.

But the closer you look, the more apparent it becomes that, over-all, the cinema has somehow got enmeshed in the static and nega-tive elements of contemporary life. The positive, creative forces moulding the present and the future, in short – the dynamic es-sence of our era – has hardly begun to be filmed. This, of course, is the cinema's gravest omission, and, incidentally, an opportunity missed for making money: since the beginning of the species, humanity has loved a tale of daring, striving and achievement. The builders of the ideas and material wonders of our times have stories full of adventure and romance. The inspiration which im-pels them to invent, compete with rivals, master setbacks and the rest, is surely more vital than the dismal avarice of spivs, if only it were dramatised instead of appearing here and there as an irrelevant background. The same applies to the common man's struggle for survival and progress, which entails the strain of self-assertion over domineering elements, the hazards, humour and triumphs of the daily process of doing a job. Not *all* these people are drab, poky curios like the stereotyped absent-minded professor. Achievement breeds self-reliance; self-reliance de-velops individuality, style, dash and charm. In real life one meets people like that.

Film studios, eternally short of interesting rôles for their stars, overlook the interesting people of the day. Hence the ab-sence of the 'modern hero' in films. The 'ordinary man' we've seen for years. A harmless, undefinable fellow, whom each star adapts to his own personality. Even the British documentary caught the fashion a little while back, making a film in which a chap told the audience soothingly 'I'm just an ordinary man', as if it would run for safety if he weren't. This much-abused term often betrays an essentially patronising attitude towards the mass of humanity which, after all, consists of individuals with at least some character, and frequently plenty of it. There are 'modern heroes' among them, and, in a sense, they may be ordinary. But not in the sense implied by the stock characters in movies. They're not the 'modern hero'.

The film world is not without its own modern heroes – technicians evolving a medium of apparently limitless range, artists striving amidst prejudice and opposition to interpret the story of our times and to create new dramatic forms to fit the new realities. (Their own stories, incidentally, would make better entertainment than those stock portrayals of the wild-haired, maniac director.) Interpreting contemporary life, which cannot be seen in perspective, is and always has been the artist's hardest and greatest task. Nobody knows this better than the film workers in the USSR, whose chief aim it has been for the past thirty years and who, despite considerable successes, still have manifold problems to solve. That's why the few films which conquer new ground thematically gain enormously in importance. *Monsieur Verdoux, The Best Years of our Lives, The Rake's Progress, Fame is the Spur, Brief Encounter* (within the limits of its detachment), *It's a Wonderful Life, Men of Two Worlds, School for Secrets, Mine Own Executioner, Frieda, The Overlanders, The Captive Heart, Holiday Camp*, and others besides – on different levels and with varying success, using allegory, satire, drama, comedy or documentary narrative, interpreted modern characters and ideas in modern idiom. Here was thoughtful consideration of some of the problems confronting society, criticism of some of its faults and homage to several of its achievements. Here, too, was some of the best popular entertainment. Whether clothed in fantasy or realism, these are probably the post-war films which came nearest to reality. The remainder, founded as they were on detachment, evasion or distortion, could not change their unreal nature by assuming a mask of realism.

CHILDREN AND FANTASY

CHARLES CRICHTON
Director of 'Hue and Cry'

★

The time has come, the walrus said,
To talk of many things:
Of ships and shoes and sealing wax,
And cabbages and kings,
And why the sea is boiling hot ...

THERE it is ... '– and *why* the sea is boiling hot. ...' So the sea *is* boiling hot; or at least this was what my very young son thought until this year, for the first time, he got a chance to test it for himself and found to his disgust that it was icy cold. He will now, presumably, slide down the slippery chute of disillusionment, and will soon cease to believe.in Father Christmas, the Devil and George Bernard Shaw. But for the moment he still has a mind which is, at the same time, delightfully literal and delightfully imaginative. He has, for example, created for himself an imaginary black monkey who lives at the top of the garden, a monkey so fierce that he no longer dares go near its den for fear of its attacks.

Now these qualities of a child's mind, the ability to create out of an imagination unfettered by too much dull experience, and the ability to believe implicitly, to believe with a solid, concrete conviction, are very useful when it comes to making a film, especially if that film be a fantasy, for the literal side of the child's mind enables it to accept the fantasy without reservation or self-consciousness, and to use a sincere and convincing technique in putting it on the screen. At the same time, the fact that the child has not yet been schooled into accepting the conven-

44

tional allows him to embellish his part with all the power of an uninhibited imagination.

Now fantasy, to be as concise as the *Concise Oxford Dictionary*, is 'an image-making faculty, especially when extravagant or visionary; mental image, fantastic design'. That definition is broad enough in origin to include almost all films that are made, but I suppose that fantasy has now come to mean a book, or play, or film, or picture which removes us from this extremely three-dimensional world into those happier spaces where the mind is no longer constricted by the narrow dictates of reality. When Balcon first decided to make *Hue and Cry*, it was largely because the subject had this happy freedom. But every freedom creates its prison, and we soon found certain conditions imposing themselves on the treatment of our subject, and from those conditions it was impossible to escape. The story opened with an amazing coincidence, Joe reading a serial in a boys' paper and then finding himself confronted with the very events of which he was reading; it continued quickly from one improbable event to another, picking up in its course one or two extraordinary characters. But it was the improbable, the exaggerated and the extraordinary with which the story dealt, but never the impossible. Later it developed moments of genuine suspense and drama which we knew would fail if we had not already created in the minds of the audience a belief in the characters of the children, and at least a tongue-in-the-cheek acceptance of our plot. For this reason the treatment of the subject had to emphasise the possibilities rather than the impossibilities, our camera angles had to be conventional, our settings realistic with as many honest-to-God exteriors as possible, and above all our children had to be children, genuine flesh-and-blood kids lacking entirely the mincing, self-conscious, semi-adult mannerisms which have been foisted on so many child actors who have not yet acquired the ability to distinguish between the true and the false, who have no dynamic personalities of their own and who have, therefore, to rely on the conventional standards of their elders. In other words, we had to emphasise the absurdity of our story through the realism with which we stated it, to enrich our fantasy by the conviction of its telling, 'And *why* the sea is boiling hot', not 'And *if* the sea is boiling hot'.

Of course, this is all post-shooting theory. We did not work this, way because we had thought it all out this way. We did it this way because we liked it so, and waited until the picture was finished before we found ourselves in the unpleasant position of having to justify ourselves. But as we were doing it this way we were naturally confronted with a major task in finding for our gang enough boys and the right boys to satisfy our demands.

We found them. We got them from everywhere. Experienced actors like Harry Fowler, Joan Dowling and Stanley Escane. Young hopefuls like Gerald Fox, David Simpson, James Crabbe and Douglas Barr; and boys from schools and jobs with no experience at all but masses of vitality and enthusiasm like David Knox, Albert Hughes, Geoffrey Sirett and John Hudson. It is difficult in some ways to discuss what was the impact of this gang on the story, because each brought to it his own individuality. Their ages ranged from fourteen to eighteen, and each, therefore, was at a different stage of development. But they did bring as a group a straightforward earnestness which not all the sophistication of Alastair Sim and all the polished honesty of Jack Warner could produce. Their earnestness strengthened our plot in a way we had not considered possible, because they believed in our story as my son believes in his black monkey. It would be difficult for an adult to take seriously the idea of a gang of crooks using a kids' paper as a means of communication. But these boys believed it possible and by their belief made it possible.

What is more, they made light of all our heavy theories of a naturalistic treatment, because their young vitality carried infinitely more weight than all our stuffy adult cinematic technique. An examination of the last sequence of the picture from the moment when the big operation against the crooks started until Joe's final triumph over the arch criminal shows this quite clearly.

The operation divides itself into two parts. First, a very fast-moving sequence, when boys from all over London, summoned to Ballard's Wharf by Joe Kirby, rush pell-mell through the familiar streets to overpower the crooks by sheer weight of numbers; and second, a sinister, slow-moving sequence, where Joe trails Nightingale through a gutted warehouse and at last brings him to justice. Now in the fast-moving section, we might have allowed the boys to chase down the streets in ordered ranks and in step to a synchronous music. We might have used the camera with greater freedom, underlining the preposterous nature of the story by preposterous set-ups. We might have built exaggerated and stylised sets in the studio. But we followed the idiom which we had planned, and tried to get our fun and our fantasy out of the situation itself and not out of its treatment. We set out to be as convincing as we could be, we really did release torrents of boys on to an unsuspecting London, we made them run in straggling mobs. If we needed twenty-eight boys to be disgorged from one taxi, we really did cram twenty-eight boys into one taxi. We used no back projection, no studio tricks. Hundreds of boys rushed from everywhere to attack a bunch of prize-fighters on a riverside wharf – and we photographed them.

What we did to create an atmosphere of realism was negative; what the boys did was positive. The bruises sustained by some of the crooks were certainly positive. These men were prize-fighters, boxers, all-in wrestlers, with hard bulging muscles. The boys leapt on them quite fearlessly. I have often admired my own prowess on the rugger field when, on a squelchy, muddy ground, I have launched myself through the air at some flying three-quarter. But these boys were launching themselves through the air on a terrain of broken brickbats, lumps of concrete and bits of twisted iron and shattered glass. I saw one who, in take after take, flung himself clean over the lip of a bomb crater on to the ragged rubble which lay below. One of the crooks, a pugilist by profession and not very popular with the boys, gave up after two days' shooting and said he could take no more: Anaconda, that brutal wrestler with the gentle heart, whose hard head has so often cracked the boards of the ring in which he has fought, rubbed a score of painful places and called the gang 'cheeky blighters!'

The boys were, of course, living vividly the story which we were trying to tell; our fantasy was real to them, and their realism was creating our fantasy. They stressed the humour of the situation and emphasised, through realism, its absurdity.

When, however, we came to that part of the story in which Joe fights it out with Nightingale in the ruined warehouse, we were faced with another problem. We wanted to maintain the natural undistorted quality of background and action, but we had to find a new element to build up the suspense of the scene and prevent it from appearing anti-climactic after all the physical excitement of the rush through London. We were fortunate in discovering, near Southwark Bridge, a gutted warehouse whose outer walls had collapsed during the blitz, leaving a vast honey-combed shell composed of floors and inner walls. This building had in itself the quality of fantasy. The floors, warped from the heat of fire, were as uneven as the surface of the sea. Huge holes gaped in them, where machinery had fallen through from the uppermost storeys to the ground. The criss-cross iron-work of ferro-concrete showed through them like the bones of a skeleton. The crumbling walls were studded with multi-coloured patches where the plaster had fallen away. The staircases were twisted. The place was dark and sinister, although the outer walls had fallen to reveal a bright panorama of London. Beyond, the river stretched away into the distance, and everyday traffic crossed its many bridges. This setting was ideal for our purpose. The warehouse was used to emphasise the element of fantasy, as also, at the most dramatic points, were our camera angles. In the foreground we could surround Joe with the distorted shapes of the warehouse, and still leave him a normal London background to echo the realistic quality which pervaded the previous sequence, and this echo enriched the sense of fantasy engendered by the action and setting of the warehouse itself.

Harry Fowler, however, playing Joe, had more to do than just walk through the scenes provided for him looking a little frightened. He had to convey that pathetic bravery which a youngster has when faced with something a little too large for his own powers. He had to show more than Joe's physical fear of Nightingale lying in wait for him somewhere in that ghastly honeycomb. He had to convey a sense of the dreadful eeriness of the honeycomb itself. Harry Fowler is a first-rate natural actor, and he never in this sequence put a foot astray. But I think his excellence here was due rather to the impressionable character of his youth than to his acting technique. He was reflecting his surroundings because he had the imagination to feel their weird, unnatural quality.

My argument has been that the gang brought conviction to a fantasy which needed to carry conviction. In fantasy, a polished performance may destroy where a rougher one may create. There is nothing so dangerous to the spirit of fantasy as sophis-tication, the borderline between whimsy and whimsy-whamsy is very narrow. The children in *Hue and Cry* never crossed this border-line, because no one had ever taught them to cross it; the technique of some of them may have been rough, but their untutored imaginations provided something else which could only otherwise have been brought to us by an actor of consum-mate skill.

There is a tendency amongst some artists to use an almost child-like technique in order to set free from well-worn forms and meaningless conventions the force of what they have to paint. And now when John Smith, aged ten, and as yet un-spoiled, chalks on an old bit of brown paper a picture of remark-able imaginative power, we are inclined to say, 'How like a Rousseau!' It might be better to have said of a Rousseau, 'How like a John Smith!'

NEWSREELS MUST FIND
A NEW POLICY

G. CLEMENT CAVE
Editor of 'Pathé News'

*

'THE main aim of the newsreel directorate is, therefore, to be as complaisant as possible, to be inoffensive by rule, and when forced by exceptional circumstances to deal with social and political issues, to play safe.'

That sentence sums up a chapter on the news film which appeared in the Arts Enquiry Survey, *The Factual Film*. It is, in my view, a fair assessment of newsreel policy as it exists in the majority of the five British newsreels. Behind this not very vigorous mentality is the all-important truth that newsreels sell direct to exhibitors, and not, like newspapers, direct to the public. The cinema manager is anxious to please as many of his patrons as possible. In his view the audience pays for entertainment and not for thought-provoking news films on the social and political issues of the day.

This commercial caution is understandable. Should a newsreel select a topic which possesses certain highly controversial aspects from the public point of view, the reception such a subject will receive in a cinema must to a large extent be affected by the personal opinions of the audience. Thus, if the screen treatment is to be positive and not a series of compromises, some susceptibilities will be offended. And in terms of box office, the exhibitor who buys the newsreel will not regard it as good business. If he cannot please all the people all the time, he will at least do his utmost to ensure the minimum of irritation to his customers.

Unfortunately, the range of subjects within this category is considerable. I would say that something like 70 per cent of the news which fills the morning papers either comes into this class or is unsuitable for newsreels because it lacks picture value. And so the newsreel editor is left with the safe type of story that has become an annual event: the Boat Race, the Grand National, the Derby, the Cup Final and many others. All these are laced with Royal events, bathing beauty competitions and much triviality. The only bright spots are fires or death and disaster stories, and the strength of these depends on how quickly cameramen can reach the scene, with the very occasional pageantry, such as the Royal Wedding.

These subjects have a place in any survey of the news, but they do not merit the rating given them by the newsreels. All are a long way from the big issues which are nearest to the community and therefore make news.

My personal view is that both newsreel editors and exhibitors have played safe for too long. I believe there is far too much comfortable assumption on the part of the film industry about what the public does or does not want. I find very little evidence for some of the sweeping generalisations about public taste and entertainment and much that contradicts some of these almost traditional beliefs. From experience I know that one crank in an audience who, for example, complains to a cinema manager that the newsreel showing is just a vehicle for Government propaganda because it happens to carry a story involving an interview with Sir Stafford Cripps can be used, if the manager has a similar political outlook, to imply that a whole audience was practically in revolt.

The war brought a great change in public outlook and taste; the tragedy is that many in the film industry have failed to recognise this fact. In some directions the trend has been seen and anticipated. Many British features which were decried because the theme was quite contrary to the conventional formula for box-office success have been astonishing successes with cinema-goers. Despite this lesson from the feature world, most newsreels still hesitate to take a chance. Certainly the path of any-one who attempts to break away from the accepted style is hard.

A mild example was the Government's White Paper on Britain's economic situation and her requirements, published nearly a year ago. On news value I regarded this as important to the whole nation, and decided to build up a story. Cameramen were sent to factories, coal mines and industrial centres for material. There were brief interviews with national figures such as the miners' Will Lawther, industrialist Sir Miles Thomas, and Economic Chief Sir Stafford Cripps. The final story which occupied the greater part of a reel was designed to show some of the nation's resources and requirements. Emphasis was laid on the need for more production. Such public reaction as was available was favourable, but the trade considered it 'propaganda' and not entertainment.

On another occasion, following a report on the conditions in some institutions for old people, we got inside some of these homes and showed the conditions as they were. The commentary was based on the report and pointed out the public's responsibility in the matter. Throughout I was advised by Lord Amulree, who is associated with the Ministry of Health, and who has given the problem considerable attention.

The topic was in the news, and it was one of public interest. From members of the public I received letters of congratulation; from the trade the opinion that it was far too controversial for the cinema. The list is endless.

My own newsreel is the only one to have attempted to face these issues, and while the trade has argued the merits or otherwise of such stories, adverse criticism from the public has not reached me. Very largely it has meant revising policy and taking the ditches one by one instead of two at a time. As a compromise I have developed the technique which gives the product a March of Time treatment. There is one main title and one story which form the theme and shape of the reel. Into that setting is packed the world news, supported by a commentary which reviews, explains, comments and is all of a piece. It is an editorial must that the commentary is positive. There must be no 'ifs' and 'buts', no sugary, old-world phrases. At least this gives the reel precision and character.

But there is still a long way to go. A great newsreel public was built up during the war, when the reels had great and vivid pictures to show and stories of great daring to tell. Through lack of imagination, much of this goodwill was destroyed. But audience interest will have to be captured again and soon. For on the horizon is a new competitor – television. It may take a long time to develop and to command such an audience as is available to radio. But this possibility may come into being before the film industry has turned television to its own purpose. If newsreels wait until that challenge arrives, they will be too late. The time for new ideas and a complete change of mentality is now.

By all this is meant a reorientation of thought. The assessment of news by the criterion of what exhibitors are supposed to want is venal and bad journalism. Neither do I believe it essential to be overawed by this bogy. The answer is to move forward slowly and to demonstrate that audiences have a wider interpretation of the word entertainment than is generally supposed. At home the nation is in a stage of transition and uncertainty. This stage brings problems and questions. In their hands newsreels hold an immensely powerful medium which can be used objectively to report, to inform and to explain. Any medium that can fulfil those aims may be said to meet the demands and requirements of the moment.

Abroad the peoples are caught up in international politics which must ultimately influence their lives. The news film can show the ordinary man in this country how his counterpart in other lands is meeting the problems of the day. By such interpretation the newsreel would be meeting the obligations it has. In a world where so much is confused and where explanation is so necessary there can be little room in a balanced news film for the nonsense of a Texas rodeo or a Miami beach parade. A new set of values must take over.

A new form of technique in presentation is required. The formal method of title and then story is as old and out of date as some of the news carried. It needs streamlining, and tricks used which give the reel a punch. News is always urgent and often vital. It should be handled that way. The most prosaic story in the world can be given life and meaning if the imagination is there when it is conceived.

There will be room for television and a bright future for the news film only if newsreels become invigorated. By this I mean the adoption of a real and understanding news sense, the imagination to think of something to say and the courage to say it, a relegation of much of the present trash which is at present given importance and a far deeper faith in themselves and in the part they should play in national and international affairs. It will take a long time to convince all exhibitors of the common sense of this new policy, but it is a move that will have to be made if the news film is to hold its place in the cinema.

IN MEMORIAM: URBAN GAD

IN February 1948 Urban Gad died. The part he played in the early history of European film art can be compared with that of D. W. Griffith in America. The film which won him international fame was *Abgründe* (*The Abyss*), with which, in 1910, he created new standards in film-making. Urban Gad was a Dane, and had been a stage producer before turning to the film. The leading actress in *The Abyss* was Asta Nielsen, his wife, herself no less important in the art of film acting than her husband in that of directing. Both left the Copenhagen studios for Berlin, where he continued directing films.

However, besides his practical studio work he wrote a book which made him the leading theoretician of the time. Entitled *The Film: Its Means and Ends*, it was published first in Danish in 1919, then in Berlin in German in 1921.

His last position was director at the Grand Theatre, Copenhagen, which he made the leading theatre in Denmark.   H.H.W.

THE FIRST GENERATION
OF THE CINEMA

JOSEF SOMLO

★

Is it possible that one single nation should control the screen entertainment of the world through its film industry? This is by no means a theoretical question, considering Hollywood's share in the screen time of this and other countries, and its ambitious moves towards international film supremacy. Nor is it a question which should concern merely the film industries of this and other countries. In view of the importance and the influence of the cinema in contemporary life, it is a question which has a general bearing and ought to interest everybody, certainly all those who take the phenomenon of film seriously.

We will try to find an answer derived from the history of the comparatively young medium on the strength of forty years' practical experience. For it was in 1908 when this writer entered the film industry, then in its early stage. At that time the word 'film' was virtually synonymous with French film. Pathé, Gaumont, Méliès were the names and trademarks which absolutely prevailed on the film programmes. The French film industry dominated the then film markets of all countries where screen entertainment was steadily progressing. Compared with this predominant position of the French film companies, the early American film effort, as represented by Edison's Vitascope, Essanay, Biograph, and so on, was irrelevant internationally in the years preceding the first World War.

In 1912, however, the world's attention was focused on the film effort of another nation – Italy; for the Italians were the first to produce feature-length films in the modern sense. Companies such as Ambrosio, Itala and Cines soon overshadowed the French. Above all, it was Cines which set new standards in film-making by its first production of *Quo Vadis?*, the well-known Sienkiewicz novel set in ancient Rome. This production had the effect of something like a miracle upon the public. Nothing perhaps is more revealing than the fact that, whereas so far a sum of £12 to £15 per week had been the normal price paid by exhibitors, *Quo Vadis?* fetched something like £500 per week. I remember this amazing development the better, since my own company handled the Continental distribution of *Quo Vadis?* Italian actresses, such as Francesca Bertini and Menichelli, became stars of world fame in those few years of Italian supremacy in the international cinema.

France's counter-move was the development of her *films d'art* movement. Of greater influence in the international scene, however, were surprising developments which were then taking place in another country – Denmark. It throws light on the question put at the beginning of this article that so small a country with about two million inhabitants should be able to rise to the leading position in film-making. The simply amazing growth of a Danish film industry, which soon took over a leading part in the cinemas of Europe, was due to an extraordinary personality, Ole Olsen, the founder of the Nordisk Film Company. Its trademark, the polar bear, soon replaced the cock of Pathé and the wolf of Cines in importance on the screens. The commercial significance of the Danish film can be illustrated by the fact that Olsen became the richest man of his country, and that his art collection, which he left to the nation, was valued at £5 to £6 million during his lifetime. This extraordinary industrial expansion in a small country can only be explained by the new standards of quality which were set in the Danish film. A new and more cinematic style of film-acting emerged from Danish talent.

Scandinavian stars like Valdemar Psilander and Gunnar Tolnaes became the most famous and most popular names with the film-going masses. Greatest, however, of all was Asta Nielsen, a phenomenon of artistic interpretation on the silent screen. Her film *Abysses (Abgründe)* made film history. It was produced in 1910, and wherever it was shown it made an almost revolutionary impression. Its director was Urban Gad, who became her husband and whose name is of no less importance in the history of film art than that of D. W. Griffith.

The expansion of the Danish film, which started in the last few years before 1914, still grew during the first war years. Actually the first World War had far-reaching effects on the international film situation. It caused the emergence of two film industries on an international scale – the American and the German. Germany, or virtually Central Europe, was cut off from the West by the war fronts and the blockade. Thus the German studios started to supply the demands of the cinemas by their own greatly increased effort. The German film industry worked in close co-operation with the Danish and Swedish film industries for this purpose. The main German companies, Messter, Bioscope, Union and others, became extremely active. The idea of the longer feature film prevailed. Many of the Scandinavian artists, including Asta Nielsen and Urban Gad, were now working in German studios. The Union Company was soon the most important under its managing director Paul Davidson. Neutral Switzerland was then the only European country where there was an opportunity to see films of all the belligerent countries, and it was there where Paul Davidson happened to view the fine Italian period film *Madame Tallien*. By this he was induced to produce a great historical picture *Passion (Madame Dubarry)*, directed by Ernst Lubitsch. It was this film which, right after the end of the war, won international admiration for German screencraft, and marked the newly won position of the German studios as leading in Europe.

The Union Company had then – in 1918 – already been merged with the newly formed UFA, now Germany's most important and powerful film undertaking. The great epoch of German film production began in the wake of the world triumph of *Passion*.

The other country to benefit from the war was the United States. Far distant from the fighting fronts, neutral till 1917, and enjoying a wave of prosperity, a tremendous film industry had grown up there in vast proportions. America became the supplier of film entertainment all over the world outside the orbit of the Central Powers. At the same time the American contribution to the evolution of film technique and screen art was most remarkable. It may be sufficient to mention D. W. Griffith's work, especially *Birth of a Nation* and *Intolerance*, or the rise of Charles Chaplin.

With the war over, the time had come for international film exchange. I was then director of the UFA Export Department, and in this capacity I went to New York to select from the many hundreds of American films made during the war years the most suitable for showing in Central Europe. I then got an idea of the tremendous expansion of the American film industry.

During the first few years after the war it became obvious for the first time that the war-stricken nations of Europe would not be able to keep going their national film efforts unless some protection from the impact of American film imports was devised. Germany made the start. Her protective system roughly provided for one imported film for each German film. This meant virtually that half of her cinema programmes were reserved for home production, the other half left for foreign films. In Britain, the quota regulations in the first Cinematograph Films Act, and corresponding legislation in several other countries followed soon. Almost all countries engaged in film production thought of some measures with a view to keeping their national film effort alive.

At the same time the first attempts at European co-operation in the sphere of cinema were made during the 'twenties. Their purpose was also to assist national production by combined efforts. The first and probably the most interesting venture of this kind was realised between a German and British group. The German partner was Felsom Film (Fellner & Somlo), the English partner was Gaumont-British. In Michael Balcon I found a personality full of vision and understanding in this cooperation. Yet another name should here be mentioned, the late C. M. Woolf, who, as chairman of Gainsborough Pictures, courageously encouraged the venture. The outcome were such fine films as *The Ghost Train, Moon of Israel* (directed by Michael Curtis, then still Kertesz) and *The Modern Dubarry* (directed by Alexander Korda).

America, although undoubtedly by far the most powerful factor in the international film scene, was not left unimpressed by the achievements of European studios after the war, beginning with *Passion*. Its reaction was a policy of luring away the best European talent, wherever it grew up to international recognition, by offering salaries ten times bigger than European producers could afford. It started with the director, the writer and the principal actors – Pola Negri and Emil Jannings – of *Passion*. Many more were to follow from all European countries, British and French, Austrian, German and Swedish, scenarists, directors, musicians, anybody who seemed of particular promise. This trend has gone on right up to the present. Its underlying idea is undoubtedly film hegemony by means of an overwhelming concentration of talent in Hollywood.

When in 1928-9 sound film replaced the silent picture, it seemed as though the problem emanating from language differences would be to the advantage of national film productions and would jeopardise Hollywood's international conception. In Paris and London, in Berlin and Vienna the greatest efforts were made to break American film domination. One of the most remarkable instances in this direction was the production in London of one of the most ambitious sound films of the early period. It was the film *Atlantis*, made by British International in three versions, and employing an equally fine English, French and German cast. However, in spite of a number of remarkably fine pictures turned out in French, British and German, Austrian, Czech and other European studios during the 'thirties, the American grip on the world market remained tight. The concentration of financial power and talent in Hollywood, the combination of the star-system with an overwhelming publicity machine, proved decisive.

A new situation arose with the outbreak of war in 1939. The second World War, like the first, was to bring about new developments in the international scene. This time it was the British films which came to the fore. In spite of almost unimaginable difficulties caused by protracted total warfare, air-raids and other enemy action, shortage, not only of man-power, but of every kind of facilities and materials, British film production came into its stride and found its own style. Without any bias it can be said that, during and after the war, the average standard of British films has outdone the average Hollywood product. The international response to British films, wherever they have been or are being shown, is most encouraging, and this even applies to the public and Press of the United States.

This rather brief survey of forty years of film history is sufficient to supply an answer to our question. It shows that the idea of one single nation monopolising the world film market is just not feasible; not even by means of the concentration of talent as attempted by Hollywood.

There will be no solution of the crisis which at present makes itself felt in the international situation of film production as long as the American film industry stands for total control of the world's film markets. This, not only for commercial reasons. It is only natural that in every country its national production will be preferred by the public. A fair exchange of the best that is achieved in various national productions is the true solution which should be accepted by everybody. The sooner Hollywood realises this truth, the better for both Hollywood and for everybody else.

ERNST LUBITSCH

H. H. WOLLENBERG

*

IF we review Lubitsch's work during, say, the last ten years of his life, which so abruptly, though not altogether surprisingly, ended through heart failure towards the end of 1947, we would hardly recognise the decisive part he played in the emergence of the new art. During that period his productions included *Bluebeard's Eighth Wife* (1938), *Ninotchka* and *The Shop Around the Corner* (1939), *That Uncertain Feeling* (1941), *To Be or Not To Be* (1942), the delightful *Heaven Can Wait* (1943) and *Cluny Brown* (1946).

If our assessment of Lubitsch's contribution to the cinema could be based on these films only, we would still number him among the finest and most accomplished directors, the master of subtle and highly cultured comedy. Certainly, not all the films mentioned above are of equal value, but it should be recognised that no film of Lubitsch's would ever sink below a certain standard of quality, even the less accomplished ones. It is, in fact, remarkable how Lubitsch, who went from Berlin to Hollywood as early as 1923, should throughout all those years never have lost that certain touch which can only be described as European. You will find this undefinable flavour in each of his films. The *Lubitsch style*, which radiates from all his films whether more or less important, would, as I said, probably suffice to secure him a place among the prominent directors.

However, Ernst Lubitsch's position in the history of the cinema is considerably more important. At an earlier phase he was one of the decisive influences through which the cinema was transformed into an art.

Ernst Lubitsch was born in Berlin on January 28, 1892. He was of Jewish stock and his parents were dress manufacturers. It was in his father's business that he started work after leaving school. But right from the outset he felt that producing and selling ladies' wear was not his true calling. In his spare time the young man started to study acting. His teacher was one of the best-known comedians of the day, Victor Arnold; for, right from the outset, Lubitsch's artistic leaning was towards comedy. It is remarkable how, from the beginning to the end, humour, the comic, was the distinct feature of his creative work.

Before the first World War Berlin had risen to high prominence in dramatic art in the world. For it was in Berlin that Max Reinhardt, the magician as they called him, had revolutionised the theatre. His productions of classical plays, especially of Shakespeare dramas and comedies, marked a new epoch in theatre history. Under the tremendous impression of Reinhardt's art, Ernst Lubitsch, the young salesman, turned to the stage as his career. Nineteen-year-old Lubitsch was brought to Max Reinhardt by his teacher for an audition. His wish came true and for the next two years he was cast in minor comedy parts.

During that period occurred what was to determine his future, namely, his first contact with the film. In 1913 he played his first small film part. In this rather modest form started a career, the next and most significant landmark of which was Lubitsch's first major work as a director, *Carmen* (1918).

At this stage it seems necessary to recall general film developments during those decisive years between 1913 and 1918, a period which roughly coincides with the first World War. It was the time when the German cinemas found themselves cut off from film supplies from the West, the time when home production began to flourish, the time when the UFA company was formed. And if, soon after the end of the war, the UFA trademark was to rise to international reputation, this was largely due to its top director, Ernst Lubitsch.

Before he had reached that prominent position, he had played a number of rôles of increasing importance in the primitive farces of the time. The farce which made his name known as a most popular screen comedian had the characteristic title *Pinkus' Shoe Palace* (*Schuhpalast Pinkus*). Encouraged by his success he formed, together with a colleague, a small production company to make comedies of his own. Alas, the first film they produced was a complete failure. When one day he was approached to see whether he would make a dramatic film for the newly formed UFA, he simply could not help laughing. He could not think of himself except as a maker of comedies. Pola Negri, the rising UFA star, was said to have persuaded him. Her first films in Germany (she had come from the Warsaw studios) had not satisfied her as regards direction. So she was looking for Lubitsch as her director. His first film for UFA in 1918, co-starring the Polish actress with Emil Jannings and Harry Liedtke, was *The Eyes of the Mummy*, written by Hans Kraly. Its success established Lubitsch as a director of dramatic subjects. A greater task followed: *Carmen*. Lubitsch had the chalkpits of Rudersdorf, near Berlin, transformed into Spanish *sierras*; a Spanish market square was erected in the studio grounds at Tempelhof and populated by a crowd of several hundreds. After *Carmen*, Lubitsch was marked as the director of the most ambitious and costly UFA films, the specialist in period super productions. His next film was *Passion* (*Madame Dubarry*).

Big historical subjects employing large crowds had first come from the Italian studios; e.g. *Quo Vadis?* and *Cabiria*. Technical achievements that they then were, they made a strong impression in the beginning by their novel dimensions, the sheer weight of quantity. However, the characters, with their overdone gesticulations, were anything but human beings. And now came Lubitsch. And, like D. W. Griffith (*The Birth of a Nation* and *Intolerance*) on the other side of the Atlantic, Lubitsch created a new technique, a new style. Film to him meant, not a substitute for theatre, nor a mere spectacle – entertainment manufactured and supplied by the yard on celluloid. He sensed the potentialities of the cinema as a dynamic and autonomous art whose æsthetic laws had to be discovered, whose specific style had to be developed. An exciting adventure.

A comparison with those previous period films shows beyond doubt that *Madame Dubarry* has made film history. Lubitsch's influential and creative part in the rise of the cinema is clearly defined here. When *Passion* appeared on the screen we saw, for the first time, against an historical background, characters of the period act and behave like true-to-life persons. Human relations were created between the screen and the audience. There was the rhythmical conception of vast crowd scenes; the perfect illusion of the period; the superb pictorial composition, camera work and lighting. Above all, there was the human touch, the perfection of acting under his guidance.

The effect of *Passion* was something like a revelation. And a world success. It found its way to almost all countries, and it was admired even in America. More and ambitious period productions in the vein of *Passion* followed: *Deception*; *Anne Boleyn* (with Henry Porten in the title part and Jannings as Henry VIII); *Sumurun* (1920); *The Loves of Pharaoh* (1922). However, accomplished as they were, *Passion* stood out as the landmark: the story of a king and his mistress, which ended in revolution, had its first night at the very moment the Prussian monarchy collapsed and Germany was in the throes of a revolution.

However, that native feeling for comedy was still alive in Ernst Lubitsch. And it was also Ernst Lubitsch who, in those productive years, developed screen comedy as an art form, as against the film burlesque or farce. No doubt, slapstick comedy had and has its rightful place on the screen; Chaplin made it a great art. Lubitsch looked for an alternative. He was not satisfied with clowning, grimaces, physical situations which were the means of striking fun in the earlier silent era. He attempted screen comedy equal to stage comedy: comedies based on a logical story, carried by psychologically conceived characters. His natural sense of humour combined with his film sense in his production of *The Oyster Princess* in 1919. All three ele-

FILMS FOR CHILDREN

31 and 32. 'Bush Christmas.' Directed by Ralph Smart in Australia. (Photographs 31 to 36, G. B. Instructional Children's Film Department.)

33 and 34. 'The Boy Who Stopped Niagara.' A fantasy, directed by Leslie Macfarlane.

35. 'The Little Ballerina.' Directed by Lewis Gilbert; with Margot Fonteyn.

36. 'Under the Frozen Falls.' Directed by Darrel Catling.

CHILDREN AT THE CINEMA

37 and 38. 'Children Learning by Experience.' A Realist Film Unit Production for C.O.I. These scenes show children's reactions to a 'Thriller' in a cinema, and were taken during an actual performance.

THE RED SHOES

39 to 44. 'The Red Shoes.' (Archers Films.) Written, produced and directed by Michael Powell and Emeric Pressburger; with Anton Walbrook, Moira Shearer, Leonide Massine, Ludmilla Tcherina and Robert Helpmann.

BONNIE PRINCE CHARLIE

45 and 46. 'Bonnie Prince Charlie.' (Edward Black, for British Lion.)
Directed by Anthony Kimmins; with David Niven and Margaret Leighton.

SARABAND FOR DEAD LOVERS

47 and 48. 'Saraband for Dead Lovers.' (Ealing.) Directed by Basil Dearden; with Stewart Granger, Frederick Valk and Flora Robson.

OLIVER TWIST

49 to 59. Further stills from 'Oliver Twist.' (Cineguild.) Directed by David Lean; with Alec Guinness as Fagin (49), Robert Newton as Bill Sikes (52),

John Howard Davies as Oliver Twist (54) and Kay Walsh as Nancy (57).

ments – story, superb acting and grand décor – blended together by Lubitsch's direction, combined in another international success.

In the same year he tried his hand at an experimental comedy, *The Doll* (*Die Puppe*). Fairy-tale, operetta and farce were mixed in an attempt to create a novel type of comedy. In 1921 Lubitsch and his scenarist, Kraly, went even a daring step farther into unexplored territory. They tried to apply expressionism in film comedy as it had been used before in film drama (*Caligari*). The result was *The Wildcat* (*Die Bergkatze*), the action of which was set in a surrealistic castle within the (real) Alps. No doubt it was an interesting, if not completely successful, venture. However, it was *Kohlhiesel's Daughters* (*Kohlhiesels Töchter*) which showed Lubitsch's mastership in the craft of screen comedy: interpretation by cinematic means of human characters watched through the spectacles of the humorist.

Meanwhile, America had begun to watch this outstanding director. He had already left the UFA studios to direct for the European Film Alliance in Berlin, a new company financed by American capital. Then, in 1923, Hollywood called. His last work made in Berlin was *The Flame* (*Die Flamme*). Hollywood offered the directorship of a film with the greatest star of the time, Mary Pickford. The result was *Rosita*. From then onwards until his death he remained faithful to the American film industry which could place at his disposal tremendous resources such as the Old World could not muster. However, he went on making neither 'German' films nor 'American' films, but Lubitsch films. He remained faithful to himself, as his Hollywood films of the silent period show: delightful comedies such as *The Marriage Circle*, *Forbidden Paradise*, *Lady Windermere's Fan*, or as a dramatic film, *The Patriot*, with his star of former days, Emil Jannings.

And then came sound. I recall a talk I had with Lubitsch shortly before he left for Hollywood. We happened to meet at a first night, and the conversation turned to the possibility of new technical developments and their potential influence on screen art. The sound film, owing to the first Tri-Ergon experiments, was then much discussed. Lubitsch expressed his doubt in the prospects of the talking screen; he thought it would not lead to artistic advance. And the use of colour, he pointed out, could possibly lead to the most disastrous aesthetic results. What interested him, he said, were the potentialities of the stereoscopic film, if this could be technically achieved. Here, he added, seemed to lie really great possibilities for the artist.

This remark, revealing Lubitsch's artistic convictions, occurred roughly six years before the talkie became reality. In view of his scepticism of sound as an advance, it seems almost paradoxical that as early as in 1929 he was to be the first to make a really accomplished musical film, *Love Parade*, which created a new type. Its origin sprang from the operetta, which was adapted to the requirements of the screen, integrating music, song, melody and dialogue with the pictorial style of the moving camera. With Jeanette MacDonald and Maurice Chevalier as his stars, Lubitsch delighted film audiences all over the world and, once more, initiated a distinct film type.

Some of his best films that followed were *If I Had a Million*, *One Hour with You*, *Trouble in Paradise*, and, in 1933, *Design for Living*, probably his finest effort. Productions to follow included his *Merry Widow* (1934), *Desire* (1936), *Angel* (1937) and the subjects of his last decade mentioned earlier.

An analysis of his work as a whole shows that, above all, acting was his first and foremost concern. In most carefully directing his cast, from the leading star down to the smallest part, he saw the overriding job of the director. It is characteristic that, for instance, Marlene Dietrich has never been as accomplished as under Lubitsch's guidance in *Desire*, and that, directed by him, Greta Garbo played her first comedy rôle, in *Ninotchka*, to perfection. Nobody had ever expected her to play comedy. Lubitsch knew how to get the actor or actress precisely where he wanted him or her to the finest shade in visual and aural expression. Jovial as Lubitsch was in his private life, he was certainly most exacting on the studio floor.

Next to acting, he laid emphasis upon the pictorial composition of each scene, each shot. He had the eye of a painter, and his films were pictorially beautiful throughout. In this connection I remember an experience I had with him in the second half of the twenties on his first holiday visit from Hollywood to his home town, Berlin. He had heard and read about a Russian film named *Battleship Potemkin* which, by its direction, had made a tremendous impression in Germany. As he had no chance to see it in America, he asked me to arrange a screening for him. He said to me what probably is the most concise diagnosis of Eisenstein's novel style: 'But this film is not pictorial at all: it is made like a newsreel.' The greatest compliment Eisenstein could hope for. At the same time it revealed his pictorial conception as opposed to Eisenstein's realism.

Within the frame of this appreciation it is impossible to discuss Lubitsch's personal and more private qualities. Sufficient to say that he was a loyal and real friend to his friends, and that his loyalty was sometimes badly rewarded. However, his greatest loyalty was to the cinema. The cinema, in fact, meant everything to him. Or, as one of his friends once put it: 'Lubitsch is not made of flesh and blood; Lubitsch is of celluloid.' There was no other subject to talk about, no other matter to think of but the film. Creative artists of this psychological make-up frequently burn their energies too rapidly to grow old. Lubitsch had been suffering from heart trouble for some years. Nothing could prevent him from chain-smoking his cigars, which had become a natural part of his face. His contribution to the history of screen art will survive him.

AMERICAN CLASSIC

A STUDY OF THE
MARX BROTHERS

RICHARD ROWLAND

★

EACH year, the film classics are becoming more of a staple in the diet of the metropolitan film-goer. Few months pass, in New York City at least, when one is not able to see *Carnet de Bal, The Informer, The Lady Vanishes,* or *Chapayev.* But as one views again many of these films, the excellences of which seem to have lost so little through the passage of time, one is struck ever more forcibly by the fact that very few of them are American. *The Cabinet of Dr Caligari,* filmed in Germany in 1919, is crude and violent and shocking – and these are the qualities at which it aimed in 1919. The wit of *Kermesse Héroïque* is as sharp and wry and full of poetry as it ever was. The pre-Hollywood Hitchcock films bristle with excitement to-day as they did a decade ago, even though one knows now the outcome of each taut episode. But what can we say for American films? The sweep and splendour of D. W. Griffith's films has not been surpassed; Charlie Chaplin's exquisite pantomime still wrings our hearts with the laughter which is so close to tears; one suspects that the superb legend of Garbo would still be valid, although we cannot be sure, since her films are never revived.

But what else? These are mostly silent films, made before 1927, when the Warner Brothers and Al Jolson revolutionised the industry. Are there no talking films to equal these? The fog in *The Informer* no longer looks quite real; indeed, most of the John Ford films, excellent though they were, seem now didactic and literary in a sense that the great French films never were. The early performances of Bette Davis, a revelation in the 1930s, are now seen to be mannered – studied and clever, but rarely felt. The brilliant camera work which Orson Welles gave us in *Citizen Kane*, we realise sadly, was largely trickery and mechanical cleverness used to conceal the essential emptiness of the film.

Has nothing else survived, then? Yes; there is one series of films to which a little circle of devotees throughout the world return again and again to find a pleasure not antiquarian, not in the least diminished by the technical progress of recent years. This is, of course, the series of some twelve films which feature the Marx Brothers, made under various banners over a period of fifteen years. Almost nothing has been lost from them; when Groucho makes his sway-backed entrance into the regal palace in *Duck Soup*, the audience stirs with excitement, with the knowledge that an important personage has suddenly appeared on a screen usually inhabited by pallid phantoms.

Bits of the films, inevitably, are dated. When Groucho interrupts a passionate love scene to say, 'Pardon me while I have a strange interlude,' and, turning to the audience, unburdens his soul, I suspect that younger generations, who have almost forgotten that Mr O'Neill startled us with an aside in 1928, are not as much amused as their elders. And bobbie-soxers, who have not even literary recollections of the days of prohibition, probably can't appreciate the superb nonsense of the speakeasy in *Horse Feathers*, with its password and Garibaldi the iceman in the back room filling bottles variously labelled RYE and SCOTCH from the same sinister-looking jug. And always in the early films, when romance, in the insipid form of Zeppo, takes over, we realise that these films were not made yesterday, but a good many days before yesterday.

Even here there is more fun than in many old films, for unintentional farce nowhere reaches greater heights than in the various costumes which the late Thelma Todd sported in certain of the Marx Brothers opera. But this is not planned, while most of the fun of a Marx Brothers film is carefully planned and usually successful. To-day, *Duck Soup*, made in 1933, remains as fresh as a buttercup, far fresher than to-day's newspaper with its uncanny echoes of familiar bumblings and catastrophes, far fresher than the tears of a *Love Letters* or the pratt falls of an Abbott and Costello film.

Why? What is there in these films which survives the rapid 'progress' of our galloping atomic age? Is it due to the fact that the Marx Brothers had a competent script writer, whereas modern comedies are apparently written by twelve to fifteen semi-literates working in a vacuum? It is true that the hand of S. J. Perelman is very evident in the early films, and true, too, that Mr Perelman has a remarkable talent for torturing the English language into a sort of insane poetry, formed by weird juxtapositions of formal diction and advertising copy, of slang and preciosity, so that he becomes a slapstick James Joyce. But the Marx Brothers continued to be funny after Mr Perelman left the firm.

Or is it simply that the three brothers have comic genius? Certainly Groucho's eyebrow is raised to the precise degree where it becomes comic; certainly the sag of his pants and the eccentric contours of his body are wonderful caricature, though we are not quite sure of what. Harpo's destructive nature is clearly a brilliant release for all of us from the restraints of society; there is complete purgation in the moment in *A Night at the Opera*, when Harpo, costumed unexpectedly as a gypsy woman, saunters nonchalantly from the chorus of the opera and strikes a match across the taut belly of the female half of a superlatively dull team of adagio dancers. Certainly Chico's Italian dialect is phony to just the right degree; if it were good Italian dialect, it would be only dialect. As it is, it is uproarious comedy. And his bouts with the piano have a precision and spontaneity which make them the most amiable thing in the comedies.

But the finest comedian in the world cannot be funny without something to be funny about. Even such wit and perfection of technique as Miss Beatrice Lillie's has succeeded in boring its audience when it has been forced to work without material.

It is not hard to find an explanation of the endless appeal of these films. They deal with the gravest question with which comedy can deal. They ask us, at least the successful ones do, intermittently but irresistibly, 'What is reality?'

Theirs is an unreal world; anyone can see that. Harpo's wig is clearly a wig and, indeed, often seems in danger of falling off. Groucho's moustache is either painted or fastened to his cigar, we are never quite sure which. Chico's accent is as detachable as the wig or the moustache, and is sometimes similarly askew. When they stow away on a ship in barrels labelled KIPPERED HERRING, they have all the comforts of home with them – alarum clocks, percolators, playing cards. Harpo's pockets contain everything but the kitchen sink; if you want a cup of coffee, he has it in his pocket, steaming hot. For somehow, in their world, disorder succeeds, and the way of order becomes the way of failure. When Margaret Dumont or one of the other stooges attempts to behave logically, as if there were rules of cause and effect, she is automatically doomed. This is more than a joke: it is a moral lesson. No world, dream or real, will allow itself to be fitted into a system – though the nature of man demands that he go on trying to make it fit.

What could be more unreal than the scene in *A Night at the Opera*, in which dozens of people are crowded into a minute stateroom which obviously can hold six people at the most? And yet, is it unreal? We see it; as we tell ourselves that it is impossible, we realise that we have witnessed it. And we find ourselves doubting, not the film, but the sillier world which tells us that only a certain number of people can get into a stateroom, that one must be sedate and attentive at opera, that it matters whether Darwin or Huxley College wins the football game.

Occasionally, these films come to grips with the subject of reality directly. In *A Night at the Opera* there is a famous scene in which the Brothers are scrambling about in the flies of a theatre while a pompous tenor sings below. As they swing, Tarzan-like, from rope to rope, the scenes constantly shift behind the harassed tenor; one moment he is in a castle, the next on a dead-end street, the next on a wharf. And we, in the audience, have a weird consciousness that in an utterly unsolemn way, quite unlike the magic of Prospero which brought us the same thought, this great globe itself will dissolve – dissolve probably into pure laughter; a happier fate, this comic fission, than the fate with which the scientists threaten us.

Or again, in *Duck Soup*, there is a frenzied episode which finds the three brothers all dressed as Groucho. Two of them approach a door simultaneously, and we are lost in a dream; is it a door or a mirror? Are there two of me? Is that other figure real? Who, indeed, am I? Am I real myself? Never, perhaps, has the shifting instability of the dream world been more vividly presented on the screen.

Again, Harpo, in *Monkey Business*, tangles with a Punch and Judy show, and to the children watching the show he is not less real, nor more real, than the puppets. And it is like the child in *The Emperor's New Clothes*, the voice of sanity; for the children are right. Are we any more real than the puppets?

But usually the approach is less direct. We look at the world of anarchy and return with a curious distrust to our own sober, leaden-footed world. 'I know where the picture is,' runs the dialogue in *Animal Crackers*. 'It's in the house next door!' 'But there isn't any house next door.' 'Then we'll build a house next door.' And they whip out blueprints and start to work. And the picture, we know, will be in the house when they have built it.

Or Harpo stalks a Western gunman with a revolver which proves to be a feather duster which proves to be a revolver, and the joke is on the audience, which laughed too soon, thinking it knew reality, when the reality which it saw was no less a shadow than the opposite reality which the gunman saw.

Nothing is sacred; nothing is real. Society, as represented by

Margaret Dumont, she of the magnificent bosom which has clearly launched more ships than Helen of Troy ever contemplated, teeters and collapses into absurdity. The opera turns into 'Take Me Down to the Ball Game.' The Symphony floats out to sea, fiddling furiously and solemnly away at Wagner, drifting on into insignificance.

Politics? Football? Universities? All of them evaporate before the onslaught of the Brothers. Even sex, the sacred subject about which Hollywood must be serious, becomes a joke in these films. Groucho leers, the siren wears the most outrageously revealing clothes, there is the bed obviously built for sin, there is the predatory lope, the last word in carnality. Will Hays may have flinched now and again, but even he did not remove the ogles and the double entendres; and for once he was right, for sex, too, collapses into nothingness. No one was ever more lecherous in a movie than Groucho is; no movie, save Rin-Tin-Tin's, was ever less erotic than these.

Words, too, to which we pin our faith so easily, have collapsed. These films are, in a sense, elementary lessons in semantics. Words fail to function, somehow; nothing means what it says. 'Cut!' says the card player, and Harpo whips out an axe and cuts the cards. 'I'd horsewhip you,' Groucho threatens, and then adds, 'if I had a horse.' 'Come, come!' someone tells Harpo, 'you can't burn the candle at both ends'; but Harpo reaches into his pocket and triumphantly produces a candle which is merrily burning at both ends, and we feel the failure of words which seemed real but which have suddenly proved worse than useless, since they always mean the wrong thing.

The latest production of the Brothers has only recently been released. Critical reaction to *A Night in Casablanca* has not been enthusiastic; most of it has taken the form of, 'Yes, it's funny, but not as good as the Marx Brothers used to be'. This all sounds familiar. Probably the Marx Brothers never have been as good as they used to be. Time haloes many things; we recollect in delighted tranquillity the first shattering impact of the

Marx Brothers destructive comedy; we forget the admittedly less successful bits which link each film together.

'There is too much plot in *A Night in Casablanca*,' the critics have said. For a few moments, at the start of the film, this appears to be so. We see nothing but conspirators and corpses and sinister background. Then suddenly Harpo appears, leaning nonchalantly against a building. A gendarme approaches, clearly a New York cop strayed inexplicably into Casablanca. 'Well, what are you doing?' he growls. 'Holding up the building?' Harpo nods with a knowing leer. The cop snarls and drags him off, angrily, whereupon the building collapses into rubble, and we know that all is well in the Marxist world. There can scarcely be too much plot for the Marx Brothers; script writers may build skyscrapers of plots; the Brothers will destroy them as easily as Harpo atomises this building in Casablanca.

Their one complete failure, *Room Service*, was not caused by too much plot: it was caused by the formalities of conventional farce. *Room Service* was based on the curious literalness of the Broadway farce, where reactions are as pat and stereotyped as those of the characters in a Kathleen Norris novel. Even Groucho could not triumph over a book which depended entirely upon one set crowded with conventional fast-talking farce figures who had none of the operatic qualities which make La Dumont or Sig Rumann such admirable foils for the Brothers. No ordinary farce hotel room can hold the Marx Brothers; infinity can scarcely hold them. The well-made play – and *Room Service* was such – with its many doors, all carefully planned to supply comic entrances and exits, is too restrictive. The Brothers need Casablanca, where various worlds meet, or the backstage of a theatre, which is whole worlds in itself, or the limitless background of a battlefield or the whole Atlantic Ocean, for their comedy, opening as it does on vasty vistas of eternity.

But the plot of *A Night in Casablanca* is quickly demolished, and they are back to their old tricks, performing them perhaps not as brilliantly as they have at times, but still with a dash and imagination which make other comedians seem thin and pale. No film offers a better example of the perfection of their technique even within a fairly routine farce situation. The scene in which some six or seven people pack and unpack a trunk in an hotel room, acting out with complete conviction an elaborate pretence that they do not know the other people are in the room, is carried off with the timing of a ballet. Never has lechery been so ludicrous as in the scene between Groucho and the beautiful spy; all the paraphernalia of a seduction are there – Strauss waltzes, champagne, roses – everything indeed but the seduction, and frustration becomes the purest laughter.

In a world which becomes daily less stable, such as our world seems to be, where order is more desperately needed and more elusive than ever, perhaps the anarchy of their comedy – 'Look! No hands!' Chico exclaims joyfully as their air-liner tears down the runway with only an inexperienced Harpo in the pilot's seat – is hard for us to bear. But that is our fault and not theirs. We are driving with no hands; perhaps that is no longer a joke. Perhaps that is why they are less funny to us to-day.

What the Brothers have done in these films is not perhaps new, but it is rare indeed in comedy. Most comedians take words and ideas and the world with complete gravity. Most comedy relies upon the wisecrack; and what is the wisecrack but a wise remark about a serious subject, an admission that what one is talking about is reality?

Even those comedians who do not rely upon the wisecrack return to the pedestrian reality of the everyday world. Charlie Chaplin builds a dream world of purity and beauty, in which the girl comes to his cabin and the rolls dance for her with a heavenly grace, but in the end his little vagabond is crushed by the world of prose and he shuffles off into drab familiarity. Charlie Chaplin's films are escape literature which does not escape. The romantic fiction of women's magazines and women's radio serials is escape literature which pretends that Life Can Be Beautiful and denies all ugliness, so that those who follow such things live in a world of unreality, becoming more schizophrenic daily as they try to integrate a dream world with a real world which is cut to a very different pattern.

But the Marx Brothers offer a pure escape; they do not falsify the world as does the world in which Portia Faces Life; but they show us another world, a moon world, a world which illuminates our own, revealing our familiar surroundings as so much nonsense. We realise that we all behave with a solemnity too vulnerable to the attack of the Marx Brothers, who exclaim with the naïveté of wisdom, 'But the emperor has nothing on at all!' And we may remain a little less willing to be crushed by solemnity, aware of our own vulnerability, aware that nonsense has a poetry which sense has not, aware in the most profound way that perhaps – who knows? – this world is, if not worthless, worth less than we had thought, being perhaps less real than we had thought.

Duck Soup, *Para.*, 1933. *Director, Leo McCarey. Story, music and lyrics, Harry Ruby and Bert Kalmar. Additional dialogue, Arthur Sheekman and Nat Perrin.* Horse Feathers, *Para.*, 1932. *Director, Norman McLeod. Screen-play, Bert Kalmar, Harry Ruby and S. J. Perelman.* A Night at the Opera, *MGM,* 1935. *Director, Sam Wood. Story, James K. McGuiness. Adaptation, George Kaufman and Morrie Ryskind.* Monkey Business, *Para.*, 1931. *Director, Norman McLeod. Story, S. J. Perelman and W. B. Johnstone. Additional dialogue, Arthur Sheekman.* Animal Crackers, *Para.*, 1930. *Director, Victor Heerman. Story, Bert Kalmar, Harry Ruby, George Kaufman, Morrie Ryskind. Screen-play, Morrie Ryskind and Pierre Collings.* A Night in Casablanca, *UA,* 1946. *Director, Archie Mayo. Screen-play, Joseph Fields and Roland Kibbee.* Room Service, *RKO,* 1938. *Director, William Seiter. Based on the play by John Murray and Allan Boretz. Screen-play, Morrie Ryskind.*

(Reprinted by courtesy of *Hollywood Quarterly*.)

MONSIEUR VERDOUX

ROGER MANVELL

*

Many one-sided comments on the rare human quality of genius have been made. For instance, genius cannot be defined merely as an infinite capacity for taking pains. This pedestrian view is untrue, for instance, of Shakespeare's kind of work. His plays bear many signs of having been written at a headlong speed. Gray's 'Elegy' complies more closely with this definition, but his poem is scarcely a work of genius as distinct from meticulous talent. Charles Chaplin's work is among the best yet produced in the short, unequal annals of the film. His later films have been made over increasingly long periods of time, and in this sense show that the taking of pains is one of Chaplin's characteristics as an artist.

In the complex art and technique of the film, Chaplin is actor, writer, chief director and musical composer of his work, which means that his films of necessity must take a long while to germinate and produce. But Chaplin's films do not bear the signs of years of deliberation, as, for example, do the films of Eisenstein, each shot and each sequence of which form a complex of deliberately calculated effects. If Chaplin is to be granted the title of genius, then it is more on account of his universal humanity, the least sophisticated aspect of his nature.

Genius, in the end, is an unusually deep-rooted concern for being human, combined with an overwhelming need to express that concern. Chaplin's wistful clown, using his superb pantomimic skill to indicate in passing a thousand sly comments on human weakness, is a sentimental symbolism of a simple, kindly man living in an involved and wicked world. I do not think Chaplin's philosophy is complicated. It is rather so deeply felt

77

that it is becoming almost messianic. He hates profoundly all cruelty, vice, misery and the destructive orgies of warfare. After the pathos of his clown in the circumstances of human greed (*The Gold Rush*), of loneliness amid gaiety (*The Circus*) and of poverty (*City Lights*), to none of which he is adapted, Chaplin, in the later stage of his work, turned his attention to what he conceived to be the greatest evils of our times – soulless industrialisation (*Modern Times*), fascism (*The Great Dictator*) and now callousness towards human life and security (*Monsieur Verdoux*).

Chaplin's ideal is always symbolically simple, the little flowered cottage which is man's universal dream of home, the pretty loving wife, the kindness of domesticity. These things alone can foster in humanity its finest qualities. Deny mankind these things, and the acid enters his soul. He becomes cruel, squalid, defeatist, violent. He becomes Monsieur Verdoux, because society has brought him to so low a pass in order that he may be able to survive at all. No film made by Chaplin in his last twenty years has been without this serious sentiment, to which his clowning is the bitter comment of the professional jester, Lear's shadow. These films are laments for the human soul lost in the devil's politics of our time.

Monsieur Verdoux is the most bitterly satiric of Chaplin's films. Dean Swift, in the bitterness of his view of human kind, turned to the simplicity of the kingdom of the horses for a purge to sweeten his imagination. Swift took his satire to the very boundaries of ugliness: his art overbalanced into the pit of hatred. Chaplin, in *Monsieur Verdoux*, shows a keener edge to his satire than in any previous film. There is almost no pathos except in the revealing relationship between Verdoux and the lost girl whom he cannot bring himself to kill because she is at once too like himself and too unlike the human beings with whom he is at war. It is this satire, this comedy of murders as Chaplin calls it, which makes the action of the film as symbolic of Chaplin's state of mind as *Gulliver's Travels* was of Swift's. If you take the action of the film at its face value, it is merely puzzling, a perverse story which seems to suggest that murder is funny, provided the women destroyed are eccentric types. The film has been unpopular with reviewers (I will not say with critics), and it has undoubtedly confused the public, who are used to Chaplin only as a rather old-fashioned and sentimental funny-man who used, if they are old enough, to make them laugh in their youth by the dexterity of his clowning. Why, they say, does he now ask us to laugh at murder? Why, they ask, does he come out of character, as it were, and pose awkward questions at the audience (in the closing speech of *The Great Dictator*), or make what appear to be deeply felt remarks about the world before his execution at the end of *Monsieur Verdoux*? This is wrong, they assume, in a comedian.

The answer to these questions is not so much that Chaplin himself has changed, as that the desperateness of these times has fortified him to make his art an outspoken challenge to the aggressiveness of humanity. It is no secret that Chaplin himself, British-born, is an isolated figure in America, unpopular as a person, persecuted within certain limits. His refusal to participate in any war-work accentuated the opposition to him. It is the old story, the artist is acknowledged but his point of view disliked. Provided he will just entertain, well and good; but his social criticism is unwelcome, and invites such reprisals and ostracism as can conveniently be brought to bear.

Monsieur Verdoux reflects this. Verdoux is at war with society. He is an ordinary man, simple in his tastes, married to a crippled wife to whom he is devoted and living in an idealised little country cottage. His mysterious 'business' in the city does not rouse his wife's curiosity: he is a most respectable citizen, reproving his son for cruelty in some trifling offence. This is his true life, the life open to him only so long as his security as a bank-clerk remained. But the misfortunes of an ill-organised and acquisitive society rob him of that security, throw him permanently out of work and force him to live on the black market of his wits. He marries a series of women, all of whom are distasteful to him, and pass their time living parasitic lives of the kind which brought him face to face with his own insecurity as a wage-earner. He murders them in turn and takes the spoils, returning always to support his little family in the country.

In his criminal conduct he is always disciplined, meticulous and practical. He is at war, as much a craftsman as a general, killing with as little compunction and taking the resulting booty to support life as he thinks it should be ordered. Here the satire of the central theme is lightened into comedy, and the gay tricks of Chaplin's clowning, always more perfect in the rhythm of their timing than anything of the kind yet known upon the screen, can take over, matching the absurdities of the women with whom his business associates him. But then the incinerator smokes at the bottom of the garden, or the moon shines while Chaplin stands poised with delicate hands outstretched to kill. His pantomime is always on the verge of becoming ballet.

Verdoux is therefore the natural man dehumanised by the unnatural cruelties which are slowly strangling the civilised world. He bears the comic exaggeration of the satiric form, like Swift's characters or those of Molière. Two women soften his hard attitude to the world – his wife and the lost girl played by Marilyn Nash. Although the girl is destitute, she retains an unquestioning belief in the goodness of human nature. Chaplin shows that Verdoux cannot resist the appeal of such a faith when she so openly expects him to share it. It is notable that while Verdoux is still in doubt whether he will use the girl as a human test for the strength of his poisoned wine, there is only conversation and the tension of action in silence; when the appeal to his kindliness has succeeded and the threat to her is removed, then music is introduced. The harmony of nature is restored, the balance of humanity levelled.

Chaplin could have redeemed Verdoux from this point had he so wished, and had the Hays code allowed him to do so. But Chaplin did not choose to redeem him. By a fortuitous blow

Verdoux loses his family in some outburst of social violence
which Chaplin does not trouble to explain, but which is due to
the economic and political crises of the thirties. He is left to shift
for himself, alone and more deeply embittered than ever. When
he meets the lost girl once more, he finds she is the kept woman
of a rich manufacturer of munitions. Beauty and faith have been
sold to the destroyer. Verdoux is aged and poverty-stricken: he
sees no reason for prolonging life or humanity. Her faith, however, is not yet destroyed. 'Life is beyond reason,' she tells him;
'that's why we must go on.' But Verdoux allows himself to be
arrested.

The last section brings to a head the philosophy of the film.
No stress is laid on the process of the trial except Verdoux's last
remark after his death sentence: 'I shall see you all very soon'.
Society is merely destroying him just in advance of destroying
itself. In his prison cell he is interviewed by the Press; now that
he is notorious, space in the newspapers is at his disposal and the
photographers wait around outside to beat the prison rule of
'no pictures'. He tells the reporter that 'crime does not pay in a
small way', that robbery and murder are the natural expression
of 'these criminal times'. 'That's business,' he says. War is the
outcome of it all. 'One murder makes a villain, millions a hero.'
Then he turns the reporter out. 'My time is limited,' he says
with ironic authority.

To the priest who comes to escort him to the place of execution he declares, 'I am at peace with God, my conflict is with
man'. He even rebukes the priest, 'What would you be doing
without sin?' When the priest prays that God have mercy on his
soul, he replies lightly, 'Why not? after all, it belongs to Him'.
With a sense of relief, having stated his aphoristic creed as if he
were a minor prophet, he hesitates over a glass of rum, and decides to have it, as he has never tasted rum before. There is something superb about this moment before death, elemental, like
the loosening of Lear's button. It unites the soul with the body
for the last time. Then with the curious ritual which attends all

scenes of death, he goes out, a small man with sloping aged shoulders walking into the prison courtyard to heavy music. This time there is no long road to the horizon, no pretty girl for companion, no pathetic fatalism. It is a stark march to death.

In most criticism of *Monsieur Verdoux*, this essential philosophy of the film has been overlooked or avoided. Reviewers have said the film is unequal, that it is not very funny, that its comedy is spoilt by the intrusion of Chaplin's personal point of view, or that it is a film of many brilliant and inimitable moments, mostly moments of superb pantomime with such skilful players as Martha Raye.

The general impression is that what respect has been accorded to *Monsieur Verdoux* is a respect born of the traditional praise of Chaplin the comedian. No film which attempts so much double meaning could probably escape some faults; the comic pantomime at times seems plugged to the point of irrelevance, like the overbalanced by-play of a Lenten holiday. There are episodes, such as the long action of Verdoux's avoidance of one wife who turns up at the reception held before his marriage to another, where the delicate touch of Clair would have been more appropriate. That almost all the aphorisms are kept to the end of the film is appropriate to the scene in the death cell, but robs the last sequences of some emotion; Verdoux becomes one with his creator. But these are small faults compared with the courageous achievement of the work as a whole, which is the most serious of all Chaplin's films. It points ahead to an even more important film should Chaplin care to develop and perfect the messianic style in a profoundly felt social satire. He works in secrecy, so only he can tell if this is to be so or not.

THE STRUCTURE OF THE BRITISH FILM INDUSTRY

R. K. NEILSON BAXTER

★

THE film industry is one of the most complex structures in our national life. It is no more than fifty years öld, and yet it has already become one of the largest industries both here and in America, outstripping many others three or four times as old and more. Millions of people go to the cinemas every week; films are shown in schools, in clubs, in village halls, in factories; every age of person and every kind of person sees and understands films. In other words, as a commodity the film is so important and has so large an amount of capital invested in it that we must look upon it as part of our national wealth. 'Cinema' is nowadays regarded as an art-form; but 'film-making' is an industry with the economic structure of an industry.

The economics of any industry comprise the manufacture, distribution and marketing of its products. In the film industry these activities are called production, renting and exhibition, and until recently each represented a separate independent grouping of individuals, of capital and of man-power. The American industry has always been in the main vertically integrated, that is, ownership of the means of production, renting and exhibition has been grouped together. Five large undertakings,[1] each with its own studios, sales organisation and cinemas, have divided the industry between them. In Great Britain, until the growth of the Rank Organisation, the tendency has been for large numbers of relatively small production companies to

1. Loew's Incorporated (MGM); Paramount Pictures; RKO; Twentieth Century-Fox; and Warner Bros.

exist,[1] relying effectively on a few large renting organisations, most of them controlled by American vested interests, to place their product. Some of these renters owned circuits of cinemas, but they were of modest numbers and constituted only a small-ish percentage of the total number of cinemas in the country. The remaining percentage was owned in ones and twos by independent companies.

As a means of consolidating their interests, following normal industrial practice, the companies working in each of these fields set up trade associations, namely, the British Film Producers Association, the Kinematograph Renters Society and the Cinematograph Exhibitors Association. It is not true, of course, that any of these are *fully* representative of the companies working in the three fields. One can say, however, that they represent the major concerns in each, and each is thereby regarded as the spokesman for its section.

At the present time the BFPA is dominated by Arthur Rank. Out of thirty-two members, about half are companies financed by or depending for production contracts on the Rank Organisation. Apart from a few small renting concerns with an inconsiderable entrée to the exhibiting market, Rank controls the principal British renting combine.[2] The only other of influential size is the Associated British Picture Corporation, whose cinema circuit is smaller than the combined Gaumont and Odeon circuit owned by Rank, and whose overseas connections are of less consequence by comparison.[3] Thus, any independent producing company will almost without question look to the Rank organisation for distribution.

Most of the independent producing companies are capitalised in such a way that they must raise the major part of their work-

1. At the time of writing there are well over two hundred production companies active. Of these, probably two-thirds are feature and second-feature producers.
2. Rank's distribution companies are General Film Distributors and Eagle Lion.
3. The precise significance of the comparatively new Korda-British Lion set-up has yet to be demonstrated.

ing capital picture by picture. To satisfy the normal backer some guarantee of distribution, carrying with it the reasonable certainty of adequate returns, is necessary, and the producer therefore normally seeks a renting contract for a proposed film in advance. Before the war, this often meant hawking scripts up and down Wardour Street; now it means, to those favoured by Rank's patronage, guarantees adequate to secure bankers' loans, often the advance of part or the whole of the estimated costs of production.

The Rank Organisation owns some of the most up-to-date studios in the country and two processing laboratories. These are available on credit terms to producers with only a modest capital working under the Rank umbrella. There are, of course, other more highly capitalised companies, some of them owning excellent studios, which are nevertheless largely dependent on Mr Rank for the distribution of their product. Others, again, do not aim at the 'first-run' West End cinemas, but have made films for a great many years destined for the provinces and marketed by companies concentrating on specified regions. These are firms of long standing who have built up good commercial relationships and find little need for Rank's financial support.

ABPC also embraces a number of production concerns, but these are far less numerous than the Rank satellites. The Corporation also owns two studios and processing laboratories. It is related to the American Warner Bros organisation, which owns studios at which, before they were blitzed, production was carried on in this country.

The Kinematograph Renters Society is not dominated in quite the same way by Rank, although he controls the main channels of distribution in the home market, and some overseas. Several of the KRS members are American companies, for example Twentieth Century-Fox, Metro-Goldwyn-Mayer, Columbia, R.K.O., Paramount, Warner Bros. and United Artists. This apparent anomaly dates back to the time of the first World

War, when the British industry came to an almost complete standstill. This was only a dozen or so years after the motion picture had first astonished the public, and its novelty value was still high. The Americans (who were not then in the war, although they subsequently anticipated a later history by winning it) made the most of this state of affairs, set up their own distribution offices in this country and captured the market. Their grip has been maintained for more than thirty years, in spite of two Acts of Parliament designed to ensure the showing of a percentage of British films. The third of these Acts will be on the statute-book by the time this article appears.

Although the successive Quota Acts have obliged the American renters to acquire a given percentage of British-made product – which in turn led some of them to set up their own production units in this country – their principal purpose here has been to get as many as possible American films of all types on our screens at the expense of the British film. The size of the home market is such that we cannot afford to spend on our films more than a fraction of the sums common in the American industry if we are to be reasonably certain of covering our costs. For instance, America has always been able to offer larger salaries than we could afford, to entice any players who showed signs of acquiring 'star' value away from London to Hollywood. So the 'star system' on which their films are sold even in Great Britain was thus denied to the native product.

Since the war, the position of the British film has become progressively stronger. Before the imposition of the import duty initiated by Dr Dalton when he was Chancellor of the Exchequer, reciprocal renting agreements had been negotiated by both Rank and Korda with American companies. It is still too early to see what effect the changes made by Harold Wilson together with the third Quota Act will have on the balance between British and American influence in the KRS. Under his arrangement it is fairly certain that American companies will be more willing to distribute British-made films in the United States, but it is equally certain that they will use that portion of their revenue from the British market which they must now leave here to produce films. Thus we may get an increase, rather than a reduction, in American domination of the British industry.

The exhibiting side of the British industry has for a long time been the most cynical. Recently the secretary of the Cinematograph Exhibitors Association said in public that his members were only interested in making money, not in art or uplift. This argues no discrimination in terms of merit or quality, but only in terms of marketing rates and conditions, and perhaps explains why 'box-office' is the deity that reigns over film commerce.

Few feature films are booked on a lump-sum basis: the renter contracts for a percentage of the box-office receipts, possibly with a lump-sum minimum. Most of the films in the 'supporting programme', that is, the second feature and the shorts, are usually booked for a lump sum, but the rates have in the past been so low that the cost of the first feature is effectively the only part of the booking costs which need be considered by the exhibitor as a serious commitment. As this is normally on a percentage basis, there is little for him to worry about except covering the overhead cost of running his cinema.

Frequent attempts have been made to obtain better marketing conditions for shorts in various ways by the shorts producers.[1] Here another splitting up of the industry is involved, in that the making of short and documentary films is rarely carried on by the same companies that make the features. Most shorts companies are completely independent of the financial interests behind the feature companies. Out of about seventy companies who are members of the three trade associations – the Association of Specialised Film Producers, the British Short Film Makers Society and the Federation of Documentary Film Units – only six are part of the Rank empire. Of those six only three are pro-

1. Recently, the President of the Board of Trade said that the anomalies in marketing conditions would be considered by the committee of enquiry he proposes to set up after the third Quota Act has gone through parliament.

ducers of complete films (plus one producing religious films exclusively): the others specialise as sub-contractors in the production of animated diagrams and similar material.

The British Short Film Makers Society represents those shorts producers who aim to supply the demands of the cinemas. We have said that the price at which such films are booked to the cinemas by the renters is very small: this means that the price at which a producer may hope to sell a short to a renter is equally small. As a result, producers of this kind normally make their films as cheaply as possible. The result may be seen on most cinema screens.

The other two associations represent those units which normally specialise in films with a more serious purpose, educational, technical, scientific or generally informative. But these are subjects which must be made to the highest standard to be effective, and many times more money will be spent on them than on the films the cheapjack can make for the price he gets. So they do not reach the cinema screen unless someone is prepared to bear a loss.

In the ordinary way, this type of film is 'sponsored'. This means that it is commissioned either by a public body or an industrial concern or some other corporation. The film is made for an agreed price and usually for a specified type of audience. It is not distributed by commercial renters, but by the sponsoring organisation itself.

The most extensive of this type of sponsorship is that controlled by the Central Office of Information on behalf of the Government. The C.O.I. organisation includes the Central Film Library in London, twelve regional offices, where a nucleus of prints is kept for use at local shows, and a hundred and forty-odd mobile projection units to provide shows in factories, institutes and clubs which have no projectors of their own. The equipment used is the 16-mm. sub-standard size and the copies of the films shown are reduction prints from the original 35-mm. negatives. The Army, Navy and Air Force each have similar arrangements. This type of distribution is known as 'non-theatrical'.

Industrial sponsors will often have films made for showing to their own staff. In this way instruction can be given, information circulated amongst overseas branches and so on. Others will make disinterested films for educational or sociological purposes instead of spending money on more direct forms of publicity. In these cases, their publicity department will contain a section responsible for looking after distribution of the films. Sometimes, films of the latter type, where their content is of sufficient importance, will be adopted by the Central Film Library.

The films which have given the British documentary-film movement its reputation were all made in this way. Their cost is in accordance with their quality and the varying difficulties inherent in their subjects. In almost every case this cost would be by no means covered by the return which the picture could earn in a cinema at ordinary commercial rates – even if a renter could be found to handle what he would regard as a film of limited entertainment value. Occasionally, however, a film produced on a sponsored basis is accepted by a renter, where the sponsor is more interested in getting the picture before the public than in making a sufficient return to cover production costs. The more blatant advertising film almost invariably reaches the screen only if the sponsor pays the cinema to show it. This type of film, however, is not held in much esteem by the technicians who are expected to make them.

The interests of the technicians are looked after by the Association of Cinematograph and Allied Technicians, commonly known as ACT. It is a trade union, affiliated to the TUC, with about 8,000 members. Agreements laying down pay scales and working conditions exist with all the employers' associations relating to production excepting the British Short Film Makers Society.

The KRS and CEA maintain agreements with the National Association of Theatrical and Kine Employees, which looks after the non-technical grades in film production and all workers in distribution and exhibition. The Film Artistes Association represents actors who work solely in films: these are in the main the smaller-part players and crowd artistes. British Actors Equity is the union covering actors who work in both stage and screen parts. Other unions covering wider fields which include sections of the film industry are the Electrical Trades Union, which has a large membership among the electricians handling the lamps in studios, and the Musicians Union.

Other employers' associations covering sections of the production field are the Film Laboratory Association and the Newsreel Association of Great Britain.

Thus is the commercial structure of the British film industry made up. It is supported by a number of organisations devoted to specific purposes, such as the British Board of Film Censors, the British Film Institute, the British Kinematograph Society and the British Film Academy.[1] Of these, the first is a body which looks after the film industry's moral relations with the public. The second concerns itself with film history and film appreciation, with providing information, helping the student and maintaining the archives of the National Film Library. The third has recently turned itself into a learned society, with a membership interested in the science of motion pictures. It disposes of up to five fellowships a year amongst its members. The last is a recently formed society with a limited elected membership of film-makers, concerning itself primarily with the æsthetic and cultural aspects of film-making. Another society which may soon achieve national status is the Scientific Film Association, whose interests are evident from its name. The Royal Photographic Society has a cinematograph section, and its associate memberships and fellowships are open to film cameramen who qualify by their artistry and skill.

1. Equivalent American organisations are respectively the Motion Picture Association (the Hays Office, now known as the 'Johnston Office'); the Museum of Modern Arts, New York; the Society of Motion Picture Engineers; and the Academy of Motion Picture Arts and Sciences.

ROUND THE WORLD'S STUDIOS

H. H. WOLLENBERG

*

IF we attempt to analyse the general tendencies within the vast and somewhat troubled waters of international film production, we may discover the interesting phenomenon of two opposing principles. Both clearly indicate certain universal trends active in film studios almost all over the world; definitely in Europe, and, although far less distinctly, also in California. Almost all films recently released and worth seeing, as well as forthcoming productions worth looking forward to, appear to be centred around the one or the other of those two diametrically opposed conceptions, which may be defined as *collectivism* and *individualism* in film-making.

The development in question may be elucidated by a few films chosen from well-known British pictures of the 1947 programme. The outstanding instance of individualistic film style would obviously be David Lean's *Brief Encounter*. The individual here dominates the screen; all the superb artistry and technique displayed in the film, all the supporting parts, brilliantly as they are enacted, are but subordinated to the one individual character, its fate, its interpretation. In fact, the individualistic type of film succeeds or fails with its central figure (or couple of figures, for that matter). As an instance to the contrary, I would quote *Captain Boycott*. Although for obvious commercial reasons 'starring' Stewart Granger, his part is actually irrelevant. It represents no more than one stone in a mosaic. Launder and Gilliat were concerned with interpreting, not that individual fate (as was Lean), but the revolutionary story of social problems and national frictions in the Ireland of the eighties. Collectivism in film style is here in evidence. Or take *Frieda* and *It Always Rains on Sunday*, both from the Ealing Studios, as representative of individualism and collectivism respectively. In the former a contemporary problem is focused on an individual case, that of Frieda, while in the latter a number of well-drawn figures are combined in a true-to-life portrayal of the East End of London and its social conditions: its purpose is clearly collectivist.

Collectivism as a principle of cinematic inspiration and conception is a fresh and increasingly powerful, if not altogether new, characteristic of current developments. It was already developed by such directors as S. M. Eisenstein, G. W. Pabst or John Ford. In *Battleship Potemkin*, individual characters were so completely submerged in the story, the real star of which was the battleship, symbolising an idea, that we forgot they were enacted altogether; just as Eisenstein made us forget that his film was 'directed': the highest achievement in collectivism.

In Hollywood, obviously, the star system necessarily acts as a brake against collectivist tendencies. However, the power of those trends becomes the more noticeable, as even American studios have lately provided some specimens. Edward Dmytryk's *Crossfire*, Elia Kazan's *Boomerang*, Henry Hathaway's *House on 92nd Street*, *13 Rue de Madeleine* and *Kiss of Death* show the tendency to diminish the influence of the actor, which means that of the individual he represents, in order to emphasise the collective effect and its social or factual reflections. The part played by the producers Louis and Richard de Rochemont in this development cannot be overlooked.

As for Europe, its studios almost everywhere have, since the end of the war, received decisive impulses from collectivism which, as a style, is now playing a far more important part than ever before. This seems to apply particularly to countries which had suffered occupation with the resulting underground movement. Neutral Sweden, on the other hand, is an example to the contrary. Individualism still prevails here, keeping up a good standard of quality. *For, the alternative of collectivism or individualism is in itself not a criterion of quality.*

The spectacular rise of post-war Italian production is in the sign of collectivism, whether we think of Roberto Rossellini (*Open City, Paisà* and now *Germany Anno O*), Aldo Vergano (*The Sun Still Rises*), Vittorio de Sica (*Shoeshine*), Luigi Zampa (*To Live in Peace*), or Giuseppe de Santis (*Tragic Hunt*).

The collectivist tendency is predominant in the young national productions of Eastern European countries, where contacts have been made between representatives of the Russian, Czech, Polish, Bulgarian and Yugoslav industries with a view to co-ordinating policy, co-production and methods of film exchange and distribution.

The great achievements of the Russian studios cannot fail to make their influence felt. This holds good for the Czech and the Polish film effort, and seems also to apply to the Hungarian studios which, after innumerable difficulties, have again resumed production. Among the first subjects we find *Somewhere in Europe*, a film dealing with war orphans. Incidentally, a similar theme, which necessarily calls for a collectivist style, has been chosen by producers of other countries. In Switzerland the Praesens Film Company have a film on displaced children, directed by Fred Zinnemann, in their 1947 production, and Warner Bros., too, sent a unit to Europe to shoot a picture on Europe's children.

In German production which, before the war, largely relied on the star principle, collectivism, as represented by directors Wolfgang Staudte and Helmuth Käutner, now appears prevalent. This holds good for the revived film effort in all the four zones, or rather three, as production has not yet started under French occupation. Recent productions under British licence, such as Werner Klingler's *Arche Noah*, Hans Müller's *Vor dem Neuen Tag* (*Before the New Day*), Erich Waschnek's *Menschen in Gottes Hand* (*Men in God's Hand*), all indicate a collectivist approach. Carl·Boese, too, is again active as a director. The first production in the U.S. zone, *Zwischen Gestern und Morgen* (*Between Yesterday and To-morrow*) has been completed. Of special interest is the first Jewish film made in Munich by the International Film Gesellschaft, *Lang ist der Weg* (*Long is the Road*). As to Jewish subjects, there are two films based on racial persecution and anti-Semitism. Kurt Maetzig's Defa production *Ehe im Schatten* (*Marriage in the Shadow*), a stirring presentation of the tragedies resulting from Hitler's racial legislation, is considered the most important German post-war production so far. Another Defa film by Erich Engel is the reconstruction of a notorious trial which actually took place a few years before Hitler came to power. A very similar venture is G. W. Pabst's first post-war film made in Vienna. Tentatively entitled *The Trial*, it tells the actual story of a Hungarian Jew accused of ritual murder.

In the west of the Continent some noteworthy examples of collectivism were presented by French studios. Such films as René Clément's *Bataille du Rail* or Henri Galef's *Jericho* again reveal the influence of Occupation, Liberation, The Underground.

In point of fact, there seems to exist an inter-relationship between collectivism and documentary. This holds good even if the collectivist style is employed in fiction films. That relationship can be recognised in all the collectivist films mentioned, beginning with *Battleship Potemkin*.

Individualism, of course, has also a long and interesting tradition in the young history of the cinema. In fact, it sprang up in those almost prehistoric days when those funny anonymous figures (always including a policeman), engaged in some hectic pursuit, were for the first time replaced by an individual, an amusing little chap with a personal expression, named Max Linder. The ideal case of individualism, however, became manifest in Charles Chaplin, the rare and fortunate instance of the producer and the writer, the director and the actor being embodied in the same individual. Here is the very personification of individualism in screen art. I understand that he plans as his next subject the story of a Displaced Person coming to America to be feted and celebrated with all the spotlights on him as long as he is 'news'. Some weeks later he is completely forgotten, nobody takes any notice or shows any kindness. Disgusted, he returns to his camp, where he finds more misery but also more real fellowship.

Chaplin apart, we can distinguish between the individualism of the productive artist, principally the director, and of the interpreting artist, i.e. the actor. The individualism of the former, the creative artist, is of the greatest importance, although it does not become physically visible on the screen as does the image of the latter. Talking of creative individualists, I found the following striking characterisations some time ago in *Ciné Suisse*: 'René Clair (fantasy), Henri-Georges Clouzot (the revolting), Fritz Lang (fatalism), Frank Capra (humorous idealism), David Lean (discreet romanticism), or Jean Cocteau (hieratic poetry)'. This list, as quoted from the Swiss magazine, could easily be extended if space would permit.

On the other hand, the outstanding interpreting artist, the actor, has hardly ever the same chance of fully expressing his or her individuality. Among productions dominated by the individuality of their interpreters should be *Joan of Lorraine*, with Ingrid Bergman (director Victor Fleming), and, of course, that grand performance of *Hamlet* by Sir Laurence Olivier. However, in Sir Laurence's case we have once more the fortunate unity of direction and interpretation.

FILMS FOR INTERNATIONAL
UNDERSTANDING

The UNESCO Story

ERNEST BORNEMAN

★

UP to the second General Conference at Mexico City, the film work of Unesco had been centred in the Film Section, which formed one-third of a vast mass communication unit (press – radio – films) headed by John Grierson. The Film Section itself was headed by William Farr, who had a staff of four information officers, two programme assistants, an executive assistant and two secretaries.

Like all other sections of the United Nations and her specialised agencies, the Film Section during this period had to strike a working balance between the potential scope of an international organisation which had the sky for a limit and its actual scope, which was defined, as it had to be, by its budget.

From the beginning Unesco's potential scope was, of course, most succinctly defined by its title – the United Nations Educational, Scientific and Cultural Organisation; by definition the Film Section therefore had to concern itself with all matters pertaining to the international flow of films on education, science and culture. During the Mexico Conference, however, a decision was taken to organise the programme in terms of nine key projects:

1. The free flow of films, film personnel and film information across national and other barriers.
2. The use of films in fundamental education.
3. The use of films for international understanding.
4. The use of films for the popularisation of science.

5. The use of films in libraries and museums.

6. The use of films by governments and mass organisations.

7. The use of films in art, music and literature.

8. The reconstruction of the film industry in war-devastated areas.

9. The international standardisation of equipment, raw stock, cataloguing methods and other technical factors.

The operational methods elected to implement this programme might be defined under six headings:

I. Research and collection of information:

    (a) Through field workers;

    (b) From the United Nations and its specialised agencies;

    (c) From Unesco National Commissions;

    (d) From film organisations –

        (1) Production,

        (2) Distribution,

        (3) Exhibition,

        (4) Stock and equipment manufacture,

        (5) Laboratories,

        (6) Film societies, etc.;

    (e) From the film trade press;

    (f) From the general press;

    (g) From educational, scientific and cultural organisations.

II. Dissemination of information (catalogues, monographs, bulletins, mail-answering service):

    (a) To Unesco liaison officers abroad;

    (b) To the United Nations and its specialised agencies;

    (c) To Unesco National Commissions;

    (d) To film organisations –

        (1) Production,

        (2) Distribution,

        (3) Exhibition,

        (4) Stock and equipment manufacture,

        (5) Laboratories,

        (6) Film societies, etc.;

(e) To the film trade press;

(f) To the general press;

(g) To educational, scientific and cultural organisations.

III. Stimulation of:

(a) Film production;

(b) Film distribution;

(c) Film exhibition;

(d) Manufacture of film equipment and raw stock;

(e) Film research;

(f) Standardisation of technical procedure;

(g) International organisation in all branches of film work.

IV. Representation at international conferences, commissions and film festivals.

V. Arrangement of international film shows and film seminars.

VI. Arrangement of film scholarships, fellowships, training schemes, grants-in-aid and the exchange of personnel.

As far as the collection and dissemination of information is concerned, it is obvious that Unesco's function should be that of facilitating an interchange of film information between existing organisations rather than that of transforming itself into an international film information centre to which enquiries from individuals and groups all over the world might be directed.

As far as the stimulation of film activities is concerned, it is equally obvious that Unesco should first of all identify pressing needs; define ways of meeting them; and then bring them to the attention of the proper national agencies and thus stimulate action upon them. The Unesco Film Section is not a world film university, a world film research centre, or a world film agency; it is an inter-governmental organisation dependent for its effectiveness upon the co-operation of the Member-States to whom it may recommend a course of action. As a mere secretariat (to paraphrase the 1948 Programme), lodged in a disused Paris hotel, Unesco would be powerless; as a world organisation of governments and peoples it can exercise an influence upon film production and distribution in direct proportion to the willingness of each Member-State to act through its own film committee.

These film committees, which are the grass roots of Unesco's film activities, can be established either as branches of the United Nations Film Board (in which the film sections of the United Nations and the special agencies are represented, together with Unesco's own Film Section) or as working committees within the growing network of Unesco National Commissions which have already been established in Australia, Austria, Brazil, Canada, China, Colombia, Denmark, the Dominican Republic, France, Haiti, Italy, Mexico, New Zealand, Norway, the Netherlands, the Philippines, Peru, Poland, Union of South Africa, United Kingdom, U.S.A. and Venezuela.

Only where national information on the production, distribution and exhibition of films and other audio-visual media is made available to Unesco through such film committees, and through Unesco to other film committees in other countries, will it be possible to contemplate and plan the international exchange of such information. While these committees would therefore have a direct channel for distributing their own current information, they would also be assured of the reception of similar information from other countries.

But the scope of their activities is, of course, not limited to the exchange of information; all major Unesco projects have been developed with their aid and are continuing to rely on their assistance:

1. *The free flow of films, film personnel and film information across national boundaries* – This task has been interpreted by the Film Section, in co-ordination with the Unesco Programme for 1948, as the need for establishing equal access to films without regard to racial, social or economic restrictions. A study has been made, and is continuing, on such obstacles to the free flow of films and film information as censorship, copyright, currency

restrictions, customs, monopolies, quotas, tariffs and union restrictions.

The Film Section participated in the First Session of the United Nations Sub-Commission on Freedom of Information and of the Press in May 1947, as well as the World Conference on Freedom of Information held in March 1948 in Geneva.

A questionnaire, tentatively titled 'Request for Information', has been prepared by the Film Section to be sent to the Governments of the States invited to the World Conference. Based on the questionnaire of the Technical Needs Commission mentioned below under 8, it asks for information about legislation and regulations affecting the free flow of news by means of films in Member-Nations as well as in those war-devastated countries which have not yet become members.

The Commission of Experts on the Free Flow of Information, which met at Unesco House from October 13 to 17, 1947, also considered practical ways of promoting a freer flow of informational films, and of information on films, between countries in the presence of, and in spite of, existing political and economic obstacles. Its recommendations were placed before the Second General Conference.

Other conferences concerned with the free flow of information at which the Film Section was represented were the International Tele-Communications Union Conference in Atlantic City; Le Congrès International du Filmologie in Paris; the preparatory meeting for the 1947 International Conference of Scientific Film Associations in Paris and its first session in March 1948: the meeting of the Educational Film Libraries Association at Columbus, Ohio; the Philadelphia Conference of the U.S.A. National Commission; the Denver Regional Conference of the U.S. National Commission; the United Kingdom Mass Communications Committee for Unesco; the International Film Festival in Brussels and the Locarno Film Festival.

The Mexico Conference instructed the Director-General to transmit Unesco's draft for an agreement to facilitate the international circulation of visual and auditory materials of an educational, scientific and cultural character, as adopted by the First General Conference, to Member-States and to other States for their consideration and comments.

All international organisations facilitating the free flow of films between nations have been strongly supported by Unesco, including the World Federation of Scientific Film Associations, the World Federation of Film Technicians and the International Federation of Film Archives. Discussions are now proceeding with various Film Festival committees and Film Societies to consider the formation of an International Film Festival Association.

Scholarships, fellowships, training schemes and grants-in-aid have been among the means advocated and implemented by the Film Section in its task of obtaining an exchange of personnel in the fields of film and other audio-visual aids. Ten such scholarships have been negotiated through the British Film Producers' Association to permit a study of twelve months, at an estimated cost of £400 each, to candidates from Belgium, China, Czechoslovakia, Denmark, France, Greece, Netherlands, Norway, Poland and Venezuela.

The provision of technicians, materials and equipment to countries in need of these – another essential project to facilitate the free flow of films – is being negotiated by the promotion of a system of international credits, to be secured against services provided by beneficiary countries to technicians from other countries.

A study, for publication, of legislation pertaining to the free flow of films in twelve countries is under way.

2. *The use of films in fundamental education.* – The Film Section, like all other sections of Unesco, began to define fundamental education basically as a campaign against illiteracy in backward areas. In 1947, however, it became obvious that an approach narrowly confined to the removal of illiteracy, without taking into account other elements in audio-visual education

that are essential to health and community life, would be inadequate. The attack on illiteracy then came to be seen as a mere part of the campaign against the threefold evil of ignorance, disease and poverty. Considered from this viewpoint, it became apparent that even industrialised and 'advanced' countries continued to exhibit deficiency areas and weaknesses in their provision of audio-visual education. Aside from bringing educational, scientific and cultural films to underdeveloped areas, and aside from bringing films about such areas to the attention of the more highly developed populations of the world, the task then became one of making the whole project known among the organisations on whose assistance it would ultimately depend. Where films and film strips required in Fundamental Education Programmes were not already available, Unesco undertook to initiate and, if necessary, finance their preparation. To take the fullest advantage in 1948 of the services of Unesco's Panel of Experts on Fundamental Education, a special group of experts on visual education was consulted to assist in the audio-visual aspects of Fundamental Education. This panel of experts was also asked for advice as to how to stimulate the Fundamental Education campaign by means of films and film strips and to review the relative value of the different techniques of Mass Communication for this purpose. Film coverage for Unesco's pilot projects on Fundamental Education in China, East Africa, Nyasaland, Tanganyika, and Haiti will be provided, and films and film strips for use in the project will be donated.

3. *The use of films for international understanding.* – The Film Section has been in constant touch with international production and distribution organisations in the field of educational, scientific and cultural films, and has been able to give help and advice to many of them; the Committee for Social Information in Stockholm, for instance, in planning the production of a series of films on social subjects for the Swedish Government, expressed the wish to collaborate with Unesco on this scheme,

while the Danish Government asked Unesco for advice on the distribution of five twenty-minute films in a series called 'Social Denmark'. The C.O.I. has asked Unesco to suggest twenty foreign two-reel films for distribution in the United Kingdom, while the Rank Organisation has offered to guarantee finance and distribution, through its theatres, of three four-reel films on Unesco projects to be produced by Films of Fact, International Realist and G. B. Instructional. Metro-Goldwyn-Mayer has expressed the desire to cover international stories which Unesco might suggest if they are newsworthy and interesting. The March of Time unit arranged the showing of its film on Basic English in connection with the Unesco meeting on problems of language in fundamental education, and this screening was followed by a discussion, led by Mr I. A. Richards, on the problems and potentialities of films in the teaching of languages.

A Unesco summer seminar on international understanding was held in July 1947, and the Film Section provided an extensive motion-picture programme for exhibition and discussion.

The Unesco Film Section is also preparing a comparative study, for publication, on the methods of international news-gathering by newsreels and other actuality films, and a world list of films on international understanding to be published in the spring of 1948. Other Unesco programmes in preparation include a project to stimulate the production of films of multi-national character in the fields of Unesco by co-operative action between groups of countries concerned with each theme.

A series of forty-eight films on the special achievements of a number of nations in the fields of education, science and culture has had high priority among the 1948 Unesco projects approved by the General Conference. These films are to be produced through national organisations to an international plan, and are to be distributed internationally through national organisations. Each country is to be invited to produce films on national achievements that are of interest and value to all other countries, and each country producing films for the series is to have the right to distribute the entire series of films. The programme was drafted by Basil Wright; Britain, Poland and Holland have already given their tentative agreement, while the Danish and French Governments have discussed it in some detail, and with the approval of the General Conference, it is expected to be the top-ranking film programme on international understanding during the next year.

4. *The use of films for the popularisation of science.* – Unesco is preparing a world list of films on the popularisation of science, which is to be followed by further world lists of films on agriculture, nutrition, town and country planning, health, medicine and surgery, and by a study on the use of films and other audio-visual media in relation to the understanding of the social conditions affecting and affected by the development of science. Other Unesco projects connected with this plan are the popularisation of the history of science through films, and the possible provision of film coverage on the Hylean Amazon project and on the work of the Field Science Co-ordination Officers in South Asia, East Asia, the Middle East and Latin America.

5. *The use of films in libraries and museums.* – A study on the use of films and other audio-visual media in libraries and museums is being prepared by Unesco. This is to be followed by a world list of films dealing with the work of libraries and museums.

6. *The use of films by governments and mass organisations.* – Unesco is preparing a series of studies on the use of films and other audio-visual media (a) by governments; (b) by industries for staff training and public information; (c) by unions, co-operatives and voluntary service organisations; and (d) by all mass organisations concerned with the teaching of citizenship.

7. *The use of films in art, music and literature.* – Aware of the inherent international character of all arts, the Unesco Film Section is promoting the establishment of experimental centres in several countries for the production and distribution of films on the popular presentation of the arts. The stimulation of the

production of films on folk art and on the traditions of crafts-manship has also been given considerable attention in Unesco's international film series mentioned above under 3.

8. *The reconstruction of the film industry in war-devastated countries.* – The Unesco Commission on Technical Needs in Mass Communications, which published in September 1947 its first report on the technical needs of films, radio and Press in twelve war-devastated countries, is now preparing its second report on ten war-devastated countries in Europe and the Far East.

Taking into account the experience of 1947, sentiment in both 'donor' and 'recipient' countries, and changes in the economic and social life of the countries themselves, the Film Section of Unesco, like all other collaborators on the Technical Needs programme, has decided to move away from the division of nations into donors and recipients, and to stress the principle of exchange of services by way of mutual aid between nations. The scholarship programme, mentioned above under 1, might be quoted as an example of this new pattern in so far as it is expected that similar scholarship offers are to be made by countries previously defined as recipient. Other programmes in preparation are the promotion of a system of international credits to be secured against services provided by beneficiary countries to film technicians from other countries; an investigation into inexpensive and speedy methods of projector manufacture, and a study of the factors determining the selling price of projectors in a number of countries. Projects under discussion include one film on international schools and camps in war-devastated countries, and another one on the reconstruction of war-devastated countries to be prepared in collaboration with the Temporary International Council for Reconstruction.

9. *The international standardisation of equipment, raw stock, cataloguing methods and other technical factors.* – This subject has been given high priority in the discussions with the World Federation of Film Technicians and the World Federation

of Scientific Film Associations. Subject to confirmation by the Second General Conference, a Commission of Experts on film-cataloguing methods is to be assembled in 1948, to promote the adoption of standard practices by national bodies.

In conclusion, it might be said that all activities of the Film Section are to be viewed as part of the activities of the Mass Communications Division, and that the work of the latter is to be understood only as the implementation of the Unesco programme confirmed by the Member-Nations during the first two sessions of the Unesco General Conference.

THE IMPLICATIONS BEHIND
THE SOCIAL SURVEY

RACHAEL LOW

★

No emphasis is needed to-day on the social importance of cinema-going, and the fact that weekly attendances in Britain amount to 25 or 30 millions is common knowledge. Using the most recent Social Survey investigation of cinema attendance as a basis, it is estimated that the film public in this country includes some 21 of the 29 million civilian adults (the survey relates only to the civilian population), who spend annually as much as £85 million on cinema tickets. Nor is this all; for the unmeasured audience of under-16s is undoubtedly very large and very enthusiastic.

In the face of such a public, one's dual attitude to the film as an art and as a sociological problem takes on the appearance of an uncomfortable dilemma. A world of artistically brilliant films giving genuine pleasure to a general public seems preposterously idealistic, for at best the coincidence of great art and wide popularity is rare. For it almost seems that the two things are mutually exclusive. In so far as they do exist together in the same film at all, it seems to be at each other's expense, in a compromise achievement that is good but not brilliant, fairly but not widely popular.

The spontaneous enjoyment of great art by everybody is doubtless the ultimate perfection acceptable to both the artist and the sociologist. But in the case of films, for the most part yearnings for art are obviously swamped by other motives. Quite apart from the escapist aspect of any form of drama, the institutionalised night out is independent of the artistic value of the entertainment, which is little more than an excuse, and in the case of the cinema, this is carried to extremes. Thirty-two per cent of the adult population go to the cinema at least once a week, and 13 per cent of this percentage, again, go more than once a week. Most of these people are habitual film-goers who exercise remarkably little choice between films. No less than 70 per cent of the whole cinema-going public go regularly to one or other of their 'locals'; thus, although they exercise a limited choice between the films offered by the few circuits and fewer independents in their area, their primary reason for going is not the desire to see a particular film. Finally, a third of this group actually goes time after time to the same cinema whatever the film.

The young seem to be slightly more selective in their film-going than people as a whole. For although the under-24s attend more often and more regularly than older people, they are less inclined to become fixed in a one-cinema routine, and form a relatively large proportion of the group which exercises its limited choice between the locals. The importance of youth in the audience is one of the most striking features of the film public. Consequently, this small measure of discrimination might be regarded as a promising sign. But the bare facts leave unanswered the crucial question of whether the younger generation of to-day is going to take its selectivity with it into old age, or whether this is merely a function of youth itself, to be replaced by habits of greater rigidity as each generation grows older. Nevertheless, it would seem easier to make a habit of discrimination itself in the case of young people, and the remarkable extent to which youth does in fact dominate the cinema audience is illustrated by the report. The frequency of attendance increases from the age of 5 upwards and actually seems to reach its peak at 20. Sixty-five per cent of the 5–15s, and 69 per cent of the 16–19s, go once a week or more, while as much as 45 per cent of the 16–19s even go twice a week or more, as against only 13 per cent of the whole population over 16. Moreover, the percentage of each age-group which never enters a cinema rises steadily from only 2 per cent of the 16–19s to 61 per cent of the over 60s, and thus the vast majority of the 7 or 8 million adults in this category are older people. The most enthusiastic age-group might be even younger than it is were it not for pocket-money difficulties, but as it is, the most frequent attenders are the young wage-earners.

They, however, are presumably the most given to cinema cuddling, and although the social surveyors have not yet classified this, tabulated it and served it as percentages, we may safely feel that it is in itself an institution, and one which suggests that frequent attendance is largely a temporary habit of youth and does not indicate a continual expansion of the audience. Consequently, it is not surprising if trade-inspired efforts to mould cinema habits while the subject is young are calculated to encourage frequency, rather than artistic discrimination. The unsatisfactory nature of films shown at present to children's clubs is widely discussed, and although the Rank plans for special children's entertainment films admittedly require time for fulfilment, little in the non-ballet sequences of their *Little Ballerina* suggests that the new films will reach the technical standard of *Bush Christmas*, for example. The encouragement of a higher standard of film appreciation by constant familiarity with fine work from an early age would require efforts greater than this. On the other hand, the deliberate inculcation of film appreciation in schools, if desirable in itself, offers difficulties of its own.

In any case, the different habits of artistic discrimination cannot be ascribed solely to differences of age. The influence of social and economic factors, such as income and education – which frequently correspond to residential areas – is also very marked, and in some measure reflects the film's dual existence as an art form and as a social habit. Broadly speaking, the lower economic and education groups show the greatest rigidity in their cinema-going, tending to go very often and without exercising much choice. To them the all-important thing is that films should be available in sufficient quantity to provide one or two full evenings a week at the pictures, with all that this implies of escape from home and job, outing with friends and, for the young, a comfortable and socially accepted place for wooing. The unimportance of artistic nuances is nowhere so marked as in the Sunday-evening houses in such an area, where bad reissues and worse second features are received with indifferent tolerance by a skylarking audience, whose sole expression of emotion, whether of amusement, embarrassment or even surprise or tension, seems to be an uncontrolled guffaw. At the other end of the scale, professional and managerial workers, the higher education groups, show the greatest elasticity in their cinema habits. With a financial and educational background which encourages more diffused cultural interests, they are inclined to exercise more rigorous selection, only going to the pictures when there is a particular film they wish to see. Such attendances, since they come from the smaller class and by their nature are less frequent, presumably form a relatively small proportion of the total, although they are the mainstay of the specialist cinemas and film societies. To such audiences an unrestricted supply of films is of importance, not because it ensures quantity, but because it permits them freedom to make their own judgment of quality.

This twofold function of the film must be borne in mind in considering the many influences which affect the demand for, and the supply of, films. Opinion polls which attempt to measure preferences, for example, are like children's clubs, in that in the hands of their most likely users they are more apt to extend than to transform cinema-going; since their most obvious effect is to help the trade to sell more and more of what it sells most easily, it is likely to retard rather than to advance a rising level of artistic appreciation. And an extension of cinema-going among the undiscriminating would hardly please either the sociologist or the artist. An informed public, with a critical appreciation of entertainment as a part of well-balanced living, would have more in common with the sparser attendances among those who exercise rigorous choice.

But external influences, such as the import tax announced by the Government in the summer of 1947, cut down cinema-going without either artistic or social justification, however necessary on grounds of national policy. Such prohibitive restrictions affect the film in both its capacities. Since home production could only gradually, if at all, fill the gap created by closed cinemas or shorter programmes, the undiscriminating would necessarily be deprived of their quantity, whereas the discriminating would be affected by the irrelevant restriction of free cultural exchange. It would be superficial and insensitive to reply that the majority of fans would suffer no harm from a curtailment of their twice-weekly orgy, for their alternative leisure activities and means of escape are few enough and by no means always preferable. And although it may be felt that with a few exceptions American films are of relatively little artistic value, and that their absence might give desirable opportunities to British film producers, the argument is probably of less validity than any other protectionist argument has ever been. The cultural results are as likely to be bad as they are to be good, and, incidental as they are to the completely different aims of the proposals, they cannot logically be defended on cultural grounds.

In the end the cultural effects of such external regulation, both in the supply of an art and the demand for it, are indirect and obscure. For the supply of an art depends ultimately on the existence and nature of available artistic talent, as well as on the conditions of its operation; and however little foreign competition it has, a sustained demand can exist only if the level of appreciation is adapted to it. Most film criticism seems to perform no useful function in respect of either supply or demand. It is too much to believe that film-makers would follow the opinions of self-constituted critics in preference to either their own impulses for self-expression on the one hand or box-office on the other. At the same time, the view that a film's Press notices have no measurable effect on its box-office returns causes as much complacency among those who feel that it demonstrates the critic's essential superiority, as among those who feel that it demonstrates his complete wrong-headedness. Whatever the truth, it seems that if the critic has any function more useful than a weekly demonstration of his own good taste, it must be largely one of popular education, a task of tremendous responsibility if the artistic development of the film is not to be accompanied by a widening gap between esoteric 'art' films and undisguised 'dope' films. The very few readable and cheaply published expositions of film technique can do incalculably more than weeks of witty subjectivity for the popularisation which is of such importance to a democratic community, where some appreciation of the higher artistic values should not be regarded as the lasting preserve of a small minority. The cleavage between the high-standard critic with his circle of initiates, and the entertainment-guide critic who only outlines the film's content, is likely to perpetuate the film's already existing dichotomy.

But to resolve this dichotomy into widespread real enjoyment of good films depends only partly on popularised instruction by film books, film societies and the few responsible critics.

The voracious market for film books, the increased film-society membership and the wide popularity of numerous fine British films during the war are to be seen, not only as causes, but also as effects. For they must be seen in the broader context of the general cultured awareness which manifested itself during the war in the other arts as well. In particular, the level of film appreciation is fundamentally related to the educational level in a way which is emphasised by the Social Survey report and which suggests that isolated efforts to raise it out of its social context will merely be scratching the surface of ignorance and immaturity. The greatest possible extension in specialist cinemas is probably the best the artist and the sociologist can jointly expect during the transition period until the most ignorant of fans is given the chance, by education and economic security, to achieve some sort of critical maturity.

HOLLYWOOD'S 1948 LINE-UP

MAX KNEPPER

★

THREATENED loss of the British market provided the major
Hollywood thrill last year. It upset filmdom more than any event
since the introduction of talking pictures. After the announcement of Britain's freezing of 75 per cent of profits earned by
American pictures in the United Kingdom, the atmosphere in
Hollywood became dense with rumours of drastic purges of personnel, even in the higher executive brackets – a last-resort cure.
Retrenchment, however, if it does materialise on a large scale,
will not be reflected in the 1948 releases, which, for the most part,
were acquired in story form one or two years ago and are already
filmed or at least in studio cutting-rooms. Results of this year's
economic impact will not be manifest before 1949.

Although a great clamour had gone up regarding the depressing foreign situation, the fact remains that there was a serious
contraction in the domestic market last year. Many Americans
who went to the pictures twice a week during the war boom are
now going twice a month. One reason is the higher cost of living – the American euphemism for inflation – and the other is
the extremely poor quality of films making up the 1946–7 output.

For this box-office sickness, Hollywood supplied a palliative
in the form of re-issues. Seven of Twentieth Century-Fox's
thirty-four features last year were re-releases, of which four were
historical romances first exhibited six or eight years ago. Fox
apparently contrived to cash in on the current U.S. rage for historical fiction. Inasmuch as any income from re-issues in excess
of exhibition costs is pure profit, this trend may be expected to
continue. In fact, most studios have advised distributors that

113

they will re-issue from one to six old features during the year. Obviously, however, Hollywood cannot counteract shrinking domestic patronage and loss of foreign markets by this method alone. For one thing, the list of such films is not inexhaustible.

The solution which major studios rely on for the box-office problem is production of movies which will attract the estimated 25 million Americans who now see films seldom, if at all. To entice these 'choosy' potential customers, the large studios will concentrate on successful Broadway plays and best-selling novels.

This development can be discerned in Universal's 1948 production schedule of twenty-five films, the same number, incidentally, as that studio produced last year. Over half this company's story properties consist of Broadway hits or fiction on last year's best-seller list. Its stage properties include *Harvey, Mexican Hayride, Are You With It?, Bloomer Girl* and *Portrait in Black*. Edna Ferber's *Great Son*, Gabrielle Roy's *Tin Flute* and *Gus the Great* are among the highly popular books that Universal will bring to the screen.

Twentieth Century-Fox is following the same pattern. This studio plans to release fifty-two films during the current year, of which nineteen will come from independents affiliated with the studio. The independent releases are for the most part 'B' pictures (although Fox disclaims handling 'low-budget' films), including six horror-detective stories. Of the twenty-five major releases for this year, only two are from original stories written directly for the screen. Twenty-one are adapted from novels or short stories and two are screen versions of British plays – Wilde's *An Ideal Husband* and Galsworthy's *Escape*.

The reliance of American producers on 'proven' works of the stage or publishing world, especially in the face of depressed box-office, is interesting on several counts. First, of course, is the belief of producers – to a certain extent verified by experience – that there is less risk in producing a popular published story than an untried screen original, despite the greater initial expense of acquiring motion-picture rights. The advertising worth of a published work, even if its circle of readers is limited, has tangible value.

Second, the conclusion of this trend, this reliance on sources outside the industry for story material, will be extinction of what little originality now exists in Hollywood.

Some critics, it is true, would say that this involves no loss, since originals in Hollywood have a bad name. This is mainly because for the most part they have been the province of 'quickie' producers who lack the means of buying proven stage or fiction properties or to hire first-rate writers to develop worthwhile screen stories. Unfortunately, the present market situation will accentuate this condition among the independents, who will now not dare to risk their all on a single 'prestige' picture. In fact, some independents who last year acquired valuable story properties are hawking them among their more prosperous brethren.

Republic Pictures, one of the larger independent studios, has completed *Macbeth*, but this film will not be released this year, because the studio is afraid that the American market will not return the cost, reputedly more than a million dollars. Republic will wait until conditions are more favourable abroad. No more pictures of this kind will be produced at Republic, however, until box-office looks up.

The vast majority of Hollywood's 1948 productions will be 'escapist'—musical comedies, highly fictionised historical dramas, detective stories and just plain romance. Fortunately, there will be a dearth of gangster pictures, contrary to an earlier outlook. Credit for this is due to a new code adopted by the Johnston Office, prohibiting the making of films glorifying living or recently dead racketeers. Several producers got caught with gangster-story properties on their hands, including one of the late Al Capone. Probably some device for evading the code will be invented to salvage their investments, but application of the new decree will result in the end of this sort of film for a while.

In summing up, it appears that the current year's production trend will be towards super-spectacles in the major studios based on widely known plays or fiction, and even lower-quality films more cheaply produced among the independents. One word of caution relative to the outlook from the majors is in order. Development of expensive or prestige-story properties is no assurance of a product welcome to an intelligent, adult mind.

The producer-director Mervin Leroy, late of Warner Brothers and now back at MGM, faced the issue squarely in a Press release, in which he acknowledged that poor pictures, rather than the recent 'Red' scare, have alienated many patrons. The next day Cecil B. DeMille echoed similar sentiments, allowing himself to be quoted in these words: 'Hollywood's circus era is over. The age of mind is now upon Hollywood. An art form has grown into one of the great industries of the world. No other art form in human history has experienced such a transformation. The public is serious about Hollywood'.

Unfortunately, Mr DeMille does not seem serious about the public. His last opus, *The Unconquered*, a story of Indian massacres, intrigue, heroic escapes and romance, contains so many cinematic clichés and implausible feats that it can be fairly compared with the most banal 'horse opera'.

To cite just one example: the high dramatic point of the film occurs when the hero and heroine, in a mad escape from hostile savages, shoot the Niagara Falls in a canoe. Midway in their lethal descent, Mr Gary Cooper reaches out, grabs a handy limb from an overhanging tree, and saves both himself and Miss Goddard by a superhuman muscular effort. The audience simply howled. There were more laughs throughout this supposedly serious drama in the wrong places than in Chaplin's *Monsieur Verdoux* in the right places.

If this sort of thing is Mr DeMille's conception of 'the age of mind on Hollywood', it is clear that the motion-picture renaissance is not due in Hollywood in 1948.

THE SCIENTIFIC FILM

JOHN MADDISON

> 'Having laid bare the heart of a living animal,
> they pointed the camera lens towards it, and left
> the shutter open. The images they obtained made
> a double outline, representing the extreme po-
> sitions taken up by the heart. At these moments,
> indeed, the heart remains motionless for an in-
> stant, and its form is recorded on the sensitive
> plate. ... '
>
> MAREY (about 1882) on the work
> of the physiologists Ominus and
> Martin quoted by Georges Sadoul.

LATTERLY, critics of the fine arts have been discovering the revealing powers of the motion-picture camera in their own field.
'It sets fire to everything,' says one of them. This is flamboyant
language, and in the experimental sciences the potentialities of
the camera and its excitements would no doubt be more soberly
described. Yet even before the invention of cinematography,
the camera's extraordinary powers for observing and recording
movement were recognised; in 1874 Janssen had photographed
from an observation point in Japan the transit of Venus, and in
the 1880's Marey had pursued his series of researches into animal
movement. In their case, the camera-gun was a weapon for
analysing the movement of planets, birds, horses and men
walking, running and bicycling. The efforts of Lumière, Edison,
Paul and others provided an instrument able, not only to analyse, but also to put moving phenomena together again on a
screen. Since then, refinements of camera mechanisms, lenses
and emulsions have given the investigator a fascinating new
mastery over time-scales and dimensions. Nearly half a century

117

of scientific cinematography has brought many revelations of the beauty and harmony of the physical universe, and some notable extensions to our knowledge of it. But the story is not a coherent one. Mainly, it concerns the individual achievements of outstanding pioneers and teams of workers. If cinematography is to become what it should be, a new international language, lucid, gracious and disciplined, for recording and interpreting science, a number of obstacles must be overcome. Some of these are purely economic; some are inherent in the youthfulness of the medium. None is insuperable, and of recent years an encouraging pattern of co-ordination has been slowly emerging. In some countries, for example, Britain, France, Belgium, Canada and Switzerland, organisations have been voluntarily set up to support and to enlarge the scope of scientific cinema. Most important, representatives of twenty-two countries met in Paris in the autumn of 1947 to create an international association which aims at linking and extending effort and achievement throughout the world.

For brilliant and sustained experiment, one must begin with the biological sciences and with two cinematographers, whose origins were sharply contrasted. Some forty years ago, the cinema laid its allurements on two young men. One, Jean Comandon, was a student at the Paris School of Medicine, preparing his doctor's thesis on the spirochæte of syphilis. The other, Percy Smith, was a clerk at the Board of Education in London, with a passion for natural history. With both of them (Smith died in 1944, Comandon is still working at the Pasteur Institute of Garches), their attachment to the cinema remained lifelong.

Though, during the first World War, he made anti-T.B. propaganda films, Comandon's chief contribution has been the patience and ingenuity with which he has combined cinematography and other techniques of visual investigation. One of his first films, remarkable in its day, employed Röntgen rays; he is, therefore, a pioneer of cine-radiography. But it is in bringing together the cine-camera and the microscope that he and his assistant, de Fonbrune, have shown their greatest skill. Since 1929 they have, in their cine-laboratory at Garches, solved many delicate problems in the lighting, protection and manipulation of living cells and other micro-organisms. The Garches cine-micrographic equipment is, indeed, a unique engineering achievement. Comandon is able to demonstrate, with superb visual clarity, his surgical operations on micro-organisms, because of two other pieces of equipment devised at Garches: the micro-forge, in which infinitely tiny surgical instruments, scalpels, hooks, etc., are fashioned, and the micro-manipulator, which scales down enormously the action of the human hand as it moves at will the living organisms beneath the microscope for the camera to record. The results of Comandon's work on the screen – this remote and tiny drama of movement and change – are often breath-taking, even to the non-specialist. But it is important to remember also that Comandon is a member of a research institute; such works as *Champignons Prédateurs* and *Greffes de Noyau d'Amibe* have contributed to the common store of our knowledge of biological phenomena.

For a cinema technician of an entirely different order, Georges Méliès, the cinema's main attraction was, he said, that it was 'handwork'. There can be no doubt that this was also true in the case of Percy Smith. Those who have visited his house at Southgate all speak of the ingenious film machinery to be found there and of Smith's flair for creating these devices, often with his own hands, out of the most unexpected materials – dripping water moved the first machine he built for filming plant life. Though his other achievements in what he and his collaborators Mary Field and J. V. Durden have called cine-biology were of high quality, it was mainly in the use of speeded-up cinematography for registering plant growth that his contribution to the scientific film lay. As Bruce Woolfe, with whom Smith began to work in 1921 on the Secrets of Nature films, has remarked, his botanical films opened up fresh possibilities to the cinematograph camera. Another of his collaborators, Dr E. J. Salisbury, has pointed to the other important aspect of Smith's peculiar talents. 'It was in the patience necessary to ascertain the precise phase of a phenomenon that best lent itself to pictorial record that Percy Smith exhibited so high a degree of skill almost amounting to genius.'

Besides the stop-motion work in which Smith excelled, high-speed cinematography can be combined with the microscope to produce records only available through film. At the 1947 Paris Scientific Film Congress, the zoologist, Storch of Vienna, presented with wit and enthusiasm slow-motion ciné-micrographic studies of freshwater animalculæ. In this same field, an immense step forward has been taken by combining the cinema camera with a new kind of microscope – the phase-contrast microscope. This new technique is particularly valuable for the study of *transparent* micro-organisms. Its most spectacular use has, so far, to my knowledge, been in the German film made by Zernicke of Jena about the division of the sperm cells of a grasshopper. This film was also shown in Paris in 1947, together with three research records using both phase contrast and polarised light by Hughes of the Strangeways laboratory in Cambridge. Hughes' work is based on the techniques originally developed by Canti at Bart's, in the 1920's and early 1930's, but the newer methods have greatly increased the scope of the cinematography of living tissues and opened up important new possibilities both for research and for demonstration films. Hughes needs, and should get, the encouragement and support of professional film-makers and film-making organisations.

The motion-picture camera is immensely flexible, and a constant and untiring observer of nature. It can register, with an authenticity which continually surprises, the nuances of life. It gives us the power both to compress and to magnify time. If its most widely known applications have hitherto been in the field of biology, there can be no doubt of its usefulness in the other sciences. Some of the striking applications of high-speed cinématography to the physical sciences still lie probably shrouded in the archives of war. In astronomy, Leclerc has shown how revealing speeded-up cinema records of solar eclipses and other phenomena can be. The films he has made with the collaboration of the eminent astronomer Lyot, in the Caucasus and in Sweden and at the Pic du Midi observatory, are contributions to science as well as being dramatic portrayals on the screen. It is a sad comment on the economics of scientific film-making that Leclerc, in order to earn a living, has had to give up this work, and to join a news-reel company. Watson Watts's use of the same speeded-up technique for the study of cloud formations in *The Story of a Disturbance* demonstrated another potential use which does not seem to have been much exploited since. The only other example of this sort of cloud study I have seen has been a Kodachrome record made in America in which, against a blue sky, white clouds perform an amusing and ultimately rather monotonous Ride of the Valkyries. A pre-war German film uses an entirely different technique of research and demonstration in meteorology; authentic weather charts covering all stages of a disturbance are animated by cartoon methods. The resulting mobile patterns provide an absorbing spectacle. Few of the many films made in Germany, by UFA particularly, have been available in Britain. Here is one of a number which it is hoped specialists may soon have the opportunity of seeing.

There are other less obvious fields in which the film camera can both increase the sum of our knowledge and fire the imagination. Germaine Prudhommeau's *La Réanimation des Danseurs de la Grèce Antique* uses the camera to investigate a problem in archæology. Figures on Greek vases and in friezes have been made to dance, as the Greeks might have done centuries ago, by the employment of the ordinary techniques of the animated cartoon. Animated drawings can also provide us with moving patterns to reflect mathematical concepts. How exciting these can be visually Kysela of Prague has recently demonstrated with his film *The Hyperbole*. The pioneer in this field has, of course, been Robert Fairthorne, and it is a pity that he has not continued the experiments he began before the war. For him, the film has a place of its own among visual aids, because the events it can create are free from the laws of mechanics. In the social sciences, the main contribution has come from the British school of documentary, but the long series of psychiatric studies made by the U.S. Army Medical Services reveal the hidden motion-picture camera as a sensitive and illuminating instrument for recording human reactions.

It is usual to think only of research and investigation when one speaks of experiment in the scientific film. But experiments in the presentation of scientific data, in relating the achievements of science to society and evaluating the consequences of progress for the citizen, all these are of equal importance. Percy Smith's work, for example, was remarkable, not only as research, but also because it represented an attempt, lasting over twenty-five years, to interpret science to the ordinary cinema-goer. Experiment in the presentation of science can take a number of forms, and it is in this respect that the documentary school established by Grierson has from the beginning sought to establish links between the specialist and the technician and the general public. To my mind, two films from this school are outstanding demonstrations of documentary's power to interpret science. The first is Elton and Bell's *Transfer of Power*, in which, within the space of twenty minutes, the story of the evolution of a technical device is not only told with lucidity and coherence, but is related to the social pattern. In *Blood Transfusion*, Rotha and Nieter drive home the point, with an ingenious bringing together of actuality, models and animated drawings, that scientific achievement is a co-operative international business. The work of British documentary technicians in using films as a mass educational technique under Government and other sponsorships, and its offshoots in Canada and elsewhere, is too large a theme to be developed here. But its importance is twofold. It has illumined the social function of science in countless ways. In *Enough to*

Eat, Housing Problems and *Smoke Menace*, it first afforded a pulpit to such progressive interpreters of science as Huxley, Haldane and Boyd Orr. In war, it demonstrated with *Potato Blight* and *Scabies* and a hundred other films how laboratory findings and specialised techniques could be given a wider currency. More recently, *Personnel Selection – Officers* and *Children Learning by Experience* have shown how the camera can expound attempts to apply objectivity and good sense to the more delicate problems of human behaviour. Not less important than the new techniques of production explored has been the vast non-theatrical experiment in distributing films to audiences outside the commercial movie houses. Fresh images of scientific achievement have been carried into schoolroom, workshop, byre and forest clearing and the thousand and one places where men meet together.

Perhaps only in the Soviet Union has there been anything approaching this in scale and continuity. The Soviet scientific films we have been privileged to see indicate how great a function of their specialised studios is the popular interpretation of science. Unfortunately, examples of films from the U.S.S.R. of direct scientific interest seen by audiences in Western Europe have been too few – *Experiment in the Revival of Organisms, Artificial Œsophagus, In the Sands of Central Asia,* a handful of others and, many years ago, Pudovkin's *Mechanics of the Brain.*

A genre of film-making, in which a good deal more experiment is needed, is in the reconstruction of important pieces of scientific endeavour and in biographical studies of the great men of science. It is only through the development of these genres that we shall educate the public in rejecting the faked distortions of history which disgrace our screens. The manner in which the Dartington Hall Film Unit retraced certain parts of Darwin's Voyage of the Beagle in their film *Galapagos* was a fine effort of this sort of thing at the classroom level. The last film to be completed by Jean Painlevé is an attempt to create a new sort of scientific film biography for the ordinary film-goer. He and

Georges Rouquier have made an absorbing study out of the biological work of Louis Pasteur. Using an unknown, unprofessional actor, a Paris workman with a strong facial resemblance to the great *savant*, Rouquier has made the scenes in which Pasteur fought against the prejudices of contemporary scientists come to life again on the screen. But the main excitement of the film lies in the way Painlevé, through innumerable hours spent with camera and microscope in his cine-laboratory, has retold the long tale of Pasteur's triumph over the microbes. Painlevé's passionate and nervous commentary enhances the visual impact of the many cinemicrographic studies in the film. Audaciously he tells the public that they are seeing, through the movie camera, this drama unfolding in a manner which would have surprised even Pasteur himself. Painlevé is, of course, an outstanding worker in all the fields of scientific cinema of which we have been speaking – research, record, demonstration and interpretation. Motor-racing champion, under-water diver, biologist and creator of the most elegant of *bijouterie*, he is a strange Renaissance figure of the modern cinema. For twenty years he has been triumphantly demonstrating that scientific film can be the most engrossing of art forms. With *La Pieuvre* and *Le Vampyr* he has combined legend and the more prosaic face of reality. In *Crevettes*, his superb skill as an editor and cameraman is matched by Jaubert's evocative music. Like his fellow-countryman, Cousteau, who, in *Paysages du Silence,* has depicted the dream landscapes to be found beneath the waters of the Mediterranean, Painlevé brings an element of fantasy and imagination to everything he touches. And this is surely not the least of the contributions which the film can make to our understanding of science. Film can break down frontiers which often divide the man of science and the artist, frontiers as outmoded as those so-called faculties of the mind which are sometimes used to label them.

(*Reprinted from* Experimental Film, *a forthcoming book edited by Roger Manvell and to be published by the Grey Walls Press.*)

BOOKS ABOUT FILMS

EDITED BY R. K. NEILSON BAXTER

★

CENSORSHIP is a subject which has often concerned the film-maker, the audience, the Church and the State. The first associations of the film, from which it is only now bit by bit freeing itself, ensured bad taste, vulgarity, sometimes even indecency. In America, always a country of contradictions, 'self-regulation' was the method adopted to keep the movies clean for the susceptible youth and maiden. Hence that remarkable organisation, the Motion Picture Producers' Association of America, otherwise known as the Hays Office.

In the contemporary history of the American film it is an organisation meriting serious study. Two books have recently attempted this, namely *The Hays Office* by Raymond Moley (Bobbs-Merrill Company) and *Freedom of the Movies* by Ruth Inglis (University of Chicago Press). Of the latter, an analysis of some importance, Davide Boulting, editress of *Documentary Film News*, has provided us with the following review:

'*They sought it with thimbles, they sought it with care;*
They pursued it with forks and hope;
They threatened its life with a railway-share;
They charmed it with smiles and soap.'

The Snark may have been a Boojum, but in this case the Snark most definitely is the Perfect-Way-to-Censor-Movies-without-Censoring-Them and it is almost as certain that everyone engaged in this Hunt would 'softly and suddenly vanish away' should their particular Snark be found.

Boojums apart, a new means of communication has only to be invented for man to start finding some means of censoring that means of communication. In earlier centuries people were content on the whole to accept the regulations of the leaders of the day. With the twentieth century and wider education, man is no longer content to accept orders as to what he must do or see or hear from the leaders of his State or Church; he reserves the right to judge for himself, the right for each individual to be his own censor of what he will read or hear or look at.

On the other hand, man also realises that he is a social animal, that he must consider the effect on other people of something which he may be able to judge for himself. He may feel that it will do him no harm to read some book which he does not consider suitable for his young son. In such a case he can either keep the book from his son or he can give it to the boy accompanied by an explanation which will enable the book to be assessed at its right value and not only on its surface merit.

But the cinema, as we have heard ad nauseam, is a means of mass communication, and as such cannot be individually controlled. The cinema is open to all and is as potentially a force for evil as it is a force for good. Because of this danger some form of control had to be evolved and this control had to be wide enough not to become repressive and therefore dangerous in a world working towards freedom.

Miss Inglis has examined the position in her book 'Freedom of the Movies.' She is one of the staff of the Commission on the Freedom of the Press in the United States, and in her report she has covered every inch of the ground. Beginning with a general sketch of the social rule of the screen, she passes to the history of the development of Hollywood (this is most necessary if the reader is to understand the later chapters) and then on to discuss the various attempts at censorship and the present method which is known as 'self-regulation.' The book proper ends with Conclusions and Recommendations, but the Appendix, which gives the Production Code, makes fascinating reading.

The meat is there – good, strong and unrationed. But meat alone without any of the usual trimmings can lie heavy on the stomach accustomed to eating it with gravy, Yorkshire and Two Veg. The subject of the need for and the growth of the 'Self-regulation' of the screen is undoubtedly fascinating but one feels that it could somehow have been put over in a more interesting, a more digestible form. Dates, statistics, initials and lists of Bodies make the book excellent for reference but heavy going for anyone who wishes to get a rough picture of the general situation. The subject is important enough to be made palatable to the general public and not just to those who work in and around the film industry and may therefore be willing and able to plough through the rather dreary pages in which the pith of the argument is unfolded. It is the man in the street who is affected by the Hays Office and not, exclusively, the man in the studio.

As it stands, however, the book is obviously meant for the person often referred to as the 'serious student of the cinema' and, as such, it cannot but be acceptable. Perhaps the most interesting section is the chapter on self-regulation in operation with its dissertation on the form and general principles of the Motion Picture Production Code. One may question whether many Hollywood films (or British ones, for that matter) conform to the three general principles:

1. No picture shall be produced which will lower the moral standards of those who see it. Hence the sympathy of the audience shall never be thrown to the side of crime, wrongdoing, evil or sin.
2. Correct standards of life, subject only to the requirements of drama and entertainment, shall be presented.
3. Law, natural or human, shall not be ridiculed, nor shall sympathy be created for its violation.

No doubt these principles are highly laudable, but they do not appear, on results, to be very practicable.

Mr. Joseph I. Breen's letters to producers who have sub-mitted scripts are a joy to read. The royal 'we' occurs through-out, and in a gentle, paternal fashion he pats the producer on the head and points him the way he ought to go. I particularly liked Case H, 'Scene 226 et seq. If you plan a foreign release please have in mind that the British Board of Film Censors always deletes the Lord's Prayer,' and Case D, 'Scene 291 et seq., we assume there will be no unacceptable exposure of A's person.'

Miss Inglis is of the opinion that 'censorship can be avoided if the industry faces its responsibilities,' and that 'self-regula-tion' can be improved and made into a really effective control. She emphasises the need to raise the level of public taste and shows how this is being attempted in America. Her contention is that, with a higher level of appreciation in the audience, the film will improve and control will not be so important. It will be interesting to see how things develop – right now it is hard to imagine that the demand for 'better' films can ever become so strong that it will act as 'self-regulation.'

Anyhow, good luck to the Hunting of the Snark, and let's hope that the Banker will suffer and that the Snark will not turn out to be a Boojum.

The other book is in a different category. Mr Moley is a rather naïf neophytic type who thinks Mr Hays was quite wonderful. Through his adoration of the magus, however, comes a lot of most valuable information which does not emerge quite so clearly from Miss Inglis's book, even though hers is based on a piece of formal research. The degree, for instance, to which the Motion Picture Producers' Association is under the influence of the Roman Catholic Church and some of the more reactionary women's societies, and the degree to which Hays became a tsar whose dicta had to be accepted un-challenged are a clear contradiction of the principles on which 'self-regulation' should be based, and shows it up for the sham it is.

THE PENGUIN
FILM
REVIEW

8

CONTRIBUTIONS INCLUDE

Eisenstein on Stereoscopic Film
The European Cartoon
The Film 'Hamlet'
Contemporary French Cinema
Target for Film Societies
The Jewish Theme in the Cinema

ONE SHILLING AND SIXPENCE

THE PENGUIN
FILM REVIEW

Editorial Board : R. K. Neilson Baxter
Roger Manvell *and* H. H. Wollenberg
Executive Editor : Roger Manvell

8

PENGUIN BOOKS

LONDON

1949

First Published January 1949
PENGUIN BOOKS LIMITED
Harmondsworth, Middlesex, England

MADE AND PRINTED IN GREAT BRITAIN
by Hazell, Watson & Viney, Ltd.
Aylesbury and London

CONTENTS

*

EDITORIAL 7

EUROPEAN CARTOON
John Halas and Joy Batchelor 9

THE FILM OF 'HAMLET' Roger Manvell 16

THAT 'FEMININE ANGLE'
Catherine de la Roche 25

ABOUT STEREOSCOPIC CINEMA
S. M. Eisenstein 35

THE JEWISH THEME IN CONTEMPORARY
CINEMA H. H. Wollenberg 46

CONTEMPORARY FRENCH CINEMA
Jean-George Auriol 51

BRITISH FILMS AND THEIR AUDIENCE
A. L. Vargas 71

TOWARDS A SCIENCE OF ART
Charles Dekeukeleire 77

TARGET FOR FILM SOCIETIES
Forsyth Hardy 86

POST-WAR AMERICAN DOCUMENTARIES
Richard Griffith 92

5

PSYCHOLOGY OF FILM EXPERIENCE
                              Hugo Mauerhofer   103

THE MUSIC OF 'HAMLET' AND 'OLIVER
    TWIST'   John Huntley   110

THE ART OF THE FILM STRIP
                         Curt A. Laurentzsch   117

BOOKS ABOUT FILMS
                Edited by R. K. Neilson Baxter   123

'FULL FATHOM FIVE...'   The Editors   128

ILLUSTRATED SECTION
                      Compiled by Roger Manvell

EDITORIAL

*

YOU cannot get entertainment out of a stone. It may be polished or it may be precious, but the blood of human feeling cannot be found in it. British films for the most part have lost that human touch and vitality of theme which constantly distinguished them five or six years ago. They have turned increasingly to a polished presentation, a surface beauty which costs money but does not illuminate human relations or help to tell a story. They have adopted more than ever the stereotypes of characterisation which derive from cheap fiction, and no doubt suit admirably the impoverished acting of most of our younger stars and starlets.

It is no use increasing quota without increasing quality. If we are not to see our cinema attendances drop during the twenty-two British weeks in the film year and rise steeply during the thirty American weeks, we must make films once more which hold people in their seats, willy-nilly. Hollywood can make films of this quality when it is on its mettle. So can Britain if we pay vital attention to what our films have to say and the creative treatment they are given.

For in the end such considerations as these go to the roots of all good art, whatever medium the artist is using. We need to get back to the strong drama of present-day realities, the absorbing material of our everyday lives, problems and relationships. The new world is surely exciting enough, yet our screen-writers and film-makers isolate themselves farther and still farther from reality in a Nirvana of costume melodrama and psychological pretentiousness.

It is hard enough in the circumstances to judge the capabilities of the new actor or actress. The little empty-faced boys and girls who stare smiling from the pages of our fan magazines may serve well enough as mannequins to show off British

7

clothes to audiences overseas, but they must first of all sustain supporting parts and eventually leading characters if they are to be useful in their job, which is the profession of acting. One of the reasons why the winds of critical favour are always blowing in the direction of Continental films (whether Italian, Swedish or French) is that this obvious factor is not overlooked there in choosing the casts of important films. Their stars and supporting players have poise and mastery: they suggest they know life and have experienced something of its mystery, its tragedy and its gaiety. This in the end is the human quality which holds audiences. Most of our younger stars can only smile or look startled. They have no poise, no strength, no understanding. As far as our older supporting players are concerned, their numbers seem so diminished that they have the impossible task of appearing in practically every British film until all sense of character differentiation is lost in a series of personal appearances. The art of real character-acting is gone when parts are merely adapted to suit actors.

It is impossible to believe that British talent and imagination have burnt themselves out so soon after their prolonged triumph. Yet nowadays Press shows and premiers, which should surely sometimes be the scenes of wild enthusiasm and the fêting of artists, have turned into dim occasions for the desultory clapping of interested parties. The general atmosphere is that of having seen just another picture. Too often those responsible seem themselves indifferent to what they have done. Real films are born out of excitement, tears, intense artistic rivalries and the strongest emotional feeling. They are not just the completion of another job of work.

By the time these words are read the signs of regeneration may have appeared. Retrenchment is the rule of the day, and it was retrenchment which set the scene for our earlier successes. Imagination and ingenuity once before took the place of swollen budgets. This may again be the true way ahead.

EUROPEAN CARTOON

A SURVEY OF THE ANIMATED FILM

JOHN HALAS and JOY BATCHELOR

*

IN the opening phases of cinematography, live-action and animated films had the same objective; both regarded the cinema as an opportunity for magic, and both were, very largely, 'trick films'.

The pioneer films of Georges Méliès, for instance, are inspired by a wish to realise the impossible. In his *A Trip to the Moon* (1902) he presents a fantasy world peopled by real people in unreal situations. Up to the beginning of the 1914–18 war, directors remained fascinated by the possibility of reaching into the supernatural by means of the camera, and the work of this early period was, in consequence, highly imaginative.

Imagination was, however, gradually superseded as technique improved. Better photography, new conceptions of editing film, the discovery of optical mixes, fades, montage, led the live-action camera right away from its magic world, leaving the supernatural almost entirely to animated film. There are exceptions, of course, when the live-action camera remembers itself and gets up to some of its old tricks. The *Topper* films and *A Matter of Life and Death* are notable examples. But when the live-action camera goes out for pure fantasy as opposed to 'tricks', the results are less happy.

Jean Cocteau's film *Beauty and the Beast* could not avoid creating the impression that all the actors were *heavier* than was necessary. The mechanism of some effects was so contrived as to make the medium in which the fantasy was carried out seem unsuitable.

9

But the main, and overwhelming, trend of the live-action film has been towards realism, and in this field it has outstripped, not only the animated film, but the theatre as well. The old distinction of theatre as living entertainment and the cinema as a shadow world can no longer be made. The theatre is revealed as a box of contrivances; it becomes once again a play with players when faced with the new realism of films like Rossellini's *Open City* or *Germany, Year Zero*. The power of the live-action film when used to the full, as in these two films, lies in the fact that it is able to enlarge human emotion until it is greater than life-size. It has the power to analyse and portray human behaviour under the microscopic penetration of the camera lens, and thus create a super-realistic effect on the audience. The degree of realism thus experienced inescapably defines the rôle of theatre and animated film. The theatre, lacking the mobility of the screen and the enlarging powers of the camera, and less free to control the time element, is at a disadvantage, at least in creating realism. It may be that, as in the case of the animated film, the theatre will find it can best exploit fantasy.

While realism is the stronghold of the live-action camera, it is also a limitation. The live-action camera can select, edit, distort, dramatise, but only what is already *there* to be photographed. If it is the live-action film's job to present physical reality, animated film is concerned with metaphysical reality – not how things look, but what they mean. Animated film properly begins where live-action film leaves off, and it is important to realise that animated film should never attempt to do the things that live-action film can do so consummately.

One of the outstanding advantages of the animated film is its power of 'penetration'. The internal workings of an organism can easily be shown in this medium. The depths of a man's soul is more than a phrase to the animator: it can also be a picture.

With the departure from realism the time element gains in control. The speed of the film can be accelerated or decelerated in order to emphasise or accent ideas. Live-action film can do this to a certain extent, and everyone is familiar with slow motion and photomicrography. Animated film carries things a great deal farther by prolonging action that would normally take a fraction of a second to many minutes. Where live-action film can show only physical changes during such a time-lag, animation can portray organic change.

Animation can play another trick with time by portraying the future or the past. Here the advantage over live-action film is that it can be done without economic headaches. The past can be reconstructed at will and plans for the future can be materialised with comparative ease on the animated screen.

Selection is as important to animation as it is to live action, but it is carried to greater lengths. Live-action camera selects from what it *sees*, animation can pick out an imagined object, transport it to any required screen position, and relegate unwanted material to obscurity. Exaggeration is also used to assist in this selective process; exaggeration, not only of form and colour, but of speed, emotion and character.

Animated film is also adept at portraying the invisible. The working of radar, molecular construction, principles of sound waves, theory of sight, and the action of wind and tide, can all be visualised through the medium.

Inanimate concepts, such as distension, multiplication and division, can be made animate and visually comprehensible.

It is both easy and economical to symbolise humans or conceptions in animation. A single white dot may represent many thousands of people, an arrow may represent the flow of water in a pipe, and a circle may indicate pressure. Equally important is the power of characterisation. Germs may appear as ravening hordes, a housefly can be a monster, a car can be shown as a hardworking servant or a killer.

But with all these potentialities the creator in this medium knows that he has to start with a clean sheet – a blank page in front of him. The live-action camera searches for the best angles and selects its vision from an already existing background. For the animator no such world is in existence – he must build up his ideas from the 'germ' stage. He will be limited by the fact that whatever he conceives will have to be carried out by a hand-made process and photographed by a camera that can do only what it is told – no lighting effects, no camera angles. Nor can he expect actors to contribute their individual talents directly. The animator is thus obliged to observe the tenets of animated film if he is to show results.

From the point of view of finance this hand-made process is more expensive than most live-action filming. This fact may explain why the American cartoon film industry is more widely developed than any of the European ones. The basic reason for this fact is economic. Only the American film market, with its octopus-like world distribution, can cover the cost of a colour cartoon. This economic advantage of the last two or three decades has given Walt Disney, Fischinger, Schlesinger and others the chance to develop and exploit fully their own particular style. Indeed, in the way of comic type of cartooning, approximating to the level of newspaper comic-strips, no better work has yet been done, and in the music-hall style, burlesque cartoon from Disney and the others, excellent results have been achieved. Both the photographic quality (mostly due to better equipment) and the smoothness of animation are well above the European standard. The skill of American cartoonists in timing action is admirable too. All qualities combined add up to a technical supremacy which, in the future, will be most difficult to surpass. From the mental point of view, however, the advancement of the American cartoons was less fruitful. Apart from the full exploitation of the physical aspect of animation, most of the cartoon's potentialities were untouched. The ideas of American cartoons are based on the exaggeration of physical forces. Gravity is fully caricatured, as when Pluto and Goofy halt in the air and jump back to the rooftop again. Friction is exaggerated when Donald Duck's hammer hits a petrified tree and the vibration is transferred to his body. Pursuit, the element of most cartoon climaxes, is a calculated caricature of the time element, a physical exaggeration of speed in its extreme. Together they add up to all the bags of tricks which the average American cartoonist employs. With this repertoire he is able to achieve a series of movements full of dynamic force and is able to provide excitement with it. The spectator is drawn well into the action, given no time to relax, and his emotion stirred.

The other and more valuable contribution of American cartoons is the sense of characterisation. The vast galaxy of Disney's characters especially are conceived with full roundness. Most of his leading characters from Donald Duck to Goofy have concise one-track solidity easily identifiable and very pure. They each represent an over-simplified aspect of human character. Goofy the lovable fool, Donald the impatient and hot-tempered, Mickey the helpful and understanding. They remain, however, as far as the mental conception is concerned, on an over-simplified adolescent level.

The cinema audience, for whom other types of cartoon are so far unknown, accepts the standard established by the American ones as absolute. They hardly know that the major influences were derived from such European cartoonists as, in the early days, Emile Cole, and later Fischinger, whose work influenced Walt Disney to produce *Fantasia* and other experimental films. In spite of the very mean screening space allotted to cartoons and almost dominated by American examples, some of our own and some of the new European cartoons find their way to cinemas. Without being able to afford the expensive technical polish so characteristic of American cartoons, these new films have offered something new to the audience. Up to this period the audience automatically accepted its dose of gagging from cartoons. On the routine music-hall comedy level it has been served well, but after several years of the same diet the audience has now grown tired of it. The conception and technique remained on the familiar lines, no new ideas came along, and the stagnation of the American cartoon industry has been handed over to the audience. This may be the reason why they reacted so favourably to the new European school of animation.

While making use of the American exploits in good action timing, the new school is far more sensitive to design. The pictorial composition has been promoted into the foreground. The possibilities of presenting pictorial art, which is so deep-rooted in Europe, are considered. Colour, which is usually used as an incidental effect to increase realism, has been given a chance to show that, used differently, it could contain new experiences. By making use of chamber music and inviting eminent composers to score our music, our sound track has been lifted from the background and given equal importance with the picture.

The Czechoslovakian State-financed cartoon film unit, led by the artist Trinka, drives towards the new conception. The French cartoon film group 'Les Gemeaux', under Paul Grimault, did valuable work in the same style. The Russian cartoon film group functioning in Moscow, employing 400 artists, shows tendencies towards better understanding of pictorial composition. In fact, Disney's own animators and some of his writers formed into a new unit under the title of 'United Productions of America', and are doing work which in style and skill is much nearer to the level of the *New-Yorker* than the penny comic-strips, and pictorially much funnier.

Trinka has a pure sense of graphic design. In his *Gift*, a small abstract film, he fully employs it with the greatest charm. With the sureness of an experienced painter he reaches a higher pictorial level in all his films than has been achieved so far by the American cartoons. The same result is achieved by Paul Grimault, with the exception that his films lack the warmth and colour sense of the former. *The Magic Flute* and *The Chimney Thief* contain sequences composed in the idiom of graphic art and backgrounds designed with typical French taste.

The fact that graphic art finds good expression through the latest European cartoons is a sign of a search towards new ways of expression through animation. The work of Georges Méliès as a story-teller, Emile Cole as a designer, Fischinger as an explorer of film timing, is already a prominent record of past achievements on which to look back. The American style of cartooning has shown what can be done technically. But so far no major attempts have been made to open wide the rich fields of satire on the level of Lear or Swift for cartoon, on the one hand, or explore the fields of Cézanne's or Picasso's pictorial exploits for animation, on the other.

Animation, with its transforming, penetrating and symbolising powers, has already graduated from the very bottom of the bookshelves to higher levels. And as far as its pictorial potentialities go, it is ready to enrich visual art with a fourth dimension, the element of movement and time, and revolutionise static painting from its very base. The animated picture of the future will be appreciated, not only in terms of its comic potentialities, but for its contribution to poetry, music, ballet and pictorial art.

THE FILM OF 'HAMLET'

ROGER MANVELL

*

EVERY so often there comes along a film which is as much an occasion as it is a work of art. This was true of Sir Laurence Olivier's production of Shakespeare's *Henry V* three years ago : its *première* and opening week had all the excitement of a great public event. It is now the same with *Hamlet*, Olivier's second experiment in the presentation of Shakespeare on the screen. The royal *première* was an event, and for nearly a year now critics and film-makers alike have been speculating on the results, for the adaptation of *Hamlet* seemed an insuperable task for the cinema. It is Shakespeare's most introspective play, his most complete study of the fashionable psychological malaise of his period, the 'melancholy' man, the man who lost the powers of action through too much speculation on the nature of what he feels he should do.* *Hamlet* (like so much of Shakespeare's work) is a play for our times, since civilisation seems to be passing through a phase of melancholy in this older sense of the word. Nevertheless, to lose the name of action, as Hamlet puts it, is to present the film-maker with a contradic-

---

* Simultaneously with the *première* of the film, Salvador de Madariaga's study of *Hamlet* was published. His interpretation of the character of Hamlet represents him as a self-centred and self-isolated man unable to accept duties and relationships outside his own personal interests and emotions. He has a touch of Machiavelli about him. Madariaga wishes us to put aside the romantic, soul-sick interpretation of Hamlet usual in nineteenth- and twentieth-century criticism, and look on Hamlet with the eyes of Shakespeare and his contemporaries. Olivier's own performance in the film is interesting from this point of view, since, although he adopts the usual contemplative, melancholy and romantic interpretation of the Prince, he plays the part with a cold pride which brings him at times very close to Madariaga's picture of Hamlet's character.

16

tion in his art, for the film is the art of observing action, the art of selecting either a broad canvas or a detail which directly or by implication tells the story. Shakespeare writing for the theatre unpacks the heart of his hero in the quintessence of words, in poetry of the finest symbols of meaning. In the cinema it is always the eye that has the advantage of the ear. Words too easily lose their hold on the attention, while the eye concentrates on the actor and the scene. It was a solution to this problem which Olivier had to find, and he has gone a long way towards resolving it in this impressive and provocative film.

Let us for a moment examine the artistic problem of whether Shakespeare should be filmed at all. This is a more important and a more particular problem than the general red herring of whether films should be made from plays. That stale issue can, I think, be disposed of quite easily by saying that the themes and the characters and the stories of many plays are quite suitable for adaptation into films, provided you realise, whilst you are on the job of adaptation, that film-making and play-making are two entirely different ways of capturing an audience's interest. In the theatre the emphasis is on the words spoken by the living players, who are giving a unique performance in the theatre each night before a unique audience: in the cinema the emphasis is on what I will call the *milieu* of the story, people, places, things all presented from a thousand different vantage-points with the universal eye of the film-director in control of what the audience will see and when they will see it. Words nearly always take second place in interest to moving pictures in well-made films.

Now it stands to reason you can put two or three cameras in various parts of a theatre and simply record the living performance of a play. Television does this and captures something of that 'immediate' feeling of being in the theatre with a snuffling, coughing audience. That is all right. But if this television viewing were recorded on film and shown in the cinemas cold, as it were, we should say that it made an appalling film, that no trouble had been taken to use the advantages of the mobile camera, or to use the visual intimacies, or alternatively, the spaciousness of motion picture art. In other words, to make a film of a play you have got to transmute it, change not its theme but the whole manner of its presentation.

Now what about Shakespeare? Shakespeare is an artistic institution. He is as much a poet as a theatre-man, and there is no need to argue the importance of his words. Both the immediate effect of this poetry and the qualities of new suggestion which last a lifetime of familiarity demand that the words come first in the real experience and enjoyment of his work. There is no question here of a transmutation being possible and Shakespeare at the same time remaining Shakespeare. In silent-film days some of Shakespeare's plays were filmed, like charades from Charles Lamb's synopses of Shakespeare's plots. Because Shakespeare cannot be adapted to the screen with the same ruthlessness as Edgar Wallace and remain the Shakespeare we recognise as our supreme poet and dramatist, artistic compromise is forced on the film-maker or a vandalism worse than death. And before we go on to see how the compromise works out in practice, do not forget that producers in the theatre like Reinhardt and Komisarjevski have tried to warm up Shakespeare with the visual luxuries of production-value, only to be beaten by the overriding power of visual suggestion in Shakespeare's descriptive poetry.

The film-maker is helped by Shakespeare in the rhythm of his dramatic structure. Shakespeare wrote for the most part for an open theatre, where the actor was free to go into the audience on the apron-stage or withdraw from it to the frame of the inner or upper stages. Unconsciously Shakespeare, in a simplified way, of course, wrote his plays along lines familiar to the modern screen-writer, breaking his action up and spreading it over a range of different places and different times, and varying the kind of action he uses from battles and royal pageants to those moments of close-up called soliloquies, which in his treatment often put aside the bombast rhetoric of the theatrical set-piece and become intimate reconstructions of thought and feeling.

Here is the compromise, then. Shakespeare's lesser plays, like *Henry V*, in which the poetry is closely bound up with a variety of immediate actions and quick glimpses of characterisation, are far easier to adapt to films than modern plays written for two or three settings in a picture-frame theatre. But the greater the play by Shakespeare the more significance he compressed into lines and speeches of poetry which challenge the imagination at a pitch that has made more than one critic say (wrongly, I believe, but none the less significantly) that their real value can only be enjoyed by the single reader protected in his solitude from the hurly-burly of the theatre, where the details of poetic meaning are lost in the general movement of the action.

Now *Hamlet*, to my mind, was the most difficult choice to have made from among the obvious great tragedies to put across in a moving-picture medium. It is true much happens which offers good visual possibilities, Hamlet meeting the Ghost, for instance, and the play-scene and the last duel. But the introspective, mysterious character of the Prince is entirely dependent for its revelation upon some of the greatest and most complex poetry in our language. If this sort of character-mystery were being conceived primarily in the cinema itself and not in Shakespeare's theatre, it would be done by a balance of revealing details of movement, facial expression, action and words, a poetry of atmosphere felt through observation at least as much as by the words given to that character. But Shakespeare is an artistic institution, and we must not therefore represent the character in this way. We must use Shakespeare's poetry itself.

Now you might say as a result of all this I ought to be promoting a law forbidding the filming of Shakespeare. I do not for a number of reasons. They are mainly these. First, Shakespeare — allowing for some judicious cutting, which in any case is a convention in the theatre itself — *dramatically* speaking, makes for at least as good filming on the screen as playing in a modern picture-frame theatre with its drop curtains and scenery. Second, from the point of view of characterisation, the film-studio can offer us a cast of players unequalled by any of our great companies in any one live production, and these performances, once filmed, are available to be shown all over the world to reveal the art of Shakespeare to those whose hearts were hardened by bad school-teachers or worse amateur performances. Lastly, an artist-producer who understands the need to stress the qualities of Shakespeare's verse can contrive by camera emphasis and reticence to direct an audience's attention to what is being said for, at any rate, limited spells of time. In other words, he must recognise the problems of the artistic compromise in bringing verbal poetry into a pictorial art, and mitigate them to the best of his ability. In my view, Sir Laurence Olivier has come nearest to some kind of a solution to these problems, which will, of course, always remain insoluble. My only wish is that he had tried *Antony and Cleopatra, Julius Cæsar, Macbeth, Othello* or *King Lear* first, because I think *Hamlet* the least immediately filmable of the great poetic tragedies, the least adaptable to the compromise I have mentioned.

As a film-producer Olivier is an inspired and imaginative amateur. *Hamlet* is only his second production, although, of course, he has acted in films for many years. He therefore approaches film-making with a boldness of spirit which often shocks the skilled technician. He is not afraid to make mistakes. There are mistakes in *Hamlet*; some descriptive speeches are illustrated with silent photographed action; for example, the murder of the old King as it is related by the Ghost, or the death of Ophelia in the stream. On the other hand, when the usurping King Claudius conspires with Ophelia's brother, Laertes, to kill Hamlet, the camera three successive times leaves the pair below at their table and travels up to the full height of the great columned chamber where they are sitting together. This is unorthodox, but I found it successful. Look, says the camera, here they are with their petty conspiracy to murder a noble man; look close upon them, and now, see how dwarfed they become lost in the desolate emptiness of the castle. In other parts of the action the camera steals along backwards and forwards in a half-circle behind a group of characters, now seeing this, now that, sometimes between their shoulders, making the viewer into a veritable eavesdropper and greatly increasing the sense of tension. This technique is used at its best in that wonderful scene when Hamlet goads the King's conscience with the Players' re-enactment of the murder of Hamlet's father. On the other hand, there is far too much time lost while the camera slips up and down the staircases and corridors of the strange mediæval castle which is the main scene for the film.

This castle was designed by Roger Furse and built under the direction of Carmen Dillon. It is wholly artificial, a massive, sombre frame for the picture of Hamlet's tragic fate. It has a vast central chamber, decorated with mediæval mural paintings. It has empty corridors and staircases which lead to smaller apartments, such as the Queen's bedroom. Curving stairways lead out on to the open ramparts, which reveal that the castle is built on a pinnacle of rock overlooking the slowly moving sea far below. When the Ghost of Hamlet's father appears on these ramparts, he is clothed in sea-mists which drift round his tall and fearful figure. These settings are impressive rather than beautiful; beauty is left to the details of costume and to the effects of photography and lighting. Often the backgrounds are mere darkness, with the human figures lit brightly in the foreground. It is then that Olivier's blonde hair, dyed for the film, glistens and justifies its fairness. The effects of grandeur are enhanced by using deep-focus photography, making the details of facial expression and decor alike clearly visible at all distances from the camera, and resulting in strange distortions normally unnoticed in the cinema, when a head in close-up may well be composed side by side with a full figure in the middle distance of the background. These effects are startling and can be used significantly. I should like at this point to add a word about the importance of Dr William Walton's fine musical score for the film. There are, I am told, fifty minutes of music in this two-and-a-half-hour film; for exactly a third of the time, therefore, the atmosphere and grandeur of the picture are heightened by Walton's exciting and often macabre music.

Although Olivier experiments in film technique, he takes few liberties with the interpretation of character. Hamlet himself is always a problem for the actor. He is really a young prince, a student with a still attractive mother. Yet Shakespeare in his usual manner became so absorbed in the inner nature of Hamlet that he endowed him with the mature wisdom of a man twice his years. It is usual to accept this dual aspect of Hamlet's character and play him both young and old, a man perhaps in his early thirties. Hamlet's mother, on the other hand, has to be played at about the same age. Olivier does not attempt to make himself very young; his Hamlet is strong, brooding and ironic, seldom a figure of pathos and never of madness. All his moments of madness are assumed, for in Elizabethan times to be mad was to gain a certain licence of expression and behaviour denied to the sane.

Eileen Herlie, in her first film, gives the Queen great beauty and a passive, sensuous quality. In her case Olivier allows himself a new development in the plot; it is implied, after the famous scene between mother and son in which he wrings her heart and shows her the guilt of her hasty marriage, that she has no further relation with the King, and in the last scene drinks the poisoned chalice in a vain attempt to save Hamlet from death. This new interpretation gives an effective touch of visual acting to the last exciting scene of the duel between Hamlet and Laertes, in which Hamlet is eventually wounded by the poisoned rapier. Basil Sydney makes King Claudius coarse and cunning, a strongly played character. Jean Simmons as Ophelia is extremely young, an innocent victim of her duty to her father. Olivier has stressed Polonius's use of her as a bait with which to catch her lover Hamlet, who suspects her feeling for him and rejects her with the violence of betrayed love.

The great moments of this play are the crucial scenes of passion, and the soliloquies. These intense close-ups of Hamlet's loneliness are played in movement, but mostly with still lips, the voice recording while the face stirs in thought. Occasionally a phrase will burst from Hamlet's lips, some flashing word of anger or excitement. This method of treatment (emphasised in the film version of O'Neill's *Strange Interlude* a decade back) makes the soliloquies as visually impressive as they are moving to hear, though its overuse can easily degenerate into a trick. 'To be or not to be', the soliloquy of suicide, is pondered on the highest rampart of the castle looking down into the sea, and it is placed after, and not before, the terrible nunnery scene with Ophelia. Although we may question the wisdom of this transposition, since it gives an entirely new and more commonplace reason for his desire to commit suicide (namely, the betrayal of his love by Ophelia), it makes an effective visual climax, since this section of the film works its way up to the topmost pinnacle of the castle for the soliloquy.

Four episodes further remain in the memory – the scene between Hamlet and his mother with its terrific attack, the mounting climax of the Players' scene which ends in a fantastic flurry of images of running figures as the guilty King cries out for lights, the scene with the Ghost on the ramparts, and the last tumult of action following the duel at the end of the play.

Olivier uses the pulse of mounting heartbeats to symbolise the approach of the Ghost with a curious added sound like the singing in one's ears before a fit of fainting. This remarkable effect he took over by arrangement from Jean-Louis Barrault's stage production of *Hamlet* in Paris, where it was first used. At the close of the film after the duel, Hamlet leaps down from a balcony and drives his sword through the terrified King. Then the body of Hamlet is borne out on to the castle ramparts commanding the sea as the light is failing, and a solemn march is played as the figures of his bearers climb up against the cloud streams of the thundery sky.

Like other major British pictures, this film to a certain extent labours under the weight of a calculated technique, and so loses the heart and the sweat of passionate feeling. Months of planning become too evident; everything seems too meticulous. Nevertheless, there is a nobility in the production, a desire to give everything that the studio can muster to make Shakespeare effective on the screen at a cost of half a million pounds. Nothing is spared in the effort to bring the world's most difficult play to a world audience which will, most likely, exceed in a couple of years the total number of persons who have ever seen the play in a theatre since the time of Shakespeare himself. This is a sobering thought, both for film-maker and critic. Does it justify the streamlining and the skilful cutting, the general simplification of a play the virtue of which may depend on its complexity? Will its success justify a further experiment in filming another of Shakespeare's greater plays? Olivier's own words about his production are, 'I feel that the film *Hamlet* should be regarded as an "Essay in Hamlet" and not as a film version of a necessarily abridged classic'. Two things, however, are certain: first, Shakespeare can be filmed effectively provided the artistic compromise involved is understood properly, and second, only through the film can his work be introduced to audiences amounting in a few months to millions.

(*This article is partly based on two broadcasts given by the writer, one on the Eastern Service and the other on the Third Programme of the B.B.C.*)

THAT 'FEMININE ANGLE'

CATHERINE DE LA ROCHE

*

Is there anything special to be said about woman and cinema? Usually, to discriminate between men and women in matters which equally concern both is to forget that, as women extend their activities, old distinctions between their interests and men's disappear. And, in essence, there's nothing peculiarly masculine or feminine in cinematography. But movieland, as we know it, is made up of all kinds of elements, real and unreal, and among them we have not one, but many feminine (or is it pseudo-feminine?) angles.

They can be detected, first and foremost, in the calculations of the commercial branch, which plays an initial rôle in determining production policy. Theoretically, its policy is any and every thing that pays – exploiting new trends no less than playing safe. But how is the potential appeal to men and women of a proposition to be assessed? Past hits and flops give certain hints, but the reasons for public reactions can never be fully ascertained. Audience research might give more reliable data, but, so far, public opinion polls, fan mail analyses and the like have not been sufficiently scientific or comprehensive.

So, on the whole, front-office producers work on hunches, sometimes following trends, sometimes even leading them, but mostly, as we know, aiming to play safe and flooding the market with stereotyped productions, many of which, incidentally, flop as resoundingly as some of the experimental pictures considered so risky. But, if only by sheer weight of numbers, this kind of film cannot have failed to influence picture-goers, so, whatever their reactions, they are the reactions of a public conditioned over a period of years by standardised movies, adver-

25

tising and journalism. This makes it all the harder to sort things out in the two-way process of supply and demand, to ascertain what the public demand is and, especially, what it might be. The supply, at all events, is largely determined by speculation, and the executives who do the speculating, with very few exceptions, are men.

Aiming at the largest possible audiences, they are, of course, equally interested in both men and women as customers. (Actually, audiences seem to be representative of populations: in Britain, where men are heavily outnumbered by women, 62 per cent of the picture-goers are women; in America, where the figures are almost even, men and women go to the movies in fairly equal numbers.) Nevertheless, backers pay extraordinary attention to this thing called 'feminine interest', perhaps even more than to the things that are supposed to attract men, and one of the reasons for this is the widely held belief that it is the citizen's wife who sets the tone for the average film. The point at which their policy gets a thorough airing is when sales pressure is applied to a completed picture, and the trade press starts advising exhibitors of its selling value. This literature provides women with a first-rate opportunity to see themselves as men see them, though, unfortunately, it cannot offer the corresponding advantage to men.

Occasionally a film's appeal for men is made a specific selling-point, though showmen are usually reassured that it also has drawing power for women. This applied, for instance, to Naked City, a realistic account of the New York Homicide Bureau at work, and to Body and Soul, an exciting tale about boxing, exposing the evils of the fight racket. From film history one knows that leg shows were evolved with the particular idea of bringing tired business men to the pictures, that horse opera and gunplay are expected to appeal to the boyish elements in men and broad farce to the cap-and-muffler patrons of industrial halls, while feminine glamour of every description should irresistibly attract men of every description. But the points of appeal for men are comparatively rarely singled out. The men who work out film policy know themselves well enough at least to realise that most of their fundamental motives, good and bad, are common to the whole of humanity, and that the few which are peculiar to themselves are usually obvious enough without being stressed. It may occasionally be their policy to appeal to the baser instincts of humanity in general, but they never talk down to themselves as males, never treat themselves as an isolated species. And I have yet to hear of a 'sly masculine angle'.

'Feminine angles', on the other hand, crop up in startling profusion. Practically every other average movie is supposed to have them. According to trade press reviews the angle was powerful in *If Winter Comes, A Woman's Vengeance, The Sign of the Ram, Homecoming, Nightmare Alley*; terrific in *Life With Father*; good in *Bond Street*; sly in *A Double Life* and *Calling Paul Temple*; obvious in *Foxes of Harrow*; subtle in *My Own True Love*; and the occult theme of *Night has a Thousand Eyes* was considered peculiarly intriguing to women. In a fascinating lecture given a few years ago, W. J. Speakman, an exhibitor, ascribed the success of *Now Voyager* to the fact that it was psycho-analysis written down for the masses, giving the illusion of high-browism, and classified it as a typical woman's picture. Study advertising and trade press matter, and you will find that sentimentality, lavish and facile effects, the melodramatic, extravagant, naïvely romantic and highly coloured, the flattering, trivial and phony – these are the elements in pictures, whatever their overall qualities, that are supposed to draw women. Above all (and not surprisingly, since it's the opinion of men), woman's chief and all-consuming interest is Men. When you find a cliché stubbornly repeated through the decades, make no mistake – it might be a feminine angle: all those remorseful husbands, for instance, trying to atone for having forgotten 'what day it is' (wedding anniversary), you see them because once upon a time some business man made the discovery that women long to be appreciated, and his colleagues still think that's one of the most touching ways male appreciation of females can be put over.

That's the standard approach, the routine. Occasionally, however, film business men do manifest their appreciation of women's better qualities, even of their intelligence, by noting the compelling feminine appeal in pictures like *Gentleman's Agreement* or *All My Sons*, which were devoted to current social and moral issues. But generally, when it comes to the great serious productions like *Oliver Twist* or *Hamlet*, the appeal aimed at is universal and the pictures are recommended without any discriminations for their human interest.

Now, the executives who think up feminine angles are expert and astute. With their heavy financial responsibilities they must be. And all those routine feminine angles are well-tested formulæ. Box-office receipts and fan mail (even some of the correspondence I receive as film critic) confirm their effectiveness. Undeniably there's a widespread response among women to cheap, sensational or false elements, to the appeal of luxury and the rest. But to know this is to know only a part of feminine nature. Moreover, many of these angles are by no means exclusive to women. I suggest that love of luxury, for instance, and especially sentimentality, are pretty powerful masculine angles. And, finally, though the standards of film appreciation *are* rising, popular taste, such as it is, has unavoidably been conditioned by the narrow and superficial approach, the *idées fixes*, of these very angles. After all, the public can only choose among the movies that are there to be seen.

There is little indication how film production would be affected if women had an equal share in its control. So far, the exceptional few who have become producers have not shown themselves to be of the stuff that pioneers are made of (remember *Corridor of Mirrors*!). There are hardly any women in the other influential positions, either: they are as exceptional among the directors, though perhaps more promising – I'm thinking in particular of Jill Craigie. Among the writers they are slightly more numerous, though still a small minority, and of these fewer still have any real authority, like the brilliant dramatist and screen-writer Lillian Hellman. Admittedly, a number of pictures have been based on novels written by women – sometimes good, more often second-rate – but the men in charge of production were responsible for their choice and treatment. There are many women, of course, in other departments of film production doing expert but completely subordinate work. What their influence would be if they were given their head is anybody's guess. Not all of it, one imagines, would be to the greater glory of cinema. Especially if one reflects that much of the frivolous fan literature is devised for and flourishes on women readers. Or that some of the most pedantic censoring is attributed to the blue stockings on boards and committees, especially in America, where, I gather, women's organisations play a prominent part in local censorship, exercising an influence which, together with that of the Legion of Decency, sometimes merely encourages those lamentable whitewashing dodges. But it seems beyond question that cinematography can only benefit by giving wider scope to the intelligent and gifted representatives of womankind, especially as it may well be that their lack of pull in the industry is one of the reasons why cinema has given so very few significant portrayals of modern womanhood.

Instead it has developed the phenomenally intricate star system which, though it has undergone many changes in fashion, even in purpose, is of its essence a complex of formulas for producing types. Popular types – and this has meant that, as the film industry expanded, catering for a growing variety of tastes, it concentrated on developing the types that might please everybody – all-purpose types, in fact – even more than on increasing their diversity. It was an elaborate process, beginning in the early 1930's, when the Hollywood star system underwent a radical change, and involving colossal expenditure and a lot of hard thinking, with the big chiefs trying to outdo each other in shrewdness and subtlety. The cult of stars as fabulous creatures beyond reach had gone out of fashion, together with the vamps and angelic heroines. Instead of being unattainable, the new stars were supposed to stand closer to the average woman, representing an ideal that she could emulate, and men might admire without being unduly tantalised. Henceforth, the entire system was to depend on the identity of the stars and the rôles for which they were typed. Publicity saw to it that their private lives were an extension of their film rôles; subjects were chosen and screen-plays written accordingly. To make sure that everybody's likes and dislikes were taken into account, each star was supposed to have it both ways in everything possible (and impossible): she had to cultivate a personality, but seem ordinary; be fashionable, yet exclusive; glamorous, but approachable; intriguing, but understandable; wealthy, but with homely tastes; enviable, but deserving of sympathy; she might even champion some unidentifiable (say philanthropic) cause, yet not be unduly serious. The inevitable result of this studied levelling was that, far from representing the typical features of modern womanhood and portraying average women as diverse individuals, the stars, with some notable exceptions, emerged as synthetic figures possessing less character than real-life women. What's even more serious is that the vehicles chosen for them, whether specially written or adaptations, give a deceptive picture of the part women play in modern society, or ignore it altogether. The effect of the star system on actors isn't quite so bad, in that male characters are at least permitted to have interests, ideals and ambitions outside their private preoccupations. True, the most usual interest is making good, which means making money, but there have also been numerous films of a certain vocational interest, such as the cycle of pictures about doctors, a very good one and still going strong.

Though we had no organised star system in Britain, the fashion, the tone of the 1930's produced similar results. In those days the best of our talent either went into the theatre, or, because of unemployment, had to make a living in some profession other than acting. The film industry made only occasional use of it, recruiting its prospective stars among girls with all kinds of qualities bar temperament, which just was not in vogue. Aspiring actresses knew well enough that to admit serious dramatic ambitions was to become classified as a 'heavy' and be condemned to remain on the wrong side of the barrier of casting directors, agents (including the women among them) and those talent scouts and up-and-coming executives who had a mortal terror of 'formidable' women, which meant women of any character at all. By the end of the decade the fashion for under-acting, referred to politely as 'admirable restraint', had settled in, and, what with one thing and another, you would not have guessed, from our pictures any more than from the American ones, that this was the century of women's emancipation. The established film stars of to-day are the product of those years, and they are seldom to be seen in rôles which call for powerful acting. Anna Neagle, who did once impersonate so fine a heroine as Nurse Cavell, concentrates on coy romantic leads, now co-producing her own pictures. Margaret Lockwood has glamour and technical competence, but when it comes to 'social problem' vehicles like *The White Unicorn*, the results are best forgotten. Vivien Leigh, who undoubtedly has talent in addition to her unique grace and beauty, lacked the temperament for *Anna Karenina*, a passionate character of essential goodness, admittedly of the nineteenth century, and if, by some miracle, her modern counterpart were ever re-created in a screen-play, an artist of greater depth and power would be needed to impersonate her.

Within the star system, incidentally, fundamental goodness and a passionate nature are incompatible. It is impossible to recruit and groom girls with the idea of making them safely non-committal types and yet have brilliant and forceful heroines. So, by way of compensation, pseudo-exciting qualities have been cultivated in the sinful types, and with equal safety, since a story twist invariably provides them with the necessary penalty. 'Bad girl makes good box office' is one of the oldest formulæ. In consequence, a large proportion of the strongest (and most coveted) rôles are evil characters and, by comparison, heroines are weaker and insipid. Unavoidably this has done much to strengthen the widely spread delusion that it is of the essence of good women to be dull and of bad ones to be thrilling. The latest and, presumably, most subtle bad-girl type (actually a blonde variation of the early vamps, who were mostly dark) is the angelic criminal. She's to be seen in those psycho-analysis thrillers, alluring and gentle, a sweet thing inciting her menfolk to murder or doing the job herself. Lizabeth Scott, Lana Turner and Lauren Bacall are among those who have filled the rôle, and so is Rita Hayworth, turned topaz blonde for the purpose. The British counterpart, I suppose, is the lady spiv, but she's not so angelic. These are the 'babies' who are 'dynamite'.

But what of the élite, the stars who established themselves initially as dynamic artists, defying classification, like Bette Davis, or those who triumphed over the limitations of being typed, like Myrna Loy? What has been their contribution in portraying modern women? Their greatest merit, I think, is that they have preserved and strengthened the integrity of their personalities. Not all the screen-plays in which they appeared have been good, and exceedingly few have touched on the broader issues of the times. Most have been love stories, confining their scope to personal relationships, and the great stars have had almost as little opportunity as the average types to try their strength in characterisations involving serious conflicts and ideas. But they have saved many a trivial story by the compelling reality of their performances and, between the lines, as it were, in an undefinable way, they have often evoked the spirit of the times. To remember Carole Lombard, Greta Garbo, Luise Rainer, Ruth Chatterton, Jean Harlow is to recall person-

SERGEI EISENSTEIN

1. Portrait taken just before his death. (Soviet Film Agency.)
2. Eisenstein in Britain, 1929. Eisenstein in a policeman's helmet. Hans Richter (extreme left), Len Lye (extreme right, sitting). Michael Hankinson (extreme right, standing), Basil Wright (next, standing). Still by courtesy Jimmy Rogers (behind camera).

ANIMATED CARTOON

3 and 4. Czech cartoons: 'Hold Tight' (by Hoffman) and 'The Chimney Sweep' (by Trinka).

5 and 6. French cartoons: 'Le Voleur de Paratonnerres' and 'La Flute Magique,' by Paul Grimault and André Sarrut.

7 and 8. American cartoons: 'Flat Hatting,' made for U.S. Navy Flight Section, and 'Brotherhood of Man,' made for United Automobile Workers to combat racial hatred. (Copyright United Productions of America).

9 to 14. Halas Batchelor cartoons, London: 9 and 10, 'Magic Canvas,' an experimental film with music by Matyas Seiber.

11. 'Dustbin Parade' (M.O.I.), a salvage film.

12. 'Abu's Poison Well' (M.O.I.), a Cartoon in Arabic.

13. 'Charley's March of Time' (C.O.I.).

14. 'Big Top' (J.W.T.), Public Relations film for Lever Brothers.

INDIAN DOCUMENTARY

15 and 16. 'Mother,' one of a series of films showing the works of an Indian woman Sita Devi, in improving the health and welfare of her community. Produced by Paul Zils.

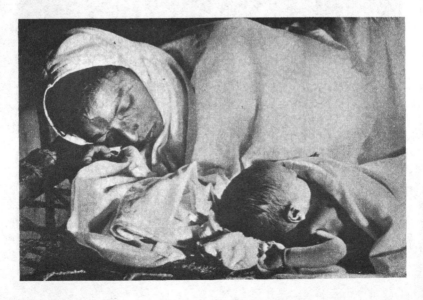

17. 'Community,' another film in the series. (Production Documentary Unit, India.)

SOCIAL REALISM IN

18 and 19. 'Gentleman's Agreement,' directed by Elia Kazan for Darryl F. Zanuck. (20th Century-Fox.) Theme: the evil of Anti-Semitism. With Gregory Peck.

AMERICAN FILMS

20 and 21. 'The Naked City,' directed by Jules Dassin for the late Mark Hellinger. (Universal-International; G.F.D.) Photographed for the most part in the streets of New York.

THE FALLEN IDOL

22 to 24. Carol Reed's new production for London Films, adapted from 'The Basement Room,' by Graham Greene, and featuring Sir Ralph Richardson, Michèle Morgan, and the child actor Bobby Henrey.

THE RED SHOES

25 and 26. Two designs by Hein Heckroth from a series of 120 made to illustrate the ballet sequence in Michael Powell's and Emeric Pressburger's colour film.

SCOTT OF THE ANTARCTIC

27 to 29. Sir Michael Balcon's new production for Ealing Studios, directed by Charles Frend, and featuring John Mills. (Stills by Dick Woodard.)

29. John Mills as Scott.

alities somehow belonging to the 1930's, even though, with some exceptions, one has quite forgotten how, if at all, the modern characters they portrayed participated in the social life of the decade. Katherine Hepburn, Bette Davis, Joan Crawford, Claudette Colbert, Irene Dunne belong to a period spanning the 1930's and 1940's, not because one has understood how the shattering world events of this period affected the modern women they impersonated (though Claudette Colbert and Irene Dunne did give delightful studies of Service-men's wives in war films), but, again, because of something reflected in their personalities. Now and again there have been films giving portrayals of women as active, or at least conscious, members of society, such as Rosalind Russell's in *Sister Kenny*, *Roughly Speaking* and *The Guilt of Janet Ames*, Mary Astor's in *A Rich Full Life*, Celeste Holm's and Dorothy McGuire's in *Gentleman's Agreement*, or Myrna Loy's and Teresa Wright's in *The Best Years of Our Lives*, though in the last two pictures the feminine rôles were comparatively passive and subordinate to the men's. But stories of this kind are rare indeed.

Of late they have been comparatively rare in British cinema, too; though during the war our best pictures were inspired by reality and showed women as an integral part of it. New and individual actresses made their mark in British pictures in those years – Celia Johnson, Deborah Kerr, Rosamund John – and since then their numbers have been swelled by fresh recruits. Nowadays our cinema is making better use of available talent, though still, I fear, not enough. Of the few portrayals of contemporary women in recent films, the most noteworthy, I think, were Rosamund John's as a politician in *Fame is the Spur* and Ursula Jeans' as a scheming cadger in *A Woman in the Hall*. But probably the most outstanding recent performances have been in pictures set in the past. In *A Man About the House*, Margaret Johnston gave a splendid study of a domineering Victorian spinster succumbing to the fascination of a younger man. Kay Walsh gave a vivid and highly dramatic performance as Nancy in *Oliver Twist*, and Eileen Herlie revealed herself as a dynamic artist with real temperament in the rôle of the Queen in *Hamlet*. She is probably the most exciting British discovery of the decade. These and a few other recent portrayals seem to indicate that the vogue for under-acting, at least, is going out.

The rest is speculation, hunches. Will the superb realism of the recent American productions such as *Naked City* or *Boomerang* eventually produce stories that will show with corresponding realism how American women participate in national life, what interests they have besides domestic ones, and will they reveal this, not as deliberate 'women's problems' subjects, but naturally, as an integral part of reality? Will the British cinema recapture the urgent sense of reality it had less than three years ago? Will those ludicrous feminine angles go out of fashion and the star system start encouraging actresses of true individuality – the only kind that can achieve universal significance – instead of the all-purpose nonentities? Above all, will screen-plays creating dynamic modern characters be forthcoming? Your guess is as good as mine. So far, at all events, the real story of modern womanhood has not begun to be told. And it cannot be told except as part of the story of modern times.

ABOUT STEREOSCOPIC CINEMA

The last Essay to be written by

S. M. EISENSTEIN

*

NOWADAYS one meets very many people who ask: 'Do you believe in stereoscopic cinema?'

To me this question sounds as absurd as if I were asked: 'Do you believe that in nought hours it will be night, that the snow will disappear from the streets of Moscow, that there will be green trees in the summer and apples in the autumn?'

To doubt that stereoscopic cinema has its to-morrow is as naïve as doubting whether there will be to-morrows at all.

However, what makes us so certain of this?

After all, what we see on the screen at present are no more than single 'Robinsonades'.

And it is almost symbolical that the best of what we have seen is precisely the screen description of Robinson Crusoe's life.

But what we have seen here is, in its turn, still no more than that raft of Robinson's, in the film itself, trying to slip through the overgrowth (one of the most convincing stereoscopic shots in Andreevsky's film) which represents the myriad difficulties that still have to be surmounted in the destiny of stereoscopic cinema.

Yet the day is not far distant when not only rafts, but galleys, frigates, galleons, cruisers, battleships and dreadnoughts will sail into the harbours of stereoscopic cinema.

But why are we so certain of this?

Because, in my view, the only vital varieties of art are those which, of their very nature, are an embodiment of the hidden urges existing in the depths of human nature itself. What matters is not only which subject is incorporated in a work of art, but also which of the means peculiar to a given art form are employed.

In the problems connected with the extinction of one or another art form, there probably exists the same law of natural selection as in everything else.

And the forms which survive are those which are so composed as to embody the deep, inner, organic tendencies and needs of both the spectator and the creator.

The deeper the questions and the fuller the answers, the greater is the reason for an art form to become realised, the firmer the foundation for its development.

Is not the so-called aimless art perishing inexorably and hopelessly before our eyes because it does not contain an answer to the latent need for enlightenment existing in every progressively minded person?

It came into being and could linger on for awhile, as a reflection of the sterility of the expiring class which gave it birth.

But it could not, of course, become an independent branch or variation capable of standing on its own among the other arts, capable of developing in its own way, of changing and growing.

At the same time, has not there existed through the centuries, and hardly evolving at all, a branch of art equally barren of content – the circus?

And the reason for this is that without touching the sphere of enlightenment (which is much more perfect and expressive in the other arts), the perfection of skill, strength, self-control, will-power and daring which gives brilliance to the circus will always be an expression of the natural urge for the fullest development of the qualities which are of the essence of our physical nature.

For the same reason sport is unchangingly popular – both as an occupation and as a spectacle – for here the powers inherent in us are given the possibility to develop in the most perfect forms and on the widest scale, not only as a commonly shared intuitive experience, but in our own actions and behaviour.

Can it be said that the principle of three-dimensional cinematography responds as fully and as consistently to certain of our deeper needs, to some kind of latent urges?

Further, can it be affirmed that, in its striving for the realisation of these latent needs, mankind has for centuries been moving towards stereoscopic cinema, as to one of the most complete and immediate expressions of such strivings – strivings which, at different stages of social development and of the developments in the means of artistic expression, in different and incomplete ways, yet invariably and persistently – were attempts to realise some such latent need?

It seems to me that it was precisely so.

And I should like to try to reveal the nature of this striving, glancing at the historical modifications through which the arts of former times realised these tendencies, before discovering the most admirable and complete form for its incarnation in the technical wonder of stereoscopic cinema.

Let us try to define for which of the spectator's latent urges the technical phenomenon of stereoscopic cinematography can serve as an expression, just as the phenomenon of cinematography has in its very nature the independent, absolute attraction of the fundamental sign of developing vitality in the universe, mankind and progress – movement!

In order to do this, let us first establish the nature of the phenomenon itself.

Let us note in a few words what it is that strikes the spectator on his first acquaintance with stereoscopic cinema.

Stereoscopic cinema gives a complete illusion of the three-dimensional character of the object represented.

And this illusion is as completely convincing, as free from the slightest shadow of a doubt, as is the fact in ordinary cinematography that the objects depicted on the screen are actually moving. And the illusion of space in one instance and of movement in the other is as unfailing for those who know perfectly well that, in one case, we are looking at a rapid succession of separate, motionless phases which represent a complete process of movement, and in the other, at nothing more than a cunningly devised process of superimposing one upon the other of two normal flat photographic records of the same object, which were taken simultaneously at two slightly different, independent angles.

In each case the space and the movement is compellingly convincing, just as the personages in a film seem undeniably authentic and living, though we know quite well that they are no more than pale shadows, affixed by photochemical means on to kilometres of gelatine ribbon which, rolled on to separate reels, and packed into flat tins, travels from one end of the globe to another, giving spectators everywhere the same compelling illusion of their vitality.

The stereoscopic effect can be of three kinds:

Either the image remains within the limitations of the ordinary cinema – resembling a flat alto-relievo, balanced somewhere in the plane of the mirror-screen.

Or else it pierces through to the depth of the screen, taking the spectator into previously unseen distance.

Or, finally (and this is its most devastating effect), the image, palpably three-dimensional, 'pours' out of the screen into the auditorium.

A cobweb with a gigantic spider hangs somewhere between the screen and the spectator.

Birds fly out of the auditorium into the depths of the screen, or perch submissively over the very heads of the spectators on a wire palpably extending from the area which used once to be the surface of the screen up to ... the projection booth.

Branches of trees are suspended all around, overhanging the auditorium.

Panthers and pumas leap out of the screen into the arms of the spectators, and so on.

Different calculations during the filming force the image either into Space, endlessly extended to the sides and in depth, or into three-dimensional Volume, moving in materially towards the spectator and positively palpable.

And that which we have been accustomed to see as an image on the flat screen suddenly 'swallows' us into a formerly invisible distance beyond the screen, or 'pierces' into us, with a drive never before so powerfully experienced.

As in colour – this new stage of colour expressiveness in relation to the former pictures restricted by the white-grey-black palette – so here, in the first instance, there only occurs a more perfect, continuing development of the tendencies towards the realisation of which cinematography was striving already in the 'two-dimensional' period of its existence.

Incidentally, one of my favourite types of exterior (in particular) shots was composed quite distinctly in the spirit of these tendencies.

It used to be composed (and continues to be) by means of exceedingly sharp emphasis on the foreground, very much enlarged, while keeping the background almost completely in focus, and toning it down only to the extent required by the air perspective in order to obtain the maximum distinction between depth and foreground.

By creating a feeling of a vast interval in scale between the foreground and the background, the maximum illusion of space was achieved.

The distorting powers of the 28-lens contributed in creating this effect, sharply accentuating the perspective, diminishing in depth – the only lens which is technically capable of giving clarity to the enlarged detail in the foreground and depth to the entire background in the same composition by retaining one and the other in distinct focus.

The attraction of such a composition is equally great both in the case of a thematic juxtaposition of both these planes, and in the case of blending them according to the unity of the material.

In the first instance, such a construction, juxtaposing volume – space, creates the maximum conflict imaginable within a single composition.

In the second case, it creates the most plastic and distinctly expressed feeling of unity between the general and the particular.

But such a composition is most expressive dramatically in those cases where it combines both these possibilities, and the thematic unity, say, of both planes is achieved concurrently with their sharply accentuated plastic (scale and colour) incommensurability.

That is how, for instance, one of the final scenes in *Ivan the Terrible*, part I, was treated. The most memorable montage piece in this scene shows the boundless snow-covered space in the background of the composition, the general view of the Moscow peasants' procession moving across it, and, in the foreground, the greatly enlarged profile of the Czar's head bowing to them.

This shot, establishing the thematic unity between the people, imploring the Czar to return, and the Czar himself giving his consent, was composed with the maximum plastic 'disunity' imaginable between these two 'objects'.

... It is interesting to note that all these examples from 'flat' cinematography are, so far, superior by virtue of the power of their pictorial composition to that which is being achieved by purely technical means in stereoscopic cinema.

And the simple reason for this is that the technical possibilities of stereoscopic filming are at present restricted by the necessity to use only one lens, and the least expressive one at that – the 50.

But at the same time, from the anticipated potentialities of stereoscopic cinema, we can foresee developments that will enable us to achieve a hitherto undreamed-of quality, using the self-same means.

One way or the other, though not yet creating a complete impression, these, precisely, are the two equal possibilities for depicting space as a physically palpable reality that the stereo-scopic cinema has given us. The capability to 'draw' the specta-tors with unprecedented intensity towards that which was once the plane of the screen, and, with no less reality, to 'hurl' at the spectators that which formerly remained flattened out on its mirrored surface.

Well, what of it?, you may ask. And why should these two 'astounding possibilities' of the stereoscopic screen have some-thing so hugely attractive for the spectator?

... Of course, not in any other art – throughout the whole of its history – can there be an instance so dynamic and so perfect of volume being transfused into space, and space into volume, both penetrating into each other, existing simultaneously, and this within the process of real movement.

In this sense stereoscopic cinema is superior also to architec-ture where, at times, the mighty symphony of the interplay be-tween massives and the delineations of space is hampered in its dynamics and alternations by the tempo and sequence in which the architectural ensemble may chance to be traversed by the spectator, who has no other means of 'penetrating' this architectural ensemble – dynamically.

... Belonging to the category of histrionic arts, stereoscopic cinema should, of course, be regarded not only as the grand-nephew of Edison's and Lumière's inventions, but also as something like the great-grandson of theatre, appearing, in its present form, as the youngest and newest stage in the theatre's development.

And the riddle concerning the validity of the principle of stereoscopic cinema (if one exists) must, of course, be sought here, in theatrical history, in one of its fundamental tendencies which threaded its way through practically every stage of this history.

But of all the diverse questions concerning theatre, the one which interests me most at the moment is this same problem of analysing the relationships and connections between the spectator and the spectacle.

... And the remarkable thing is that, almost at once, from the moment there's a 'parting of the ways' between the spectator and a participant, a 'longing' sets in for the two severed halves to be rejoined.

Not only in the intelligent writings which flourished in the epoch coinciding with the most extreme and acute individualism, not only in the countless practical experiments which were particularly characteristic of the newest times – not only in these endeavours to realise the tendency towards the renaissance of the original collective 'entity' of a spectacle, but also during the entire course of theatrical history, which, in the innumerable examples of past theatrical techniques, through the centuries, at practically every step, unfailingly and consistently reveals the self-same tendency – distinct in its forms, yet single in purpose – to 'cover' the breach, to 'throw a bridge' across the gulf separating the spectator and the actor.

These attempts fall into various categories, from the most 'crudely material' external devices, such as the lay-out of the auditorium and of the area of action and the stage manners of the actors, to the most subtle forms of a 'metaphorical' incarnation of this dream of unity between spectator and actor.

Furthermore, the tendency to 'penetrate' into the midst of the spectators, no less than the tendency to draw them towards the actors, invariably and of equal right, either compete, take turns, or try to move hand in hand, as if to presage those two peculiar possibilities which represent the essential signs of the technical nature of that which we have noted as the fundamental plastic characteristic (the fundamental optical phenomenon) of stereoscopic cinema!

... The bourgeois West is either indifferent or even hostilely ironical towards the problems of stereoscopic cinema – problems to which the researching and inventive thought of the country of Soviets, its Government, and the directorate of its cinematography devote so much attention.

Does not the musty conservatism, with which news of work

on the stereoscopic front is met in the West, sound absurd and, in its way, insulting to the eternally developing tendencies of a genuinely vital art?

Do not these lines about stereoscopic cinema, for instance, written by Louis Chavance in 1946 (!), sound like sacrilege and obscurantism:

'... In what is the dramatism of a situation enriched by means of this new technical discovery?

'Does a three-dimensionally represented comedian find some additional means of expressiveness in this stereoscopy?

'A physical roundness?

'Will this be the triumph of fat people?

'What can anger, jealousy, hatred gain from the fact that they will occur in three dimensions?

'And laughter. ... I cannot believe that one could induce more laughter than is induced by a custard pie hitting Mac Sennet's flat personages. And intrigue? Comedy? ...

'Is there any need of further proof that stereoscopic cinema is a fruitless, sterile instrument?

'Of course, other hypotheses could be put forward, and I could speak of the purely visual aspect. But we should not become analogous with the plastic arts, and quote the sculptors after having talked of painters. Of course, Michelangelo's life could be filmed in relief and Titian's in colour. ... Charming result! But what pleasure for the eye? Sculpture evokes the idea of tactility, but, in any event, we do not touch the screen. ...'

In what is Chavance mistaken?

His mistake, of course, lies in the fact that while making a pose of his contempt for the analogies, he is entirely their captive, completely encircled by the limits and conceptions of former arts, the norms of theatrical drama, the actors' functions and 'sculpture evoking the idea of tactility'.

But is it possible that Chavance does not think with us that there is bound to be an explosion and a complete revision of the relationships between the traditional arts in their encounter with the new ideologies of new times, the new possibilities of new people, the new means of controlling nature possessed by these people?

Is not the eye capable of seeing in the dark with the aid of the infra-red spectacles of 'night-sight'?

The hand capable of directing shells and aeroplanes in the distant spheres of other skies by means of radio?

The brain, by means of electronic calculating machines, capable of completing within a few seconds calculations on which, formerly, armies of accountants worked for months on end?

Is not consciousness, in the tireless, post-war struggle, hammering out a more distinct and concrete form of a genuinely democratic international ideal?

Will all this not call for absolutely new arts, unheard-of forms and dimensions ranging far beyond the scope of the traditional theatre, traditional sculpture and traditional ... cinema, which, in the course of such development, must needs become mere palliatives?

And will not the new dynamic stereoscopic sculpture cast out beyond the confines of dimensions and peculiarities the former, static sculpture, according to which Chavance would set his standards?

There is no need to fear the advance of this new era.

Still less – to laugh in its face, as our ancestors laughed, throwing lumps of mud at the first umbrellas.

A place must be prepared in consciousness for the arrival of new themes which, multiplied by the possibilities of new techniques, will demand new æsthetics for the expression of these new themes in the marvellous creations of the future.

To open the way for them is a great and sacred task, and all those who dare to designate themselves as artists are called upon to contribute to its accomplishment.

(*Translation by Catherine de la Roche.*)

EISENSTEIN IN LONDON

The following extract from a letter by Basil Wright explains something of the background to the photograph of Eisenstein in London published elsewhere in this volume.

'In the autumn of 1929 the London Film Society instituted two study courses, open to a limited number of its members on payment of a fee. The first course was a series of lectures on "The Film" by Eisenstein. The second course was the actual production of an avant-garde film under the direction of Hans Richter. I joined both the courses, and I still have the notes I took at the Eisenstein lectures. The second course became a bit of a muddle, and the film never got completed. What shooting there was, was done partly on location in London and partly in the little film studio which used to be upstairs in Foyle's in Manette Street. It was in this studio that the photograph was taken, on the afternoon when Eisenstein called in and dislocated production by dressing up as a policeman and dancing a ballet. Some shots of this were taken both by Jimmy Rogers on the camera which you see in the photograph (which is an Eclair), and by one of the members of the group on 16mm. As far as I know, neither of these have survived.'

THE JEWISH THEME IN CONTEMPORARY CINEMA

H. H. WOLLENBERG

★

A SURVEY of the world's screens during recent months will
hardly show any common denominator in present production
trends: small wonder at a time when mankind seems more
deeply divided than ever into groups of different if not fundamentally contradictory outlook. All that can be said is that this
baffling situation is somehow reflected in the films we see. Those
in control of film business, with rare exceptions, consider it
wisest to play for safety. Controversial subjects, in times like
these, mean greater risks at the box office. And what subject,
concerned with the real issues of human society and contemporary life, would not turn out to be 'controversial' these days,
at least in one or another part of the world market? The 'Un-
American Activities' trials in Washington have certainly been
taken as a warning by the executives of the most important
studios commercially in the world, and outside Hollywood as
well. At best this attitude can only result in somewhat colourless
productions (even if they dazzle us in glorious Technicolor); at
worst the result inevitably is an attempt to take advantage of
political trends by a crude blend of propaganda and what is
hoped to be popular appeal. And this, indeed, applies on both
sides of the 'Iron Curtain'.

The almost inevitable effects of the 'witch hunt' were clearly
seen at the time by some British film critics. One of them,
Stephen Watts, while reviewing Elia Kazan's *Gentleman's*

Agreement last summer, predicted that this was a subject of a kind which would not be coming again from Hollywood for the time being.

As a matter of fact, even before *Gentleman's Agreement*, America's Jewish problem was brought to the screen by *Crossfire*, and significantly its makers were among the foremost 'un-Americans'.

Anyhow, both pictures were ventures by feature producers into the field of a contemporary issue, and the venture in either case was successful artistically no less than commercially: public reaction was positive and encouraging. Both films are valuable inasmuch as they dramatise efficiently an important contemporary issue and make people think about it, but both show the *symptoms* rather than the causes; both (perhaps deliberately) avoid going to the roots of the problem.

Anti-semitism certainly has been a latent problem throughout the last two thousand years, erupting again and again long before the word was coined, erupting periodically and in such varying forms as racial hatred or religious fanaticism. Its most horrible outburst in all history, accounting for six million defenceless victims, has just taken place in Central Europe from 1933 to 1945. But it would be a fallacy to think that the defeat of Hitler and the collapse of the Third Reich have eliminated anti-semitism as a corrupting force, or to assume that this phenomenon has ever been confined to a single country or political party.

Crossfire and *Gentleman's Agreement* show bluntly the forms in which anti-semitism is rampant in the U.S.A. and the specific social and psychological conditions of its existence in that country. They will be understood even in countries where certain aspects of the same problem are different though no less menacing; indeed, in some respects the conditions shown in these two Hollywood productions are very like the symptoms prevalent in certain European countries prior to Hitler's rise to power.

Hitler himself, of course, and even more so Goebbels, were well aware of the singular power of films as a medium for disseminating racial hatred, the most outstanding example being Goebbels' own version of *Jew Süss* which, of course, was not based on Feuchtwanger's well-known novel (filmed in this country by Gaumont British); as a matter of fact, what Goebbels attempted (and achieved) was the age-old demagogue's recipe of distortion. It is easy enough to appeal to the basest human instincts and to stir up the most evil emotions against any race, nation, class, or other group by putting on the screen its most unsavoury (and by no means representative) specimens in a skilfully distorted and deliberately repulsive manner. Just so, it would be easy enough to take a character such as Shylock and to make him appear, not as the great tragic figure his creator meant him to be, but as a ludicrously distorted figure of fun and scorn.

This was, obviously, the method of Nazi film producers in trying to put across their own version of the Jewish problem. But at the same time outside the Nazi orbit (or wherever else a more objective treatment of this issue remained possible), little enough was done to contradict it. Among the relatively few attempts, the two outstanding were *Zola* and *Mamlock*, both released in this country before the war.

In *The Life of Émile Zola*, its director, William Dieterle, clearly set out to show his hero as the fighter for a just cause rather than as the great novelist he happened to be, the particular cause being the notorious *Affaire Dreyfus*, with its great dramatic as well as ideological possibilities. In the mid-thirties, with Nazism rampant, nothing could have been more 'topical' than this presentation of an event forty years past. It was meant to be, and it certainly was, an answer to Nazism on the Jewish issue.

Even more directly does this apply to *Professor Mamlock*, a completely anti-Nazi production based on Friedrich Wolff's story of a Jewish doctor resisting Nazi persecution.

There were, of course, several anti-Nazi films in which the Jewish theme appeared as one of the facets, though not the central issue of the subject: for example, Chaplin's *Great Dictator*, to mention but one film where the Jewish theme is only incidental, and the British production of Louis Golding's *Mr Emanuel*, in which the Jewish theme, though much more predominant, is still used merely for its story-value rather than as a basis for serious thought.

As for current productions adopting a more serious approach to the problem, it is perhaps significant that many of these are being made in post-war German and Austrian studios. They seem properly and particularly alive to the task of providing an antidote to the poison systematically spread by years of Nazi indoctrination.

While their American contemporaries *Crossfire* and *Gentleman's Agreement* are based on fictional events and characters, these new Central European productions make their case against anti-semitism almost invariably by referring to actual events and persons.

G. W. Pabst's first post-war film *Der Prozess* (The Trial) deals with the notorious Ritual Murder case in Tisza Eszlar, an Hungarian village, where in 1882 the Jews were indicted for the murder of a girl for allegedly ritual purposes.

While this picture was produced in Vienna, D.E.F.A. in Berlin turned to *Affaire Jakob Blum*, another notorious trial with the anti-semitic background of the late twenties and the beginning of Hitler's ascendancy. Robert A. Stemmle wrote the script, Erich Engel was the director. Another D.E.F.A. production, *Ehe im Schatten* (Marriage in the Shadow), is based on the tragic story of the actor Joachim Gottschalk, who committed suicide rather than accept Goebbels' order to separate from his Jewish wife. Author and producer of this impressive film is Kurt Mätzig.

Finally, there is one interesting contribution from the Geiselgasteig studios near Munich, *Lang ist der Weg* (It's a

Long Way), produced by I.F.O., an independent unit. Unlike the other three productions, this one is not based on an actual event; nevertheless, with its strikingly real reconstruction of the terror of ghettoes and the concentration camps, it succeeds in creating the impression of being a documentary film.

Outside Germany, the young and promising Polish film effort has contributed two new productions: *Border Street* and *The Last Stage*. Their respective backgrounds are the Warsaw Ghetto, its heroic last fight and ultimate annihilation by the Nazis, and the notorious death camp of Auschwitz. Both are stirring and realistic. To the same category belongs the new Italian film, *The Wandering Jew*.

Similar themes seem to be developing elsewhere. This one great contemporary problem at least is being given full attention by film producers in many lands.

CONTEMPORARY FRENCH CINEMA

JEAN-GEORGE AURIOL

★

AT the best period of French cinema, the critic had to consider scarcely twelve films a year and finally to select three or four, or perhaps only one.

To-day as yesterday, we do not concern ourselves with current film fare – the weekly programme at the local cinema – any more than the literary critic pores over magazine fiction.

Nevertheless, since our art can only express itself as an industry, and since the film-maker's freedom and even his chance of self-expression depend on unique economic conditions, we must briefly look at the economic aspect of French film production over the past ten years.

THE 'CORPORATION' IS ORGANISED

Ten years ago the French cinema was that of Rénoir, Clair, Feyder, Duvivier and Carné. To-day the influence and even the activities of these directors are still important; but the great masters have more or less given way to their disciples, probably because the first four of these left France just as it was being occupied by the German Army.

At the beginning of the occupation, production was brought to a standstill. Everyone withdrew into himself, examined his conscience, indulged in dreams: hopes and fears together created an atmosphere suitable to a revival.

Since the cry for bread and circuses is heard under every régime, the Vichy Government soon obtained the right, within certain not too narrow limits, to start up this industry as being of the first importance.

A director-general of cinematography was named, a Cinema Corporation was set up, whose administration and methods of control were approved by both those with fascist and those with Marxist leanings. Bit by bit, from November 1940 to June 1944, the supply of electricity current, film stock, wood, paint and raw material, was reduced to such an extent that the producers and technicians had more and more to draw upon their reserves of imagination, ingenuity and even cunning.

It is not true that films were made without the knowledge of the authorities (*Pontcarral*, 1943, was first hailed as an anti-British film and later claimed to be anti-German); but it is very interesting to note that Jacques Becker and Robert Bresson were engaged on subjects as remote as possible from the events of the day during the weeks when, in the spring of 1944, in the studios as elsewhere, electricity was supplied only at night, and when the noise of the battles of Normandy was coming nearer day by day.

Falbalas, by Becker, and *Les Dames du Bois de Boulogne*, minor successes because experimental work, are nevertheless films of the first significance, as displaying the director's search for an ultra-spectacular style, and for expression of his own personality as one not so much looking on at an activity which he is directing, as making a film from within himself.

Before the actual projection of the film on the screen, there has taken place a projection of the imagination on to the film through all the normal stages of production, adaptation and cutting, rehearsal, shooting, montage and mixing.

This is not to claim that these films have revolutionised the art of the film, but that in its inevitable and haphazard evolution they mark a step comparable to the first films of Orson Welles, on the one hand, and the films of Rossellini on the other. But neither Bresson nor Becker had seen *Citizen Kane* any more than Welles had seen *La Règle du Jeu*, the last film that Rénoir made in France and the most important one to study in considering his influence on the young French cinema.

Before we further consider this work and the measure of its originality, we must complete our examination of the psychological circumstances of French production during the German occupation.

IT'S AN ILL WIND ...

As soon as film production began again in Paris, old methods of making films were abandoned, and to begin with, thanks to the intelligence (or the indifference or the stupidity) of the new producers, new themes were adopted. Censorship was far from severe, and the post of official Director of Cinematography was held almost throughout by a courageous and altogether admirable man* whose skill, in the midst of the worst material and political difficulties, allowed a series of minor miracles to be accomplished with the assistance of the goodwill and active willingness of all concerned.

Censorship was quite mild, but it was obviously useless to attempt to bring to the screen subjects that were either patriotic or related to contemporary problems. Similarly, whether tacitly or not, there was a general agreement to avoid stories that were unduly depressing; hence the flight towards the whimsical, the fantastic, the supernatural and the past. Never were so many costume films made as at the time when fine fabrics were scarce. This came about because no one knew how long our isolation would continue, and because the financial backers, who were anxious to change their capital into solid value, did not have to fear that historical productions would become unfashionable along with the wardrobe of the stars.

Before discussing these newcomers, let us turn to the older directors. In his last film before the war, *Le Jour se Lève*, Marcel Carné created a drama out of the cobbled streets and grey walls of a Paris suburb of 1938. He was already planning to make

* This refers to Louis-Emile Galey, an architect, subsequently engaged in production.

Fleur de l'Age, a story of children in an approved school from a script by Jacques Prévert, which he finally began in 1947, only to find himself compelled to abandon it a short time later. Turning away from the sooty skies and 'fantastique social' of the working-class districts, he thought of filming a fairy-tale, *La Clef des Songes*, from a play of Georges Neveux, then had models made for a film taking place in the year 2040, only to return to Prévert, who meanwhile had written the legend of *Les Visiteurs du Soir*.

In Jean Gremillon we have a musician who also has a sensuous and eager eye, taking in the essentials of an environment before he introduces his characters into it. Gremillon, never forgetting the reality behind his images, gives to the construction of a great hydro-electric dam a richness that is both unusual and imaginative. Also working from a story by Prévert, he easily passes from the mundane to the fantastic, and gives a romantic aspect as well as a sense of sustained violence to a drama consciously removed from the merely journalistic. The result is *Lumière d'Été*.

Marcel L'Herbier, one of the best-known figures of the earlier post-war period and one of the most fertile experimenters of the *avant-garde* of the silent film, who had been gradually driven to producing vehicles for the big stars, pounced upon a story by Louis Chavance. This was coloured by a quite individual surrealism, and he used it to mould a style, employing wholly orthodox techniques that had been usually neglected through indolence. Unfortunately, his producer lacked money, and this film, *Nuit Fantastique*, confined to the sets by the hard winter of 1941–2, was not quite the masterpiece it might have been.

THE INFLUENCE OF JEAN COCTEAU

Now the most famous sorcerer and poet of magic in the inter-war period waved his wand to set the stage for the new mood. Jean Cocteau's mission in the decadent art of our time is quite clear – to prevent people from slumbering in conventionality and to reveal to the artist his true abilities.

Unfortunately, he brought to the screen the trappings of his macabre farces and the striking but monotonous symbolism of his mythology of sex. Although over fifty, Cocteau is younger than many a young man still dreaming. Unluckily, he learnt to make films only after having engaged in all other forms of expression, and always experimentally. On the screen his magic remains cold, just as the tricks of a Western fakir would fail to interest a Hindu crowd, or as a Chinese painter who had learned nothing from our art galleries but the technique of perspective would make us smile.

Nevertheless, the influence of Cocteau on the cinema has not been worthless.

In fact, it is better not to discuss Cocteau's rôle as a scenario writer in *L'Éternel Retour*, that sombre incident, nor even the rather gripping *Baron Fantôme*, made in the dust-covered store-shed of German expressionism (although he did bring a ray of moonlight into this barn). And *La Belle et la Bête* (1946) is still the film of a rich amateur, a series of challenges from the dilettante setting out to ginger up the listless technicians.

Cocteau is, after all, the author of one masterpiece, irritating and trivial, but with a moving introspective force, a film which illumines with flashes of lightning one of the abysses of the human soul, *Le Sang d'un Poète*. This dramatic poem, in which everything is the deliberate effect desired by the author, has been a constant inspiration in the field of photography, direction, décor and psychology; in its descriptive music and echoing images; in its writing and its numerous so-called technical suggestions (that is to say syntactical or prosodic). To give but one example, and a score – the heartbeat throbbing like a drum was used again, among other things, by Carné in the scene of the petrified lovers at the end of *Les Visiteurs du Soir*.

With that teasing jocularity of which he is such a master, Cocteau, when he showed *Le Sang d'un Poète* privately to a few friends in 1943, said, 'This film is thirteen years old and already has wrinkles. And remember that in those days the technique of sound was still in its infancy'.

Nothing could be less true. Except for Orson Welles (and of course Disney) no one has used sound on the screen to better purpose than Cocteau, and if one looks at Périnal's photography in this film, one would doubt whether Périnal himself could serve the inspiration of the poet as perfectly to-day. While as for Georges Auric, his music in this film is the finest, with the exception of that for *A Nous la Liberté*, which he ever wrote for the screen.

THE BIRTH OF THE SUBJECTIVE CINEMA

The cinema must, of necessity, be a collective art, especially since it is bound to be a synthesis of all the arts, and since the poet, who is the creator, must work in harmony with his collaborators, the architect, the composer and the photographer. This does not absolve the ideal director from knowing, if not how to draw up the plans of his décor, or write his musical accompaniment, at least how to imagine, suggest and dictate them, in the same way as a director knows what photography he wants, decides on it, and then leaves it to the cameraman to carry out. On the other hand, if the set designer builds sets which are only buildings, without dramatic value, or technique, or rhythm, if the dress designer then brings on costumes which were not created for particular characters and particular actors, and to be photographed in a particular frame and a particular manner ... if the composer writes his music only when the film is finished ... if the script is written by one man (or two), then adapted by another one (or six) and finally yet another writes the 'dialogue' like trimming embroidered on a frock ... then one gets that horrible mixture which too often calls itself cinematography.

It is against this that French directors have been struggling with considerable force in the past few years; and to begin

with, once the older directors had gone, the younger ones as-
serted with all their strength the principle which we have been
proclaiming in writing for so many years and which an American director summed up in this simple formula: 'Creativeness
cannot be diffused'.

We do not claim to have rediscovered the cinema. This would
be as ridiculous as the discovery of prose in *Le Bourgeois
Gentilhomme*. But it was a matter of recognising the facts. At
the moment when films were first being made again, and many
people were making them for the first time, all those who had
something to express said, in effect: 'If it's just a matter of
starting again as before, it's not worth the trouble. We want to
try to make our own cinema'.

On the screens of Paris in the summer of 1940 the only competitor was the German films, by now quite undistinguished.
The Italian films did not arrive until 1942, and neither those of
Blasetti nor those of De Robertis broke any new ground in the
matter of style, in spite of their lyric power, overwhelming in
the one and harrowing in the other. The lack of American films
was extraordinarily beneficial to our directors. The less honest
ones took advantage of it to make imitations of Hollywood,
caricatures which brought out the defects of mass production
and industrial process; the better ones acted as if they were the
only ones left, in a narrowed world, to make films; and the
reproach which foreign friends were able to level against them
of retiring into an 'ivory studio' is, in our opinion, a compliment, or at least the acknowledgment of a fortunate circumstance; because the cinema, which is always in such a hurry to
paralyse its artistic right hand in the grip of its commercial left
hand, is perhaps the only industry which has no 'back rooms'.
Pooling experience, making – if one may borrow the jargon of
other expressions – prototypes and experiments in new artistic
methods, is an economy which the film industry finds more
expensive than financing a production X more lavishly than
productions A, B and C. ... One can reproach, and always for

rather petty reasons, the French cinema of the Occupation for a tendency to interest itself excessively with literature. We have the best of excuses— and we say this without rancour – in comparison with our friends in countries whose literary endowment is poor; but we cannot but be more conscious of the exact value of three and a half years of self-sufficiency, of forty months of isolation that were, ultimately, less stultifying than fruitful.

RÉNOIR – ABSENT BUT ALWAYS PRESENT

The period in the French cinema called 'realist', or, to be less vague, the '30s, ended with *La Règle du Jeu*, Jean Rénoir's film that disconcerted the public and more than one professional. Marking the end of an era, it also marked a new beginning.

It could be objected that Rénoir represents the typical director who is at home on the set like a painter in his studio, and only considers the subject as a pretext. One can easily quote his remark about *La Bête Humaine*: 'To hell with old Zola, I wanted to play at trains.'

As a matter of fact, the opening of *La Bête Humaine*, with its long stretch of railway lines, is one of the finest pieces of cinematography that French artists have created. I, for my part, have always shown it with success to illustrate my lectures, in France and in various European cities, confirming each time the effect of exaltation produced by this lyric-didactic poem on the least film-minded of audiences. This comes in part in the passages detached from the film as a whole and consequently free from the necessities of the plot and from any of the sentimentality of the novel.

Without the slightest strain, recalling the *avant-garde* of Gance, L'Herbier and Clair, this fragment of film becomes a fragment of abstract cinema, created by the director with concrete images as with words and as freely selected with the weighty and complicated instrument of the cinema as with a pen.

We stress the importance of Rénoir for two reasons: first because *La Règle du Jeu* is an innovator, and secondly because Rénoir, universally admired and accepted as the most forceful, the most mature and most versatile artist in French films, is usually appreciated for his gifts as a 'painter'. Illiterate critics are so pleased at knowing that Jean is the son of Auguste and at being able to drivel about the 'seventh art' being above all else a visual art (thus confusing the mechanical function of the eye with the intellectual apprehension of vision), that they want to imprison this tireless and creative experimenter in a kind of workshop-cum-studio where, as a jolly painter-director, he can follow the whims of his sensuous temperament. This would be a slightly laughable parody of the reporting of some gushing female all agog at the chance of bringing Rénoir down to the level of her readers' understanding, but we must after all remember that Rénoir is so far from being a mere 'orchestra leader' or technical virtuoso, that immediately *La Bête Humaine* was finished, he wrote down the play that had been germinating in his mind, namely *La Règle du Jeu*, which, with its theme, images and dialogue united into one integral whole, is his work alone.

Just as we have seen that *Le Sang d'un Poète* has been extensively borrowed from, so do we find traces of Luis Bunuel's *L'Age d'Or** in a number of French films of the '30s. Even in *La Règle du Jeu* there are traces of this film of baroque revolt, this parody drawn with bold humorous strokes that is at the same time a 'critical essay' rich in poetic treasures.

But these reminiscences have been coloured by the emotion of the creative artist; it is, in fact, Beaumarchais by whom Rénoir claims to have been inspired in his attempt to paint – not without affection – the breaking-up of a society – the self-

* A decisive proof of the need for Research Schools or experimental laboratories and for a Cinema Review not on paper but on film. ... For these two works, *Le Sang d'un Poète* and *L'Age d'Or*, were both made in the year 1930 at the expense of a Mæcenas whose name is thus enshrined in the history of talking films: Vicomte Charles de Noailles.

styled aristocratic bourgeoisie. This script is so profoundly his own that he felt the need, although he is an indifferent actor, to play the rôle of the witness – or, if you prefer, the chorus of ancient drama – in this film, not caring, or not considering it worthwhile, to tell his story in the first person, as the Americans were shortly afterwards to do.

But film wears out, and in spite of the vigilance of the *Cinémathèques* – unfortunately founded all too recently – important works have vanished. Nevertheless, it is ridiculous to consider the value of a film just by the length of women's skirts in it.

In contrast to a symphony which is recreated more or less happily at each performance, a film is for ever fixed in its form, which may or may not be perfect, but is usually adequate. Even in this form it is sometimes beyond the understanding of the public from its first appearance.

Everyone knows the story of Bizet's *Carmen*, how it was hissed from the stage of the Opéra Comique for ten years until it was quite naturally popularised, first by the music-halls, and then by half the house-painters and laundry-women of the world. To a public which knows all the films that have followed *La Règle du Jeu*, this work, first held to be ill-constructed, badly arranged and full of distractions and irritations, is now revealed as a brilliantly integrated composition. One would have to read ten novels of the interwar period to understand as clearly the drama which Rénoir has caught and condensed into eight thousand feet of film. Borrowing once again from the vocabulary of the concert-hall – some parts have been spoiled by being played on indifferent instruments: naturally not all actors are equally good. And in the cinema, 'it is the actors who are the language'.

But in the cinema, everything is language – beginning with the descriptive and concrete image which may be general or detailed and going on into the boundless field of images within images of evocative juxtapositions (Eisenstein), of

associations, of contrasts, of metaphors, of the imagined and
realised vision, of poetry traced by a camera which can then
easily take the name and the rôle of a camera-pen (i.e. camera-
style). If young men were not crushed on entry into their
professions by the routines that take the place of dogma, they
would even steal in order to buy a camera and miniature film
with which they would make – not documentaries, not even
poetic documentaries, but poems, short stories and essays. I am
the son of a creator of modern typefaces, and have inherited
his notes, addresses and lecture courses. When someone asked
me to write the book that this master typographer had neglected to complete on the history and design of letters, I replied that I would not make a book but a film. I could not make
myself understood. Shortly afterwards, Étienne Lallier turned
out his little masterpiece La Lettre, which in five minutes can
do more to instruct the ignorant than half the standard works
on the subject.

Any thesis – medical, sociological, philosophical, written or
unwritten and not at least partly made into a film – is either
incomplete or dead. There is not a critic, a psychologist or a
metaphysician worthy of the name who has not taken cogni-
sance of the film and of the artistic, moral and intellectual
revolution it has brought about. Since this new language exists
and since it has already influenced the mind, the methods of
knowledge and the moves of modern man, it must be used in
its totality.

LANGUAGE AND LITERATURE

The rôle of a poet like Jacques Prévert is, then, of the greatest
importance in the evolution of the French film. Without him,
without the characters he has provided, for Carné, without the
adventures he has put in the way of Jean Gabin, Arletty, Jules
Berry, Pierre Brasseur, Louis Salou, Jean-Louis Barrault, without that mythical being to whom he has, in Le Quai des
Brumes and in Remorques, given the face of Michele Morgan

(the popular star who has brightened the nights of a whole generation of film-goers), without his felicities of expression ('*Vaut mieux cette tête-là que pas du tout,*' etc.), without his own kind of despair that never despairs of love, without all these, the French cinema would not have the shape it has to-day.

In any event, we should perhaps never have had so fine a demonstration of the qualitative meaning of time as that given in *Les Visiteurs du Soir*: the long waking dream of the enchanted couple which covers that fraction of a second during which the dance seems to stop. We should not have had that heart-warming film-stream in which nothing of importance happens, but only those things that are so delightful to watch at ease, the sort of thing that can happen to a woman like Garance (Arletty) in a Paris as teeming with life as that of Balzac (*Les Enfants du Paradis*). In any event, Marcel Carné would not have been the same Carné — that is, the Carné of *Jenny*, of *Drôle de Drame*, of *Le Jour se Lève* or even of those *Portes de la Nuit* which close upon a period that is rich in beauty and which will remain, even if it is thanks to Carné, the period of Jacques Prévert.

Sound reproduction is so bad in two-thirds of the cinemas of Europe, film-goers so lazy and French so far from being the universal language it was, that strict commercial logic would have the French Cinematographic Corporation pay Jacques Prévert to do nothing but make suggestions, of which only the 'action' would be retained. ... One thing that is worse than literary dialogue in a film is dialogue that is flat, stupid and ugly.

For our part, our fancy runs to the quite pure and 'utilitarian' words, such as were dictated to Jean Cocteau by Robert Bresson for his *Dames du Bois de Boulogne*. But in the present state of development of film language, the most satisfactory dialogue is that of the director who has written his own films, even if it is sometimes clumsy.

This will sometimes be the actual phrases which the characters would utter in the circumstances in which they appear, as
in *Farrebique* by Georges Rouquier, and, in a different way, in
Les Dernières Vacances by Roger Leenhardt, two of those
very infrequent films which illuminate without realism some
aspects of the real France: a particular peasant society, a particular provincial middle-class society. Sometimes it will be
much less discreet, the shouts of Clouzot or the poetic epigrams of Jean Aurenche and Pierre Bost, at once true novelists
of the cinema and authentic scenario writers. The last two, who
always work together, could film their stories even if they had
not, as they have, the ideal collaboration of a Claude Autant-
Lara.

If, then, film language is the actor, and also the lighting and
décor and the famous 'atmosphere' (*Stimmung*) which derives
from the photography and from the mysterious and subtly
deluding harmony of details appealing, through the eye or the
ear, to the heart as well as to the head, to the senses as to the
intellect; if all this is the rich and precious material of the film-
maker's language, he is still much less the master of this
material than the poet of *his* language or the painter of *his*
colours. Particular words coming from a particular mouth in
the tones of a particular voice have not the same value when
spoken by another actor. So much so that there are a few films
quite prepared, in fact written, sketched out, realised, that cannot be made for lack of certain actors. So much so that Gabin
has imposed his charm, his manners, his expression and his
vocabulary on a whole epoch of French cinema, which could
have been just as well dominated by a character such as Drieu
la Rochelle's *Gilles*, cousin to the *Rake* of British films, if we
happened to have an actor of the type of Rex Harrison.

In her silent *Anna Karenina*, Greta Garbo made us hear
words of grief and passion which were missing from her – admittedly excellent – talking *Anna Karenina*. This is because
out of its very weakness the silent cinema had to make itself

heard; besides, the best of the silent films stirred our imagination until one might say that they were 'heard' as well as seen. (A famous example is Dreyer's *Jeanne d'Arc* who succeeded in making herself 'heard'); but the human element is not less important in the story presented by a talking film; and the admirable picture of Gerard Philippe in *Diable au Corps*, learning that he is to become a father and immediately placing his head against the belly of Micheline Presle to listen to his child, would not be half as satisfying if the woman, moved and surprised by her boyish lover, did not say with beautiful naturalness, 'I have two children!'

In the same tone she also says, summing up the drama of a love-affair abhorrent because abhorred by nature: 'Why are you a man only when you are in my arms?'

Later on, the *tragedy* of this drama is given a more terrifying form by the very elegance of a heartbreaking vow: 'I shall never deceive my husband; that will be my way of remaining faithful to you'.

NEW FILM WRITERS

I quote these speeches only because it is not possible for the reader to see here the passages of the film which they illumine; and because they would never have been either written or heard if the screen had not made it possible for them to be created by those three lovers of their art, Autant-Lara, Aurenche, Bost, to whom we owe, not only the perfect success of a *Diable au Corps*, delicately translated from the novel of Raymond Radiguet, but also the earlier films: *Le Mariage de Chiffon* (1942), a charming 'water-colour', *Douce* (1943), a near masterpiece, and *Sylvie et le Fantôme* (1945), an honourable failure.

Autant-Lara passed through all the active rôles of production costumier (Rénoir's *Nana*), set designer and assistant, and he also visited Hollywood without being able to find the means of expressing himself in his own way until after 1940. Similarly,

PAISA

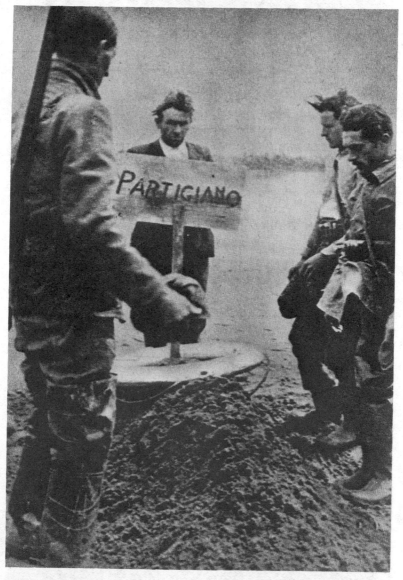

30 to 32. Roberto Rossellini's film of episodes from the war of the liberation of Italy. 30. Burial of a Partisan.

31. The American soldier with the Italian girl turned prostitute.

32. The American army chaplains at an Italian monastery. (Stills by courtesy of Academy Cinema.)

ITALIAN FILMS

33 and 34. 'Caccia Tragica' (The Tragic Chase), a film of the black market in Italy, directed by Giuseppe de Santis, and featuring Carla del Poggio (above) and Vivi Givi (below). (Lux Films.)

35 and 36. 'L'Ebreo Errante' (The Wandering Jew), a new version of the old story involving the tragedy of the concentration camp, directed by Goffredo Alessandrini, with Valentina Cortese and Vittorio Gassman.

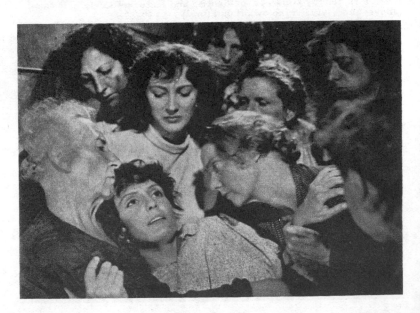

37 and 38, 'L'Onorevole Angelina' (Angelina, M.P.), a film about a working class housewife who fights for better conditions, directed by Luigi Zampa, with Anna Magnani. (Lux Films.) Stills 33 to 38 by courtesy of the International Film Bureau.

DANISH FILMS

Films remarkable for the handling of children are being made in Denmark by Bjarne and Astrid Henning-Jensen. 39 and 40. 'De Pokkers Unger' (Those Blasted Kids) is a story of the struggle for room to play by chil-

dren in the Copenhagen tenements. 41 and 42. 'Ditte, Menneskebarn' (Ditte, Child of Mankind) is the story of the unhappy life of an illegitimate girl.

43 and 44. 'Der Prozess' (The Trial), directed by G. W. Pabst, with Max Brod (above) and Maria Eis (below). (Star Film, Vienna.)

GERMAN AND AUSTRIAN FILMS

45 and 46. 'Ehe im Schatten' (Marriage in the Shadow), directed by Hans Maetzig, with Ilse Steppat (above) and Paul Klinger and Alfred Balthoff (below). (DEFA.)

FIRST YUGOSLAVIAN POST - WAR FEATURE

47 and 48. 'Slavitsa,' directed by Vjekoslav Asric, was made on the Dalmatian coast, assisted by the local people, and is a story of the later part of the war. (Stills by courtesy of Progress International Press Service.)

CANTIFLAS

49 and 50. Two stills from the films of Cantiflas, the famous Mexican comedian. 49. 'Grand Hotel,' and 50, a burlesque of 'Romeo and Juliet,' (Stills by courtesy of Dore Silverman.)

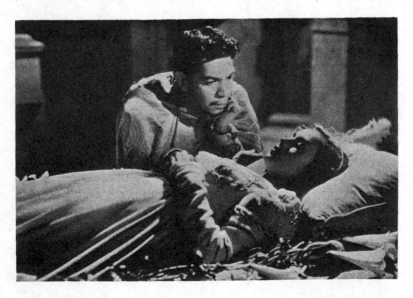

SOVIET CINEMA

51 and 52. 'Alexander Matrosov,' directed by L. Lukov for the Children's Film Studio, tells the story of a young man who died in the war. (Stills by courtesy of Voks.)

53 and 54. 'Pirogov,' directed by Kozintzev, is the story of a pioneer of Russian surgery distinguished during the Crimean War.

55 and 56. 'Russian Question,' directed by Mikhail Romm. Story of an American journalist who suffers because of his sympathy for Russia.

57 and 58. Twin frames from 'Robinson Crusoe,' a feature film of the Russian third-dimensional cinema. Stills enlarged from frames cut from the film itself. (Stills 53 to 58 by courtesy of the Soviet Film Agency.)

AMERICAN AVANT GARDE

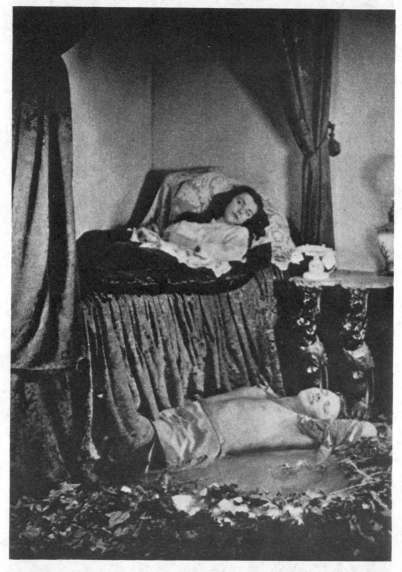

59. 'Dreams that Money can Buy,' Hans Richter's full-length film, made
with the help of Max Ernst, Fernand Léger, Man Ray and Darius Milhaud
among others. Scene from the episode created by Max Ernst, 'Desire.'
(Still by Sheila Ward.)

his artistic contemporaries took about the same time to overcome their own almost identical difficulties.

Considered until the war to be presumptuous and not too competent, Henri George Clouzot – thanks to the support of Pierre Fresnay, an actor always ready to help young authors – was suddenly given the opportunity of influencing the production of an entire studio as chief scenario writer. He went so far as to rewrite himself half the films of his company. First making it possible for Georges Lacombe to make the best film of his career, *Le Dernier des Six* (1941), Clouzot then began to produce his own stories, culminating in the famous *Corbeau*.

Open to discussion as a work of art, *Le Corbeau* is yet a masterpiece of skill. Without hesitation, without losing himself in the senseless rituals of technique employed since the beginning of talking films, Clouzot brings to life his story and his characters (who are very numerous) because he is a novelist. The over-curious little girl is not playing ball here merely to provide certain tricks of the camera which will arouse the admiration of the mechanics or ushers, but because she acts the child the better to play her part in the build-up of the drama as a girl on the verge of adolescence.

Le Corbeau is a film which must be seen, even if only to be disliked. Here for the first time in many years is found, in the hysterical state of a community tormented by anonymous letters, the true feeling and psychology of provincial France. We have here as well the collaboration, as co-author of the script, of Louis Chavance, one of the few French film writers who have written only for the screen, and to whom detective stories are a means of expression adapted to the spirit of enquiry of an acute intelligence into problems at once psychopathological and poetic.

Another film of Clouzot's which must be seen is *Quai des Orfèvres* (1947), an equally unusual example of true depiction of Parisian scenes: that inhabited by the police and that of the small music-halls. It is another detective story, but a perfectly produced one. It must be considered a necessary experiment for an artist who has waited ten years for the right to make films and who until now, in spite of success and his slightly demagogic gift of pleasing the public, has had practically all the original subjects which he has proposed turned down, while others, prisoners in Germany, still young and until then reduced to building castles in the air or to dragging along in subordinate positions, were dreaming of their future films. Returning to France in 1941, Jacques Becker, previously an assistant to Rénoir for eight years, made (from a story by Chavance) an imitation American detective story, *Dernier Atout* (1942), so successfully that a young producer entrusted to him another by Pierre Bery, which became a film of character, peopled with earthy peasants; this was *Goupi-Mains-Rouges* (1943).

For his part, Robert Bresson, who had recently written an extravagant little burlesque film, but who had never succeeded in breaking through the doors of the studios – usually barred by the most strident vulgarity – also returned, ill from captivity. He outlined so persuasively his ideas for a drama set in the Convent of Bethany, a kind of Foreign Legion for women, that the producers finally recognised in him a potential author-director. Roland Tual, a producer himself attracted by direction (*Le Lit à Colonnes*), allowed Bresson to make this film, which impresses one by its noble perfection, its latent strength and the state of lyrical exaltation in which the artists found themselves, from Renée Faure, Sylvie, Jany Holt and Paula Dehelly down to the most obscure (*Les Anges du Péché*, 1943).

Les Anges du Péché, *Le Corbeau*, *Goupi-Mains-Rouges* and *Lumière d'Été* are all films which reach a certain level of fantasy; not by the usual methods of fairy-tales, the picturesqueness of romantic bric-à-brac or the old technical, scenic, photographic tricks, but by the magic of a poetry springing from the intellect and the style of each director, and by the special quality of his vision of truth.

FILMS BY NEW-COMERS AND OTHERS WHO ARE MORE SETTLED

Do I have to analyse all of these films? If I did I would only be able to urge you to see them and help you to understand them. To repeat once more, to make a real survey of the cinema one must have a room where the screen itself would be allowed to speak and where the lecturer would be able to quote the films which he has been describing, comparing and studying. Failing that, I should have to compile a sort of catalogue of titles, names and fragments of my choice. I would have to quote all the minor technicians who have fallen by the way and all the lieutenants who have since become captains ... or even colonels; from Jean Delannoy (*L'Éternel Retour*, 1943) to Christian Jacque (*L'Assassinat du Père Noël*, 1941). There would be so much to say about some men and some works and so little to say about others that this catalogue would become involved, doubtful and dull for the reader.

Le Ciel est à Vous, a film of Jean Gremillon, 1943, is unfortunately dull, very solid and rich in moving emotional scenes. It is about an adventure, a little in the manner of Dickens (but a Dickens who is as grey as the print of a daily paper), of a lower middle-class couple who have a taste for aviation. One does not know whether the moral of the story, which was written by Albert Valentin and Charles Spaak, is that this mechanic, who implants in his wife the nostalgia of the one-time hunter of the sky of the First World War which he himself feels, ought to have been content to stay in his own middling station; or whether he is a symbol for the popular hero who ought to be allowed to rise as high as he wants to. The result is rather disappointing, owing to a certain melodramatic key which spoils an honest and often beautiful piece of work.

Jean Gremillon has not yet given us his masterpiece, but all his films have a very pure and personal style, although unfortunately they have not fought themselves free from the descriptive, passive and frequently imitative style of the silent days. Within this powerful artist, the creator is hampered by gifts of observation which prevent him from picking out the figurative and the dynamic quality of the frame.

Gremillon has, however, made a film both descriptive and presenting his own personal point of view, in which he thought out the scenario, the visual images and the music. This was *6 Juin à l'Aube*, which conjured up from a purely subjective point of view the battle of Normandy in 1944 after the Allied Armies had landed on this war-devastated province. I must see this sixty-minute film again in several years' time – and the public does not want to see it for the moment – to know for sure whether it is really a personal work of art, as I believe it to be, or merely a piece of good reportage or a reconstructed documentary like René Clément's *Bataille du Rail* (1944).

It would seem to me useless to cavil about *Le Silence est d'Or*. Personally, I consider that René Clair in Hollywood has taken on a new lease of life, and that *I Married a Witch* and even *It Happened To-morrow* can be counted among his successes. On the other hand, he could have made *Le Silence est d'Or* just as well in 1939 or even 1935.

THE PRESENT AND THE FUTURE

And to-day? It would be an exaggeration to say that the German occupation was the cause of the success of the French cinema, but it is true to recognise that the artist is the only one who knows how to draw a new creative inspiration from suffering, repentance and compulsion.

The theatre and cinema were the only entertainments for a population deprived of the means of travelling, for youth deprived of amusements. ...

As to the difficulties, increased for those who were trying to rebuild the film industry, the cinema saw their audiences grow and their receipts increase, while at the same time American competition was completely non-existent and German competition was hardly worth noticing. For the younger men, there was the desire to assert themselves quickly in order to gain their place and their right to express themselves; for others the duty to give the public entertainment to make them forget their worries for the evening. Finally, for all of them, from the most ambitious producer down to the most humble workman in the studio, the pride of getting over, by their ingenuity, good taste and intelligence, the lack of materials for film-making which grew a little worse every season. From this arose a kind of pent-up enthusiasm sometimes coloured with dreams or anger, and bringing to birth one of the most brilliant periods of the French cinema.

To-day the industry is paralysed by lack of initiative and the weight of an all-controlling bureaucracy more than by a lack of financial credit.

In fact, the majority of the French film-makers would like to see the nationalisation of the film industry. Half-paralysed by an ever-growing heap of new rules and regulations, French industry must either be freed by the re-establishment of free enterprise or reorganised by socialisation.

The French film costs twenty times as much to produce now as it did in 1939, while the price of cinema seats has only gone up about 60 per cent. French films which used to sell well abroad are now not selling so well; and this is due to a number of reasons, some of them psychological, others due to quotas and above all to bureaucratic organisation. Left alone by itself, the French cinema industry has taken a liking for isolation. A forced self-sufficiency has left it with the idea that it could live voluntarily by these means. When the French citizen has a hankering after Napoleon, it seems that he must also have a hankering for blockades.

In other words, the French cinema has become parochial and has retired into itself. To-morrow, because it will have prevented the artists from expanding their talents freely after the healing influences of the occupation, it risks being engulfed by a tide of foreign films. In order to ensure a stable French film industry there must be a series of social reforms, which in the past have been purely formal, whether they be made by an ingenious economic policy or by the bounty of the State. Meanwhile, one can only advise every film-maker to make the films he wants to make on 16-mm. film stock. And that is what the partisan of the 'camera-pen' will not hesitate to do.

Excessive individualism, intellectualism, films with restricted showings, esoteric art, will cause the best friends of the French cinema of yesterday to sigh. I regard the present crisis of the French cinema not without due consideration; not tragically but seriously. But I am not the only one to prefer the laboratory, intellectualism and the rule of the amateur to the production of spectacular balloons and the triumph of journalism over art.

Even for this year, the best French films will only be visible on the secret screens of those who imagine them without being able to put them on to celluloid. It is not entirely the fault of the artists, for, indeed, I almost forgot to say that the French cinema has barely one or two producers capable of handling this difficult, thrilling, tremendous and magnificent craft.

(*Translated by Cynthia Morris.*)

BRITISH FILMS AND
THEIR AUDIENCE

A. L. VARGAS

★

THE 1939–45 war saw the emergence of an artistically mature
British cinema. It was a cinema which grew healthily and
naturally out of the people of Britain under the impact of war,
and gave us such works as *In Which We Serve, Target for
To-night, The Way Ahead, The Way to the Stars,* and hosts
of others. These films won for Britain critical acclaim wherever
they were shown, and an international film market began to
occupy the minds of film producers. At last, it seemed, the era
of the great British film had arrived. No more did we avoid
cinemas showing British films as we did in pre-war days. Instead we went eagerly to see all British films, confident that the
product would be the equal of, if not superior to, all other films
being shown. And the important thing to remember is that the
new British cinema was essentially a native art, reflecting the
British outlook on life and the determination to see the war
through, cost what it may.

If we attempt to take stock of our position to-day, two and a
half years after the war, what conclusions can we draw? Have
we consolidated our position and made further progress, or are
we just marking time?

Let's face it. British films are in grave danger of slipping back
to the bad pre-war days. The technical efficiency is there; the
settings, costumes, lighting, and camera work are invariably
beyond reproach. But let us probe deeper than mere technical
excellence. The films Italy has been sending us in recent months
are proof enough that great films can be made, even with

71

slender technical resources. No, the root of the trouble lies deeper, in the theme or idea behind the stories which are filmed.

The best British war films never lost sight of their theme: the common struggle of the British people to persevere and win through under the stress and strain of war. It was from this theme that they drew so much of the strength which enabled them to reach the high standard hitherto so rare in British films. Here were films which were not only satisfying as entertainment, but boasted that little bit extra the others had not got. How often do we leave the cinema nowadays after seeing a British film with that feeling of renewed faith in ourselves, that refreshment of the spirit which we derived from such films as *In Which We Serve* or *The Way to the Stars*? Very seldom indeed, I imagine, if the truth were told. Our films to-day supply us with entertainment, thrills and glamour. They amuse us, excite us and sometimes stimulate our imagination. They seldom move us; and there lies the whole trouble. They have lost their personal contact with their audience.

British films are at the crossroads. Our studios can either continue to supply us with an unending stream of well- and not-so-well-made novel and play adaptations, with a handful of thrillers and comedies thrown in, or they can get down to brass tacks and tackle the urgent problem of making films with stories and themes that bear closer relation to the pattern of life as it is in Britain to-day.

The lessons drawn from our successes during the war years seem to have been quickly forgotten. The debt owed by film producers to British documentary is given little more than a passing thought. Yet it would be true to say that it was the documentary approach to film-making which put the film industry on the right track during those first few months of war, and whose influence did much to guide the hand of the new school of directors and screen-writers which the war brought into prominence for the first time. Thanks to documentary, our screen stories were ruthlessly pruned of their novelettish flavour (a bad legacy from the days when we took the Hollywood film for our model), and films were made from incidents which had actually occurred or could be authentically related to the background of Britain at war. As a result our films grew daily in stature and importance.

Here was a cinema which took its audience into its confidence and produced films which treated with candour and perfect sincerity the everyday problems of a people at war.

But to-day the reverse process seems to be at work. Film producers have decided, quite firmly apparently, that, as we are all a little tired and the outlook for the future is none too rosy, we should welcome a large dose, even an overdose, of romance and glamour, having duly noted that there is precious little of these two commodities about these days. Here, I fear, they have been led astray by a dangerous half-truth, and have badly underestimated the intelligence of British film-goers. The public will always pay to see a well-made film on a subject of topical interest provided that the approach is sincere and the audience is taken into the confidence of the film producers. In my opinion British film producers since the war have let the film-going public down badly. The success of the war years has gone to their heads. They have got into the dangerous habit of thinking that they have found the magic formula for making good pictures, and from now on it's plain sailing to turn out winners every time. They have given us glamour, but it's the meretricious and outdated glamour of the blonde cutie singing in a night-club, not the glamour of the charge of the French cavalry in *Henry V*. We have had the 'Spiv' thrust down our throats till we wince at the mere mention of the word. We have had precious little healthy laughter in our films of late and hardly any of the integrity and poetry that were wrung out of the war years to put the British product high up in the top flight of films.

The main trouble is to be found in the fact that too many films are now being made which have nothing to say and are frankly pure entertainment. It is obvious that we must expect a fair quota of films which seek to do no more than entertain film audiences, but it is equally obvious that British films will not maintain, but will in fact soon lose, their hard-won prestige unless they also give us a fair share of films which have something to say and say it intelligently. It is the dearth of the films of the latter class which has become such a matter of concern to those in the industry, to critics and discerning film-goers in recent months.

Our studios have now reached the stage where, in their quest for higher and higher standards of technical efficiency and professional slickness, they find themselves turning out pictures which are technically impeccable but often quite without point or purpose. Whilst we have been worshipping the false idol of efficiency, the soul has gone out of our pictures. It is ironical to remember that this same technical gloss, which now comes so pat with every new British film, was once the reason why we cast envious eyes at the Hollywood product. 'How tasteless that American film was', we used to say; 'but how beautifully made.' The wheel, it seems, has now come full circle. Whilst in Hollywood the rise and steady growth in the number of independent producers has led to a more mature and realistic approach to film subjects, culminating in productions worthy of serious attention, such as *The Best Years of Our Lives, Crossfire* and *The Unfaithful*, our films are tending more and more to waste their time and energy on cheap sensationalism, vapid novel adaptations and costume melodramas.

We are also being regaled with occasional spectacles, such as *An Ideal Husband*, gorgeously arrayed in Technicolor. Having seen how brilliantly effective Wilde's comedy can be on the stage, one wonders why a little more serious thinking was not done before the decision to film it was made. The result is a splendid feast for the eye. The settings, costumes and colour are magnificent, but one can hardly call it a film. The sparkling, epigrammatic flavour of Wilde's comedy is wholly lost and the treatment throughout is entirely uncinematic: the only possible result to be expected when the cinema tries to improve on the stage instead of standing on its own two legs and seeking after suitable subjects for filming.

I seem to remember a film called *Brief Encounter*. It was made in 1945 by David Lean for Cinéguild from a story by Noel Coward. It was not in Technicolor and was certainly not studded with stars. Celia Johnson, one of our finest stage and screen actresses, played the lead opposite Trevor Howard. It was a very simple and straightforward story about a middle-aged woman who falls in love with a doctor. Both of them are married, and the main thread of the story concerned itself with the manner in which both come to realise the hopelessness of their love and decide to part. He goes off to a post in Africa and she returns to her husband and child. There is no sub-plot. We are concerned only with two people struggling to find a way out of the dilemma in which their love has placed them.

It was not a very original story and it contained none of the usual safe box-office clichés. It was a story, in fact, which would have been turned down flat as uncommercial by an average producer who had some experience of the film business. Yet Noel Coward, David Lean, Celia Johnson and Trevor Howard, and in fact all concerned in making this film, evidently had faith in the story. The result, as everyone knows, was that their skill and team work produced one of the finest British films ever made. For acting, direction and passionate sincerity it will remain as a landmark among British films. Producers to-day could hardly do better than to take to heart some of the valuable lessons to be learned by studying this film. For it proves over and over again the much-neglected truth that what matters in film-making is not a script cluttered up with incident or a film audibly creaking under its burden of stars, elaborate sets, gorgeous costumes and brilliant camera work, but a story which has something to say and whose characters are not the colourless puppets of some schoolgirls' weekly, but creatures of flesh and blood, drawn in the round with all their faults, impulses, hopes and fears like ourselves. The story should mean something to every Tom, Dick and Harry engaged on the production, from the director down to the clapper boy.

One feels this must have been the case with *Brief Encounter*, and that is one measure of its success and the reason why it lingers in the memory when countless other more ambitious productions have been forgotten.

As one who has serious misgivings about the way British films are tending rapidly towards slick commercialism, I would like to make a suggestion to film producers. Let them turn their attention to the serious problem of recapturing that contact between their audience and themselves which accounted in such great measure for the success of the war films. Let us give melodrama and romantic backgrounds a rest and concentrate more on stories with simple, everyday themes featuring well-drawn characters. The humour and characterisation of such modest film successes as *Holiday Camp* and *Easy Money* were brilliantly handled, and one feels that there is ample room for development on the lines followed by these two films.

To-day, more than ever, the urgent need is to cut costs and increase the output of British films. Here is one way we can achieve this end.

TOWARDS A SCIENCE
OF ART

CHARLES DEKEUKELEIRE

★

THE natural histories of a few centuries ago used in all seriousness to describe the griffon and the unicorn among the fauna
of this earth. Art and the other branches of learning were not
yet widely separated in origin. Empiricism and imagination
held the place of science in human knowledge, all forms of
which could serve the contemporary social order as appropriate.
If only the dreamers practised alchemy, it was art that built the
cathedrals, for art had a social and constructive rôle in civilisation, and one which was never in doubt. I stress this initially,
because to-day we are accustomed to consider art only as a form
of entertainment, and seldom question whether the unrest of
modern society may not be due to the collapse of certain disciplines by which the great social orders of the past were held
together, however markedly the material conditions of their
various classes may have differed. A society is a living body, and
to remain healthy all its organs must function normally. The
body of our society is in process of growing, and certain of its
organs as yet are only potentially in existence.

Though the artist ranks to-day as a dreamer, while chemical
science, evolved from mediæval alchemy, is the key to modern
production, it is too soon to say that art has definitely lost its
constructive rôle in society. In fact, with the whole of human
knowledge growing a new skin, now is the time to revise every
spiritual discipline and mode of understanding necessary for the
creation of a stable society.

When the rudiments of mathematics, first of the sciences,

were established, man entered history. Elementary geometry drew up maps and plans for navigation, irrigation and building, and the abacus aided business transactions. But antiquity never completely discarded the imaginary significance of numbers: it recognised male and female numbers, the perfect number and the unlucky number. Even in mathematics its culture remained charged with a mythical spirit which was the foundation of its unity, and which enabled all the spiritual disciplines, including art, to collaborate in its development.

In modern times mathematics has completely discarded the myth, and we have passed decisively into a period of scientific knowledge. Experimental calculation extends to spheres where previously fantasy reigned, for example in anatomy, botany and medicine. When knowledge had advanced sufficiently from the mythical to the scientific, a new mode of work, the industrial system, was created which strikingly confirmed the power over nature yielded by the new method. Industry progresses as the accurate sciences advance. Psychology and pure thought entered the laboratory not long ago. To-day, of all forms of knowledge which attempt to understand the universe, art alone remains exclusively empirical. Forty years ago industry never dreamed it would turn one day to a still non-existent science of psychology, which to-day renders it immense services. It barely suspects that art, if it became a science, could do still more. Even less do art lovers realise what services industry could render their ideal. For industry possesses the means of action and ability to finance researches, however costly, to the limit of their usefulness. It is industry which assured the necessary researches for the contemporary development of the sciences. We need as precise and practical a collaboration between the machine world and a science of art.

Only in modern times has art lost contact with the production of material goods. Of the six traditional arts, painting, sculpture and architecture are directly related to the artisan mode of work. Earlier still we find as direct a relationship between the primitive forms of work and poetry, music and the dance. These three arts not only accompany the traditional work of surviving primitive peoples in Africa and Oceania; they mould the spirit in which it is performed, infusing it with a certain humanism. Although values multiplied as civilisation developed, and art became less closely linked to daily work, the arts evolved by the artisan world fulfilled an analogous purpose; the artisan knew that manual labour could create masterpieces of art, and this enlivened the monotony of his daily work which to-day we compare favourably with the mechanical labour of the worker on the production line, though the latter creates more finished products and the monotony of movement is often the same. The science of psychology, while improving working conditions, cannot solve the problem of making the rationalised system of the factory more attractive in itself, and the source of a true humanism. This is the province of a science of art. Its usefulness is obvious. There is a latent spirit of revolt in the working class against the industrial system for the very reason that they must perform work unproductive of any emotion, as were all the traditional modes of work which were raised by art to the level of poetry. The worker thinks, feels and imagines, and, like every human being, demands that his activity should serve his whole personality. He will be a rebel until his work opens the door to emotion, until the industrial system leads to emotion and he can discover in his work itself the satisfaction of his desires and his psychological equilibrium. Indeed, peace and social order depend on this: art is the crowning glory of technique, the means by which an economy attains its perfect internal equilibrium.

To collaborate, art and industry must be linked in spirit and in technique, just as art in the past served the economy by taking as its starting-point the contemporary mode of work. But the multiplying activities of industrial civilisation, directed in the main to the measurement and domination of something essentially dynamic – energy – cannot be crystallised in some great architecture such as the cathedrals. The appropriate art, the cinema, has already been born out of industry. In order to function, the cinema requires the modern products of mechanics, chemistry and electricity. Its very principle, the reconstitution of movement and sound after its analytical disintegration into twenty-four units per second visually and many hundreds per second aurally, was inconceivable for mankind only three centuries ago. The concept of measurement proper to all science is inherent in this analysis. The cinema can translate into images and sound, according to a universal measure, everything that occurs. It can become a scientifically exact reflection and analysis of the universe, the human mind only intervening, as in every science, in order to interpret – or in cinematic terms to edit – the results which have been objectively recorded by the apparatus. Industrial in its equipment, scientific in its processes, this cinematographic art demands our systematic study, and must be raised to the level of a science of contemporary emotion.

This, then, is our aim. It is clearly defined and is not the subject of any other science. Psychology has been called the science of behaviour. Certainly it can assess the qualities of an existing emotion, but a science of art should create new emotions. This claim might provoke some scepticism at first sight. I will define its exact meaning by an example from the past of humanity. There is a profound difference between the primitive type of humanity such as we find to-day in Africa and Oceania and the Occidental type in so far as we can consider him apart from the machine. In both types we can find qualities and refinements, particularly of a sentimental kind, which are identical. But there are others which differ, and certain forms of understanding, certain emotions do not exist, or exist only in embryonic form among the primitives. Much more than any physiological differences these differences of a spiritual kind are attributable to racial selection, and above all to modes of living and education which are diametrically opposed. The life of artisan and industrial societies differs as greatly as the life of primitive and artisan societies. Consequently, just as national artisan civilisation led to a flowering of new emotions and philosophical conceptions, so we can expect from industrial civilisation a fresh flowering in humanity. I will not dwell on the processes which must lead our civilisation to new philosophical conceptions, but as far as new emotions are concerned, the rôle belongs to a process of artistic creation. Chemistry not only analyses what is in its own domain, but deduces from its studies the possibility of creating new products. In the same way the science of art will enable us not only to analyse the emotions – in one respect it has this in common with psychology – but also to create the new emotions that are essential for the continued development of industry, and above all of man himself.

The preliminary task of information to be undertaken by the cinema is certainly vast, but the very fact that our civilisation with its diverse specialisations has given rise to a far greater number of activities than previous civilisations is a reason for hoping that a science of art will generate far subtler emotions than the empirical arts of hitherto. Furthermore, the services of the cinema to industry will be judged by the exacting standards of modern output calculations, thereby excluding all fantasy. The empiricism which so far has governed art must under the conditions of industry give way to a strictly methodical approach. And with our mode of work as the starting-point, we can easily draw up the main groups of films to be made.

The first is that of instruction – of apprenticeship in the widest sense of the word. It covers, for example, elementary, secondary and university education, scientific study, industry, administration and the liberal arts. Each of these types can be subdivided, the industrial film for instance into personnel selection, trade apprenticeship, the study of new manufacturing processes and so forth. Under this definition the instructional film is really the basis of the science of the film. As every form of knowledge is a subject for study, it comprises in fact the whole domain of learning: its field of experiment is as vast as humanity, its laboratory is the universe. But in all this immense field, to which the huge scope of art is well suited, there is no place for faults or omissions, for we are dealing with the formation of those on whom will depend the development of society: we are confronted with a true science.

The problem of acquired skill, of mastery of the activity, gives rise to the second group of films. Once an activity is mastered it must be practised, not only to earn a living, but also to obtain the maximum satisfaction from it. This group consists of films dealing with the key problem of raising the activity to the level of humanism. Above all it is a question of films primarily aimed at those who to-day carry out jobs from which they gain no satisfaction. It concerns the rationalised tasks which no longer have any connection with a manner of working whose beauty we have been taught by tradition – the rationalised work of the factory hand, of the employee and even of certain executive posts where the task has been deadened by routine. In reality the rationalised activity of the factory worker is more precise and calls for more human qualities than that of the artisan, as is proved by the fact that education became compulsory as soon as industry felt the need for a massive recruitment of new elements. This spirituality must be given its true value: it must be linked to the universe of the worker and it must be used to extend this universe. I am always astonished when people inveigh against the monotony of the factory worker's activity: as long as it remains within certain limits monotony is not in itself inhuman. It is only inhuman in so far as it does not lead to any emotion. We all perform certain activities which lead naturally, so to speak, to emotion; those which I have described above as being common to the primitive and to the artisan. We perform others which lead to emotion because they bear a resemblance to the former. It is precisely this world of resemblances, of symbols and images, which is the world of art, the world which must be linked up with the activity of the factory worker. A possibly over-simple analogy is that of reading a book – we sit and turn the pages and follow the lines by the hour. The ideal is to make rationalised work like an open book which the worker reads as he carries out his task. Here again the output of the worker who has been educated by films of this kind will be the measure of their success. The film of mastery, which is already intensely lyrical – for it must by its very definition link together the whole of humanity – also answers to practical aims which will keep it to the path of the greatest efficiency for civilisation.

The third group is an extension of the first two, and comprises films of synthesis destined to reveal to all mankind the full splendour of their work. The film of mastery will evoke a new world whose richness and subtlety we cannot imagine to-day, not only because of the subjects with which it deals, but because of the way in which they will be treated. Indeed, the film-makers will have to solve extremely delicate problems, and to succeed they will have to deploy a refinement of means of which the crude psychology of the dramatic film of to-day gives no idea. In the film of revelation it is a question of making known all this new beauty to the whole people and of making a synthesis of it for them. The films of revelation have no place either for fantasy. Their task is precise – the integration of society for which every responsible person is seeking.

A science of film, then, based on our work, gives us three groups – films of instruction, of demonstration of mastery, and of universal revelation. The task is complex but the plan is simple, and in each of these spheres the cinema has already taken its first steps. All we lack is the necessary co-ordination of effort to make the project economically practicable and useful, so that the cinema may really become the science of contemporary emotion. We must seek the creation in every country of a Film Institute of Labour, whose task will be to collate and edit all the existing documentary film material in the world and to put it at the service of the industrial effort, and to issue regularly new films answering the needs I have outlined above. By establishing this under the ægis of industry we guarantee not only its true scientific basis, but also the necessary resources to ensure its fullest development.

One may ask what will become in all this of the so-called entertainment film with its vast finances. For many it is the whole of the cinema, but its evolution is essential. It is absurd that a civilisation should seek for its emotions outside the active life of its work, absurd both economically and morally. If our schools of literature and our entertainment films transgress through pessimism, disgust with life and through immorality, it is because they seek for emotions outside active life which is inspiring and creative. In the factory and the laboratory there is no place for the unhealthy thought of a Sartre, but only for virile qualities of creation. Our hope is to set these qualities up as an example through a science of the cinema and to raise them in a wonderful synthesis to the heights of a perfect humanism. In the great ages the life of entertainment lay in an extension of the life of work: it grew out of work and led it to spirituality. The great temples of antiquity and our mediæval cathedrals were at the same time works of entertainment, of piety, of spirituality and eminently practical works to which the people went to draw strength from this expression of their attachment to the collective whole. To-day there is a division between the works of entertainment and those which are directed towards social or industrial propaganda. The latter are somewhat slightingly referred to as publicity, and not incorrectly so, for publicity is a poor manifestation which expends itself in a display of fireworks. Economically this division is a heresy, for it compels society as a whole to pay a double tax – one for its entertainment and one for learning to make use of the goods which the community provides for it. Economically and morally it is essential to combine these two taxes. One day the whole entertainment side of the cinema will be at the service of the contemporary ideal. The films will be entertaining just as they are to-day: they will appeal to the sensibility and the imagination, but at the same time they will be useful, because they will take part in the constructive work of the community, and from this useful task they will derive their grandeur. When the cinema reaches this point industrial civilisation will approach maturity. Its art will bring into the realms of emotion, preceding somewhat the appearance of a system of thought appropriate to our age, works which will no doubt surpass in greatness those of the empiricism of hitherto, even as the different sciences and modern industry surpass in their respective domains the creations of the past.

(*Based on an address given at the University of Louvain; translated by P. S. D. Furse.*)

TARGET FOR FILM SOCIETIES

FORSYTH HARDY

*

THE film society movement has been expanding so rapidly in
the past two or three years that a critical glance at its aspirations and achievements seems overdue. What is the film society's
rôle in the community? What service does it render to cinema?
Does it get the assistance it needs? Does it get the recognition
it deserves? Is it doing its job? What reforms are necessary?
These are some of the questions which seem worth answering
at a time of expansion, when the movement ought to be keeping its objectives clearly in view.

The film society is cinema's minority audience. In the main
the film industry is organised on the basis of broad appeal and
big battalions. It produces pictures for the million, not for the
thousand: pictures designed to make the circuit of the cinemas
quickly and easily, on the sure basis of star appeal. Difficult
themes, unusual forms of treatment and foreign languages do
not make for popularity. A film society recognises that, cinema
being a mass medium, films must be made for the majority;
but it also argues that there should be an opportunity of seeing
those films which, by accident or design, lack the broad appeal
necessary for the cinemas.

In London and some other cities, the needs of this minority
audience are met to a large extent by the specialised cinemas
(although, of course, specialised cinema and film society can,
and do, exist side by side). In most communities, however,
there would be no opportunity of seeing the films which diverge
from the box-office track were it not for the activities of the

86

film society. The audience is too small for the commercial
cinema to bother about, and too exacting in its taste. It can
best be served by a voluntary organisation with the patience
and resource to compose programmes consistently to the
standard necessary for its satisfaction. If the programmes do not
satisfy, then the members have the remedy available in all good
democracies.

In so far as they make available the freaks and flowers of
film-making, the specialised cinema and the film society have
similar aims; but the society which merely provides a replica of
the Academy and Curzon programmes is doing only one part
of its job. The film society's existence recognises the art of the
film and accepts some responsibility for its study and advancement. That responsibility is not discharged by showing the
latest films from the Continent. The cinema is an ephemeral
art: films are out and away and in again while the trumpetings
of the West End *première* are still echoing in the distant villages
(which presumably explains why the trumpets are blown so
loudly). There is little opportunity for a second glance at a contemporary film. The older film of merit, and particularly the
silent film, is so rarely seen that the study of history and traditions common in the other arts is virtually impossible. It is the
responsibility of the film society to provide these opportunities
for study. The society can combine old and new elements in its
programmes; or it can arrange a supplementary series of programmes to set the outstanding films of yesterday against the
background of contemporary achievement.

Study infers criticism. A film society ought to be a critical
clearing-house. It should stimulate discussion and invite
analysis. The discussion session after a performance should be
as important in the society's scheme of things as the performance itself. Some of the discussions I have heard following
film society performances have astonished me by the critical
acumen revealed and the knowledge displayed of the film's history. I think that some of our film critics would find it stimulat-

ing to drop in on one of these evenings. If the experience I have had is a reliable guide they would find themselves drawn into a keen and lively debate; and they would not get out of it again without stating clearly why they thought a film was good and what was good about it.

Similarly, I think there should be a closer contact between the film-makers and the film societies. They would find it helpful to discuss their work in an atmosphere free from the distraction of star worship and the like. I recall an occasion when a director with the star of his new film was attending a film society meeting before making a personal appearance at one of the city's cinemas. The star was welcomed politely, as befitted her decorative value; but the director soon found himself involved in a quick, keen discussion of his work. As the moment for the personal appearance approached he showed no inclination to leave; and eventually the star was hauled off by the agitated publicity man to make her appearance alone. The director clearly did not wish to miss the stimulus which an informed and critical audience can give to a creative worker. Many of the film-makers realise this, but their opportunities for breaking away from the studios are limited. I am not sure, however, how hard on the one hand the film societies are pressing their invitations and how easy on the other the film companies are making it for their technicians to accept the invitations. Such personal appearances would not pay a dividend in headline publicity; but it would be a poor film society which did not send a director back with an idea or two and a welcome feeling of refreshment.

This is one of the services which the film society can render the cinema. Another is to provide an inlet for new men and new ideas. It is worth recalling that it was through the film societies that the dynamic work of the Russian directors first made its impact in this country; and that it was the unwavering support of the film societies which helped to sustain the documentary film movement in Britain during its early struggles. It should be a first aim of the film society movement to seek out experimental work wherever it is being done and to give it wider currency. Between Oscar Fischinger and his abstract studies of twenty years ago and Arne Sucksdorff with his poetic nature films of to-day, there have been many instances of talents discovered and introduced by the film societies, and cinema is the richer for them. Since the sound-film threw language barriers round the producing centres, the film societies have become one of the few channels for the free circulation of experimental work.

I am not satisfied that the societies are sufficiently alive to their opportunities in this connection. Perhaps travel difficulties have limited first-hand exploration of foreign sources; perhaps currency problems hamper importation. There may well be other reasons. But if fifty foreign films and more can be imported by a single society for the Documentary Film Festival at the Edinburgh Festival of the Arts, it suggests that the difficulties are not insurmountable and that there is experimental work waiting to be discovered.

The film society ought to be able to take a generous view of its responsibilities. It should be the focal point for film activity in its area. It can, for example, take the initiative in arranging special performances for children if this is not being done by any other agency. It can help to form an educational film association or a scientific film society to supplement its work in these fields. It can form a production group or take a friendly interest in the activities of amateur cinematographers among its members. It can provide lecturers to help to meet the great unsatisfied hunger for information about the cinema which exists all over the country.

It would be misleading to suggest that all film societies are at present hitting this target, or even aiming at it. Some of them are content to repeat locally the programmes of the London specialised cinemas. They have no additional activities to justify the term 'society', and their claim to remission of entertainment tax on educational grounds is decidedly meagre. I am not surprised that there has been criticism from the film trade of organisations which are film societies in name only. The privileges which a film society enjoys cannot be justified by putting 'The Study and Advancement of Film Art' on its notepaper and leaving it at that. It is not enough to offer lack of numbers as an excuse. One of the most successful film societies I know is in a town of no more than two thousand inhabitants. It gives performances (on 16 mm.) of foreign and other films which would not otherwise reach the community. It shows documentary and educational films, holds regular discussion meetings, and maintains a library of film books. It has fewer than a hundred members, but without any doubt it is doing its job in the community as a film society.

Film societies in England and Wales are now combined in a Federation which is represented, with the Scottish Federation (founded in 1936), on a Joint Committee. Through this organisation it is possible both to protect the interests of film societies and to maintain standards within the movement. There are many advantages to be obtained through co-operative working, difficult though that has always been to achieve in the film society movement. The first advantage is a central booking agency. During the war the British Film Institute agreed to act in this capacity for the Scottish Federation, and is now the centralised booking agency for both Federations. By this means film society secretaries are saved the nightmarish explorations of the sources of films which made colourful chapters for their records in the early 'thirties. Acting for the Federations, the Institute has made available a greatly improved information service. It is now unlikely that any film society with *Extase* in its programme would announce it, for want of better advice, as 'an experimental musical film'. The film societies, however, could have still more information without feeling that the service was being overdone. We have still little to compare, for example, with the information sheets about films and directors prepared by the French association of Ciné Clubs.

A beginning has also been made with the importation of films for film societies. In the early days of the movement this was done most effectively by the Film Society in London, and many of the films introduced by this means are still being shown by the societies. If the new arrangements can equal this record, a major problem of film supply will have been overcome. The specialised cinemas are, of course, constantly on the look-out for programme material and, since the revenue they can offer producers is much greater than the resources of the film society movement, it is unlikely that any masterpiece will remain undetected or neglected. There are other films, however, which may go rather farther in experiment than the specialised cinemas are prepared to accept, and there are also the smaller production centres to explore. There is a wide territory for exploration; and the explorers should remember that film society programmes cannot be too rich and strange.

The principle of co-operation is sound, and there are services which the film societies can secure only through a pooling of resources. The price of these advantages is too high, however, if it means the loss of independence. The film societies grew up as free and independent bodies. Much of their value in the community and to cinema would be lost if they became subsidised agencies. As the only articulate demand for a better type of film than normally fills the screens, they must not be muzzled.

POST-WAR AMERICAN DOCUMENTARIES

RICHARD GRIFFITH

★

FLAHERTY aside, the first American documentaries were made under strong Soviet influence, and partook of an agit-prop flavour which was already slightly out-of-date even in the early thirties. Although these were depression times, such films never really reached the American public; they were expressed in an unfamiliar idiom and tied to a crudely dogmatic dialectic. Meanwhile, Grierson was building his successful British documentary movement on a principle of compromise between the interests of adult education on the one hand and the interests of big business and big government on the other. Reluctant as Americans might be to admit it, this was the only possible model to follow – indeed, a model peculiarly appropriate to the atmosphere of the New Deal period. Pare Lorentz was the first to see this and to act on it. His *Plough That Broke the Plains* and *The River* opened the way for big-time Government sponsorship of documentary, and showed the world of education and business what could be accomplished both inside and outside the theatres.

The opportunity was there, but was hard to realise upon. A Congress growing increasingly restive under Roosevelt's hand looked upon Government film production with suspicion, and finally choked it off altogether. Industry and advertising circles were even more suspicious of a movement which had come into prominence under New Deal auspices. The academic world was cautious; perhaps it had interests of its own to protect. Above all, the documentarians instinctively drew back from the job of selling the propagandist potential of documentary to the alien worlds of politics and business. They understood the necessity for this salesmanship, but they were mostly craftsmen who had a hard time putting their minds to business.

Still, selling documentary to potential sponsors was the essential job, and nothing could be accomplished without tackling it. At this point there appeared on the scene the significant figure of Mary Losey. Miss Losey had no interest in films as such. A recent college graduate, she was interested in projecting what colleges teach about economics and sociology to an audience big enough to matter. Film happened to be the mass medium which seemed most readily accessible. She got herself a job at the March of Time and did the research and script outlines for the period which now seems its golden age. But neither this assembly-line method of interpreting fact, nor the sporadic efforts of the independent documentarians, seemed to her to meet the need for a planned attack on the citadels of sponsorship and distribution. About this time Grierson, Rotha and Anstey visited the United States, and she came under the influence of their ideas – or rather, was struck by their affinity with hers. She quit the March of Time, and went to England to find out how they did it there.

Returning here in 1939, she set to work, after the Grierson pattern, to organise the jangling sects of documentary into a purposeful group geared to continuous action. The Association of Documentary Film Producers was formed, and, with Miss Losey as secretary minus salary, set out to attract teachers, journalists and social workers, organise distribution, and allot film work fairly among its members. Working with American Film Centre, a rather watery version of Film Centre, London, the Association also began to try to open new sources of sponsorship. A nucleus of unity formed itself at the centre of this organisational pattern. American documentary was developing the *esprit de corps* which was the mainstay of the Grierson group in England.

But the war was too close. Even before Pearl Harbour, the documentary people had been drawn into some form of war-related activity, and, by 1942, the members of the Association of Documentary Film Producers were dispersed to the ends of the earth and the Association itself disbanded. The seed of unity that had been planted had no time to take root.

This seemed no tragedy. Everybody was working, and documentary itself was sensationally on the upgrade. No other medium so specifically met the needs of the war for men's minds. The Army, the Navy and the Office of War Information received with open arms the pioneer documentarians, to whom was added plentiful talent from Hollywood. At first hostile, these two groups at length combined their methods to produce films whose brilliance, power and exciting promise are familiar to everyone. After the *Why We Fight* and *Fighting Men* series, and the Overseas OWI films, there seemed no limit to documentary's American future. A vast audience, in service and out, had been conditioned to understand and like factual film. A greatly increased number of men and women had been grounded in the skills and crafts of film-making. And, most important, Government, industry and education were now thoroughly convinced of the power of the medium. Documentary had proved itself in action. No one any longer questioned its power to inform, to persuade and to incite.

No one questions it to-day. The power is there, but for two years it has been used so feebly as almost to cancel memory of documentary's wartime supremacy. Let us look at the reasons.

The scores, if not hundreds, of young men who received their film training in the Services were sanguine of their future. Universal acknowledgment of the success of the training and orientation films they had made had convinced them that they had only to apply the same methods to peacetime themes. The first problem they confronted was one all too familiar to the documentary pioneers, but entirely new to the Service men, that of selling themselves to sponsors. In the Army, their only problems had been those of script and technical ingenuity; the themes and ideas were created by the exigencies of the war and the money and machines for expensive film-making had been provided by the taxpayers. Now, all was to seek, and the young producers discovered that they had more to do than convince a potential backer that they knew how to make films. They had to convince him that they could analyse and solve his particular problem of public relations or propaganda or information, and solve it, not only better than other film-makers, but better than other mediums. It was, again, a task, not for the mentality of the craftsman, but for that of the educator, the propagandist, the social analyst, and most of the ex-soldiers were interested in film-making for its own sake, not for the purposes it could serve. They had formed themselves into a myriad of small production units which competed intensely for what business occasionally offered itself, and mostly lost it. Discouraged and bewildered, some of them drifted to Hollywood to offer their skills to the studios, giving up their independence and what interest they had in the documentary form and purpose. Some went so far as to rejoin the Army and resume the now rather dreary business of making training and propaganda films for peacetime soldiers. Some few others – and these generally were the ones who had grasped the documentary idea in more than its technical aspects – got themselves jobs in industry or Government or education, from which vantage-points they began the long pull towards the creation of some new base for production.

Meanwhile, the pre-war documentarians tried, on the basis of their longer experience, to exploit the improved reputation of documentary. Grierson, after his great achievements in Canada, came to New York to set up World To-day, with Stuart Legg and Raymond Spottiswoode as producers and Mary Losey as liaison with sponsors. World To-day's strategy aimed in part to repeat the Canadian pattern, that is to say, to produce a monthly theatrical series comparable to *World in Action*, backed up by non-theatrical sponsored films made for special purposes. Willard van Dyke, Irving Jacoby, John Ferno and Henwar Rodakiewicz pooled their resources as Affiliated Film Producers, and set out to capture sponsorship for either theatrical or non-theatrical films. Robert Flaherty signed contracts with the National Sugar Institute and the Standard Oil Company for sponsored films. Of the others, Joris Ivens had again set out on his travels, Pare Lorentz remained in Government service to supervise films to be shown in occupied countries, and Joe Losey, Irving Lerner and Ralph Steinter had gone to Hollywood.

All these had been leaders in the pre-war documentary group as represented by the Association of Documentary Film Producers. Two other factors of great importance developed in isolation. Louis de Rochemont had left the March of Time during the war and gone to Hollywood, where he adapted documentary technique to semi-fictional themes in *The House on 92nd Street, 13 Rue Madeleine* and *Boomerang*. Through these films, and the increasing number of their imitators, the documentary idea has been thoroughly acclimatised to southern California. De Rochemont has now temporarily forsaken Hollywood to supervise the production of several score films about geography, human and topographical. Three facts about his new programme are of the greatest significance: (1) the de Rochemont films represent a carefully planned attempt to produce a connected series of films covering every aspect of global geography that could be useful in the schools and out; (2) these are not sponsored films, but represent an investment which is expected to be recovered, with profit, through non-theatrical distribution alone; (3) de Rochemont's producer is United World Films, the instrument through which Universal and J. Arthur Rank are entering the non-theatrical field on a big scale. The second development of major importance is not dissimilar in plan from de Rochemont's project, though very unlike in backing. With the vigorous aid of Mary Losey, and under the direction of Nick Read, a graduate of Grierson's Canadian National Film Board, a Southern Educational Film Association has been set up to meet the school and adult education needs of all the southern states. It is officially supported by these states, is charged with the responsibility of planning to meet their film needs on the basis of close analysis of their actual informational problems, and has a grass-roots support from prominent citizens throughout the south.

The potentials of these two forward thrusts of documentary are readily seen. One has an economic base in the needs of a region united culturally and economically as well as geographically. The other is speculating on eventual profit from a distribution field just now opening up – and has the capital power to wait for returns on its investment. Both are compatible with the actual structure of American life as we find it, if not as we would wish it to be. And both possess a characteristic essential to documentary effectiveness: each film is a part of a programme designed to attain cumulative effect over a period of time.

The efforts of the Grierson group and of Affiliated Film Producers have also been directed towards planned film *programmes,* rather than the making of individual films, but they have lacked the economic base and clear-cut purpose of de Rochemont and the Southern Film Association. Grierson's operating margin was small; and when his distributors, United Artists, decided to get out of the short-subject field, the results were crippling. More crippling still was Grierson's departure for Paris to work for UNESCO. Since that time, his organisation has lived on the numerous little films which Mary Losey has been selling to institutional and organisational sponsors. Some of these have been good, and some not so good; but the salient point is that the financial necessity to make films for all comers has prevented World To-day from developing the unique style and outlook which was Grierson's original purpose. This can be seen in the films themselves, which derive either from the pre-war impressionist school or, as in Legg's *Searchlight on the*

Nations, repeat the diffuse journalistic attack of *World in Action*.

Affiliated Film Producers began by working for a division of the State Department which continued the work of the Overseas OWI Division, by whom they had been employed during the war. Such films as Van Dyke's and Jacoby's *Journey into Medicine* refined upon the flavoursome, folksy style of pre-war documentary, but could not innovate, because sponsorial purpose forbade any but an official approach to American life in these films intended for propaganda abroad. Both the Affiliated Group and World To-day have also made films for the Motion Picture Association's educational film project, a Hollywood-financed effort to discover whether teaching films could be made to the satisfaction of teachers. Jacoby's *Osmosis* and Spottiswoode's *Subtraction* were strenuous, indeed strained, attempts to obey Fénelon's injunction, 'Anything which excites the imagination facilitates learning'. My own feeling is that both, and especially the first, tried so determinedly to interest the student in the subject-matter as almost to lose sight of the subject itself. In any case, the Motion Picture Association's project seems to have benefited documentary but obliquely. Its end result has been to stimulate Hollywood producers to set up their own educational film units, just in case there turns out to be profit in non-theatrical films.

There *is* potential profit in non-theatrical, and it is being determinedly pursued by groups whose interest is profit only. American textbook publishers, alive to the threat to their product represented by the school film, are meeting that threat by entering production themselves, tying the films they make to the books they publish. This would seem a natural source for documentary sponsorship, but so far the publishers have been markedly reluctant to employ recognised documentarians. The tie-up between textbook and film requires complete script control by the sponsor, and they find it easier to exercise this control by employing small commercial firms which make films at so much per foot (Britain is familiar with similar semi- or so-called documentary groups which offered some competition to Grierson's unit in the thirties). The results may be correct enough, but their very correctness tends to restrict the imagination-kindling techniques which are the essence of documentary, and, we are told, of the learning process.

In short, the documentary story here has been a struggle for survival, in which the fittest have by no means always survived. Actually, documentary's plight reflects the world situation. Government sponsorship, the principal source of wartime documentary achievement, has almost dried up. Congress dislikes information services, and what films are made are tied to the shifts and expediencies of a confused national policy. This characteristic is not, of course, peculiar to U.S. Government agencies. John Ferno's brilliant and moving *The Last Shot*, produced for British MOI, was forbidden U.S. distribution by its sponsors, lest it shift the American public's attention from dollar-starved Britain to food-starved Holland. American business, eagerly looked to as a source of big-time documentary sponsorship, has proved coy. Documentary's war-record is well known to business men, but a favourable political climate has produced growing lack of interest in public relations designed to 'sell' business to the public, and besides, the excess-profits tax no longer operates.

In addition to these sponsor difficulties, documentary faces a public apathy in direct contradiction to the bright wartime hopes for a post-war audience which would not only welcome but demand fact films. That ideological fatigue, of which Siegfried Kracauer writes in connection with fiction films, operates most severely on documentary. Since few people now have much hope or belief in the causes which documentary customarily promotes, it is hardly strange that they are indifferent to the documentaries themselves.

Yes, it is hard to make documentaries in America to-day, hard to serve the cause of public information in a civilisation so divided and well-nigh paralysed as ours seems to be. But the fault does not lie wholly with the world situation. There are growing points here. The users of informational films, the teachers, organisation executives and the scattered groups of people who are hungry to be informed, have banded themselves together in what they call the Film Council of America, whose purpose is to stimulate the use of documentary on the community level, with the long-term aim of wider distribution and the eventual resulting possibility of self-supporting production. This organisation of film-users and see-ers, the most encouraging event in American documentary history, is not matched by any organisation of documentary producers and receives only perfunctory support from them, or has so far. And, in spite of the apathy of business and Government towards sponsorship, there do exist public servants, and servants of industry, whose influence could be thrown in documentary's direction. They have not been adequately proselytised, and the reason seems to be an assumption on the part of the documentary people that the case is hopeless. That it is not is evidenced by Robert Flaherty, whose activities in the field of sponsorship make more sense to me than anything that has been done here since the war – and perhaps before.

There were those who were of the opinion, a few years ago, that Flaherty's concept of documentary belonged to the past, and could have no relation to a world polarised around big business and big government. Yet, when the Standard Oil Company set out to make a public relations film, they selected – not without careful consideration of the other film people available – the man whose *Nanook of the North* was hailed round the world as a classic, with never an outcry at the taint of commercialism implied by the fact that it was financed by a firm of furriers. If it be granted that Standard Oil knew what it was doing in making this decision, may it not also be supposed that Flaherty did? Now his long-awaited film on Louisiana is released, it has been attacked because it serves none of the public causes with which documentary is identified. Perhaps – perhaps not, but it serves the strategy of documentary as well as anything could. What Flaherty's sponsor wants, what any sponsor wants, is, first, public goodwill for the sponsor, and second, the highest possible film quality. If the film-maker wants his picture to serve another purpose as well, it is quite possible that it may do so – provided only that the first two conditions are fulfilled. To put it mildly, many documentarians still do not see this. They are determined their films shall serve their own purposes first. They are quite willing to throw in film quality, in fact they assume that they do so. But they balk at serving the sponsor's purpose, because they cannot see how to accommodate it to their own.

That is their fault, not the sponsors'. As Grierson demonstrated so long ago and so many times, documentary can survive in the modern world, or any conceivable permutation of it, only so long as it knows how to confront the sponsor with the necessary identification of his own interest with the public interest. There really is no other way of it, and I cannot conceive of any other problem which deserves the attention of anyone seriously concerned with the documentary film in its real meaning. That documentary can easily achieve high quality is to be taken for granted from the existence of so many admirable film-makers of proved ability but mostly out of work. That documentary as a *technique* still has enormous persuasive power is evidenced conclusively by the popularity of Hollywood's documented fiction films. If the heart seems to have gone out of the documentary movement here, that would seem to be because its practitioners are not thinking sufficiently about what is the heart of the documentary idea.

I hope I have said enough to indicate what I think may be done to better the situation. First, documentary must achieve the unity as a movement towards which it was headed before the war. That unity is essential, because to survive and progress documentary must plan – plan in terms of all its members and of a series of over-all goals. I believe its planning should be based on an analysis of the most promising sources of sponsorship, whether those sources lie in the kind of regional film-making represented by the Southern Educational Film Association, in the capital-investment gambit represented by de Rochemont's programme, or in busy exploration of business sponsorship after the fashion of Flaherty. Somewhere in these three fields the future of American production lies. Until their possibilities have been analysed and there has been a planned attempt to exploit them, little progress can be made. The organisation of audiences represented by the Film Council of America, the reviewing and publicising activities of the National Board of Review, wait upon a stream of films worth recommending and seeing. The whole potential system of education-through-films must and will lie paralysed until usable films are available.

It may seem that I have devoted small space to the discussion of individual films in this survey. Entirely aside from the fact that so few films worthy of good report have made their appearance in these lean years, it should not be necessary to apologise for pointing out that there is now only time enough to point to essentials – to deal with essentials. America lacks any such system for the support of documentary production as has been built up in Britain. To build this system is the only legitimate business of documentarians just now – or at any time, until it has been built. The rest – æsthetics, techniques, the personal convictions of individuals – had better be silence.

PSYCHOLOGY OF FILM
EXPERIENCE

HUGO MAUERHOFER

*

WHEN modern man, particularly the city dweller, steps out of the natural light of day or the artificial light of the night and into a cinema, his consciousness undergoes a decisive psychological change. Subjectively he goes to the cinema in most cases to find diversion and entertainment, or possibly instruction, for a couple of hours. He does not bother about the technical, economic and sociological background of the industries which in the first instance enable him to see films; indeed, he feels no desire to bother about this. However, besides these subjective motives, certain objective factors come into play, namely, that psychological change of consciousness which automatically accompanies the everyday act of cinema-going, and which shall now be analysed.

One of the main symptoms of this everyday act, which we shall call the *Cinema Situation*, consists of the most complete possible isolation from the outside world, with its visual and aural causes of disturbance. The ideal theatre would be one where there are absolutely no sources of light (such as emergency and exit lighting, etc.), except the screen itself, and where not even the faintest sounds, other than the sound-track of the film, could penetrate. This radical elimination of all visual and aural disturbances not connected with the film originates from the fact that only in complete darkness can the best results in film presentation be obtained. The perfect enjoyment of cinema-going is restricted by any visual or aural disturbance, for it reminds the spectator, against his will, that he has just been about to elicit a special experience by excluding the banal reality of everyday life. These disturbances remind him that there is an outside world, which is by no means in accord with the psychological reality of his cinema experience. The inevitable conclusion is that a voluntary escape from everyday reality is an essential feature of the *Cinema Situation*.

In order to assess accurately the psychological effects of the *Cinema Situation*, it is necessary, from the standpoint of experimental psychology, to recall the reactions produced by a person remaining for some time in a more or less darkened room. In such a situation, first of all the *Sense of Time* undergoes a change, in that the course of ordinary happenings appears to be retarded. The subjective impression is that time is passing more slowly than it does when we are kept at a distance from our experience of time by light, whether natural or artificial. The psychological effects of being in a darkened room can be gathered under the common denominator of experiencing *boredom*. This experience is characterised by the absence of 'Something Happening', and simply expresses the hollowness of the bored person.

Another psychological result of visual seclusion in a darkened room is a change in one's *Sense of Space*. It is a known fact that inadequate lighting causes objects to lose something of their distinct shape, thereby giving greater scope to imagination in interpreting the world around us. The less clearly the human eye can recognise the real shape of objects the greater is the part played by the imagination, which is extremely subjective in registering what still remains of visible reality. This change in the sense of space partly removes the barrier between consciousness and the unconscious. Consequently, the rôle of the unconscious in film experience cannot be overlooked.

Decisive parts in the *Cinema Situation* are played by the psychological effects of the changed sense of time and space, i.e. the incipient feeling of boredom and the intensified working of the imagination. The moment the cinema is plunged into darkness, these psychological changes take place. The film on the screen meets both the incipient boredom and the keyed-up imagination, relieving the spectator, who now steps into the different reality of the film.

Immediately there are two significant results: the roused imagination takes possession of the film, which records a specific action on the screen by visual means; at the same time, the changed sense of time creates a desire for *intensified action*. With certain exceptions it is simply intolerable to watch a story recorded on the screen at the same pace as events would occur in reality. The spectator is not satisfied with the action on the screen passing in the usual rhythm of real life. He feels a sub-jective desire for a concentrated form of film narrative. He ex-pects the continuity of the action to be intensified. Unless this psychologically motivated desire is satisfied, his feeling of bore-dom, so far dormant, will inevitably reawaken. In other words, such a film is registered as boring. In this connection it is im-portant to point out that this impression of a film being 'dull' originates, not in the film as such, but in the changed state of the spectator's consciousness. Only for symbolic purposes or for the purpose of intensified dramatic effect may certain scenes from everyday life be presented in the real rhythm of everyday life. In these cases, the continual threat of boredom is temporarily removed by the inner tension and symbolic impli-cation.

Simultaneously with the changed sense of time (i.e. the evoked latent boredom), the effects of the changed sense of space (i.e. the unrestricted play of the imagination) become ap-parent. Their readiness for action is stimulated by yet another essential element in the *Cinema Situation*, namely, the *passive state* of the spectator. He arrives at this state of his own ac-cord. He sits comfortably and anonymously in a room which is shut off from everyday reality, waiting for the film in complete passivity and receptiveness. This condition causes a psycho-logical affinity between the *Cinema Situation* and the state of sleep. Between these two there is a significant relationship. Both cases comprise a withdrawal from reality, darkness as a prerequisite for sleeping or film viewing, and a voluntary state of passivity. For this reason Ilya Ehrenburg was right in calling the film a 'factory of dreams'. While in sleep we ourselves produce our dreams, in the cinema they are presented to us ready-made.

This *Cinema Situation,* with its results of continually imminent boredom, intensified power of imagination and voluntary passivity, causes the unconscious to begin to communicate with the consciousness to a higher degree than in the normal state. The whole arsenal of our repressions is set in motion. As the experience of film-viewing takes shape, a decisive part is played by our unfulfilled wishes and desires, our feelings of incomplete resignation, the daydreams which we do not or cannot realise, and which grow up on the edge of the *Cinema Situation,* so to speak.

The spectator gives himself voluntarily and passively to the action on the screen and to its uncritical interpretation supplied by his unconscious mind. There is no doubt that the reason why film critics so often contradict one another is that the difference between their unconscious minds plays tricks on them. For no two people experience a film in the same way. The experience of Film is probably the most highly individual of all experiences. Even the course of sexual experience, fundamentally speaking, seems more monotonous than the experience of Film in the half-light of imminent boredom, unconsciously fomented imagination at work and passivity in voluntary seclusion. It is just this radical switching off of everyday reality and this voluntary renunciation of all dealings with it which cause that strange phenomenon now under investigation.

Recent psychology, in particular psycho-analysis, has frequently tackled the problem of daydreams as well as dreams experienced while falling asleep; in other words, those border-line phenomena between full, wide-awake consciousness and the real deep dream. It is characteristic of these phenomena that, while the consciousness of reality is not yet completely cut off, it is largely deprived of its critical faculty, although at the same time the unconscious has not taken over full control of the psychic activity. The affinity between the *Cinema Situation* on the one hand and daydreams on the other cannot be ignored. Film experience supplies countless people with acceptable material for their daydreams and the dreams with which they fall asleep.

In this connection let us mention in passing the terrifying lack of imagination in modern man; the Press, Radio and Cinema are by no means suitable for bridging to any noteworthy degree this lack of imagination, which is an essential symptom of contemporary man. The position of the cinema is therefore that of an unreal reality, half-way between everyday reality and the purely personal dream. The experience of Film canalises the imagination, at the same time providing it with the material it urgently requires.

A tangible example of the above may be given. It is a fact that for quite a while after leaving a cinema the entire state of mind of the cinema-goer is changed: a change which is actually apparent to those with him. If for unconscious reasons he has identified himself with certain actors or situations, this mental co-ordination lasts until the film experience recedes before the claims of everyday reality and consequently fades away. In the case of sensitive people with a strong imagination and considerable repressions, the effect of film experience can even be observed in their attitude, gait and gestures.

Finally, let us indicate another psychological effect of the *Cinema Situation*, namely, the *Anonymity* of the spectator. Neither in the dimly lit concert hall nor in the darkened theatre are the spectators, in relation to one another, subjected to such anonymity as in the cinema. In the first place, neither of the former is darkened to such an extent as the cinema is for technical reasons. Secondly, the intervals serve to make at least visual contact with our neighbours as well as with the orchestra or theatre cast. For this reason, too, it is impossible for a 'community', in the original sense of the word, to be formed in a cinema. This is prevented by the individualising effect of the experience of film, as well as by the almost complete anonymity of the spectator. We only sense the presence of our neighbour. He is usually already there when we arrive, and is gone by the time we leave. In the legitimate theatre and at concerts the individual spectators are frequently fused together in an emotional community of objective experience. In the cinema the private and personal participation of the individual is intensified. There is no more than a diffused mass formation. Apart from this, the individual is thrown back upon his most private associations. A factor which adds to this situation is that our feelings make no objective contact with the artists on the screen. To the individual film-goer they are not so much creative artists as representatives of his most secret wishful thoughts. He identifies himself with them uncritically.

These psychological elements – namely, the *boredom* lurking continually on the brink of the *Cinema Situation*, the increased readiness of the *imagination*, the uncritical, voluntary *passivity*, and lastly, the *anonymity* which guides the spectator into his most private sphere – these are the mainstays of the 'Psychology of Film Experience' which we have sketched above. Its effects are manifold. The part played by the film in the life of modern man can hardly be overestimated. It originates from its peculiar psychological conditions and the extraordinarily wide range of its influence, in many cases increased by the modest intellectual demands on the film-goer, who, indeed, has simply to follow his eyes and ears.

One of the decisive elements of the *Cinema Situation* may be called its *psychotherapeutical function*. Day by day it makes life bearable for millions of people. They salvage the shreds of the films they have seen and carry them into their sleep. The reaction produced by the film rids them of their belated longings and daydreams. The cinema offers compensation for lives which have lost a great deal of their substance. It is no less than a modern *necessity*, as yet unsung by any poet. The film makes us sad and it makes us gay. It urges us to reflect and delivers us from worries. It alleviates the burden of daily life and nourishes our impoverished imagination. It is a great reservoir for our boredom and an indestructible net for our dreams. Every day millions of people seek its seclusion, its warm anonymity, its non-committal appeal to the *ego*, the concentrated stories it tells, the colourful interchange of emotion, force and love which passes across the screen. And then, changed for a short while, they step out into the daylight or into the night; each one his own film now, each possessed by the 'bright reflection' of life – or at least the image of this reflection – until reality leads him relentlessly back to its characteristic harshness.

(*Translated by V. H. Adams.*)

THE MUSIC OF 'HAMLET'
AND 'OLIVER TWIST'

JOHN HUNTLEY

★

'A composer must, right from the start, adjust his approach to the composition. In writing for the concert hall, he can work out his ideas to suit himself. His symphony may run for twenty, thirty, or fifty minutes. Not so in films. The form and content of the music is governed absolutely by the exacting requirements of the pictures on the screen.' – WILLIAM WALTON on *Hamlet*.

'Composing for the film was hard work, and I found I had to adapt my normal musical approach quite a bit; it was nevertheless an interesting experience, and I was particularly impressed by the ingenuity and skill of the music director in the actual process of recording the music with the picture on the screen.' – SIR ARNOLD BAX on *Oliver Twist*.

IN the cinema, the demands made on the mind by a really good film are so varied and complex that the work of the individual artists and technicians is not always apparent – which is as it should be. When the composers of these two outstanding British films, *Hamlet* and *Oliver Twist*, speak of the problems of film composition, their words mean little in the cinema when the audience is or should be entirely preoccupied with the end, and not the means, of film craft. Technique for its own sake is nothing, we are told; every technical trick must be justified by some point in the telling of the story or the creation of an effect.

Nevertheless, there is a fascination (that comes with many viewings of a good film) in exploring the various elements that 'make it tick', in the same way as the studio technician who created a particular effect may have found himself completely engrossed in his task to the exclusion of the general pattern of the picture. In such cases, it is the function of the director and producer to see the film as a whole and maintain the balance between the departmental technicians engaged on the various composite parts of the picture. Similarly, the film-goer can adjust his attention to accept the film as a whole or to analyse the separate elements from which it was assembled. With a film, the analytical approach is hampered by the fact that the facilities for examining a film are limited: a visit to a specially designed and equipped building at certain times of the day is necessary. Home projectors can help, but films such as *Hamlet* and *Oliver Twist* are not yet available outside the professional cinema.

In the case of music and dialogue, however, the gramophone is beginning to offer considerable possibilities for people who are interested in finding out more about the construction of films. There are, for example, three records of *Hamlet*, presenting the recorded voices of Laurence Olivier, Basil Sydney, Stanley Holloway and Harcourt Williams, a quantity of natural sound, and the music of William Walton, taken directly from the sound-track of the film by Walter Legge and an E.M.I. mobile recording unit at the Dubbing Theatre in Denham Studios where the picture was made. The first record (H.M.V. C.3755) carries two of Shakespeare's soliloquies. 'Oh that this too too solid flesh,' spoken by Laurence Olivier as Hamlet, is delivered to a musical accompaniment by William Walton, recorded by the Philharmonia Orchestra conducted by Muir Mathieson. Olivier's technique of partly off-screen, partly spoken dialogue is illustrated here, though the effect loses much of its clarity when divorced from the picture. The music flows smoothly, never clashing with the words, expressing thoughts and feelings that even Shakespeare's great command of language cannot fully convey. At the end of the speech, the Ophelia theme is heard as the mobile camera moves rapidly along the corridors and alcoves to the room where Laertes and Ophelia are in conversation regarding 'the Lord Hamlet'.

The roar of the sea, mingled with the turbulent sounds of music, introduces the famous pronouncement 'To be or not to be', spoken on the high battlements of Elsinore. As the speech proceeds, music and the noise of the waves on the rocks below alternate in accompanying Hamlet's musings; divorced from the film, the words come slowly, but there is no questioning the depth of meaning Olivier gives them.

'Speak the speech' (H.M.V. C.3756) consists of Shakespeare's text-book notes on play acting. There is a prelude provided by a gay and sweeping march theme of Walton's which is heard as the Court enters the Council Chamber prior to the Play Scene and later the Duel Scene. In view of the fact that the music was written after these scenes had been shot, the synchronisation is magnificent; even the Queen's graceful sitting-down on the royal chair is perfectly rounded off in a musical phrase.

'The Play Scene' is almost entirely musical on the sound-track, the play itself being enacted in mime. The players make their entry, accompanied by their own small group of instrumentalists, who sit in an alcove above. Here the composer hints at the idiom of the period, and uses an orchestra consisting of two violas, 'cello, oboe, cor anglais, bassoon and harpsichord. He opens with a sarabande, music in slow, three-in-a-measure dance time, often encountered in seventeenth- and eighteenth-century music; there is a sinister passage later for the entry of the poisoner. As the camera moves round to show the reactions of the audience, and particularly the King, the stage music dissolves into a theme expressing the dramatic undercurrent in the Court as the tension rises. The camera, from its tracking, circular orbit, returns to the actors, and the music reverts to the quiet accompaniment of the play. The actor-king has been poisoned; Claudius can no longer stand the strain ('The play's the thing, Wherein I'll catch the conscience of the King'). The full power of the symphony orchestra of sixty players rises up, swamping the soft sounds of the oboe, 'cello and harpsichord, ending in a tremendous 'crash chord' as the King cries, 'Give me some light'. King Claudius thrusts away a torch, offered by Hamlet with a mocking laugh, and flees from the Council Chamber. Complete confusion breaks loose as the cries of the courtiers for 'lights' and the screams of the women are emphasised by the riotous music. The recording ends with Hamlet's triumphant song: 'Why, let the stricken deer go weep, The hart ungalled play; For some must watch, while some must sleep: Thus runs the world away'.

On the third record (H.M.V. C.3757), one scene – 'How long hast thou been gravemaker?' – has no music; it ends on Hamlet's discourse on Yorick's skull. Backing this on the disc is the Funeral March, heard over the opening titles, and then, in a longer form, at the end of the film, starting from Horatio's final speech (spoken in Shakespeare's original play by Fortinbras): 'Let four captains bear Hamlet, like a soldier, to the stage'. Interspersed with Walton's stately and tragic march, the sounds of the soldiers' footsteps and the roar of the cannon on the battlements are heard as the picture moves to its close. *Hamlet* was William Walton's third Shakespearean film; he wrote the music for *Henry V* and also for *As You Like It*, produced in this country in 1936.

Imagine Winston Churchill, a little less flamboyant but equally stocky and formidable at first sight, smoking a pipe instead of a cigar, with a pork-pie hat jammed down over his eyes as he watches a county match at Lord's Cricket Ground – and you have a good idea of Sir Arnold Bax, Master of the King's Musick. With six symphonies, a violin concerto and many other works to his credit, Bax is well known to all followers of contemporary music. His tone-poem 'Tintagel' and the fanfares for the Royal wedding have made his name familiar to many more. In 1943 Bax wrote his first film music for a documentary picture entitled *Malta G.C.*, a production of the Army,

R.A.F. and Crown Film Units. Afterwards he wrote of his impressions on music and the film: 'I do not think the medium is at present at all satisfactory as far as the composer is concerned, as his music is largely inaudible, toned down to make way for – in many cases – quite unnecessary talk'. To-day, having written for his first feature film, Bax feels happier in the cinema.

Oliver Twist contains a number of interesting musical points, and it is very important to see how the director, David Lean, the musical director, Muir Mathieson, and the composer, Arnold Bax, visualised the music, conveyed their ideas, and collaborated in the final result after discussion on all the points involved. For example, here are David Lean's original notes for three sequences, showing how the working out of the music was effected in each case; the result on the screen you must judge for yourself.

'Titles: I haven't the faintest idea what sort of music should accompany the titles, but I should like it gradually to fade away – a fade into an orchestration that suggests that something is about to happen, so that the last two titles on the screen will be in silence, and the first shot of the picture – that of dark clouds – will have a rumble of distant thunder.' The title music was eventually worked out with the two main musical ideas of the picture. Firstly, there is the 'locket theme' – the locket being the key to the mystery of Oliver's birth – and secondly, the theme associated with Oliver himself, heard first on divided strings in the upper register. Lean's idea of 'something about to happen' and the 'last two titles on the screen in silence' eventually became incorporated in the form of a tremolo string sound that quivers through the last of the titles and acts as a bridge into the opening scenes of Oliver's mother in the storm, struggling on to the workhouse.

The next example, taken from the sequence in which the infant Oliver is carried through the workhouse, shows how discussion may sometimes alter the director's original conception of a scene if he hears an idea he likes better. David Lean first

wrote: 'The mother has died in the lying-in room, and the doctor has said "It's all over, Mrs Thingummy". As daylight pours
in, I should like the music to start again. Hopeful: a new day:
new life. I should like the music to "accent" the locket round
the girl's neck, as it is a very important plot point. The music
over the walk through the workhouse changes to a more sombre
note'. The sunlight music and the locket theme were incorporated into the score as Lean indicated, but for the scenes of
the workhouse an experiment was tried. It was decided that
Oliver himself was the primary factor in the scene that introduces the dingy, sordid surroundings of the workhouse. Therefore Bax wrote a part for the piano (played for the film by
Harriet Cohen), and as Oliver is carried, crying, through the
monstrously ugly and dimly lit hall, the tentative sounds of a
piano are heard to emphasise Oliver and act as a contrast to his
miserable surroundings. The piano music has been criticised as
'inappropriate', probably because the significance the director
and composer were searching for has been missed; it may be
therefore that Lean's original conception was the correct one.

A piece of music which came to be known as 'Fagin's Romp'
started life again as a note on the director's files: 'The boys have
sat down to supper with Fagin, and after the Dodger has
brought out his spoils for the day, Fagin raps the table with the
toasting-fork and says "To work". I should like music to accompany the whole scene of Fagin donning his hat, taking the
walking-stick and walking round like an old gentleman, and
finally having his foot trodden on and his pockets picked,
causing him to search frantically for his lost wallet and watch,
which makes Oliver laugh so much. I think the music should
start immediately after "To work" and end on the dissolve to
Oliver lying asleep. This is to me almost the most important
piece of music so far, and I should like it to transform the scene
into a comic ballet, with only one angry jar in it – the moment
when Fagin gives the two boys who have failed to pick his
pocket successfully a kick. This is important because, although

I should like to emphasise the comedy in Fagin, I also want to retain his viciousness which is to develop more and more. In other words, Fagin as a character starts off in Oliver's eyes as an amusing old gentleman, and gradually this guise falls away and we see him in all his villainy.'

Sir Arnold Bax's music does full justice to Lean's requirements. It is highly rhythmic, starting lightly and ending in a rich, vulgar tune. Three chords open out into the main idea, which begins on the strings; the development is interrupted with string chords and a rising phrase for trombones. The fun increases with a tune for the horns, with off-the-beat accompaniment by the full orchestra, going on to the trumpets and trombones as the noisy climax is reached, and a coda, based on the opening theme, brings the musical sketch to an end. It is interesting to note that, at the recording session at Denham with the Philharmonia Orchestra conducted by Muir Mathieson, the music (known then as '4M1' – that is, the first section of music in reel 4) was first recorded straight through and then an additional sharp roll on the side drum (known as '4M1X') was recorded to obtain the vicious effect of the kick mentioned in Lean's notes.

Hamlet and *Oliver Twist* are two films that will bear many viewings. With the aid of gramophone records, a close study can be made of the music alone, which can afterwards be heard in its correct context in the cinema; in the case of Walton and Bax, it will be time well spent by anyone interested in the art of film music.

THE ART OF
THE FILM STRIP

CURT A. LAURENTZSCH

★

DURING recent decades a conscious widening of the scope of the visual arts has been going on by their application to what are now called the applied arts. We can see examples of it every day in advertising, decoration, and modern design generally.

One of the latest additions appears in the rapid development of visual aids in education. It has been realised that the graphical or pictorial representation of things, processes, or principles gives a much better chance of imparting them to the mind of the scholar than merely verbal explanation; and that a series of pictures showing different or successive stages is of still greater value. Modern facilities in photography and the necessity for training the Services, rapidly and soundly, during the war evolved the film strip, a rather glorified magic-lantern affair, the difference being less bulk and more convenience. The projector weighs only a few pounds, and the pictures are photographed on non-flammable cine-film, so that now one small film strip containing twenty to sixty pictures replaces a heavy box of glass slides.

Film strips have come to stay, and those pioneers in Visual Aids who see many of their hopes realised can be congratulated on their success. Active interest is growing, strips and projectors are forthcoming, and helpful discussion is in full swing.

Very little has been heard from that section which is most intimately concerned with the production of film strips: Art Directors, Artistic Advisers (if there are any, as compared with

117

technical advisers), and the individual artists whose craft may make or break the film strip.

Whatever the type of strip – diagrammatic, drawn, or painted, or purely photographic – the artist's help is always needed. And yet his views are seldom asked for.

Nevertheless, his connection with this type of work looks back on a long line of precedents in history. It began, of course, with the cave drawings, where in certain places series of representations can be found, the purpose of which might have been edification according to one view, instruction according to another. Primitive writing followed, beginning with Bushmen, developed by higher cultures like those of the Red Indians, and culminating in ancient Egypt's hieroglyphs. Rome placed the stories of her wars on columns and triumphal arches, and one of the finest examples of pictorial story-telling is certainly the Bayeux Tapestry. Great moral tales can be found in the *danses macabres* of medieval Gothic churches. England produced her own eminent artist in serial picture-story: Hogarth creating his 'Industry and Idleness'. Wilhelm Busch, of 'Max and Moritz' fame, came along with the humorous popular picture-tale, anticipating both comic-strip and cartoon. Many will know that priceless gift of the picture-postcard industry, the harmonica picture album, for the less tasteful examples of which no better word has ever been found than 'kitsch'. Certain modernist painters turned the idea into more serious channels again, picking up where the Gothics had left off. They reintroduced the moral tale, but not having the long walls of churches and cathedrals at their disposal, they divided their canvases into a certain number of equal sections and then painted into each section one small picture to fill the frame with the required number, like Segal, a Continental expressionist whose picture 'Our Daily Bread' comes to mind.

The contemplating artist generally feels concerned with the story of these pictures (which in themselves present a pretty mixed bag) only in so far as content and form reveal their essential harmony. The first view he takes is that of formal achievement. Very little doubt is left with regard to the artistic unity which all of them show by treatment, technique, and the hand of the individual artist concerned. Here it is that the film-strip man links up. His first concern is to make any job æsthetically as satisfactory as lies in his power. That the individual picture must pass this test is understood. His personal skill and artistic understanding are the basis of his work, anyway. But in our case the individual picture does not stand any more alone than those we considered above. Beyond the theme and subject-matter the strip must be held together æsthetically.

What is there initially that makes a film strip? The subject-matter in the form of a script and some pictorial reference material. The easiest way would be to rely on the unity of the material provided and use it as it is, or perhaps to copy it and incorporate such improvements as seem necessary for photographing it. The result is bound to be dull and uninspiring. It would probably be rejected outright.

To put over the lesson effectively, all those principles must be applied which in other forms of visual guidance and influence, as, for instance, in commercial advertising, have been recognised as fundamental and which we find as a matter of course in our historical examples: artistic unity, inner dynamic, and organic coherence.

We can do worse than study the æsthetic laws which govern the *danses macabres* or the Bayeux Tapestry. As we follow their picture-stories we feel at the same time how the artist worked for climax and anti-climax in colour or tone harmonies, for parallel and contrasting movements and subtle direction. We walk along those pictures in churches or museums, or follow the story on some carved altar-piece. The mental movement of our mind is supported by the purely physical movement of our body, thus adding subconsciously to the experience of contemplation. All these æsthetic considerations, which are inherent in the artist's treatment of his job, get an added importance when we try to apply the findings of Gestalt psychology, the importance of which Herbert Read stresses so strongly in his book, *Education Through Art*. Leaving aside the probably controversial nature of Gestalt psychology, it must be recognised that most of its principles have a strong appeal to the artist, especially when working in education. Formulations like symmetry, balance, proportion and rhythm, which in Gestalt psychology attain such an importance, are the very elements of his own work. Then it must be his duty to make the maxim 'Productive thinking must have a close relation to artistic production' work from his end. He must try to provide the æsthetic patterns which made 'progressive apprehension of and comprehension of our environment possible'. He will not be able, nor is it his task, to provide ready-made patterns in the sense of Gestalt psychology (as they, of course, are being produced mentally by the individual himself), but what he can do is to provide at least an artistically satisfactory representation. This will help the film strips to be what an educationalist, in an attempt to define visual aids, called 'supports to the process of thinking'. In this sense the artist is quite prepared to accept the extension of his æsthetic experience into the field of perception in the sense of Herbert Read's quotation of H. J. Eysenck's 'Perception tends towards balance and symmetry, or, differently expressed, balance and symmetry are perceptual characteristics of the visual world which will be realised *whenever external conditions allow it*; when they do not, unbalance and lack of symmetry will be experienced as a characteristic of the whole field, together with a felt urge towards better balance'. The artist with his work can help to create these external conditions in and through visual aids, and thereby cut out to a large extent the need of readjustment for better balance.

The formal content in some of the historical examples mentioned above as artistic unity, inner dynamic, and organic coherence must be considered as fundamental in any work of an artist. They all have this importance in visual aids of our type, too. In appreciating them, especially the last one, we come near enough to their application in the sense of Koffka, who, as Herbert Read quotes, says: 'The facts of a case are not grasped by enumerating them, but must be felt as a coherent pattern'. Not only the artist, but the script-writer, technical adviser, and all the others should indeed ask themselves repeatedly how far a relation may be as significant as the data between which the relation holds. It will be the artist's task again to work his design in such a manner that it gives due consideration to those points which might not be the immediate concern of the frame in hand. All these views must be brought to bear upon the technical approach to our film strips.

It should not be forgotten that the sometimes used expression 'Still Strips' tends to fog the possibilities which are given by the movement from frame to frame during projection. It must be said, however, as will be seen later, that the projectors available at present do not help much in this respect. The lack of a shutter gate which blacks out the screen during frame change makes it impossible to take into account, for instance, the effects of persistence of vision. As things are now, we cannot even speak of a 'cut' in the accepted movie sense. The visible change of frame, which is aggravated when the mechanism gets sloppy, presents a most awkward problem for artist, teaching projectionist, and student alike. With the shutter gate a proper cut could be effected and, considering persistence of vision, even a 'mix' could be obtained. Given a certain design of strong contrasts, projected in a fairly dark room, the shape of it will be kept on the retina and carried over into the next picture. This, of course, calls for very careful planning of design from frame to frame.

Beyond that it would be possible, by thoughtful placing of related objects within the lay-out, to create an imaginary movement, somewhat replacing the above-mentioned physical movement in front of museum pieces, which by its own harmony reinforces the lesson.

Actual movement of objects or pointers can be put over much

more effectively in film strips than on still pictures. The interposition of a few auxiliary frames, showing intermediate positions, will easily establish the relation between two points in distance and so help to clear the meaning. It is simple to do, with hardly any additional cost. But here again, only the improved projector will make the intelligent use of such helps possible.

The practice of animated diagram supplies any amount of ideas for adaptation which can be usefully applied by those who have had experience in it.

Many other considerations will have to be taken into account, for example the caption, a most awkward part of the design, full of controversy. Or the frame number, an utterly alien part in its surroundings. The presence of these things, as well as that of numerous requests and restrictions from all sides, calls for a special effort to give film strips that well-rounded appearance which will make them a real visual aid.

It seems clear that much more preliminary work will have to be put into film strips than has been done so far. The co-operation of all concerned will have to go far beyond the purely technical aspect to include the artistic and psychological factors. Only then can we hope to create in film strips a really effective branch of visual education.

BOOKS ABOUT FILMS

EDITED BY R. K. NEILSON BAXTER

★

WHILE we have been busy over our last few issues exploring
some of the literary output of the continent, British publishers
have been catching up on us. Waiting for review are a number
of books of which I have selected six, three technical (more or
less, as our reviews will show) and three descriptive.

The technical trio is headed by Ken Cameron's *Sound and
the Documentary Film* (Pitman, 15s.). The first nine chapters
of this are devoted to Mr Cameron's personal views on the way
documentary films should be made. He is, as most of our readers
will know, the chief sound-recordist of the Crown Film Unit,
and before that of the G.P.O. Unit of pre-war days. As such,
he has had the experience of working with most of the documentary élite. One wonders in consequence why many of the
opinions expressed in those first nine chapters seem so bitter,
even at times vindictive, when directors and their production
staff are under discussion.

Throughout the book, however, and particularly in the final
chapter there is much valuable and interesting information
about sound-recording methods and technique. The treatment
is neither so erudite nor so specialised that it is unintelligible to
the lay reader, yet it will be acceptable to the knowledgeable
technician or student of the cinema. It is, moreover, easily and
quickly read, since it contains only a hundred and fifty-odd
pages. Nevertheless, it is of lasting value as a reference book and
worth the rather high price at which it is published.

Number two is *The Right Way to Write for the Films*
(Right Way Books, 5s.). Again a volume written by experienced
film workers, but this time, judging by the views expressed by

John Shearman who has reviewed it for me, not so happy an achievement.

In case we are not clear what we mean by 'formula picture' Mr Moresby White and Mrs Freda Stock have published all the rules for writing every 'formula' screenplay in The Right Way to Write for the Films. They reiterate all the elementary truisms in an effort to persuade the amateur script writer to think before he submits. The rules are illustrated by a synopsis, treatment and excerpts from the scenario of an imaginary film, Miss Adventure. This piece breaks at least two of the rules ('The audience must be convinced that it could happen' (p. 5) and 'Avoid coincidence at all costs' (p. 27)) and horrifyingly out-formulas the formula to an extent which becomes hysterically funny.

There are occasional gross inaccuracies; for example, sixty feet of film are wrongly stated to take a minute to show on the screen (p. 89); the authors get four out of four documentary film titles wrong (p. 108), and on p. 112 a film is said to go 'into production' before locations or floor space have been found, or the art, camera, casting, wardrobe and music departments have had a copy of the script. This would be difficult if not impossible. Nor are the authors lucky in their guesses. 'An excellent story set in the Himalayas or on the banks of the Amazon will probably be discarded on the grounds of expense alone' (p. 19). Like Black Narcissus and The End of the River? 'Suppose that we showed the start of a race and tracked with the horses right round the course ... we should have lost all sense of filmic movement, the movement that keeps audiences on the edge of their seats' (p. 84). Like the charge of the knights in Henry V? Was this book written before the war? If so, it has not been revised since.

Altogether aside from such unfortunate lapses the authors seem depressingly unaware that if it is a fact that a 'formula' script stands most chance of acceptance, then this is a tragic comment on picture-makers and audiences, and not a matter for complacency, self-congratulation and perpetuation.

One is forced to the conclusion that script-writing is an almost impossible subject to be analysed and well described. All of the books about it that I know are unsatisfactory and some are downright bad.

In the third book of our choice every job in film-making is described, including scripting. This is *Working for the Films*, edited by Oswell Blakeston (Focal Press, 10s. 6d.). It is a pretentious book because it aims to be encyclopedic about nineteen of the key jobs in various kinds of film-making. This, I submit, is an impossibility in two hundred pages. Its intention is to provide information for the would-be film technician. What are the attributes he needs for any given job; how can he best get the job for which (having read the book, presumably) he thinks himself most suitable? The nineteen contributions, each by an established and well-known technician, vary in quality. Some are too subjective, like Freddie Young's 'Cameraman' section. Some are nothing but a sales-talk, like David Rawnsley's piece about the art director. But on the whole they measure up well enough to what the publisher has asked for. But will you tell me why it is so necessary for us to have books telling the world how to get into the film industry? I am not conscious of similar books relating to other industries, yet *Working for the Films* has had several forerunners. The film-production industry in this country has never yet succeeded in directly employing more than about ten thousand workers, and that is the size of the labour force now. By the time expansion demands more workers an official apprenticeship scheme, which is the only satisfactory method of regulating recruitment in any industry, will be in existence. The answer, then, to the question 'How do I become a film technician?' will not need two hundred pages or even two.

Of the three descriptive books to which I referred, one is intended for children. This is, I believe, the first such book on film-making with a serious purpose. It is by Mary Field (another technician) and Maud M. Miller, and is called *The Boys' and Girls' Film Book* (Burke Publishing Co., 10s. 6d.). Cynthia Whitby reviews it as follows:

The Boys' and Girls' Film Book by Mary Field and Maud Miller has a great deal to be said in its favour and a certain amount against it. It is both interesting and instructive, but whether it would maintain the interest of the average child it is difficult to say. I feel that Miss Field and Miss Miller would have done better to have made their minds up a little more firmly for what age-range of children they were writing. One moment the book is giving a comparatively technical description of a piece of equipment and the next breaking out into approved 'bed-time story' language interspersed with rather coy slang.

Also, I question whether the present generation of children would be interested in the rather long and detailed descriptions of the big personalities who participated in the history of motion pictures. I doubt if people such as Mary Pickford and D. W. Griffith are more than vague names to most present-day youngsters and the fact that they formed companies and made films years ago will not impress them much.

However, there is also much that may hold their attention and many amusing anecdotes if they care to search for them. The section headed 'Making a Film' is full of interest for both old and young, though one or two of the stills have silly inaccuracies – for example, having explained at great length in the caption underneath the still of a fourway synchroniser that three of the tracks are effects, music, and speech, and having taught you on the previous page how to identify a sound-track, the picture then shows you a synchroniser with three obvious picture strips running through it.

In spite of all this, I recommend you to buy this book for your children, and if they don't read it, you will find in it much to enjoy yourself.

But if Mother and Father, or the older children, really want to get down to an appreciation of the basic principles of film æsthetics, the two remaining books in my pile can be fairly recommended. *The Art of the Film* by Ernest Lindgren (Allen and Unwin, 16s.) is one of the best books of its kind written in this – or indeed any other – country. This, be it noted, is a considerable statement, for the subject is a favourite one, with both the initiated and the uninitiated author. There are, however, few classics, Arnheim's *Film* being almost the only one to endure, and it is now fifteen years old.

Lindgren is not a technician. He is curator of the National Film Library, and his job has made him a keen student of the way the screen is used by its *aficionados*. His book is therefore a detached analysis, free from personal idiosyncrasies of technique and methodological biases. It is also refreshingly unconcerned at the implications of its own title – it recognises that artistic creation requires craftsmanship, and it is with the skills of the film craftsmen that it primarily deals. This is a book that takes the cinema seriously, but without all the æsthetic chi-chi which we have so often to read; knowledgeably, without making a great mystery of it; devotedly, without phoney glamorisation. I would almost use the adjective 'scholarly' if I were not afraid that it would put some people off.

Lastly, we have *Anatomy of the Film* by my colleague, H. H. Wollenberg (Marsland Publications, 10s. 6d.). This too is a valuable book, though in a curious way unsophisticated. It is a collection of lectures, and tends therefore to read badly, and Wollenberg is a critic and writer and the jargon of film production is unfamiliar to his tongue – and his pen. But these lectures were intended as an introductory course in film appreciation, and the book should not be regarded as anything more than a primer. As such it is good.

'FULL FATHOM FIVE...'

★

Two years ago *Penguin Film Review* began, and in our first editorial we said that, as soon as practicable, we hoped to publish regularly. The time has come, and with Issue 9 we cease to be an occasional volume and become an annual, appearing each spring as a full-size Pelican Book.

Although the *Review* has never had a readership less than 25,000, the costs of publication and distribution are now so high that it is no longer economical to print the *Review* even for a circulation considerably exceeding this number. Both the publishers and the editors, however, think that a valuable contribution can be made to film studies in an annual Pelican volume, which will give scope for long essays on various aspects of the cinema as well as for a survey of the achievements of the film during the previous year.

Irregularity of publication is one of the factors that tells most against the establishment of a stable circulation; however that may be, the 50,000 regular readers we need have not been forthcoming since the earlier issues of *Penguin Film Review* went out of print. We hope they will come forward once more to support us in the annual volume we are now planning to publish in 1950.

THE EDITORS

THE PENGUIN
FILM
REVIEW

9

CONTRIBUTIONS INCLUDE

Harry Watt on Film Making in Australia

Eric Ambler on Turning Novels into Films

Articles on film censorship, design, colour and
the two-reel comedy

Critical Symposium on 'Paisa'

ONE SHILLING AND SIXPENCE

THE PENGUIN FILM REVIEW

9

THE PENGUIN
FILM REVIEW

Editorial Board : R. K. Neilson Baxter
Roger Manvell *and* H. H. Wollenberg
Executive Editor : Roger Manvell

9

PENGUIN BOOKS
LONDON
1949

First Published May 1949

PENGUIN BOOKS LIMITED

Harmondsworth, Middlesex, England

MADE AND PRINTED IN GREAT BRITAIN
by Hazell, Watson & Viney, Ltd.
Aylesbury and London

CONTENTS

*

EDITORIAL   7

YOU START FROM SCRATCH IN AUSTRALIA:
Harry Watt   10

THE MAGAZINE FILM: Edgar Anstey   17

THE FILM OF THE BOOK: Eric Ambler   22

THE PRE-FABRICATED DAYDREAM:
Maurice Cranston   26

DESIGN BY INFERENCE:
Oswell Blakeston and David Rawnsley   32

THE TWO-REEL COMEDY – ITS RISE
AND FALL: Arthur Knight   39

THE DOCUMENTARY FILM: Jean Painlevé   47

'PAISA': HOW IT STRUCK OUR
CONTEMPORARIES: Roger Manvell   53

FILM CENSORSHIP IN BRITAIN:
A. T. L. Watkins   61

PSYCHOLOGY AND THE FILM: Gertrude Keir   67

A TECHNICIAN'S VIEW OF THE
COLOUR FILM: J. H. Coote   73

'THE MAN WITH THE BOX BROWNIE':
R. K. Neilson Baxter   82

NO DEMAND FOR CRITICISM?
Catherine de la Roche   88

5

THE MIRROR UP TO NATURE:
Siegfried Kracauer   95

HOLLYWOOD REPORT ON A 'TREND':
Martin Field   100

THE RETURN OF ROMANTICISM:
H. H. Wollenberg   103

EXPERIMENTS WITH CELLULOID:
Hans Richter   108

BOOKS ABOUT FILMS:
Edited by R. K. Neilson Baxter   121

ILLUSTRATED SECTION:
Compiled by Roger Manvell

EDITORIAL

★

THE Film Industry has been passing through one of its almost regular periods of mortification. The new vitality created by the war, which gave the British film a tradition and a respect it had never had before, has already drained away as the frustrations of American, Government and financial influences have attacked it. By the beginning of this year a large number of studios were shut – pathetic shadow-haunted places with only the echoing footsteps of a caretaker to break the silence. Hundreds of technicians were out of work. Deputations of employers and workers alike were visiting the Board of Trade almost daily. Panicky articles were appearing in the Trade Press, and 'Cut costs!' was the universal cry. However much one agrees with the concern at rising costs, a mere exhortation to the producers to reduce them is useless as a panacea.

The main reason for the slump is, as it was in 1937, the lack of confidence of the City. Film production has always been a bad investment, because it is comparatively rare even for production costs to be recovered, let alone a profit made, wholly within the home market. The only overseas market of any importance is America, and America commercially is mainly notable for its vindictiveness. The raising of the British film quota under the 1948 Act to 45 per cent brought to a rapid end the beginnings of reciprocity. There are, too, strong American interests in many British distribution companies.

It has been obvious for many years that the distributor is the anomaly in the industrial set-up. He is an agent who can control the amount of revenue that reaches the producer, which would be crazy in any industry. The Portal Committee may have found a remedy, but short of legislation controlling the operation of the distributing companies it is difficult to see how fair marketing conditions can be ensured.

The cynicism for which the distributor is noted is well demonstrated by the plight of the 'supporting programme'. The quality of the shorts one sees most frequently in the cinemas reflects the price paid for them. Once again it is the distributor, not the exhibitor nor the public, who establishes the price – often no more than a few shillings for a week's booking. So the reputable documentary film must rely on sponsorship and non-theatrical distribution – primarily official, through the Central Office of Information – if it is to have a sum adequate for good quality spent on it.

But at present it is almost as difficult to overcome the obstacles to this form of promotion as those in the way of commercial production. It is recognised that integration of Government information policy needs constant attention and is of major importance. But to make it effective, the Government must have at its disposal a soundly based organisation for promoting the films required. For a time this was ignored, but even when recognised, speedy and economical working is prevented by the 'system' with which the Treasury surrounds it. This is a system which, from top to bottom, appoints one man to put up ideas and another to veto them, one man to establish the cost justified by each project and another to say it is too expensive. Thus, it is claimed, the minimum amount of taxpayer's money is wasted – and the inevitable corollary is that the maximum number of films remain unmade.

This post-war world is a puzzling world. Complexity piles on complexity till a structure of wonderful unwieldiness is created. Rationalisation is so easy – if the right people were to be given the freedom to carry it out.

★

Pelican Film Annual 1950

As announced in Issue 8 of Penguin Film Review, this present number will be the last in the Series. From the spring of next year the Review will be replaced by an annual Pelican Book devoted to the film. This book will have 228 pages of text and 64 pages of illustrations. The Editorial Board of the Film Review *will be responsible for editing this new volume.*

The book will contain as its main feature a fifty-page essay by a prominent writer. A large section will give detailed critical analyses of important films shown during 1949; these will be contributed by leading film critics, film-makers and writers not professionally connected either with the film industry or film journalism. There will be essays on technical progress in the cinema and on recent experiments with the film. Other sections will survey critical writing during the year and review the film festivals and production abroad; important films made during 1949 will be listed with their main credits. The volume will be fully indexed for reference.

*

An Award from India for 'Penguin Film Review'

The India Film Journalists' Association, Mysore City, working in co-operation with India's leading editors, has awarded Penguin Film Review *the 1948 title of 'The World's Best Film-Journal'. The Award Scroll is signed by the President of the I.F.J.A., Faqir Mohammed, and the President of the Awards-Presentation, Palghat Subramanya Iyer, and contains many other goodwill signatures of prominent film journalists, writers and radio workers. We are very proud to announce this, and in return send our greetings, thanks and best wishes to our colleagues in India.*

YOU START FROM
SCRATCH IN AUSTRALIA

HARRY WATT

★

'THE OVERLANDERS' was an experiment. I was sent out to
Australia by Sir Michael Balcon purely on 'spec' to see if it was
possible to make films there and, if so, to make one. We had no
set plans, no ideas. We agreed I should take three months seeing
the country. That, of course, just showed how little we knew
about it. In five months I travelled 25,000 miles and had only investigated three States with any thoroughness. And during
that five months I'd had five ideas and scrapped the lot.

I was influenced, of course, by what I found going on in the
film industry of Australia. In 1944 there was only one film being
made, the *Rats of Tobruk*, a reconstruction of the part played
by the Australians during the siege of Tobruk. As this seemed
to be an excellent subject and was getting complete co-operation in its making from the army, I decided against trying to
compete with another war subject. *Rats of Tobruk* was being
directed by Charles Chauvel, one of the two established directors in Australia, who made the only Australian film to have
much prestige abroad, *40,000 Horsemen*. This film, made about
1940, had some of the finest mass cavalry material ever seen on
the screen. Chauvel has been struggling to make films in Australia for many years under appalling difficulties. He is usually
independently financed, and practically every production has
meant a heart-breaking struggle to raise capital. His films are
made on a shoe-string, and generally with equipment that
should have been junked years before. Unfortunately, his *Rats
of Tobruk* proved disappointing, but he is at present engaged

10

on a pioneering story, *Sons of Matthew*, which promises better.

The other established director in Australia is Ken Hall, who has directed more than 20 films for Cinésound Productions. This company specialised in comedies in the early thirties, and scored considerable success with the *Dad and Dave* series, starring an excellent Australian character comedian, Bert Baily. These films had a huge success in Australia and were shown overseas. Other comedies, starring Australian comics George Wallace and 'Mo', followed, and then a number of dramas were attempted with much less success.

Studying these films convinced me of one thing – that studio facilities and equipment were so poor that indoor films were useless to attempt in Australia and that that had been the basic mistake of Australian film-makers. Their huge, exciting, hard country had never been used by them at all. So I set out to find an almost 100 per cent exterior subject. And I found it in a Food Office!

I was being constantly called upon to advise Government Departments on their documentary films. I was finally summoned to the Ministry of Food and wearily trudged there, expecting to hear endless statistics about dried peas and dehydrated potatoes. The Minister had a way with him, however, and I soon got interested. He finally said: 'You see, we do everything here. Why, in 1942 we even brought 100,000 head of cattle across half Australia.' As he went on to talk of something else, I suddenly did a mental 'double takem', got him back on to the cattle theme, and the film was born.

Then began the really hectic rush. You start from scratch in Australia. So, leaving a researcher to hunt out everything she could about every cattle trek that had ever happened, I tore off to the Northern Territory with a photographer, and in three weeks surveyed the whole route and established basic locations. We spent four days in the saddle with a travelling mob of cattle, and returned drunk with exhaustion. But mountains of hard work had to be done. We investigated all equipment in

Australia and found two Mitchell cameras, one tucked away in a business man's safe, where it was held against a bad debt! The script was written at odd moments between 8 a.m. and midnight, when casting and collecting the unit allowed. We had only two tiny offices, shared with the Ealing Distribution man, who had long ago decided we were mad. We were besieged by the usual masses of crackpots who turn up when they hear a film is going to be made. The passages were crowded with children showing off their dancing, and in the street outside men waited with performing dogs and horse-dealers paraded their wares. Films were a rarity in Australia, and our life was made a hell.

Out of it all the unit began to take shape. As it was war-time and Chauvel had the only experienced technicians available, I decided to look for young enthusiastic amateurs or semi-amateurs. The unit finally consisted of artists, scientists, young documentary workers, an ex-impresario, circus hands, writers, cattlemen and a waiter. I was lucky to get Ralph Smart, who had considerable European experience, released from the R.A.A.F. as associate producer. Osmond Borrodaile, the cameraman, and a production manager came out from England. But of the whole unit of thirty-five, including cast, only six had ever worked on a feature film before.

We had to design and get built practically everything – reflectors, dolly-tracks, tripods, even mike booms. We had to buy 1,000 head of cattle and hire drovers to look after them. We had to find film horses, which must look like racers and behave like mice. And as it was war-time we had to get permits and coupons and priorities and passes. But eventually it all worked out, and the whole unit embarked in two Dakotas for Alice Springs, somewhere near the geographical centre of Australia.

I was again told I was mad to go to Alice Springs. Film-makers said there was every type of country I needed within fifty miles of Sydney. But I was obsessed with putting on the screen the limitless spaces I'd seen in the Northern Territory.

And Alice Springs was the nearest central point to them. At that it was 1,500 miles from Sydney, and our horses and heavy gear took a fortnight by rail to do the journey we did by air in a day.

There is no room here to give a detailed description of how we made the film. In fact, much of it was such a nightmare that it is best forgotten. But when I say that every road, every track, every cattle-yard and most of the close bush in which the cattle appeared on the screen was built by the unit, it will give some idea of the work we put in. And built by the unit means built by the technicians, the actors, the drivers, the cooks and the secretaries. The night stampede sequences were made, for instance, in a huge yard. They had to be, or the cattle would have been lost for days. The floor of this yard was as bare as a board. In it we planted trees, scrub and grass. And the production staff planted the trees, the actors and camera crew planted the scrub and the girls planted the grass. Every time the cattle rushed through them they knocked the lot down! So again the production staff planted the trees, and so on.

We had five months of it. We lived in army camps, usually about 200 miles from anywhere. We saw our rushes once a fortnight on a portable projector with a screen like a postage stamp. We had, of course, a series of crises. We had a threatened outbreak of pleuro-pneumonia amongst the cattle. A horse fell on Chips Rafferty. Some of our trained wagon horses were killed in an accident. Our second lead nearly took his eye out with a stock whip, and had to be flown 1,000 miles to a specialist. Our leading lady eloped. But eventually we got through it, and after a few interiors in Sydney (made in a studio the size of a recording theatre) we delivered the film and I vowed 'never again'. But I got it with *Eureka Stockade*.

This was one of the subjects I'd found when investigating the Australian scene. We documentary people had never tackled history, and here was an important historical moment that fell so perfectly into film shape that there was no need to distort events or create false situations. It could be treated completely realistically. So, as *The Overlanders* seemed to be popular, it was decided to have a crack at *Eureka*.

It needed, of course, much more of the 'feature' approach than *The Overlanders*. We decided to import the main artists from Britain and a key technician in each department. Walter Greenwood and Ralph Smart came in on the script. And large quantities of equipment were to follow us out. As there are no professional extras in Australia, the Government agreed to letting us have soldiers for the crowd scenes. The Australian Government has been always exceedingly co-operative and long-sighted in helping the creation of an international film industry there. Everything was ready, the seventy speaking parts had been cast, the 800 costumes prepared, Australia combed for period muskets, stage-coaches and the like, when, with a few weeks to go, we were hit by the 75 per cent *ad valorem* duties. These were aimed, of course, primarily at saving dollars. Unfortunately, they applied to all films made outside Britain. Which meant us. And for ten weeks we sat and fretted while complicated arguments went on at home with the Board of Trade. At last a formula was reached, whereby, by importing some more artists and technicians, we could become a British film on location. But that initial knock started a run of bad luck from which we never quite recovered. In fact, we more nearly came a 'gutser' on *Eureka* than any film I've ever worked on. For instance, that ten weeks' delay pushed us into the bad weather, which turned out to be the worst for ninety-two years! We had by this time an enormous unit with 250 soldiers and 100 technicians and actors in one camp. And we had only five shooting days in the first five weeks! We took over a complete valley, and built in it a replica of Ballarat in 1854, with a main village street and more than 600 tents scattered around the diggings. Our complete tent town was blown down twice! We had to transport the complete unit sixteen miles each way in buses every day, and our roads became so bad that we had to walk the last two miles, which, after the luxury of studio cars, disturbed some of our actors somewhat. But we plodded on, and as before, the young technicians did wonders. This time we had George Heath as cameraman, an Australian who is in world class on exteriors. But again 80 per cent of the unit were new to the business. Our dreams of easy film-making had gone with the tax. As the order for our fine new equipment had been cancelled, we improvised again, and shot most of the film on a camera made by Heath himself!

When the good weather came we decided the only thing to do to catch up was to split into two units. I was fortunate in having Les Norman and Julian Spiro with me, so we divided up the script fairly arbitrarily and ran two units almost continuously. We shot all our night exteriors on the location, using a generator, and latterly built many interior sets in the open air to shoot on in bad weather. The most time was lost organising our big crowds, but as it was essential that this film should always give an impression of a mass of people, we never skimped on this, and saw to it that even behind close-ups there should always be about a hundred extras. I think this policy was justified. To do it we developed intercommunication throughout the location by walkie-talkie with a central office in direct phone communication with the outside. Of course the usual day-to-day problems arose. The police uniforms, hired from London, were made for West End chorus boys. As soon as the hefty Australians put them on, they split in the most awkward places! The period straw hats, known as 'cabbage trees', were too much of a temptation for the soldiers when they discovered that one sharp tug removed the brim. We lost dozens a day. We had the inevitable accidents. Chips Rafferty broke a rib in a fight scene. Jane Barrett was overcome with the heat. And Jack Lambert got acute tinea. On many days it was well over 100 degrees in the shade, and the period costumes were terribly trying. But worst of all, a strike deprived us of beer for eight weeks! This nearly caused a mutiny!

Eighty per cent of the film was shot on location. We are very proud that, although it is in the big action class, not one shot is back-projection. We did several tracking shots more than 100 yards in length, with dialogue, crowd reaction and even play back, and all without studio tricks. I still think this is worth it, because the public always smells unreality, even if they don't know how it is done.

We finished off the film in Pagewood Studios in Sydney, which we re-opened after it had been shut for eleven years. It is by far the best studio in Australia, with one excellent stage and a good dubbing theatre, and it is going to be, I am glad to say, the headquarters of Ealing Studios in Australia from now on.

Reading this back, it sounds like a hard-luck story. But the real physical labour involved in making films in Australia is almost unbelievable compared to present-day filming here, and maybe I'm a bit obsessed with it. Although I'm dog-tired of it, I wouldn't have missed it for worlds. And it's been worth it. We have started to put Australian films on the screens of the world. We've raised the pay of both technicians and actors in Australia by about 100 per cent. And we've given creative work to a lot of people who otherwise were smothering with frustration. And it looks as though they're going to get a bit of continuity of employment now. The Government National Films Board, under Stan Hawes, is doing excellent work, and many of the young people who started with us are working there. Ealing is continuing. Local feature production is on the increase. Most of this, unhappily, is of very poor quality and does more harm than good. But there are immense film potentialities in Australia and a lot of good stories. I'll go back some time. But I wish it wasn't such sickeningly hard work!

THE MAGAZINE FILM

EDGAR ANSTEY

★

BY the time this is in print it is likely that the Central Office of Information will have put into production a regular screen magazine in the same class as the *March of Time* and *This Modern Age*. It will be under the supervision of Stuart Legg, and will fall within the administrative parish of John Grierson in his capacity as C.O.I. Controller; so that we may expect the new release to show some of the characteristics of the old Canadian *World in Action* series which Grierson and Legg, in their Canadian National Film Board days, developed into *March of Time's* first serious rival.

The *genre* has been known by a variety of names and never neatly defined. It is a combination of Press leader and feature article translated into pictures and sound. Let us for simplicity (and stressing regularity of appearance rather than content) call it the magazine film. In attempting an examination of accomplishments and status, I should begin perhaps by renouncing any claim to objectivity. As a practitioner who has been responsible for items in both the *March of Time* and *This Modern Age*, I am likely to be more conscious of aim than of achievement. At any rate I am expert in the good intentions with which the paths of screen journalism have always been so lavishly paved. For these films have – first and foremost – been films of purpose; they have had something to say of more consequence than the manner of the saying. And they have survived nearly fifteen years of criticism by the æsthetes.

There is something of a paradox in that the preponderant importance of content has not prevented the form of the magazine film from becoming individual and immediately recognisable whatever the subject-matter. This may or may not demonstrate that quick-fire picture and vigorously didactic commentary provide the only means of bringing to the screen direct sociological and political comment. Certainly it is the most constantly effective means yet devised. Yet let us not ignore the likely limitations of a film form that so frequently eschews the full-blooded screen creation of people, place and mood in favour of illustrated phrases. At its infrequent best this type of film can achieve a counterpoint of word and image rising near to poetry; it is of consequence that it more often rivals a lantern lecturer over-anxious about a last train home.

Let us try to recall some of the outstanding magazine films. Do you remember, for example, *Inside Nazi Germany 1938*, *Nazi Conquest No. 1* and *King Cotton*, all from *March of Time* in its hey-day? They were made in the two years immediately prior to the war, and no films did more to arouse public (and official) opinion to a belated awareness of the power of the film as a sharp instrument of sociological and political comment. The weight of the argument as expressed in commentary would find its emotional overtone in picture; or sometimes the cold objective comment of an unremarkable shot would be given pulsating life by the turn of a commentary phrase. I shall never forget the grim, proud climax in *Rehearsal for War* (how sadly prophetic were the *March of Time* items of that period), when an account of the steady retreat of the Loyalist forces in the Fascists' Spanish Rebellion was brought to a halt by the ringing, defiant sentence, 'Then came Madrid'.

Generally the trick was to create a counterpoint between sound and image. The favourite exhortation of Louis de Rochemont, *March of Time's* inventor and for many years its producer, was 'Never call your shot', meaning that precious commentary wordage should never be squandered upon what was already sufficiently obvious to the eye, that commentary should always add some new idea, should be complementary to the image and not alternative to it. Commentary, as de Rochemont understood it, was to contribute what was impossible to the unaided picture, whether that contribution took the form of ideas or feelings. Too often to-day one hears commentary that is merely descriptive of the scenes portrayed, or sees images which merely illustrate in a pedestrian manner ideas that already have complete and self-sufficient existence in the narrator's words.

Like others of the more experimentally-minded producers (notably John Grierson and Basil Wright), Louis de Rochemont is a great editor in his own right. He has an eye for the foot of picture wherein lies the instant of maximum eloquence; and can cap it with just the word of commentary or phrase of music which will bring the idea or emotion home to the target of all good editors – the human stomach. Yet I am not sure that Stuart Legg, in a shorter run with his *World in Action* series, did not achieve enough hits in the solar plexus even to rival de Rochemont. I call to mind in particular *And Now the Peace* – the best boost the United Nations has ever had – and *Churchill's Island*, a film about Britain which came at a time in the war when our friends overseas were anxious to hear that there was life and a few kicks still left in poor old Britannia.

The World in Action combined in its editing shrewd political insight with what often was sheer brilliance in the selection of the appropriate images. And selection was an especially true description of the process, for Stuart Legg employed – often of necessity – a very high proportion of library material originally photographed for quite different purposes. He combed the film vaults of the world for material of historical value, or scenes which seemed to symbolise or dramatise some mood or emotion of significance to his audiences. The other side of the medal is that the photographic quality of the *World in Action* series was, on the whole, low, and sometimes shots seemed over-familiar – an inevitable consequence of using so many duplicated scenes.

Yet for my money coherence and vitality of exposition is

more to the point of the magazine film than beautiful photography. Ideally one employs both, and this has sometimes been achieved by the *This Modern Age* series, notably in *Palestine Problem*; but in other releases of the new magazine, editing has been loose and undynamic, and the consistently beautiful photography has given us a kind of travelogue of ideas rather than an integrated conception of the theme. The editors of *This Modern Age* could well devote some study to the precision of the ideological and emotional relationship between word and image achieved in the early *March of Time* items. The more so since they are undoubtedly seeking and finding a higher degree of precision in their commentary wording than the *genre* has yet experienced. Moreover, *This Modern Age* is showing healthy signs of being less stereotyped in its camera-work than the older magazines. *March of Time*, for example, has been traditionally opposed to the use of camera movement except on those occasions when it is virtually unavoidable. It was argued that shots in which the camera moved required to be left too long on the screen if they were to make their point, and this would interfere with the brisk, staccato manner of cutting which was held to be obligatory in screen journalism. *This Modern Age* has demonstrated the validity of a slower tempo for certain purposes, and there has been a consequent gain in the freedom and power of the camera.

It appears to me, however, that if the magazine film is to develop beyond its present stage (and it has been stuck there all too long), more is required than eloquent counterpoint in the editing and a new freedom for the camera.

Let us look back to the origins of the *March of Time* in 1927–8. During those years Louis de Rochemont and Jack Glenn were making for the U.S. Navy a series of recruiting films. They were not documentaries in the generally accepted sense of that word, but consisted of short acted stories played against the real background of the Navy. Subsequently the same team made *March of the Years* in 1933, and began work on the first experimental issues of *March of Time* in 1934. The first release was made in 1935.

During this whole period the idea of 're-enactment' was not lost. More importantly the creation of character by script analysis and screen synthesis was not regarded as the exclusive prerogative of the feature fiction film. In such early *March of Time* items as *Father Divine, The Lunatic Fringe, Fiorella La Guardia* and *Father Divine's Deal*, leading personalities of America were re-created on the screen with understanding and often with delightful humour. These were tiny screen bio-graphies; they were full of the life and warmth of real people. All of them were directed by de Rochemont's first associate, Jack Glenn, and there is no doubt that they represented an important part of the original de Rochemont-Glenn conception, a part which now has been quite lost. To-day the magazine film has become a medium for the editor rather than the director. The shooting is rarely imaginative and the characters are eliminated rather than interpreted.

It may be argued that two reels are too short to create character, and some support for such a thesis may perhaps be seen in the fact that Louis de Rochemont now devotes most of his time to documentary story films of feature length like *Boomerang*. Yet I remain unconvinced that characterisation cannot play its part in our magazine films. Jack Glenn used often to create character in a single scene, and I suspect he would be doing it still if these films were coming out of film-makers' heads and hearts and not off assembly lines. Of course, you may argue that people, characters, have no business mixing in with the sociology of the magazine film, anyway. In that case we must be prepared to find them soon deciding they have no business in the audience either.

THE FILM OF THE BOOK

ERIC AMBLER

★

'I READ it quite by accident,' said the producer. 'It was published over ten years ago, you know. My wife and I were staying in Cannes. I was looking for something to read and found it lying around the hotel. *Henceforth to Seek*, by Jeremy Kitchworth. I'd never heard of the book or the author. But I read the first page and it had me at once. By the time I'd finished the book I was very worried. You know how it is. The thing was such perfect picture material that I couldn't believe that Selznick or Korda hadn't got the rights already. I got the office busy on it, and they had quite a job even finding Kitchworth. Where do you think he was? Working in an advertising agency just round the corner from the office! And he still had the rights! Metro had taken a three months' option on it originally but they'd let it lapse. The publishers were a bit sticky at first. They had a percentage interest in the rights, and tried to bump the price up; but the thing was ten years old, and they hadn't got U.S. copyright, so I soon got them back to earth. And of course the author was delighted. I had a long chat with him. You know what fantastic ideas novelists have about film-makers. And not without reason.

'In my experience most film-makers tackle a novel they've bought for production as if it were an enemy that had somehow to be defeated. Why buy it if you don't really want to use it? No, I know it isn't as simple as that. The producer badly wants a new subject. Usually he's in a hurry for one. Something comes along that he thinks is just possible. Perhaps there's a good part for a star he has to pay anyway and wants to use. Or perhaps he needs a tangible proposition to convince the financial boys that he really is worth talking to. A novel, especially if it's a best seller or a Book Club choice of some sort, gives him something to tell them. And if the rights are expensive, that fact may determine the scale of the production. I think too that lots of them feel more comfy if they've got a literary property of proved appeal on their desks. In some curious way the very fact that the thing's printed and between stiff board covers gives it a sort of magic. The title too. When he's asked what his next picture's going to be, he can say right out, "So-and-so", instead of having to mumble something about not being quite decided yet. And, even if everyone knows that the picture's going to be a turkey, he's somehow in the clear. He *chose* the novel, yes, but he's not responsible for it. It had an independent life of its own, and he in his innocence was deceived by it.

'But you know all that. The point is that I feel differently. I like *Henceforth to Seek,* and that's why I'm making it. And I'm going to make *Henceforth to Seek* – the book, I mean, not some half-baked travesty of it. I think I set Kitchworth's mind at rest on that point. I know we're going to run into censorship trouble, but I say: "All right, let's run into it. We'll deal with that problem when it arises." What's more, I'm getting Kitch-worth to work with me on the adaptation. I think I've got him really enthusiastic about the picture. And that, after all, is the main function of a producer as I see it – to create enthusiasm within the small creative group which really makes the picture, to give that group a dynamic of its own.'

'I think the man's mad,' said Kitchworth. 'I told him so too. Not actually in those words; but I did say that I couldn't by any stretch of the imagination see a film in it. Oh, he just smiled rather patronisingly, and said he was paid to stretch his imag-ination in terms of pictures, whatever that means. It'll be inter-esting to find out. The money's good, anyway.'

'*Henceforth to Seek,*' said the producer to the woman from the newspaper, 'is a lyrical love-story based on an old legend of the Bolivian Indians dealing with the search for the ideal woman. Jeremy Kitchworth spent his childhood in Bolivia, you know. The title comes from a poem he wrote when he was eighteen:

"Drive me not out; I go unbound henceforth to seek
Another love beyond the ice-drenched slopes of Mana."

Lovely, isn't it? And that's the feeling I want to get on the screen. Of course, the hard-currency situation may make it impossible to go to Bolivia for our exteriors. We shall probably have to do them in the Alpes Maritimes.'

'I think I'm beginning to respect him,' said Kitchworth. 'He has an extraordinary grasp of story construction. It makes me feel like an amateur. If only he wouldn't generalise so mellifluously about the creative impulse I think I'd really like him. One thing; I'm beginning to realise how little I know about film-making. You know that bit in the book where the girl about to marry thinks of the lover she has killed? It took me three pages to describe what she was thinking. He does it in one shot of her looking down at a cup of water and then slowly letting the water dribble away into the sand. I wish I'd thought of that. Do you know, I think this might turn out to be a rather better film than it was a novel. Anyway, I'm enjoying myself.'

'It's a pity,' said the producer; 'and I do understand how Kitchworth feels; but if we're going to have Garry Roper playing the lover – and he's absolutely ideal casting – we have got to think again about the story. It's not that I object particularly to his being killed off so early in the picture – I hope I can rise above that sort of consideration whatever pressure his agent brings to bear – it's the economics of the thing. Roper's expensive. That means I daren't gross less than two hundred thousand in this country. I'll do it with him all right, but not if I have trouble with the censor – I mean, trouble over the basic-story idea. You know I liked the story as it was, but one's got to be practical. You see, I've been wondering, anyway, if they're going to like the girl killing one lover then marrying another in

the one-and-ninepennies. I think they'll think it's rather sordid.'

'Far, far worse than kicking against a brick wall,' said Kitchworth, 'is kicking against a wall of blubber.'

'Kitchworth didn't do a bad job on the whole,' said the producer; 'but the thing needed a complete reshuffle and drastic
tightening. There were too many characters and not enough
action. I got impatient with the girl. The man behaved like a
fool. You see, the trouble with a story of that kind is that it's
so easy to be seduced by the writing in the original. Now *I*
could look past all that to the essential story, which was about
a girl and two men, with one or two variations and an unusual
setting. One of the variations was the killing of the lover, and
quite obviously it had to come out in the end. Another thing;
the real story didn't begin in the book until chapter eight.
With all the dead wood cleared away from the remainder, I was
left with very little to work on. I *had* to invent fresh incident.
Naturally, Kitchworth resented things like the introduction of
the Cockney sea captain with the lisp, but I felt it needed some
humour. And I was right. A good showman has an instinct
about these things.'

'I hear,' said Kitchworth, 'that *Henceforth to Seek* is now
called *Beyond the Hills*. You'd think he'd have the primitive
courtesy to send me tickets for the première, wouldn't you?
After all, I wrote it.'

'I don't really mind much what the critics say,' said the Producer. 'The audience seemed to like it well enough. It's not a
great picture, of course, but then, I didn't expect it would be.
When you consider what I had to start with I don't think it's
turned out too badly at all. I always knew it was a very tricky
subject. Did you ever read the book? Curious stuff. My wife
never quite liked it, did you, dear?'

THE PRE-FABRICATED DAYDREAM

MAURICE CRANSTON

★

SALVATIONISTS and some other Christian sects consider it a sin to go to the cinema. For my part, without any greater claim to theological exactitude than the Edwardian curate who called himself a liberal high-churchman of evangelical views, I think it would be better to speak of a *vice*. And I define a vice, again without authority, as something which is nice while it lasts, but which leaves one feeling the worse for it afterwards.

I enjoy films, especially a comedy directed by the late Ernst Lubitsch, a Bette Davis melodrama or a slapstick piece with Mr Hope, but the enjoyment lasts only for the duration. Two or three hours in the stalls at the Empire or the Warner and I become for quite a time afterwards as sour and disgruntled a man as ever moved outside of Scotland.

A friend has suggested that this may be an occupational disease, arising from the circumstance of my having been for a little time a newspaper film critic. But my trouble goes back farther than this, back to the days when, as a fifteen-year-old schoolboy, I cut games every Wednesday to see these same Lubitsch comedies and Bette Davis melodramas and the slapstick pieces featuring – for this was 1935 – the late W. C. Fields.

The explanation? Certainly, it is not a case of an anticlimax. Finding myself in reality in Leicester Square after having been, if only in fancy, in Fifth Avenue or Hollywood Boulevard or the Kansas Highway, could cause only the deepest relief and satisfaction. For me to be acquainted, however briefly, with the glamorous is to become all the more attached to the homely

and the shabby. No, it is not a matter of coming down to earth
and not liking it. It is more likely a matter of coming back to
the self and not finding it encouraging.

Several distinguished gentlemen, such as Mr Eisenstein, Mr
Rotha and Mr Grierson, have evolved theories of Film (with a
capital F and no article), but no one has pointed out what seems
to me to need particular stress; that is, what a film is *not*. And
what a film so significantly is *not* is an exercise for the imagination of those who witness it.

A novel, coming to the reader in the form of little black
marks on sheets of white paper, calls for a creative effort if it is
to become a definite experience. A play demands only a little
less strenuous imaginative participation, for any actor will explain that he needs an audience 'with him' if his work is to succeed. At the cinema it is quite different. The enjoyment of a
film is a passive process. The shapes and sounds from the screen
occupy the whole mind, and, like one of the more pleasant
drugs, cut off that clear awareness of the self and not-self which
is the mark of waking life.

A film doesn't 'take us out of ourselves'. It comes into us. To
use a word of Mr Andrew Buchanan's, it *embalms* the mind. It
induces oblivion, an almost mystical elevation above consciousness of separate identity. I always emerge from the experience
like a swami from an ecstasy of nothingness or a medium from
a trance.

I have often read of films providing 'vicarious' thrills, delights and hazards. But is there not something direct and immediate in the experience? I doubt if it is possible to watch a
film with conscious detachment and still to enjoy it. It is not
simply that one identifies oneself with the hero or heroine, although there may be an element of this. Rather it is a matter
of being involved, without any responsibilities or duties or
choices, in an adventure. In real life we seldom have adventures
without anxiety, and the anxiety kills the pleasure. At the
cinema we can be genuinely carefree.

The excitement of the film, then, is not so much vicarious as ersatz imaginary. Not authentic imaginary. We do nothing. We do not imagine ourselves in interesting situations, for the work of the imagination has already been done. Our fantasy is effortless. We put ourselves in a receptive mood, and the pre-fabricated daydream steals over us.

Hollywood knows its business better than many people are generous enough to admit. Those unlettered film producers with their deep Jewish sense of human frailty and their American zest for smooth delight have worked out formulæ that are more often successful than not, while the theorists of Film, for all their intelligence and culture, have yet to articulate any lucid principles of criticism. The theorists have looked for art and reality. Is a daydream, by its nature, likely to embody either? Not reality, certainly, nor art, if the imagination is dormant.

An interesting situation occurred some little time ago when Hollywood made a film of Mr Thurber's story, *The Secret Life of Walter Mitty*. Walter Mitty is a man who has daydreams. In real life a timid, henpecked American husband, he visualises himself in his private fantasies as in turn a war-hero, a brilliant surgeon, a gallant sea captain, a great lover. The point of Mr Thurber's story is the ironical contrast of the miserable fact with the glorious fantasy. Hollywood took eagerly to the fantasy, but it could not stomach the fact. So in the film this timid henpecked Walter Mitty is represented as having *in fact* a final adventure which proclaims the heroic Mitty as the true Mitty and the timid Mitty as ultimately unreal.

Thus to have robbed Mr Thurber's story of its irony was to rob it of its art. And deliberately so. For art demands imagination for its appreciation. And it has been suggested by a French writer – Georges Bernanos, I think – that our age is lacking above all else in imagination, and that when a people is without imagination it cannot be given to them.

Hollywood films are the true folk entertainment of our times in the sense of being enjoyed by almost everybody. If they are designed for a world that 'lacks imagination' and 'cannot be given it', is it relevant to introduce the categories of art? Or of reality?

We might better speak of mythology. For it is not the men and women of this world that we meet on the screen, but twentieth-century heroes and goddesses moving in an international wonderland. This myth, like most myths, has been taken as literal truth by the simple-minded; literal truth, in this case, about life in the United States of America. I think not only of those G.I. brides who supposed that to enter America was to step straight into movieland, but of the vastly greater number of cinema patrons who, equating the Good Life with the Hollywood myth, think of it as being actually lived, not quite here and now, but now and there in California, Florida, New York.

The Marxists say that religion is the opiate of the people. I think it would be more correct to say the opiates of the people are their religion. For it is in this way that the cinema has come to furnish the popular values, heroes, ikons, rituals. Thus that the utterances of movie stars have come to be received with the respect which, in more primitive and superstitious times, attended only the deliverances of oracles and priests. In America Mr Eddie Cantor is the modern patron-saint of charity, Mr Bogart of political liberty, Mr Chaplin of social righteousness. And while Protestant enlightenment precludes the adoration of sacred images, photographs of Mr Mason, Mr Henried and Mr Sinatra are an evident source of emotional stimulus to many humble souls in Britain as well as in America.

The Victorians read novels and went to church. The twentieth century has in its cinema a substitute for both. There is, of course, the notable difference that the cinema offers only the occasional repetition of its pleasurable languors, where the Church promised everlasting bliss. Whether the age is cynical enough to accept indefinitely this lesser consolation I do not know, though the football-coupon habit in Britain, drinking, necking and neurosis in America all point to a general frustration. A frustration which the Hollywood myth can only aggravate. For although its films are not of this world, their ethos is wholly worldly.

We have come to the question of morals. Not what Hollywood would itself regard as morals: its by-laws about covered bosoms, twin beds and perpendicular embraces. I am thinking about the principles of good and bad, right and wrong, praise and blame implicit in the Hollywood mythology. It is, I suggest, an ethos to which guilt is alien and failure the only sin, which cherishes success and physical comeliness above everything else – except perhaps 'sophistication', which means, if anything, a suave maturity in worldliness.

America, a country created by men possessing either too much or too little of the old-fashioned morality, has taken to this ethic more readily than Britain, but even here the Hollywood standards are acknowledged as those appropriate to the never-never land of films. Hence the difficulty of making films that specifically embody another morality – Christian, Buddhist or Nineteenth-century Rationalist. Mr Rank's efforts in the realm of 'religious' films were as marked a failure as his activities with the 'secular' film have been successful. Myths won't mix.

There is, however, at least one thing to be said for Hollywood. Any myth is better than a political myth. Significantly it is the two countries which consciously approached the film as an instrument of art or reality – Weimar Germany and Revolutionary Russia – which succumbed to the most monstrous political myths of our age.

It would be pleasant to believe, but it is not true that the British public taste in films is considerably higher than America's. I have seen *Henry V* at Muswell Hill, where the audience was bored and restive, and again in Massachusetts, where the audience was spellbound. A British audience may be detached in its attitude towards American exuberance, but its desires in the way of daydreams are still better understood in Hollywood than in Denham or Pinewood or Twickenham.

Minds habitually doped with pre-fabricated daydreams cannot stir themselves to a new and active awareness. If this were possible, the many French films, the several Italian and Scandinavian films that have achieved such critical success would be universally shown and not confined in the Anglo-Saxon world to the few specialist cinemas in London, New York and the university cities, and Britain's documentary industry would not be near extinction.

The imaginative film loses money because the ordinary experience of the movie-goer, as I understand it, involves no use of imagination. Artists, realists, theorists, moralists, Continental film producers and Mr Rank's more gifted units have expected more of the public than the public has been used to giving. Winning the public round promises to be as hard as making motorists walk. Harder, for while most motorists have legs, there is no such certainty that the movie-going millions have the imagination to use.

DESIGN BY INFERENCE

David Rawnsley, inventor of the much-discussed independ-
ent-frame technique, talks about some of his ideas for the
simplification of film design and presentation in an inter-
view with Oswell Blakeston

★

THE majority of cinema-goers forget the titles and stories of
the films they saw last year, last week, last night. 'Yes,' they
say, 'it was quite a good little picture; but I can't for the life of
me remember what it was all about.' Quite obviously, the film
has made no demands on the spectator's imagination; and
within a few hours it has paid the penalty of its facility – it has
found oblivion.

This may seem of little concern to those who are interested in
film *business*: so long as the audience enjoys the picture, what
does it matter if, a few hours later, patrons can't remember
what the film was called? Yes, for the business man this would
seem to be a valid argument, were it not for the fact that a film
which does not attempt to exploit the imagination is a film
made in the most expensive way. The spoon-feeding conventions of film-land are the inflationary elements in so many pictures' budgets.

Oh, the dreary spoon-feeding sequences. A street scene is
built to show a taxi arriving outside a house. An actor is engaged to play the part of the taxi-driver. The star steps from
the taxi and pays her fare. She knocks on the front door. An
actress is engaged to answer the door in a maid's cap and apron.
The maid leads the star down a corridor, through a door and
into a room where her lover is waiting. Yet all this elaboration,
which simply holds up the story, could be inferred from a design of sound. We could see the lover waiting for his mistress
and hear the sound of a car, the ringing down of a taximeter,

ITALIAN FILMS

1 and 2. 'Senza Pietà.' A Universalia production, by Alberto Lattuada, featuring Carla de Poggio and Johnny Kitzmiller, and dealing with the problems of a Negro sergeant in love with an Italian girl.

3 to 5. 'La Terra Trema.' Luchino Visconti's film, made with local people in Sicily (Universalia.)

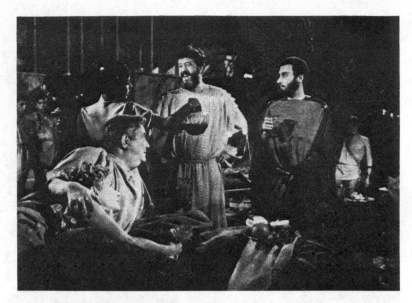

6 and 7. 'Fabiola.' Alessandro Blasetti's spectacular film, with Michèle Morgan and Michel Simon, set in fourth-century Rome. (Universalia.) (Stills 1-7 International Film Bureau and Centro Sperimentale di Cinematografia.)

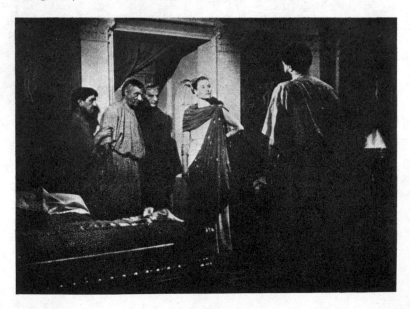

CHINESE FILMS

8 and 9.'Under a Shanghai Roof.'A domestic comedy of overcrowding and inflation as it affects a clerk whose family arrives from the country to live with him. Director: Fu Shen.

10 to 13. 'On the Sungri River.' The story of a family of lodging-house keepers at the time of the Japanese invasion of Manchuria. Apart from the

leading characters, the film is acted by non-professionals, and was shot on location in Manchuria. Director: King Shan. (Stills by courtesy of Lo Tsin-Yu.)

A FRANCO - NORWEGIAN

14 to 17. 'The Battle for Heavy Water.' The struggle, directed from London through the agency of the Norwegian guerillas and British parachute

WAR DOCUMENTARY

forces, to blow up the Norwegian heavy-water plant at Vemork. Directed
by Titus Vibe Müller and Jean Dreville.

NILS POPPE'S SWEDISH COMEDY

18 and 19. 'Soldier Bom.' In this film, written by Nils Poppe, the famous Swedish comedian plays the perfect station clerk who becomes the perfect soldier. (Svensk Filmindustri.)

LE DIABLE AU CORPS

20. Gerard Philippe as the adolescent lover in Claude Autant-Lara's film. (Still, Studio One.)

RUBENS: A BELGIAN DOCUMENTARY

21 and 22. Paul Haesaerts' and Henri Storck's feature-length study of the art and technique of Rubens. Above, animated lines indicate the painter's composition; below, twin-shots in the single frame are frequently used for demonstration.

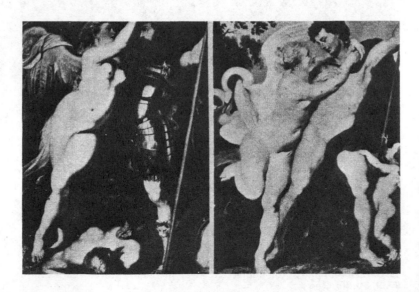

JEAN PAINLEVÉ

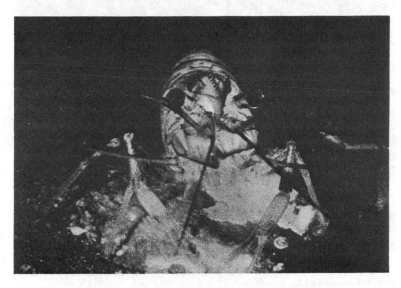

23 to 26. Jean Painlevé has been making scientific and other documentary films in France for over twenty years. 23. Close-up of a shrimp's head from 'Crabes et Crevettes' (1933). 24. Close-up of projecting spike on the forehead of a shrimp from the same film.

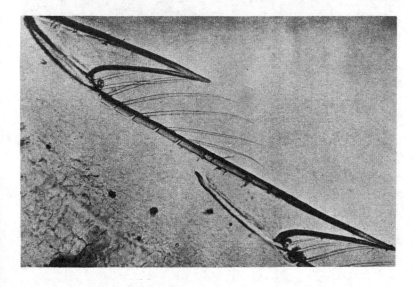

25. Sea anemone, with its poison tentacles, from an unfinished film on mutual poisoning by animals.

26. 'La Vie Scientifique de Pasteur,' made by Painlevé, with Georges Rouquier (1948).

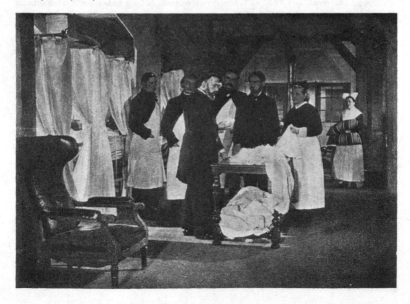

CALL NORTHSIDE 777

27 and 28. Henry Hathaway's film for Twentieth Century-Fox, featuring James Stewart, about a man wrongfully charged with murder and saved by a journalist. Another film in the American realist style, using actual locations.

HANS RICHTER

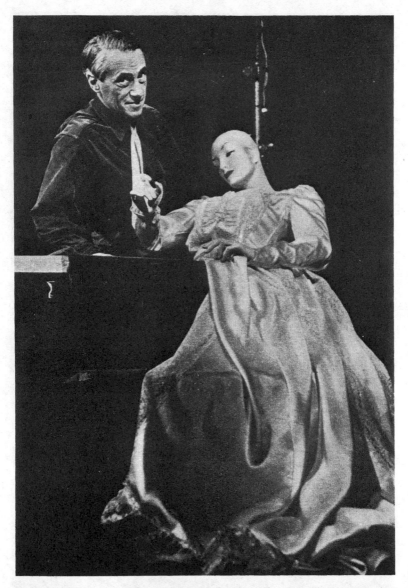

29. Hans Richter, with the mechanised leading lady suggested by Fernand Léger for the 'Girl with the Pre-fabricated Heart,' second part of Hans Richter's 'Dreams That Money Can Buy.'

and the slamming of its door; and this inference could eliminate an orgy of set-building.

An æsthetic case against the film which ignores the universal power of imagination is too easy to formulate; yet it is worth stressing that sequences which, from the artistic viewpoint, rob a picture of its vitality, are often the most expensive.

It would seem, then, that the business men and the æsthetes should be allies in fighting the sustained contempt of directors for their audience. But, alas, the film industry is dominated by conventions of fifty years ago. Out-of-date sheds still comprise the centre of film-making, and the shed-mentality flourishes even in the construction of theatres which are, presumably, to last us another fifty years. Cinemas are not planned to enhance the audience's experience; and cinema-goers are still confronted with the black-bordered screen, with its 'black dazzle', instead of the new screen which fades off gradually, the borderless screen, into which colour could move from the edge to the centre without shock. (On the conventional screen, all colour is thrown into the eyes' focal centre; and colour-shock becomes a problem where such inference is not required.)

And film-makers have become a small clique who no longer trouble to identify themselves with the audience. The film is a story-telling medium, and the clique manage to convince themselves they are specialists of the medium. In fact, they have forgotten the lessons of the nursery and of everyday life. It is the public who are the experts in story-telling and the film-makers who lack imagination.

You meet a friend who tells you that yesterday he ran into a man in a rage with you. You say: 'Why? What's it all about? What did he say? What's he going to do?' Not: 'Was it raining? Was the sun shining? Was he standing in the street, or did you meet him in a house?' Such matters, surely, are incidentals which, unless they have some direct bearing on the story, need not even be mentioned. Why, therefore, do film-makers go to vast expense to provide information of this kind? Entire sets are built for a meeting between two people, when the manner of their meeting is utterly unimportant to the story. Elegant ballrooms and lavish restaurants are presented for a distant view of a character who is as yet unknown to the audience.

Is this the experts' way of telling a story? The living story is told in people and the things they say, with an occasional essential prop necessary for the progress of the story. Was there ever a child who stopped the tale of the Three Bears to inquire about the colour of the wall-paper or the 'production-value' of the ceiling?

Naturally, though, it takes more talent to tighten the story than to pad out a thin story with 'production value'. If the executives did not suffer from shed-mentality, they would acknowledge this elementary fact. They would not try, when they are flustered, to impose temporary economy measures through the agency of efficiency experts and accountants. It's no economy to take the towels out of the lavatories, and keep a star, who is angrily looking for a towel, off the set. Economy must begin in the fundamental design of the film: for it *is* practical to economise, and to make better films, by using the people's imagination. If every room has a door, and if everyone who comes into a room must have passed through the door, why show the actor dealing with the door unless this humdrum has some relevance to the scene? Why go to the expense of building solid sets with doors?

From a piece of column the audience will automatically assume the rest above it, from the mantelpiece mirror the fireplace beneath, and from a lighting effect on a wall an audience will naturally assume its source. But there are vested interests in the old ways. The colossal set helps to inflate the ego of the art director, just as a producer imagines his prestige is increased if he is allowed to spend a fortune on a production. These are the psychological difficulties which, apart from the failures of imagination, work against the acceptance of design by inference as the filmic way. At this minute, in this country and in

America, the studios are full of purely three-dimensional buildings, static and immobile, accurate in every detail at a grandiose cost. 'Production value,' say the executives; for this is the term which has been invented to cover the fact that producer, director, art-director and lighting cameraman are trying to make a shop-window for themselves.

Actually, the whole idea of an immense, static set is unfilmic. One does not make a motion-picture move by tracking a camera round a gigantic static set. (Witness *Hamlet*.) The movement of a film is in the thought line, the continuity of inference; and, of course, the film which is to stir the imagination of the audience must be designed in inference as a whole, as a 'concept in time'.

The sound-track should be part of the design, and not spread on the film, afterwards, like butter. Sometimes the sound may help to tell the story by inference (as in our example with the taxi), and sometimes the picture may have to be fitted to the sound instead of the inevitable sound to the picture. Lighting should have its pre-determined values and be able to explain moods and situations by inference, and not be the whim of a lighting cameraman. (A recent example of a ruined inference: an art-director's careful design showing a man in real and emotional shadow speaking to a woman in sunlight, was changed by the lighting cameraman to a picture of a woman in shadow and a man in a halo of light.) Sets, again, should be inferential; not static, but pliable backgrounds which can take up the task of telling the story. The sets should be capable of changing – as they can with independent frame technique – without interrupting the continuity of performance.

Design by inference of the film as a whole calls for pre-production conferences, such as are held by technicians using the new independent-frame technique, when writer, director, designer and sound-man go into conference to plan the shooting script.

In a short article it is impossible to cover all implications of design by inference; but let us take, as a subject for closer consideration, that of colour inference. Colour is probably the most neglected of the new dimensions of the screen: few directors who use colour to-day have taken the least trouble to study the inferential possibilities. How, then, can they build a new cinema world of colour? The concern of most practising colour technicians is simply to photograph as much objective colour as possible. If, however, we make a scientific analysis of the old masters we find that in any one picture the artist is using a far smaller range of colour sequence than that which is embraced by (say) Technicolor.

If it is to have inference colour must be used selectively; and we must remember, in order to exploit, the basic facts. For instance, the eye is slow to adapt to the dark and quick to adapt to light. One can cut from a dark, sombrely coloured scene to a brilliant one; but one must use a slow dissolve to turn a light scene into a dark one. Again, the technician who would use colour for psychological inference must remember that when the eye is saturated with a colour it becomes thirsty for that colour's complement. If it is important, inferentially, to show a woman in a marvellous yellow dress, the eye should first be saturated with blue; then the yellow dress, when it appears, will be exceptionally vivid. If the yellow dress is held against a blue background and the camera tracks in, the yellowness of the dress will dim as the area of blue is reduced. So, in all these examples, we see how there are times when the picture may have to fit the inferential design of another element in the film.

Yes, colour inference, if it is understood, can be used to exploit the audience's imagination.

Firstly, colour has time. Time seems to pass more slowly in warm lighting; warm colour can therefore be used to imply that an incident has taken longer than is actually the case.

Colour has size – a yellow ball will look bigger than a blue one which is in fact the same size – and colour has distance, for earth colours belong to the foreground and cold colours to the backgrounds. A man in a red cloak in the background will appear to be nearer the foreground than he is; so, to achieve separation — the illusion of depth in a scene — earth colours should never be used in the background. A similar point can be made because colour has texture. A dozen different materials, dyed with the same colour, will present different appearances. In this case rough textures belong to the foreground. Again, the handling of colour distance can be made a story-point by the inference of emphasis.

Colour has temperature. Certain 'hot' colours, when played continuously on the screen, affect the audience and raise the physical temperature in the auditorium. Here is a clear opportunity for the inference of passion.

Colour has weight. Under red lights, athletes find it harder to lift weights. Colours, then, can infer exertion, and suggest, too, a lack of vital concern.

Once the inference of colour is understood, the selective colour changes from scene to scene have a new impact. The scenario of a film which is designed for inference must indicate these changes, which must be planned in accordance with basic, physiological facts. Colour can help the picture's flow or it can punctuate the story.

The film-maker must constantly identify himself with the audience when estimating colour suggestiveness. The clique go to rushes to see if the colour is 'good'; they do not consider the imagination of the audience. Design by inference, on the other hand, strengthens the bond between audience and film-maker. The technician who is using colour as sound was used (in our example) to conjure up a street scene must not ignore the fact that 'seeing colour' is a thing of light and not of darkness; and so the auditorium could be flooded with colour to stress colour inference on the screen. A character is outside in the cold, and then comes into a fire-lit room. The fire and the room might become almost completely inferential with the extra accent achieved by changing the lighting conditions in the auditorium.

But perhaps this is enough to show the difference in approach between a technician who aims to appeal to the audience's imagination, who tries to tell a story in the way people have learnt to understand a story in life, and the film-maker who just wants to advertise the fact that his picture is in colour.

Meanwhile, one wonders how soon it will be before new blood is born and the tools which are available to the makers of pictures are used to their maximum advantage. How much, or how little, will be made of the tremendous opportunities afforded by the introduction of electronics into the studio, when the true artist of film can use inference scientifically in all cinematic elements?

THE TWO-REEL COMEDY–
ITS RISE AND FALL

ARTHUR KNIGHT

★

ONE of the rare blessings of the double feature is its virtual elimination of the two-reel comedy in its present form from most theatre programmes. Because of this, old film fans who may still treasure the memory of early Chaplins or Keatons or Sennetts are apt to believe that the two-reeler has merely died out. Relatively few have learned the sad depths to which this familiar and once popular programme feature has sunk. For the two-reel comedy is still being ground out industriously by at least two of Hollywood's eight major studios, while other companies release an occasional series from time to time. But Mack Sennett, the old master, would in all likelihood cheerfully disown these offspring.

Comedy, like all other forms of film entertainment, found its origin in the brief, minute-long films turned out by the picture pioneers. Lumière's *Arroseur et Arrosé*, Edison's *Fun in a Chinese Laundry*, Kuhn's *Washday Troubles* – all contained the seeds which, varied and expanded, were to become the two-reel, and eventually the feature-length, comedy. They were short, intense chases, skits in which the tables turned unexpectedly, snatches of laugh-provoking violence. They were the delight of the first film audiences.

Film comedy has since taken two turnings. There is now – thanks largely to the sound film – the comedy of wit and manners, a comedy derived chiefly from the theatre and from fiction. This is the comedy patterned by *It Happened One Night,* and seen currently in such features as *Mr Blandings Builds His*

Dream House. The other is the comedy of pure clowning, the comedy of the grotesque and of the impossible – a comedy that found its fullest development in the two-reelers.

Through the early 1900s, from 1900 to 1910, the French made their contributions. Zecca, Cohl and a host of anonymous others worked up the chase technique to a state of new perfection, introducing into their comedies such specifically filmic devices as rapid motion, slow motion and stop motion. After 1905, the dapper and skilled Max Linder, one of Chaplin's greatest teachers, introduced into films the visual surprises and stunts which are to film comedy what gags are to the radio comedian.

Widely shown in America, these French comedies exerted their most notable influence upon Mack Sennett. American screen comedy had by 1912 developed into a vaudeville type of humour that was merely an extension of the early, primitive skits, and played stage-fashion by such obviously funny people as John Bunny and Flora Finch. Sennett, working for Biograph, had other ideas for film comedy. But D. W. Griffith was then the great Biograph director, and the firm itself was dedicated to the more serious sort of film. Just about the time that Sennett left Biograph for Keystone, Griffith succeeded in convincing his superiors that pictures need not be limited to a single reel: Griffith introduced the two-reel film (about twenty minutes' playing time).

And Mack Sennett, his own master at Keystone, appeared as the genius of comedy. Closely studying the work of Zecca and Linder, he brought slapstick to its final form. His contributions are almost beyond computing. He trained and directed a whole generation of fun makers – actors, writers, cutters and directors – many of them still active in Hollywood to-day. His Keystone corps of screen grotesques, including Fatty Arbuckle, Mabel Normand, Ben Turpin, Louise Fazenda, Ford Sterling, Marie Dressler, Wallace Beery, Gloria Swanson, Harry Langdon, Harold Lloyd, Bebe Daniels, Buster Keaton, Charlie Murray, and, of course, Charlie Chaplin, provided virtually all of Holly-wood's top-flight comic talent up to the coming of sound. He worked out and perfected a gag technique without parallel. It was his idea that comedy must move swiftly and ceaselessly, with barely a pause for audience comprehension. His favourite maxim was that a situation should be introduced, developed and pointed all within twenty feet of film. Sennett, inevitably linked with custard pies and Keystone Kops, deserves recognition as a great satirist as well. Often his satires had a direct, contemporary reference; but always the satire was there, poking fun at polite society, at conventional manners, and at the machine world that America was becoming.

But Sennett's greatest single contribution to two-reel comedy – and to cinema – will always be Charlie Chaplin. It was at Keystone that Chaplin began his fantastic career; from Sennett he learned the rudiments of his art. His first dozen pictures were all directed either by Sennett himself or by Henry Lehrman, at that time Sennett's chief assistant. Chaplin, however, quickly discovered that Sennett's type of humour was not for him. He began to work out longer gag ideas, slowly milking a situation, or even a locale, of all its inherent comedy. Gradually the famous tramp character began to emerge. Leaving Sennett, Chaplin was able freely to explore and develop its comic potentialities in the notable series of two-reelers he then turned out for Essanay and Mutual.

Chaplin's earnings during this three-year period provide a good index to the popularity of the two-reel comedy at that time. He started work for Keystone at $125 a week. A year later, in 1915, he joined Essanay at $1,250 a week. In 1916 Chaplin went to Mutual for $10,000 a week, plus a $150,000 bonus. Chaplin's salary was exceptional – is exceptional, even for stars to-day. But by 1916 the two-reel comedy had become a standard part of every programme, and a producing company could afford to pay its talent as much – and sometimes even more – for shorts as it paid its feature players. Between 1916 and 1920 such personalities as Harold Lloyd, Buster Keaton, Raymond Griffith, Gloria Swanson and Wallace Beery began working in two-reel comedy series. With the single exception of Douglas Fairbanks (who appeared in features from the start), all the major comedians of the 1920s had their grounding in this field. It is pertinent that, even after 1918, Chaplin, working under a million-dollar contract calling for eight pictures of any length, interpolated two-reelers in among his feature films up to 1922.

Undoubtedly, as the film industry began to consolidate through the 1920s and stars began earning fabulous salaries, it was the economic factor that carried the top two-reel comedians into features. But a host of lesser clowns – Laurel and Hardy, Harry Langdon, Larry Semon (immensely popular in Europe), Hal Roach's famous 'Our Gang', Lloyd Hamilton, Charley Chase – maintained the two-reel tradition. Later in the 'twenties, some of these too were to graduate into features. But by that time whole studios (Educational, Hal Roach, Mack Sennett) existed solely for the production of the two-reelers, while virtually every major studio had its short comedy department as well. The two-reel comedy had reached its peak.

The situation then was quite familiar to Hollywood's present-day set-up for cartoon production, cartoons having in large measure supplanted the two-reel comedy on the theatre bills. Unlike the cartoon studios, however, the two-reel school was able to make important contributions directly to the entire film industry. It was for the industry at once a school and a proving ground. Through the late 'teens and early 'twenties, the two-reelers continued to provide a major source of talent, both in front of and behind the camera. The roster of actors and actresses who are graduates of the two-reel school is, as indicated above, an impressive one. No less important is the list of writers, directors, cameramen and cutters, which includes, among many others, Frank Capra, Eddie Cline, Leo McCarey, Charles Reisner, Hal Roach, Mal St.Clair, Alfred Santell, Lewis Milestone, George Stevens, Eddie Sutherland, etc.

The conditions for two-reel comedy production through the 'twenties fostered their talents. Having a regular place on the theatre programmes, the comedies could be produced on a fairly elaborate budget.* Time could be spent to develop and perfect situations. And salaries were large enough to attract and hold first-class talent.

The revolution began in 1928, with the arrival of sound. A host of new comedians immediately appeared to supplant the established favourites. Clark and McCullough, Robert Benchley, W. C. Fields, imported from the New York stage, all made comedy series; while established film comedians of any merit at all, provided only that they could talk, were promptly promoted to features. Soon even the imported stars were playing in features. Almost overnight the two-reel comedy became a despised relation of the feature film, holding out only the meagre reward of a star's billing to the bit players who acted in them.

Sound brought a revolution that shook even the long-established feature comedians. Raymond Griffith, Harry Langdon, Douglas MacLean and Johnny Hines, all popular through the 'twenties, were unable to make the change. Buster Keaton starred in a scant half-dozen pictures, then fell into obscurity. Harold Lloyd's early talkies never touched his silent films. Chaplin's long unwillingness to come to terms with the new medium is famous ; the change-over to sound delayed *City Lights* (silent, with effects) for almost two years. In their places appeared new masters of a purely verbal humour – the Marx Brothers, Will Rogers (whose occasional appearances in silent features had won him but scant following), Bob Hope and Jimmie Durante.

Coupled with this drainage of talent to rout the two-reel comedy was the great depression of 1929. Through the years that followed, studio budgets were pared – particularly in the

* In a late silent Laurel and Hardy, for example (*Two Tars*, 1928), M-G-M seems to have bought out the entire Los Angeles used-car market to provide the climax of the picture.

shorts departments. Then, as theatre patronage dropped, the double feature appeared, with its lure of two shows for the price of one. But, of course, these were not two *complete* shows. Programmes became rather two features, a newsreel, and a single-reel cartoon or novelty. Band shorts, variety acts and travelogues became the standard programme fillers; while *The March of Time* and, later, the *This Is America* series made further inroads on whatever two-reel playing time might still exist. Against this combination of odds, the death of the two-reel comedy as a creative form was inevitable.

But the two-reel comedies are still around. One sees them occasionally among the "selected shorts" in the newsreel houses, or in those converted burlesque theatres that promise four hours of laughs from cartoons and comedies. They are also shown fairly widely in America through the South and the Middle West, in houses that book horse operas and Monogram melodramas as their main attraction. And occasionally – but very occasionally – they turn up as programme filler in the key houses of key cities, in houses that are more often than not affiliated with the producing company.

For that is what two-reel comedies have become to-day. They do not pretend to bid for playing time on the strength of their merit. Practically given away, they represent for their producers less a source of income than a means of holding on to playing time for their features.

Small wonder then that little time and no effort is spent on their preparation. Shooting schedules are a few days, sets are either quick run-ups or paint-overs from features, scenarios are stereotyped, and dialogue is just short of improvisational. Most of the comedy series in recent years have been built around a once-great name – Buster Keaton, Harry Langdon, or, to come down a few pegs, Leon Errol, Edgar Kennedy, or the Three Stooges. But it would be pointless to compare one of Keaton's Columbia comedies with, say, his early *Electric House*. They just were not made the same way. Comedy needs time to grow; its development cannot be constricted and forced. Chaplin, whose constant battle in his early days was for more production time, understood this well. The others, whether they understood it or not, all profited from the comparatively leisurely schedules. And dialogue comedy, it would seem, requires even more planning and rehearsal than pantomime to achieve its optimum success.

Until the studios can find this kind of time in their production schedules and budgets for two-reel comedies, they seem doomed to their present ignoble position. And with retrenchment again the watch-word in Hollywood, certainly the present outlook is not an auspicious one.

There are a few possibilities out towards the horizon, however, that bear looking into. Double features, long the subject of ineffectual attacks by audience groups, have been slightly weakened in recent years by the appearance of numerous 'super-productions'. Running two hours and more in length, they have forced many theatre managers to use shorts rather than a second feature in rounding out their programmes.

Far more telling, and of greater practical concern to Hollywood itself to-day, is the positive dearth of new comic talent. The present crop of film comedians is ageing, and few new ones have been developed. Where are they to develop? An occasional Danny Kaye is plucked from Broadway and transplanted, but Broadway too leans heavily on an earlier generation: Beatrice Lillie and Jack Haley star in the year's top musical revue. Vaudeville and burlesque, once primary sources of talent, are now a long time dead. Radio's best-loved comedians have produced some of Hollywood's most terrifying flops. (Bob Hope, it might be well to recall, reversed the usual order: he came to films from vaudeville and musical comedy, and only then added radio.) Where are the new comedians to come from?

Well, why not from Hollywood itself? The two-reel comedies of the 'teens furnished all the major comedians of the 'twenties, much of the major talent. Those same two-reelers still exist, an ignored but potential source of talent – indeed, the logical place for talent development – in the studios to-day. More time, more money, more care would be required for production than the studios now grudge them if they are to show any dividends. But if the dividends would be another Chaplin, another Keaton, another Capra, another McCarey, might that not be worth it? And as for playing time for these new productions, what theatre manager would dream of turning down a series of two-reelers as popular as the Chaplin Mutuals?

THE DOCUMENTARY FILM

JEAN PAINLEVÉ

*

Jean Painlevé, son of the famous Prime Minister, is well known in French film circles. His primary interest is the making of scientific films, to which he has devoted a large part of his own not inconsiderable private funds. 'L'Hippocampe' and 'Le Vampire' are among the best known of his films: he has specialised in underwater photography, and recently, in London, has achieved the first successful transmissions of television from a microscope. The problem of general distribution for such films is as great in France as in England, and it is virtually impossible to recover their production costs, however praiseworthy their object.

During the war Painlevé was a member of the French Resistance Movement, and when it ended he became the head of the Direction Générale du Cinéma. Later he resigned from this position. Now he continues to try to develop his first love, the use of films for science teaching and information generally. Recently he helped to start two international bodies, the International Scientific Film Association (l'Association Internationale du Cinéma Scientifique), of which he is now Secretary-General, and the World Union of Documentary. The first of these, as its name implies, exists for the promotion and interchange of ideas concerning the making, distribution and use of scientific films of all kinds. In those countries where they exist, national associations with similar objects, such as the Scientific Film Association of Great Britain, are affiliated.

World Union of Documentary is a body, loosely constructed at present, representing the views of the technicians who make documentary films in all countries. In Britain, a national group was started last year as a forum for the British technicians concerned with films of that kind. In other countries national groups are in process of formation, with the hope that a fully ratified membership can be published after the Union's first official Congress in August 1949. Jean Painlevé, in spite of some early differences of opinion, is still prominently connected with the running of the organisation.

He is also head of the Centre de Production de Films Scientifiques et Techniques of the French Conservatoire National des Arts et Métiers.

★

LET me establish that I am talking only about the sincere documentary, and not those in which the authors satisfy themselves with any old subject irrespective of whether they have any real feelings about it. When at the Department of Agriculture, for example, the happy idea of making a film on the beetroot comes up, there is always some hanger-on to exclaim, 'But the beetroot! I have thought only of that since I was born! And my grandfather is a diabetic.'

In fact, making any documentary worthy of the name is hard labour. It has proved over a long time its undisputed qualities for ruining the honest and independent film-maker. The head of that permanently drowning man can only be kept above water by grants from public funds or trusts. If it is commercially exploited, it is generally at a loss, for the financial climate created around it smells of the swamp.

Touchstone of cinematographic skill, the documentary formula has always attracted the most authentic cinéastes; often those who have made none dream of doing so, and only the fact that they are caught up in big productions stops them. But in many countries, documentary is very sickly; to safeguard it, documentarians must at least understand each other, have similar points of view about the conception, exploitation and distribution of their films. In each country one must fight against the export of bad national films and, reciprocally, put everything in hand to distribute in each foreign films of good quality. Naturally, the kind of film proper for one country is not attractive to another; nevertheless, many nationalities have a cinematographic language in common, above all in documentary, and each has a natural appreciation of the other's production. And it is obvious that they have special characteristics too; thus the English school always goes for films about people and their work, many Frenchmen follow the cult of art for art's sake, Soviet production popularises for all even the most complex ideas, and so on.

More and more it is acknowledged that classification is indispensable. First, about general order. For the last twenty-five years I have adopted the following categories: scientific research, specialised teaching, general teaching, special mass information, general mass information. There is not always a dividing-line exactly drawn. One is obliged to be even more precise still when one analyses the different categories.

Some people employ the term 'scientific film' in the sense of demonstrational film – with the result that they cover everything – it can lead to vast lists. I consider as scientific only the scientific research or technical progress film, and the film for the dissemination of new knowledge. All the rest can come under education or general mass information ... and that will allow the pedagogical or documentarian associations to exist. They can, if they so wish, utilise the scientific film; the opposite is not valid. A film on personal hygiene or the use of vaccination comes into the social-propaganda-film category – general mass information: a film on a new way of vaccinating is a scientific film.

In teaching itself, one should consider two distinct branches. Although specialised education, close to research itself, addressed to trained minds, may utilise every sort of film, the same

is not true of the general education given to the majority up to
the age of sixteen years. It is in this kind of teaching that the
use of film is most confused. Anything is put on to celluloid,
although not every subject is cinegraphic; or sometimes the
subject would be more interesting presented in an abstract form
(to which indeed all young children are very sensitive); or again
the film may with advantage be replaced by still pictures, wall
boards, etc. But no: the cinema is the fashion. Most of the time
the teachers know nothing of the really useful possibilities of
the cinema, and the film-makers have no knowledge of peda-
gogy. But one must realise first that teaching worthy of the
name should make the subject understood, learnt and remembered. Nothing is more dangerous than to *believe* that one has
understood or that one knows. And the film too often has such
magnificent clarity that nothing of its lesson remains a little
later except the satisfaction of having avoided the need to
make any effort.   Beware of superficial culture!

Play and the vital necessities of life should be the basis of any
modern teaching method which is to be rapid and effective; but
it is equally necessary that the pupil should take an *active* part;
and the cinema can be dangerous, in that it creates a passive
attitude.

One should first, then, be able without ambiguity to justify
the necessity for a film; next, to know what is the use to be
made of it. There is the teaching film of which the master can
make use during class, a teaching instrument as easy to handle
as the blackboard. This is the kind of film, very brief, which
deals with one precise point: it can be projected several times
and commentated by the master and the pupils. (This kind of
film, in fact, is yet to be created.) There is the recapitulation
film, which may be projected at the end of the study period, and
needs previous knowledge duly acquired; this film will be a
sound film, and may last ten minutes. There is, finally, the
educational film in the widest sense of the word, multiplying
centres of interest and exciting the imagination, most often at

the expense of mental concentration. One can find many of them among the documentaries intended for public showing. What must be avoided at all costs is the film becoming a '*pense bête*' for teachers, a film made by teachers with an eye to its effect on other teachers.

Of the teaching film, one expects a well-demonstrated affirmation; on the contrary, the documentary for the public or for general mass information should not be didactic. This does not in any sense justify bluff, the useless parade of images, the fallacious presentation. Strict reality always exceeds imagination, and if one finds oneself tempted to deck it out or liven it up, it is because one has not been able to get to grips with it and that one is using cutting or commentary as a palliative for that impotence. How many times has one been able to replace, for the uninformed spectator, a missing crucial gesture (always difficult to record) by cleverly contriving the continuity of what precedes and what follows?

A complete phenomenon in fact requires enormous patience for an exact recording of it. The seeker who has succeeded is proud of his achievement, and will not relinquish a single detail. Generally, he is in consequence irritating even to an informed public. And it goes without saying that he will not tolerate cuts in his work if one wants to make another version. Some of these people feel themselves compromised if the film serves any purpose other than the demonstration of a piece of research before learned societies: and by that they are allowing their film to be lost. The ivory tower is no longer acceptable in our time. This attitude is all the more serious, as the scientists are numerous who deny the film any value as an instrument of research. Although up till now, in the absolute, there are few interesting results, one can say that, relative to the meagre use made of the cinema for this purpose, there have been a good number. It is therefore of some interest to catalogue the films which have contributed to the development of a piece of new knowledge – those that earn their place by using the film's ability to show what one cannot see without it, thanks to time lapse, slow motion, infra-red, ultra-violet or by a more accept-able visualisation of phenomena already stated otherwise (for example, frame-by-frame analysis with repeated projection in front of several observers – a very useful method for anything that is unusual, fleeting, difficult or expensive to reproduce, visible by only one person at a time, etc.). But the cinema, like every means of observation, carries within itself the soul of a false witness, and for that reason the critical spirit must remain wide-awake. For example, in the same way that one employs several magnifications with a microscope, one must in the same way look at any given subject in close-up, as it were, as well as in long-shot.

One thing is certain, that only when the camera is used to the same extent as the microscope will the importance of the cinema in scientific research be convincing. From now on it should be obligatory for the date of production to appear on the titles of these films (as it should, indeed, on all document-aries): this will avoid some of the abuses – multiple recapitula-tion of the same subjects, wasted effort. To avoid confusion; to obtain unanimous agreement from directors on their ap-proach; by comparing the intention and, via the user, the achievement, to create in a practical way international co-operation in the production and distribution of the document-ary film; such must be the constructive objects both of the World Union of Documentary and of the International Scientific Film Association.

'PAISA'

How it struck our Contemporaries

ROGER MANVELL

★

ONCE upon a time there was a journal called *World Film News*.
One of its features was to put together a series of contrary notices by different critics writing about the same films. This is always an instructive thing to do, especially about a film which
may well rank as 'great' when our period of film-making is seen
in perspective. Let us have a look at what some of the critics
have said about this initial quality of greatness ascribed by
many of them to *Paisa*.

'PAISA' IS A GREAT FILM

Basil Wright: '*Paisa* is a full-length feature film. It is made up
of six short stories not in any way connected with each other
either in characterisation or plot. All the stories have a carefully and deliberately contrived twist to them.

'It may well be asked therefore why this film is considered as
documentary. The answer is that *Paisa* may well prove to be,
not only the climax of all documentary development, but also
an influence on all types of film production as profound and far-
reaching as that of *Potemkin*.' (*Documentary '47.*)

Stephen Watts: 'One of the great films of our time.' (*Sunday
Express.*)

Richard Winnington: 'It cannot be doubted that Roberto
Rossellini's *Paisa* will stand as one of the few great comments on
the Second World War to be made by the contemporary cinema. ...

'*Paisa*, humorous and tragic, fully earns the depleted title

9   54   THE PENGUIN FILM REVIEW

"great". ... A splendidly positive film of our tragic times.' (*News Chronicle*.)

Matthew Norgate: 'There are the bones of greatness in *Paisa*.' (*Tribune*.)

'PAISA' IS NOT A GREAT FILM

Jympson Harman: 'These incidents have no apparent link of purpose and the continuity within them is poor.' (*Evening News*.)

A Special Correspondent in the *Observer:* 'He may one day feel ashamed at having merely done well in haste by a theme that deserved to be done better at leisure.'

THE HUMANISM OF ROSSELLINI

The film critic of *The Times* says the following about the new realistic school of Italian films in general: 'Its impulse is a kind of imaginative realism which knows how to take into account the inconsistencies, the paradoxes, the maddening inconsequences of human behaviour; it spreads out generously on the counter rather than ties up neatly in a parcel.'

Of Rossellini he adds: 'Rossellini and the cast he controls are creating while they seem to be doing nothing more than giving a random, disconnected report.'

Milton Shulman, in the *Evening Standard*, speaks of the film's 'stark reality and warm humanity', and other critics write in these terms:

Leonard Moseley: 'Almost intolerably moving.' (*Daily Express*.)

Stephen Watts: 'Few films have said so much about war – and about humanity – and never with more perceptive economy.'

Richard Winnington: 'His belief in men and women is evident in almost every foot of the film, through all the disillusion and irony.'

Matthew Norgate: 'Here, at least, is an artist with the ability to express himself. Not that Rossellini has anything more precise to say than that war is a soul-destroying business, but his medium is humanity rather than words or pictures, and he has that rare gift of being able to present humanity without being sentimental about it.'

Dilys Powell: 'It brings to the picture of war a pity at once savage and tender which is quite foreign to the studio-made film.' (*Sunday Times*.)

William Whitebait: 'It is no exaggeration to say that *Paisa*, with its warm shifting episodes, gives a greater and more heart-rending sense of the totality of war than any other film, more than the same director's *Open City*. He shows again the same careless genius for welding document and story, actors and actuality.' (*New Statesman*.)

THE TECHNICAL QUALITIES OF 'PAISA'

Basil Wright*: 'Rossellini's direction may be particularly noted for his brilliance in depicting action in extreme long-shot (especially of the passage of the Negro and the boy through the crowded square); his unerring sense of rhythm and tempo, and his highly individual system of editing, which may be described (inadequately) as a kind of shorthand.'

M. T. McGregor: 'Reactions to *Paisa* were in my case delayed by doubt, frustration and the shock of so much passion conveyed in crude news-style photography. There may be room to doubt Rossellini's judgment, none to question his vision and power to communicate it; frustration is the result, perhaps intended, of the episodic treatment. At least one episode is quite ineffectual, and the whole a less mature work of art than either *Open City* or *Germany Year Zero*. But I have not been able to get it out of my mind.' (*Time and Tide*.)

Matthew Norgate: "There is no getting away from the fact that it is technically slovenly. The six episodes of which it is

* It should be remembered that Basil Wright is a director and producer of documentary films of nearly twenty years' standing. His films include the beautiful *Song of Ceylon*.

composed are slung on to the screen without any regard for continuity, the cutting is positively slapdash, and the acting uneven. ...'

'Even if you were working in rough-and-ready conditions, can you get away with meretricious trick endings to your episodes, however successfully you bring off some of them?'

Milton Shulman: 'Loss of unity makes it less satisfying than those other two Italian masterpieces *Open City* and *Shoe Shine*.'

Jack Davies: 'Each story he has to tell is simple and straight-forward; but each has a cynical twist at the end.' (*Sunday Graphic*.)

Richard Winnington: 'With the exception of the fifth (the monastery) each one is permeated with a sense of tragic irony and given a de Maupassant flick at the end.'

Observer Correspondent: 'Its direction is often crude and its acting amateur . ... Rossellini had to get this story off his subjective chest and tell it crudely at once rather than delicately later.'

'The matter of these *contes* is often as artificial as that of any by O. Henry or de Maupassant, but the manner of their telling carries a passionate conviction beside which all other films this week seem flat and unprofitable.'

But the *Observer* Correspondent compares Rossellini's approach to his work with that of an undergraduate.

ROSSELLINI'S NATIONAL ATTITUDE

Nearly every one of these critics takes up the point of the anti-British attitude shown in the film. The *Observer* Correspondent speaks of the anti-British jibe* spoken by a G.I. in the last episode as placed 'with cunning or possibly with cowardice by Mr Rossellini into the mouth of an American soldier'.

Richard Winnington writes: 'It is an all-American-Italian

* These people (i.e. the Italian partisans) are not fighting for the British Empire – they're fighting for their lives.

film, distinctly disparaging in representation of and comment on the British. And I take it that Rossellini, to gain on the American market, was prepared to lose in objectivity.'

The *Daily Mail* film critic also hints at the dollar-earning possibilities behind this touch of dialogue. Matthew Norgate says: '... if he made his film again now, would he not, I wonder, be more discriminate?'

Dilys Powell, however, while noting the lack of consideration for the British part in the liberation of Italy, is prepared to concede that 'we must not be too sensitive'.

Campbell Dixon says of Rossellini in the *Daily Telegraph*: 'He has imagination, a passionate sympathy for the underdog, great skill in selecting incident, and even greater skill in giving his work a political slant the more telling for its subtlety. ... Rossellini ingeniously contrives to load the dice against the Allies.'

On the sequence showing the two British officers admiring the architecture of Florence whilst the Partisans die, he adds: 'Italians who fought these same dilettanti in Africa are permitted to laugh on the other side of the face.'

M. T. McGregor, however, writes as follows: 'I didn't share the general umbrage at a couple of anti-British cracks. I never see why we should expect foreigners to like us all that much; I certainly don't see why they shouldn't make fun of a nation that thinks all foreigners are ludicrous. *Paisa*, anyway, is more concerned with the Americans who have swarmed on Italy. These strange new barbarians are taken apart gently, like a mechanical toy, to see how they tick. And here they are: indifferent, obtuse, kindly savages.'

THE BEST EPISODE

Paisa is divided into six episodes or short stories. They are:

1. Sicily. An Italian girl avenges a G.I. member of a landing patrol killed by the Germans.

2. Naples. A street boy buys the right to rob a drunken Negro M.P. of his boots.
3. Rome. A drunken G.I. fails to recognise in an Italian prostitute the decent girl who welcomed him to Rome on its liberation six months earlier.
4. Florence. An American nurse crosses the city through the street fighting to find her Italian partisan lover killed.
5. Countryside near Bologna. Three American Army Chaplains (Catholic, Protestant, Jew) visit a remote monastery.
6. Po Marshlands. The scattered and tragic resistance to the Germans of a party of Italians, Americans and British.

Critics had various preferences among these episodes. M. T. McGregor finds the Naples episode 'the most perfect, the most irresistible episode of the six'. Jack Davies prefers the last ; so does Matthew Norgate, who writes: 'This monastery story is the only one of the six which is, to my mind, beyond reproach on æsthetic grounds, and it contrasts exquisitely the simple faith of the monks with the worldly sophistication of the padres.' Richard Winnington claims: 'The Naples, Monastery, and Po Valley sequences display Rossellini's unique talents to the full. The last, brave, disillusioned and full of forlorn beauty, contains the whole core and meaning of partisan warfare, and owes not a little, one would say, to Malraux's forgotten and unrecognised masterpiece *Espoir*.'

On the whole, the second, fifth and sixth episodes have gained the most favourable comment.

★

Among British film-makers I have found in conversation a similar divergence of opinion. One found it disconnected and unconvincing, the action of some episodes not at all clearly defined. Another prominent documentary director thinks it a work to rank with *Potemkin* in the development of the film. A distinguished director of feature films said he could no more work like Rossellini than fly, but said he thought Rossellini's complete disregard for the technical values he himself always worked for did not matter, because the effects at which Rossellini was aiming were completely different.

Rossellini works when the mood is on him with complete absorption, normally on location and not in a studio. The writer Serge Amidei is an important influence in his films.* Dialogue is often worked out on the spot with the speakers, the actors being mixed professional and amateur (such as the monks in the Bologna sequence who are friends living in a monastery actually located near Amalfi, where several of the episodes of *Paisa* were actually shot). He can therefore be called an inspirational film-maker, shooting 'off the cuff' in accordance with what seems to him to feel right, to fit in with his conception of the human element in his film. For it is always the human element that concerns him. There is no overt theme to his films, though it is always possible to invent themes for this kind of work by trying to find a highest common factor or lowest common denominator to the outcome of his stories or the attitude they seem to represent. I believe Rossellini's prime concern is to take a bunch of people whose characters and faces attract him, and let them work their way through situations which involve acute human emotion, conflict or simple humour.

Like many artists in literature, notably Flaubert, Rossellini is objective, keeping any views he may have out of his work as far as possible, observing the sentiment, the squalor and the glory of life with an eye to getting it as nearly as may be on to the screen. This may well be the reason for the so-called anti-British element in the film: it came to the lips of the particular people in the particular situations they were in, and was not pruned away by the kind of censorships and reticences which attend the script conferences of more consciously metropolitan pictures. Rossellini gives his stories a 'twist' or 'flick', because he thinks it necessary, in translating the raw material of life to any medium of expression, to round it off, to point it for the sake of

* I am grateful to Paul Rotha for some of the details mentioned here.

emphasising its quality and giving it climax before withdrawing from it to deal with other facets of human experience he fancies worth recording. His films may feel raw because he lets human emotion and human indifference come over alike with as little dramatisation as possible, and certainly without letting himself or his audience indulge in the same emotionalism as his characters, which, of course, is the essence of melodrama or romance, where author, audience, and characters are all in the thing together. For this reason Rossellini is praised for his authenticity or condemned for his cynicism.

Paisa is roughly acted (except for those happy performances by professional and amateur alike which roundly and naturally succeed before the camera), roughly photographed with no attempt to be beautiful pictorially except when the surroundings or the faces make it so inevitably and without conscious tricks of composition, seldom lit with that smooth continuity of photography so carefully and lengthily devised in the studios, and edited always to drive home the human element and not to play games with rhythm. The music by Renzo Rossellini, little mentioned by the critics, is excellent. It is reticent and yet evocative, as in the Florence episode or in the terrible scenes of the rescue of the body of the Partisan from the swift river current carrying it to, from and past the camera.

The position of *Paisa* in the development of the realist branch of film-making cannot be determined until we see whether it will remain a sort of respected monolith (like *Intolerance* or *October*), or whether it will give heart and courage to other film-makers and make them more ready to strip off the reticences and show the face of humanity on the screen without conventional make-up. For this is Rossellini's real achievement in *Paisa*.

FILM CENSORSHIP
IN BRITAIN

A. T. L. WATKINS

(Secretary of the British Board of Film Censors)

★

CENSORSHIP is only news when it makes a mistake. The
fact that the British Board of Film Censors has been viewing
films at the rate of 3,000 a year for many years is a matter of indifference to the majority of cinema-goers. And rightly so.
The effect of a good censorship should not be noticed. The
result of its work lies on the cutting-room floors of the studios,
and although the trade may be all too aware of this, the cinema
public, which sees only the completed and apparently untouched film, is happily ignorant. Indeed, they might reasonably be pardoned for wondering why censorship is needed.
They well might ask, 'Who is this Censor? Why should he take
upon himself the duty of saying what I should or should not
see? What does he mean by "should not"? Because I may suffer
harm? Well, if I am in that danger, isn't he in his examining
theatre? What is there in his mental equipment that enables
him to emerge unscathed from seeing the things I'm not allowed to? Surely intelligent adults may be allowed to look after
themselves in these matters?'

The answer is that intelligent adults could be. But the world
is not made up of intelligent adults, any more than it is made
up of morally balanced individuals. The cinema public in particular represents all ages and all stages of mental and moral
development. And while an intelligent adult audience might be
relied on to reject bad taste and to remain undisturbed by im-

moral influences, he would be an optimist who would expect such qualities of resistance in the average patrons of the local Odeon or Granada. Bearing in mind the mixed audience which attends the ordinary cinema, imagine what would be the result if no obstacle were placed in the way of films which misrepresent moral values, condone cruelty, debase marriage and the home or mock at religion. Does anyone believe that such films would have no ill-effect, particularly on the young people who represent such a large percentage of the thirty million weekly cinema-goers?

But, it may be said, no director would make such films. The answer is that, even with a censorship, he occasionally tries to. And if the Censor so much as nods in his direction, a storm breaks. Angry members of the public reach for their pens. Responsible public bodies demand an inquiry into the methods of censorship. The Board has no right or desire to resent criticism when a mistake is made, but from the letters which from time to time reach the office, it might be inferred that some of the critics never visit a cinema and have little or no knowledge of the principles on which censorship works. Though the best censorship may be one which works with due reticence, not seeking advertisement or expecting commendation, it must rely for its success on public support and co-operation. For this reason it may be useful in this short article to clear up one or two of the commoner misconceptions.

The Board is an unofficial organisation which was set up in 1912 by the cinema trade to ensure an acceptable standard in the films it produces. From the fact that the trade set up its own censorship critics have hastily deduced a sinister liaison between the Board and the trade. Nothing could be farther from the truth. The trade, through a representative committee, appoints the President of the Board, but there its association with censorship ends. The President, once appointed, is completely independent, and has a free hand to appoint his examiners and staff. There is a clear understanding that no one who has any connection whatever with the trade may serve on the Board. The idea that, in practice, the Board is influenced in its decisions by its obligation to the trade would cause some surprise in Wardour Street, where its impartial decisions have given too many painful headaches.

The Censor is not an arbiter of taste. It is not his function to improve the quality of films or the public taste in films. The public will in the long run get the films it desires or deserves, and nothing the Censor can do will alter this. How much pleasanter indeed would be his task if his work were conducted on æsthetic principles – if he could reject what he did not like and allow what pleased his artistic taste. But such an approach would be far from his proper function. Dismal trash must be passed, if it does not offend; and conversely, even a film of artistic merit may require the blue pencil where the handling of its theme would be objectionable for a mixed cinema audience. The Censor's function, then, is strictly limited, to take out of films what is likely to offend or likely to do harm. The quality of what remains the public must judge, and on their ultimate verdict must depend the artistic development of the cinema.

The Board has no written Code, no neatly docketed list of things which are allowed and things which are not. It has been suggested that such a Code would help producers. The Board thinks it would have the reverse effect. The absence of a Code enables it to treat each picture, each incident, each line of dialogue on its merits. No two pictures are alike, everything depends on the treatment and the context. If the Board worked to a Code, it would have to stick to the Code. Films would be dealt with on the basis of hard-and-fast rules, no discretion would be exercised – and producers and public alike would be the losers.

But if the Board has no Code, there are certain broad principles on which it works. In judging a film there are three main questions to be considered:

Is it likely to impair the moral standards of the audience by extenuating vice or crime or by depreciating social values? The Board does not assume that because a screen gangster successfully brings off a coup, the ordinary husband will be tempted to crack a safe on his way home, or because that wife in the film gets away with a clandestine affair, a respectable housewife is likely to break up her home in Brixton. But the boy or girl in the next seat to them? The young wage-earner with too little in his pay-packet, the weak, impressionable girl for whom all is unquestionably gold that glitters? Remember, the Censor is not dealing with single pictures. Single incidents or lines of dialogue are not likely to corrupt anyone. The Censor is dealing with the cumulative effect of a continuous output of pictures on people who see films regularly, many of them two or three times a week.

Secondly, is the story, incident or dialogue likely to give offence to any reasonably minded section of the public? Repeat 'reasonably minded'. The Board does not cater for cranks or their susceptibilities: if it did, no film would remain intact. But it tries to keep out of films the things which it believes the normal audience would not welcome as entertainment: harrowing death or torture scenes, gruesome hospital and accident sequences, unnecessary physical brutality, cruelty to animals or children; indecency, vulgarity; flippant references to religion or any sincerely held belief; ridicule of respected public figures or institutions.

Thirdly, what will be the effect of the story, incident or dialogue on children – that is to say, children of all ages under sixteen? This is one of the Board's most important considerations. Because, whether we like it or not, the children are in the cinema and they have come to stay. The cinema in this country has developed as a family entertainment. In this respect it differs from the stage or radio. The theatre, except at Christmas time, is largely an adult entertainment; and while the radio caters for everyone, it is a selective entertainment,

LOUISIANA STORY

30 to 33. Stills from Robert Flaherty's film made in the bayou swampland of Louisiana, and showing the personal reactions of a bilingual Acadian family to the drilling for oil in their locality. Photography by Richard Leacock, editing by Helen van Dongen, music by Virgil Thompson.

The stills show Lionel Le Blanc as the father and Joseph Boudreaux as his son.

THE TREASURE OF SIERRA MADRE

34 to 36. John Huston's production for Warner's, featuring Humphrey Bogart. Its theme is the degeneration of men's characters through the search for and discovery of gold.

OLIVER MESSEL'S DESIGNS FOR

37 to 40. 'The Queen of Spades,' produced by Anatole de Grunewald, directed by Thorold Dickinson and designed by Oliver Messel. The designs were exhibited in the Leicester Galleries, November 1948. 37. The young

'THE QUEEN OF SPADES'

Countess leaving her coach to visit Count Saint-Germain. 38. The ballroom scene. 39 and 40. In the Cathedral, the design and the actual set. (Photograph 40 by Edward Mandinian.)

THE PASSIONATE FRIENDS:

41 to 44. The recent Cineguild film produced by Ronald Neame and based on H.G. Well's novel. Featuring Ann Todd, Claude Rains and Trevor Howard.

DAVID LEAN'S RECENT FILM

The story is that of a married woman whose passion for her past lover revives after her marriage. (Stills by Charles Trigg.)

THE SMALL BACK ROOM

45 to 49. The Archers (Michael Powell and Emeric Pressburger) have filmed
Nigel Balchin's novel for London Films, starring David Farrar and Kathleen Byron. The film includes an hallucination sequence symbolising the

temptation of whisky to David Farrar, who plays the crippled scientist, Sammy Rice (45). The climax to the action concerns a German booby-trap bomb, an example of which, isolated on the Dorset seashore, has to be investigated by Rice (46 to 49). (Stills by Anthony Hopking.)

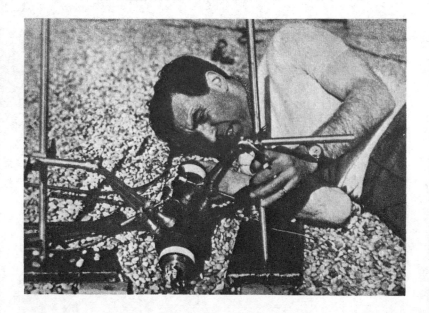

EUREKA STOCKADE

50 to 57. Scenes from Harry Watt's film, made in Australia for Sir Michael Balcon, and described in his article in this issue. 50. Left to right: Sydney Loder, Chips Rafferty, Gordon Jackson and Peter Finch. 51. Part of the crowd of miners.

52. The police arrive after the miners have burnt down the Eureka Hotel.

53. A scene in the goldfields.

54. The beginning of the revolt of the miners against the police.

55. The military arrive to quell the revolt.

56. The miners hold protest meetings throughout the goldfields.

57. The miners form the Diggers' Reform League and fly, for the first time, the Southern Cross flag.

and children do not as a rule tune in to the programmes which attract their elders. Added to which, the radio lacks the tremendous visual influence of the cinema, perhaps the most important of all influences on the juvenile mind. The Board must take into account the fact that the films it passes may, and probably will, be seen by children of all ages. Adults may rather resent this. They may regard with disfavour the idea of the children's presence limiting the scope of their entertainment. Well, the remedy is simple and has been suggested. Exclude the children from the 'A' films. Let these films be truly adult – and confine children to the 'U' films.

This has been the solution adopted in some foreign countries, but, as already pointed out, the cinema in this country has grown into a family entertainment, and any proposal in the direction of excluding children would destroy the basis on which the industry has developed. For the effect would be that large numbers of parents could not go to the cinema at all. The 'A' Category has been devised to meet this difficulty and to preserve the cinema as a family entertainment. Under the conditions commonly imposed by licensing authorities, the 'A' Category allows children to be present if accompanied by their parents or a *bona-fide* guardian. The 'A' Category leaves the decision to the parent. It says in effect, 'This film is not, in the view of the Board, a suitable one for *all* children under the age of sixteen, though it may be suitable for some, having regard to their mental development. Is it a film which is suitable for your child? You know your children better than we do. We are leaving it to you to decide.' This is a compromise, a liberal solution which trusts the parent. The alternative would usurp his function of deciding what entertainment is suitable for his children. The compromise has worked over a number of years, and its continued success will depend on the degree to which the parent exercises the responsibility conferred upon him.

I have outlined above the general principles on which the

Censor works. His task is not an easy one. The balance between passing films which will be such as the general public wish to see, and can approve, and those which, in their subject or treatment, may have some objectionable features or incidents, is often delicate. It is difficult for him to please everyone, nor is it likely that every one of his decisions will be universally acceptable. There are times when he must stand between a disappointed public and what it thinks it should see, between aggrieved producers and what they think they should show, between jaded critics and what they believe they should be spared, between the educationist and the theorist and the commonsense of the average man. Moreover, while it is right that the Censor shall pay regard to the preservation of a high standard of entertainment in the cinema, he must be careful not to provide any needless impediment to the development of an important art. The successful accomplishment of his task depends on the sympathetic co-operation of all who are interested in the welfare of the cinema: of the producers and the public, and of the Licensing Authorities in whom is vested the final responsibility for the standard of entertainment offered in their area. The degree to which the Censor's work is in accord with responsible public opinion is the measure of his success.

PSYCHOLOGY AND
THE FILM

GERTRUDE KEIR

*

'To-day the artist (the film-maker is the artist of our time) has a truly tremendous scope. The moving talking picture is such a colossal power that the man in the director's chair might be forgiven for imagining that he is God in locum tenens. To show the world as it is is art: with the precepts of Aristotle well in mind, the maker of films proceeds to put the world on celluloid' (D. A. Yerrill, 'The Technique of Realism,' *Sight and Sound*, Spring 1948).

A statement such as this (which conveniently ignores the restrictions imposed on film-makers by economic and political considerations) offers us an extreme view as to the power of the film and the film-maker to-day. Extreme but by no means unusual. Even if we do not accept the film-maker as God in locum tenens, there is a widespread acceptance of the film as an instrument superior to any other devised for mass communication and the inculcation of ideas, opinions, attitudes and behaviour patterns. 'Every form of human communication ... has a cohesive effect, but the moving picture has had a tighter, more lasting, binding effect because of its infinitely more powerful emotional impact upon the minds of the people' (Robson, *The World is my Cinema*).

What produces this emotional impact, why should the film audience be thought to differ from any other type of audience? Are the effects of the film powerful enough to produce lasting effects upon attitudes, sentiments and beliefs, and to change subsequent behaviour? In trying to answer some of these questions we shall be considering some of the psychological aspects of the film.

Two main reasons have been given for the supposed power of the film over its audience: (1) the conditions of mass film showing; (2) the technique and content of the films themselves.

(1) The conditions of mass film showing bear a strong resemblance to those utilised when putting a subject under hypnosis. The warmth, the comfortable seats, the darkness and the fixation of moving objects upon a lighted screen: add to these the feeling of communication with other members of the audience, and you have all the features which increase suggestibility, diminish logical thought and criticism, and enable opinions, sentiments and attitudes in the film to be accepted more easily by the audience.

It is very probable that this contention is true. At the same time it should be remembered that the problem of heightened suggestibility during film shows has never been subjected to scientific research. We do not know by how much suggestibility is increased at film shows, the extent to which it may vary with sex, age and economic-social background, nor to what extent it persists. We assume, possibly with truth, that the conditions within the cinema heighten suggestibility, but we do not really know.

(2) The technique and content of the film itself are such as to diminish logical thought and heighten suggestibility, since the power of the film to by-pass the barriers of time and space, to mingle fantasy and reality, is almost unlimited. By its themes, which make direct appeal to the unconscious desires and motives of its audiences, the film greatly increases its emotional impact.

It is with this point of view in mind that Dr Kracauer has lately attempted a psychological analysis of the content of German films over a certain period. He says, 'It is my contention that through an analysis of the German film, deep psychological dispositions predominant in Germany from 1918 to 1933 can be exposed, dispositions that influenced the course of events during that time. I have reason to believe that the use made of the film as a medium of research can profitably be extended to studies of mass behaviour in the United States and elsewhere' (*From Caligari to Hitler*). This is so, since, for Dr Kracauer, 'films are able, and therefore obliged, to scan the whole visible world. In recording the whole visible world, films therefore provide clues to hidden mental processes. Permeating both the stories and the visuals, the unseen dynamics of human relations are none the less characteristic of the inner life of the nation from which the films emerge.'

For Dr Kracauer films 'reflect, not so much explicit credos as psychological dispositions, those deep layers of collective mentality which extend more or less below the dimensions of consciousness'.

For him the relation between films and audiences is, then, twofold – films reflect the collective unconscious and in turn reinforce it, and from this unconscious follows decisive action. By analysing the latent content (as opposed to the manifest content) of films, one can gain knowledge of the instinctive forces which mould nations and drive them to subsequent action. Thus the central figure of *The Student of Prague* is symbolic; it is 'a dreamlike transcription of what the German middle class actually experienced in its relation to the feudal caste running Germany'.

Dr Kracauer's investigation has been ably evaluated in other places, but it may be worth while pointing out some of the pitfalls which await the worker adopting this particular approach. Any research worker must perforce select his material before he proceeds to analyse and interpret it. But the process of selection should take some account of facts which do not fit into the general theory. Dr Kracauer does not make very clear the explicit grounds on which he selects or rejects films for his analysis, but he tends to brush aside as unimportant, because they do not support his theory, a large number of German films produced in the period under scrutiny.

The whole question of the symbolic interpretation of films is fraught with difficulties, since objects will differ in their symbolic meaning according to the school of analysis to which you adhere. What may be a symbol to a Freudian may have a very different significance to a follower of Jung. Parker Tyler analyses latent content according to Freudian interpretations. In an article in *Sight and Sound*, Autumn 1947, 'The Horse – Totem Animal of American Films', he writes thus: 'America is the land of, among other things "the open prairie" and "the lone cow-boy"; alone, save for his eternal partner – the horse. This coupling is paradigm for the pagan myth-creature, the Centaur. ... The horse is not only a power-symbol as a fleshly engine, but as an extension of the man's personal power, more specifically, of his sexual power. ... In more serious films, the riderless or yet untamed horse becomes a symbol for man himself, objectively or subjectively, father or son – and sometimes symbol for woman, the woman to be sexually rejected or obtained.'

Speaking of the horse-race in the racing picture *Homestretch*, he says: 'Let us not be squeamish about the horse-race as a symbolic variety of the sexual act. ... The obsessional temper of racing fans and the emotional build-up to a minute's long suspense (the race itself), accompanied by the wildest excitement and breathlessly climaxed, are factors of racing that testify to its sexual parallel. ... Moreover, we are compelled to recognise in horse-operas of a significantly totemic kind the presence of the Œdipus-complex.'

He is not alone in this analytic approach to the content of films. The Robsons in *The World is my Cinema* also make the statement that 'Decline of the social subconscious towards introspection or Romanticism would therefore undoubtedly find its expression in the widespread concept of the horse and its rider'.

This is obviously an entrancing game, which can be played

by anyone with imagination and a smattering of psychoanalytical knowledge. If one chooses to interpret objects and situations in this way, there is no one to say Nay (with the possible exception of the horse).

It is as well to realise that the most devout follower of Freud might shy at the above interpretation. It is true that certain classes of objects have certain fixed symbolic meanings for the Freudian. Nevertheless, the particular symbolic meaning which an object has for a particular person can only ultimately be determined by its interpretation in the psychoanalytical interview, and by the subject's subsequent behaviour in the light of that interpretation. One cannot therefore really analyse a film, one can only analyse the person producing the film, or, of course, the person seeing and interpreting the film.

Turning from the theoretical to the practical researches carried out upon films and their audiences, we can ask: What have been the principal topics investigated and with what results? The field is disappointingly bare. Among the best-known studies, and in some respects still the best, are the early researches of Thurstone and Peterson, Shuttleworth and May, carried out under the auspices of the Payne Fund in America 1929–33. The former investigated the influence of selected films upon the attitudes of a group of children towards such social issues as War, Gambling, Capital Punishment and Racial Stereotypes. The children were shown films with these as their themes. They were given a questionnaire before and after seeing the film in question. Certain slight but positive results were obtained. The showing of a racial film such as *The Birth of a Nation*, for example, altered the attitude of the children towards Negroes in an unfavourable direction. This change of attitude endured for some eighteen months, when another questionnaire was given to test persistence of impression. Positive changes also took place in their attitudes towards War and Capital Punishment. A cumulative effect was also established. If two films on a given subject were shown, the effect was greater than if only one was seen. These investigations were unfortunately never followed up.

In this country work is only now beginning on the effect of films upon adolescents. Meyer's book, *The Sociology of Film*, while interesting, lacks simple controls which would have made his results more scientifically acceptable. The Department of Education in the University of Birmingham has recently completed a first investigation of the influence of films upon certain attitudes and aspects of behaviour of a group of adolescents. Very little work has as yet been attempted with adult audiences. Much more investigation is needed before we can accept in its entirety such a statement as Rotha's when he says, 'In one form or another, directly or indirectly, all films are propagandist, negative or positive, for their place of origin. Whether it is aware of the propaganda or not, the general public is influenced by every film it sees.'

In particular it seems essential to have accurate information on some of the following points:

1. The amount of suggestibility induced by the special conditions of the cinema house and the special medium of the film, as opposed to other media of mass communication.
2. The extent to which opinions, attitudes and sentiments of the film audience undergo change as a result of seeing films.
3. The degree to which subsequent behaviour is altered as a result of these changed attitudes, sentiments and opinions.
4. The difference in all these respects between audiences of various age-groups, different sex and varying socio-economic backgrounds.

Admittedly these problems would be difficult to tackle on a scientific basis. Speculation is more fascinating, easier and productive of more startling results than scientifically controlled research, but the latter forms a more reliable instrument. It is only by investigating some of these points and many others that we will begin to shape, slowly and tentatively, something of what might be called a psychology of the film.

A TECHNICIAN'S VIEW
OF THE COLOUR FILM

J. H. COOTE

*

YEARS ago, when Technicolor had to sell colour as well as Technicolor, potential customers would ask Dr Kalmus, who was president of the Technicolor companies then as he is now, how much more it would cost to produce a feature film in colour than in black and white. In reply, Dr Kalmus would say: 'You have seen Disney's *Funny Bunnies*; you remember the huge rainbow circling across the screen to the ground, and you remember the Funny Bunnies drawing the colour of the rainbow into their paint pails and splashing the Easter eggs. You all admit that it was marvellous entertainment. Now I will ask you, how much more did it cost Mr Disney to produce that entertainment in colour than it would have in black and white? The answer is of course that it could not be done at any cost in black and white, and a similar analogy can be drawn with respect to some part of almost any Technicolor feature.'

Whatever doubts others have had, colour technicians have seldom lost a moment considering whether colour film is more entertaining than film in black and white; why should they, when they have helped to make films like *Henry V* and *Black Narcissus*? Instead, they turn their thoughts towards perfecting existing processes or to the development of others, and it is the main purpose of this article to outline what they are doing at the present time.

All the colour processes which are in general use to-day are known as 'subtractive processes', and these have one thing in

73

common – three* negatives must be made, one recording the red light which is reflected from the subject, one recording the green and one the blue. The methods by which these colour 'separation' records are obtained can be divided into two classes – the first, in which special cameras exposing three films at once are used, and the second, in which the colour separation occurs within the superimposed emulsion layers of a single film or 'monopack'.

Examples of processes which operate with special cameras are Technicolor and Dufaychrome, while the monopack processes are represented by Kodachrome, Anscocolor, Agfacolor and Gevacolor.

Monopack processes seem on the face of things to offer an almost ideal method of working; ordinary cameras can be used, and furthermore, the negative or positive monopack film, after exposure and development, can be printed on to more monopack film for copies. However, after much consideration and practical experience, more and more colour technicians are arriving at the conclusion that there are serious disadvantages and limitations associated with the use of multi-layer colour materials.

Let us examine the principal steps involved in making colour film by a typical process from each of the two groups. As it is by far the most important process using a colour camera, Technicolor is the inevitable choice on the one hand, and because we have been told more about it than any other 'monopack' process, Agfacolor will be the principal example of the other group, although it is known that there is a great deal of similarity between that German process and the American product – Anscocolor.

Technicolor really began as a three-colour process when the first three-colour camera came into use in 1932. That same camera, together with twenty or thirty others, is probably still be-

---

* Two in the case of two-colour processes such as Cinecolor, Magnacolor, Trucolor and Technichrome.

ing used to-day, and what is more significant, despite the complaints and criticism which at times have been levelled at the practice of using the 'three-strip' camera, many more of them are at present being made for Technicolor by the Newall Engineering Company in this country.

A three-strip or 'beam-splitter' camera enables all three of the required colour separation negatives to be exposed at the same time. Such a camera usually employs a prism block, which is made up of two 45° component prisms, so that part of the light from the camera lens is reflected from the dividing surface between the prisms, while the remainder is transmitted. By such an arrangement two exposing beams are available, and in one of them is placed a 'bi-pack'* of two films, while the third film is exposed, behind the appropriate colour filter, in the second beam.

Disadvantages do arise when using a three-strip colour camera – the weight and size of the outfit being particularly troublesome when synchronised sound shooting is required and the 'blimp' must be used. Because of these difficulties, a great deal of effort has been spent during the last few years in attempting to ally the unquestioned convenience of any monopack process when used at the taking stages to the undoubted capabilities of Technicolor as a release printing process. This compromise procedure has been employed for the production of several feature films – the *Lassie* series, for instance – as well as for sequences in several others – more recently in *Scott of the Antarctic* and the Winter Sports section of *XIV Olympiad*.

On the whole, however, it is now generally agreed that the quality which can be obtained on the screen by a combination of monopack and Technicolor cannot equal the results which we have come to expect from the three-strip camera, and this is quite apart from the rather serious inconvenience which arises when a producer must wait days, and sometimes weeks, while

* A bi-pack is a combination of two films which are run through the camera emulsion towards emulsion, the front one recording the blue end of the spectrum and the rear film recording the reds.

the monopack original is processed in America and then re-separated for printing in Technicolor.

It is usual, with a Technicolor production on which the colour camera is being used, for the laboratory to return 'pilots' in colour and rushes in black and white about twenty-four hours after shooting. The pilots are very short strips of finished colour film intended as a guide for director, art director and cameraman.

The broad principles of the Technicolor printing process are fairly well known, although there has often been an undesirable tendency to compare the procedure with lithographic repro-duction on paper. The first operation involves the making of positive prints from the three-colour separation negatives and processing these prints so that hardened gelatine relief images are formed.

Each of the three relief films – known as matrices – are im-mersed in appropriately coloured dye-baths, and then success-ively brought into contact with a blank film which is coated with plain gelatine; thus building up a composite coloured image.

The blank film which is used in Technicolor to receive the three dye impressions is a relatively cheap material – costing only about the same as a black-and-white print. In this low cost of starting material lies the most significant difference between an 'assembly' process such as Technicolor and the monopack or multi-layer processes.

The initial cost of making three matrices before any result can be obtained in colour is naturally a problem, and it makes Technicolor a relatively expensive process when only a few copies of the film are required. However, since a hundred prints can sometimes be obtained from a single set of matrices, the process is ideally suited for feature-film release printing.

When the picture has finally passed the editor, it will usually include a number of special effects – in fact, it has recently been estimated that the optical effects contained in an average feature film necessitate the duplication of some 50 per cent of the negative finally employed. This reason for duplication is of course in addition to the overriding importance of duplicate negatives for the purposes of safety and making foreign releases.

It can be seen that there are several imperative reasons for duplicating the original camera negatives in any production of importance, and it is because the Technicolor and other 'assembly' processes permit the satisfactory duplication of the silver-image negatives without appreciable loss of quality that they have a tremendous advantage over the multi-layer processes; all of which suffer from considerable, if not fatal, colour degradation upon duplication.

One of the results of the recent heavy tax on American films was that Technicolor began to look for some means of utilising the printing capacity which became available with the drying up of American releases in this country. All American Technicolor films are printed in this country from matrices sent over from the Hollywood laboratory. It was not possible for the number of Technicolor productions to be increased in this country, as the only colour cameras available (four of them) were all in continuous use, and it was unlikely that more than the first of the batch of new cameras being built in this country would be delivered during 1948. As a result, a scheme was worked out by which it was possible to produce two-colour prints without altering the standardised three-colour imbibition printing process,* and furthermore, without the aid of anything more complicated in the way of camera equipment than bi-pack magazines and pressure-pad gates in standard black-and-white cameras.

The first examples of Technichrome, as the new process is called, were seen in the recent film of the Olympic Games. Some twenty cameras were adapted for two-colour photography, and besides the track and field events at Wembley Sta-

* Imbibition print is the name given to the matrix mentioned earlier.

dium, they were used to cover the marathon, the cycling in Windsor Park and the yacht racing in Torbay.

The idea of Technicolor returning to two-colour cinematography has seemed to many to be a retrogressive step, since the company graduated from its earlier two-colour process as long ago as 1932. Whether Technichrome will ever become widely used remains to be seen, but it is at least interesting to note that the combined footage printed by two American two-colour processes – Cinecolor and Magnacolor – last year equalled the total three-colour footage of Technicolor in America.

Cinecolor prints, like most other two-colour films, carry emulsion on both sides of the base – a very convenient arrangement when printing from bi-pack negatives, as it is possible to print with one negative in contact with the emulsion on each side of the positive stock in a double-headed contact printer. It is true that the finished print is somewhat more susceptible to scratching than a normal film, and that it is impossible to project both images in perfect focus at the same time, but these disadvantages have often been exaggerated. After all, some 200 million feet of two-colour prints were sold in America last year – and all of it had emulsion on both sides of the base. The real limitation of a two-colour process is that colours such as violet, green and yellow just cannot be reproduced.

We have now seen enough of the 'assembly' processes to be able to say that they all make use of cheap printing materials as their starting-point, although it is equally true to say that they all involve considerably more complex processing than anything carried out by a laboratory making only black-and-white prints.

It is the special handling and control which has led so many existing laboratories to wait and hope for a colour process which, while perhaps entailing the use of a costly starting material, will nevertheless permit the application of more or less standard processing methods and machinery. To such laboratories it seemed, at the end of the war, that Agfacolor was their answer, for there is no doubt that that process represents one of the greatest achievements in the history of photography. However, it is gradually being realised that Agfacolor is essentially a triumph of the manufacturer of sensitive materials, and that it does not necessarily follow that such a material – however great the achievement it represents – is well suited for the production of large numbers of 35-mm. theatrical release prints in a world market.

From their earliest work in the field of 35-mm. motion pictures, Agfa chose the colour-negative to colour-positive printing procedure, and it is said that Ansco, the American company which until the war was associated with I.G. Farben, will shortly change from processing by two reversal stages to a negative-positive sequence.

The idea of a colour negative is rather difficult to grasp, for not only are the densities of the image negative in value, but the colours of the colour negative are complementary to the corresponding areas of the subject. For instance, blue sky will be found to be a dark yellowish-grey in the negative, while the negative image of a red rose will be quite a bright green.

Part of an official report on the Agfacolor process, made by American technicians, says: 'The cameras employed were the Debrie Super Parvo, the Eclair and the Arriflex. Each scene was photographed three times by the same camera; one negative was set aside for safety, while the other two were available for making the release prints. Whenever possible, dissolves and fades were made in the camera to facilitate the laboratory work of special effects.'

In these short sentences we can see at once the strength and the weakness of the Agfacolor type of process: you can use any normal black-and-white camera to shoot your picture, but when the time comes to make release prints, you cannot afford to duplicate the colour negative for fear of loss in quality.

We will assume that the colour negative has been exposed and sent to the laboratory for development. The first point which has to be realised in processing Agfacolor, no matter whether it be negative or positive, is that the material is panchromatic, and must therefore be printed and developed in a low level of suitable green light – in fact, almost in darkness. A further point of difference between Agfacolor and black-and-white film is the considerably longer time of treatment which is involved in the case of the colour film.

When developing colour film, developer constitution as well as development time and temperature must be held within finer limits than are necessary in black-and-white laboratories, as any alteration in one of these factors will not only result in differences in density and contrast, but also in a change in colour balance. Quite apart from resisting such differences in processing conditions, with multi-layer colour materials it will always be necessary to contend with batch to batch changes in the sensitivity and contrast balance of the stock.

We can be sure that by the time a production has been edited, the negatives of the different scenes are likely to vary considerably in their colour balance, and will therefore require a good deal of preparatory colour grading and testing before they are levelled out.

The next factor which must be considered is the provision of a satisfactory sound-track on Agfacolor type material, and while it is possible, with the aid of suitable photo-cells, to obtain reasonably good sound reproduction from a dye-track, it was nevertheless found desirable to devise means for retaining a silver-image track on most of the prints made in Germany during the war. A dye-plus-silver track was in fact obtained by applying a highly viscous bleaching solution to the picture area only, by means of a coating roller. This procedure removed the unwanted silver from the picture images, but did not remove it from the sound-track.

Apart from one or two documentaries, such as *Sports Parade* and *May Day in Moscow*, with a strong newsreel quality, there have been no reports to indicate what use the Russians are making of their possession of the plant and personnel at Wolfen, where all Agfacolor film has been made.

In America, Anscocolor has been used so far only for short films, although one of these, *Climbing the Matterhorn*, won the Academy Award for two-reelers. Anscocolor has been imported by the French for a combined puppet and live-action production of *Alice in Wonderland*, which all technicians will await with great interest. The prints we shall see in this country are to be made at Denham Laboratories, but whether they will be made from the original colour negative or from a duplicate has not been disclosed.

It may well be that during the next few years there will be development of processes which compromise between leaving all the work to the stock manufacturer and giving it all to the processing laboratory. All that can be said with certainty at present is that Technicolor is the only three-colour process which has been operated successfully on a commercial scale in either America or England.

The success of Technicolor has resulted in a form of monopoly for which that company is often criticised, but which can never be avoided until some other organisation makes the determined and sustained effort which will be required before any laboratory can offer a service comparable with that which the film industry has had from Technicolor for so many years.

'THE MAN WITH THE
BOX BROWNIE'

R. K. NEILSON BAXTER

*

I AM probably sticking my chin out, but no matter. Provocation is the fashion these days, and another challengeable generalisation will only create the most minor of diversions, even if it creates one at all.

From time to time, as I sample the critical plethora which the national Press places thoughtfully at my disposal, I come across the phrase 'he uses his camera ...' and the 'he' in question is the film director It is probably repetition which, acting upon my imagination like the proverbial dripping water on the stone, conjures up a picture of a lonely figure, draped in camera-cases, exposure-meters and all the other decorative gew-gaws of the snapshooter, committing his scenario to celluloid by some form of artistic parthenogenesis.

Nor, I am sure, is the camera the only thing these critics* place in the directors' hands. There have been occasions on which he has 'manipulated his sound-track', 'handled his lighting effects', even 'built his sets'. A man of parts, indeed. And the defence will doubtless claim that the charge is a trumped-up charge and the usage wholly figurative. But the prosecution is still unappeased. A fundamental misconception of the way in which most films are created is being conveyed, even if it does not exist in the critic's own mind. Most films, please note - for there are exceptions to prove the rule – films made by directors who have worked in exceptional conditions, usually without commercial entanglements, and almost always with a special

---

* Note, please, Manvell, that I have not said which, nor how many.

purpose: Flaherty, Eisenstein, Chaplin perhaps, Rossellini, many documentary film-makers, among others. But the feature film produced in the regular commercial way – which is not intended as disparagement: it is often of very considerable artistic merit – is a remarkable piece of creation, which turns the familiar biological phenomenon upside down by producing a single offspring from a veritable litter of parents.

The translation of an idea in somebody's head, some words on a piece of paper, the events of a man's life, whatever the story-origin may be, into picture and sound images on a strip of celluloid involves a very large number of individuals, a small group of whom constitute the creative team. The fact that their work must resolve into a unity, a single piece of dramatic expression, demands some unifying influence. A team, however closely knit its component individuals may be, always requires the co-ordination of leadership. The film director provides that need; his job is precisely what its name implies. He is the conductor of an orchestra.

Analogies are dangerous things, but music provides a parallel that goes a considerable way before it breaks down. A composer writes a piece of music; somebody else orchestrates it; a conductor interprets the score, rehearses the instrumentalists and directs their individual skills to create the artistic unity which is the orchestra's rendering of it. A film starts as a composition of one kind or another, as a novel or a play or an original story. It may even begin as nothing more than a theme, a simple melody, which is built up to the size of a symphony. Then it must be scored, put into a form, that is to say, which will indicate to the members of the orchestra, the creative team, what they have to do. And the conductor? Well, his job is rather more than just waggling his little bit of stick up in front – and so is the film director's.

So the first contributor to the film is the author of the piece of writing which is the story of the film. He uses words as his medium of expression, probably knows nothing about film construction, and may not even have any thought that his story will one day be turned into a motion picture (unless, of course, he writes for the *Saturday Evening Post*). The next contribution comes from the screen-writer, who is given the task of 'adapting' it. Many are the tales (and they are not all apocryphal) of stories 'adapted' beyond all recognition, but we are not concerned with the meretricious; rather with those films which have some creative pretensions. The broad conception of how a story shall be treated in film terms is a valid part of the creative process. It is more than that, for once it is adopted it will circumscribe all subsequent thought devoted to the presentation of that particular story by everyone connected with it. Much will be built on to it, modifications may alter its appearance, but fundamentally the pattern is set.

It is more than likely that the man who will ultimately direct the film has not yet been brought in. The next development, which is the writing of the script, carries the story one stage farther in its metamorphosis from a piece of verbal expression into a piece of visual expression. More and more often film directors take part in the scripting of their films. There is a mutual stimulus to be obtained by bringing together the script-writers and the man who is to interpret their descriptions and to guide the actors' interpretation of their dialogue. More and more, too, it is recognised that a script-writer must have a working knowledge of the possibilities of camera and sound techniques, is in fact a technician who needs the training of a technician before he can effectively contribute to the creative process. He may have all the ideas in the world and lots of artistic ability, but they are not much good to him if he has not the knowledge to 'visualise' them. It stands to reason that there are variations in the degree to which different directors and script-writers can contribute to the cinematographic interpretation of the story, and the amount of credit due to the director for the basic form of the film *at this stage* is impossible to assess. What is quite clear, in those cases where the director collaborates in working out his script, is that complete visualisations of scenes and sequences, as he wants them ultimately to appear on the screen, will be forming in his mind throughout the whole period of time taken up by scripting.

Now comes the point at which the director must hand over to somebody else the carrying out of the creative work required to achieve his aim. Sets, which a cameraman has ultimately to light so that they can be photographed, are designed by an art director, and planned, built and furnished under his supervision by the construction staff and property department. In them, too, a sound recordist will have to record in acoustic conditions which must be highly controllable. So that, whatever the *ideal* conception of the sets may be, concessions may well have to be made to the limitations of the technical processes involved. But the cameraman and sound recordist in their own fields are creative artists too, and in the course of discussing with the director the problems involved in interpreting his wishes, they and the art director will certainly feed-in conceptions of their own. So once again the mutual stimulus of a creative team working together will affect the final result on the screen. The director provides the essential unifying force, and once again the degree to which each member of the team contributes depends on his skill, his experience and, to a large extent, his personality.

The result is – or should be – that, when shooting starts, a full understanding exists between them of the achievement at which they are aiming. It is true that this does not always happen, and the concord which is essential to the production of an artistically satisfactory film is absent. But even when that is the case, the director does not tell the cameraman where to put his lights, the camera operator how to compose his picture, or the sound recordist how to record his sound. The factors, however, with which he must always concern himself are the choice of camera angles and camera movement, because these control the continuity of the film; and the guidance of his actors, because their performances must be consistent throughout the whole higgledy-piggledy business of playing their parts in snippets, out of continuity, over a period of weeks or maybe even months. This does not mean that he will ask them for a slavish imitation of a prototype performance. They, too, are contributors to the creative process, and will obviously be chosen for their ability to interpret the characterisations demanded by the story. Having chosen them, the director would be foolish indeed to inhibit their freedom to use their own creative ability.

Having shot his film, the director hands over to yet another individual who may have considerable influence on the final result. This is the editor, the individual whose job is popularly supposed to be to cut out the bad bits and join the rest together. In fact, it is by the editing of a film, the choice of shots, the way they are broken up, the length of each cut, that suspense and tempo are created. In the editor's care are also the precise contriving and placing of dissolves, fade-outs and other optical devices. These are points of finesse which all assist in the full achievement of the creative aim.

The assembly of tracks carrying background sounds and the scoring of accompanying music each impose their influence on the artistic unity of the finished film. The sound editor, the composer of the music, the recordist who mixes the tracks, are all of them part of the creative team, and the measure of their sensitiveness is a further measure of the extent to which the original conception will be fulfilled. It is unusual for the director to participate directly in these activities; rather does he hover like an agonised seagull (often indeed making the appropriate noises) over these end-stages of the production of the film. And in the final analysis, who can say, who even among the team that made the film will be able to define the precise contribution made by each? Who, for example, conceived those wonderful transitions in *Brief Encounter*, where music, the noise of the train, dialogue, lighting and optical work all combined to create the effect? Even in *Louisiana Story*, that highly individualistic film (because it was made by Flaherty), one finds it impossible to assess the relative responsibility of editor Helen van Dongen, composer Virgil Thompson, photographer Richard Leacock or Flaherty himself.

And come to that, it probably doesn't really matter. It's just that all those names on the screen that you probably often feel are holding up the start of the film have got some justification for being there. The director's name usually gets the screen to itself – and it should. He has a considerable task conducting his orchestra and making it keep in tune. It is a fascinating form of creative skill, and it is worth realising, I think, that it isn't all done by a man with a box Brownie.

NO DEMAND FOR CRITICISM?

CATHERINE DE LA ROCHE

*

ABOUT seven hundred journalists attend the film press shows. About half belong to British publications; the remainder send their copy overseas. Between them they represent a considerable variety of journals. Yet we have nothing that could be seriously called a 'school' of film criticism, no publication setting a standard of expertise in the appraisal of motion pictures.

Fleet Street and publishing chiefs, like their opposite numbers in Wardour Street, have definite ideas about public demand. A number of successful formulæ for film journals and columns have become pretty well standardised, and each is used, with slight modifications, by several rival publications, which means overlapping and repetition. Occasionally experimental publications, more or less ambitious but mostly amateur and without the indispensable financial backing, make brief appearances, then vanish. And though these failures are often interpreted as an indication of strong sales-resistance to any fresh departures in film journalism, all they prove, surely, is that the new ventures themselves were wrongly conceived or executed, that an adequate new formula has not yet been found and that, in consequence, the potential market remains unknown. In any case no authoritative journal for the lay reader, serving as a yardstick against which the value of the more subjective and often contradictory routine reviewing could be measured, has been put to the test in recent years; I mean no journal which could be relied on to appear regularly and to cover a comprehensive field systematically.

Whatever the public demand, actual or potential, may be, film expertise seems to be the last thing required of the writers engaged in criticism. Indeed, I imagine that only a minority of the critics themselves would claim to have a knowledge of cinema – its history, theory and technique – that could stand comparison with a creative film-maker's. And the majority probably know little more about it than what they learn as regular picturegoers. But practically all, from the effervescent, chatty profile writer on a popular magazine to the highbrow columnist, have to be expert in their particular class of journalism, if only to hold down their jobs against the savage competition in Fleet Street. Their primary task, in most cases, is to shape the subject-matter according to the journal's requirements – its intellectual level, policy, style, jargon – rather than to shape their articles according to the matter. And this inevitably diminishes the intrinsic value as film criticism of many review columns.

Fundamentally, this applies to the most independent-minded writers who would never tolerate any restriction of their freedom of criticism no less than to those who are briefed, or know without briefing, what kind of general line they should take if they are to get a contract and have it renewed. In the first case the writer is *chosen* because his approach coincides with the editor's; in the second he may have to adapt himself to it. But in both cases he is writing from a particular viewpoint for a particular section of readers.

Like movies, publications depend on circulation; like movie-makers, writers must catch the public's attention, hold its interest – they must entertain. The demand in Fleet Street, therefore, is primarily for certain kinds of entertaining copy, and, for the same reason, the qualities particularly highly valued in a writer are personality, vigour and wit. These qualities, of course, are adornments – more, essentials – of good writing in practically any field, but their importance in film reviewing seems to be so greatly overestimated as to affect the very nature of the reviewing.

Take that fashionable business of writers 'projecting their personalities'. It is really no better than a trick, comparable with some of the tricks of the star system, and has as little to do with criticism as star building has with acting. Sometimes it produces mere self-assertion, as in the case of young columnists trying to establish themselves by assuming a hard-to-please attitude. And the most common manifestation is the chatty personal column, cluttered up with irrelevancies and bits about the writer's idiosyncrasies – a highly specialised line this, and a highly paid one. Editorial demands for vigorous copy produce another set of problems. To be 'readable' one must 'make it hard', be definite, commit oneself all along the line and no nonsense. Which is fine if a movie adds up to something definite, but not so many of them do. Cinematography being a composite art, there are an exceptionally large number of elements to consider in reviewing a movie. Hardly ever can one be wholehearted in one's estimation of a picture, or even of part of it. A further difficulty is that the average reviewer does not dispose of enough space for anything like a comprehensive analysis. No wonder there is a tendency towards reckless generalising and unexplained opinionating, produced with or without zest, according to temperament.

As for the traditional linking of wit and criticism, the logic of this has always eluded me. Why should wit be more necessary in criticism than elsewhere? I would have thought it is desirable, when appropriate, in all kinds of writing. But in criticism, as elsewhere, there are occasions when it is inappropriate. Nevertheless, in writings on criticism and in high-powered debates on the air, wit is constantly described as one of the most important elements in criticism. This is an *idée fixe*, almost, and leads to a good deal of misplaced levity. Every now and again one detects writers trying to be funny at the expense of their subject, presumably because theirs is the film column on the entertainment page and they know they are expected to be bright.

There is nothing, of course, in the demand for entertainment value which need affect a writer's integrity. Certainly in my own peregrinations as a freelance I have never heard of writers saying or being asked to say things they disbelieved, nor have I ever found a suggestion of this in anything I have read. But the favoured prescriptions for entertaining copy do impose limitations; they do necessitate omissions and lead to lop-sided selection. What is more, they tend to establish conventions and to set fashions.

Now, what is the general aspect of the criticism produced in the conditions I have tried to outline above? One of its strongest suits, probably, is the assessment of the literary element in films adapted from novels and plays. And, as we know, a large proportion of motion pictures are adaptations. One can always rely on finding reviews giving evidence of literary knowledge and possessing an unmistakable ring of authority in their references to literature. Critiques of pictures like *Hamlet, The Idiot, Quartet* or *London Belongs to Me* often give a clear indication of the value of the originals in their respective spheres, and, in appraising the adaptations, they sometimes reveal more about the peculiarities of the film medium than is otherwise usual. Whether films are adaptations or based on original ideas, one can invariably see from the reviewer's description of the plot what he thinks of the story. But the art of screen-writing and the screen-writer's individual contribution to the creation of a movie are seldom mentioned at all. The acting, on the other hand, is another element which receives a good deal of attention, some of it well-informed. Perhaps it is not accidental that the criticism of the literary element and acting in films is the most authoritative, for both these branches are related to the long-standing traditions of literary and dramatic criticism. On the other hand, the same does not apply to the criticism of film music, mostly conspicuous by its absence, nor has the criticism of monochrome or colour cinematography as yet benefited from the traditions of art criticism.

On the whole, it is difficult to find criticism that is reliable as regards the technique, theory and history of cinema. Ejaculations about brilliant photography, sensitive direction, beautiful composition, shocking backcloths, wonderful cinematic movement, slow cutting and the rest, are usually safe enough, if unrevealing. But when writers risk going into details the results can, on occasion, be somewhat puzzling. (One of my recurring nightmares is the discovery of a howler in something of my own by thousands of thinly smiling readers!) *Odd Man Out*, for instance, in the expert opinion of all the film technicians and artists I have spoken to was a model of filmcraft, but open to criticism as regards the thematic treatment. Yet one national paper suggested that Mr Reed should learn to keep his camera still, while another thought that *Odd Man Out* was the first film of thematic importance in the British cinema.

Several writers allowed themselves to be misled by the publicity about deep focus photography in *Hamlet*, and gave the impression that it was something new. In fact, of course, deep focus lenses have been used for years – some of Eisenstein's favourite compositions depended on them, and both Carol Reed and David Lean are among the directors who are keenly aware of their possibilities. The point about deep focus in *Hamlet* was Dickinson's virtuosity in handling it, and Olivier's insistence on using it over-extensively. The exact function of the various film-makers is a constant stumbling-block, leading to many invalid generalisations. One critic says the French cinema is essentially a cinema of actors, another attributes its strength to its directors. Both would have been right if they had realised that in films the creative collaboration between actors and directors is so close that their functions in interpreting a character are almost indivisible.

Are cases such as these somewhere on the borderline between opinion and intrinsic standards, or are they mistakes arising from an insufficient knowledge of cinema? In any case, nothing comparable can ever be found in the writings of the few critics who are also experts by virtue of having been engaged in film production.

An appreciation of the social aspect of cinema need not detract from the entertainment value of criticism, but for proof of this one must again turn to exceptional critics whose writings reveal an alert interest in the connection between cinema and life's broader issues, be they philosophical, moral, political or commercial. These matters, however, may be controversial, and, more generally, controversy is eschewed, partly in order to play safe and partly because ... it is bad form. In a radio interview once, discussing aims in film production, Miss Anna Neagle came out squarely on the side of 'pure entertainment' and referred to film-makers who want to express themselves as 'blush-making'. There you have it – an attitude, a code of ethics, almost, according to which it is an abuse of privilege and an unseemly indiscretion for the artist to let his work be affected by his own ideas and feelings (as if he could prevent it!). This attitude is not anything like as prevalent among journalists, whose job it is to discern the news value of controversy, as it is in the film industry. Indeed, the exceptional films that are overtly controversial usually get corresponding notice, and it should be added that in this respect the views expressed by the critics do not necessarily match those in the editorial column; it even seems to be the policy of certain right-wing papers to have pinkish critics, while left-wing papers have sometimes been indulgent in their appraisals of reactionary films. Nevertheless, the attitude I have just mentioned does exist among critics, most of whom, especially the æsthetes, take note of social and political implications in films only when they positively cannot be ignored. More often the tendentiousness implicit in a picture, especially the tendency to gloss over or misrepresent the more long-standing problems and diseases of modern society, is given no notice at all. In other cases the passionate political or moral convictions which were the inspiration of an artistically important film are also passed over in silence, as if to safeguard its respectability. One critic, I remember, actually said that Eisenstein was not particularly concerned with politics in making *Ivan the Terrible*.

However, despite everything I have written, it does not seem to me that there is either a need or a possibility of any great changes in the ordinary run of film criticism. On the whole, good films get a good press and bad films get panned! There is much brilliant and often illuminating writing to be found in film columns, some of which are a joy to read, and, on the other hand, it is a physical impossibility for reviewers to deal with all the aspects of a film in the small space at their disposal. No, the need, as I see it, is for a journal that would do the jobs which cannot be done in weekly reviews, a journal which could be relied upon to give critiques of all the creative elements in the most noteworthy movies, appraisals of the most important personalities and reviews of general developments. Tougher subjects, goodness knows, have made entertaining copy.

THE MIRROR UP TO
NATURE

SIEGFRIED KRACAUER

*

THERE is no doubt that our films meet with increasing criticism and, even worse, disaffection. Among the possible reasons for this regrettable state of affairs one seems to me essential: Hollywood's realistic-minded films – that is, the main body of its output – are strikingly lacking in real-life experience. Perhaps it was always this way, except for a few gangster films or so. But people themselves have changed. Exposed to the impact of the post-war world, they can no longer get a thrill out of films which, under the pretence of reflecting this world, either misrepresent or elude it. As matters stand, the average spectator knows more about reality than is offered him in our movie houses. It should be the other way round.

What is wrong with Hollywood is driven home to us by a glance at various European films. They differ from our own productions precisely in that they grow out of a closer contact with life. All of them draw on first-hand experience of real persons and situations. *Brief Encounter*, one of the better British films, though by no means an exceptional one, perfectly illustrates the kind of experience I have in mind. It is one of those frequent extra-marital romances between middle-class people which invariably end in resignation. There is nothing to get excited about. And yet the film-makers manage to elicit from this commonplace incident a maximum of suspense. Their secret is that they are observant rather than showy. They never slur over details, as is done in so many Hollywood films.

Brief Encounter renders a brief railway junction with loving care, while, for instance, *Cass Timberlane* distorts New York society life into an unrecognisable rush of gay parties. And the heroine of the British film is not a Mrs Miniver who rarely lets you forget that, besides being Mrs Miniver, she is also a Hollywood star. This woman, instead of feeding on borrowed glamour, is, or appears to be, nothing but a housewife with a careworn face and a timid dream behind it. She exists, we are led to believe, independently of the screen, a plain woman waiting for her lover at a railway junction that also exists. The film simply records their clandestine meetings – records them, however, with an accuracy intensified by true compassion and a sense of human values. Life is here explored on many levels. Thus, by sheer dint of inclusive observation, a seemingly banal affair is transformed into a tense experience of sporadic joy and lasting sorrow.

These examples can easily be multiplied. Whatever its shortcomings, the French screen surpasses ours in the expression of iridescent moods, amorous feelings and emotional tangles. Such films as *Children of Paradise* and Rénoir's *Une Partie de Campagne* afford an absorbing insight into melancholy passion and love become stale. Where the French transmit real experiences, we as a rule confine ourselves to stereotyped patterns. Even otherwise superior Hollywood films are strangely lacking when it comes to handling inner conflicts. They drown bright aspirations in phony emotions. *Gentleman's Agreement,* for instance, combines a sophisticated crusade against anti-Semitism with a ready-made love story that rings so hollow as to belie the seriousness of the crusade.

And, finally, there are the new Italian films, with their reliance upon lay-actors and their whole documentary approach. I know of no Hollywood production – nor of a British or French film, for that matter – which could match *The Open City, Shoe-Shine* and *Paisa* in power of observation and compassion for ordinary people. These films seize upon the raw material of life, embracing it so fervently that all its humanly essen-

tial meanings are brought to the fore. You can almost touch and
taste the horror, the suffering and the generosity they depict.
As compared with them, Hollywood movies look particularly
inexperienced. In *The Open City* Gestapo tortures grow out of
the fully substantiated interplay between the persecutors and
their victims, while in most of our anti-Nazi films they merely
mark the sensational climax of plots calculated to lead up to
them.

Of course, life in Europe is more exacting than it is here.
Bombed cities and years of Nazi terror, followed by years of
starvation, have done their share to open eyes and stir the
senses. It would be a miracle if films emerging from such a background fell short of authenticity. Nor should it be forgotten
that some of the best among them have been improvised under
incredible difficulties. Wrung from life, they bear its inefface-
able stamp.

Our films are what they are because of the circumstances of
their production. Hollywood film-makers are concerned less
with reality than with its dim reflection in best-sellers and
Broadway hits. In tapping these doubtful sources, they are
greatly hampered by the large size of our major film companies,
a factor conducive to the mechanisation of production methods.
Improvisation yields to organisation, personal daring to the
team work of specialists. The whole set-up tends to smother
that adventurous spirit with which alone the screen can capture reality. Nor does the Production Code encourage such
ventures. Reality thus becomes an indistinct rumour in a
vacuum, crammed with formulas which further falsify this
rumour.

Hollywood is not unaware of its remoteness from life. In his
Sullivan's Travels, of 1941, Preston Sturges exposes this attitude
in an attempt to justify it. The film is an autobiographical
tragi-comedy, born out of qualms of conscience which do hon-
our to Sturges. Sullivan, its protagonist, is a Hollywood film
director who is so fed up with the comedies for which he is fam-

ous that he determines to devote his next film to the plight of the masses. In his compassion for their suffering he holds that our usual escapist entertainment should be superseded by films which come to grips with life as it is. But how to perceive life in a place like Hollywood? Realising that film people live in splendid isolation from their fellow-men, Sullivan visits several hobo camps in the guise of a tramp to experience what he wants to depict. He eventually lands in a Southern prison, and there learns, or thinks he learns, that he was all wrong in trying to reform Hollywood. The turning-point of the film is that scene in which he and the rest of the prisoners get a good laugh out of an old Mickey Mouse comedy – a laugh that makes them forget their hardships. Sullivan, the rebel with a mission, feels greatly elated about this lesson which permits him to conform to Hollywood standards with a clean conscience. And back home at the studio and his swimming-pool, he gaily resumes his comedies.

This brilliant film with its cynical moral is all the more revealing, as it anticipates the course Hollywood actually took in the years subsequent to its release. After the manner of Sullivan, many a prominent film director left Hollywood for the war, acquiring a knowledge of the seamy side of life he would never have been able to acquire on Sunset Boulevard. And exactly as in the Sturges film, these excursions into blood and tears turned out to be an intermezzo of little consequence. Post-war Hollywood, whether or not adopting Sullivan's belief in the redeeming effect of laughter, continues to do what it did before the war.

And yet the analogies should not be pressed too hard. After all, there are slight differences, and they hold out a promise, however faint. Sullivan's counterparts in real life have brought back from their travels such documentaries as *The Fighting Lady*, *San Pietro* and *The Memphis Belle*, which record the war without any Hollywood flourish. These films are valid statements, because they are modest, sincere and humane. And at least William Wyler, the director of *The Memphis Belle*, has profited more than Sturges's hero from their common lesson. His *The Best Years of our Lives*, though on the whole too compromising, is a far cry from his *Mrs Miniver*. In particular its opening part, with the three soldiers returning home, each in his own way frightened by the task of readjustment ahead of him, testifies to an awe of facts which challenges our most sacred screen traditions. Here for once life is not cut to pattern, but laid bare, layer by layer, in a slow process.

Other films breathe a similar spirit. Differing widely in purpose, they nevertheless coincide in penetrating segments of reality that have been blurred or ignored before. A certain freshness of approach distinguishes all of them. Perhaps *Mourning Becomes Electra* is not so much a film as an animated mural; but as such it is an expert depiction of grandiose compulsions and passions. *Boomerang*, outstanding for its brisk and sympathetic observations, seems to have initiated a whole trend of films in documentary style. Unfortunately, most of them have been confined to police cases, misusing newsreel shots as trappings for otherwise conventional plots. *The Naked City* is symptomatic in this respect.

Yet it need not be so. This is demonstrated by *The Search* in which a Hollywood director – the Austrian-born Fred Zinnemann – avails himself of documentary techniques to explore life in its fullness. The film, set against the background of displaced children camps and bombed German cities, is a fascinating blend of American and European mentality. There are still vestiges of artificial emotions and Hollywood rhetoric in it, but they all disappear among a mass of scenes which, shot on location, render real distress with real understanding.

People themselves have changed, as I have said above. Hollywood will have to change also. *The Search*, a farmed-out Hollywood film, points in the right direction. What is asked for are films that search the core of life, films founded on unadulterated experience.

HOLLYWOOD REPORT
ON A 'TREND'

MARTIN FIELD

★

TEN years ago, Preston Sturges, a successful Hollywood writer, persuaded Paramount to allow him to direct his own original screen-play, *The Great McGinty*. To get the studio to agree to this unorthodox procedure – a writer directing his own story – Mr Sturges 'sold' them his script for ten dollars. Mr Sturges, the director, showed respect for the screen-play of Mr Sturges, the writer, and *The Great McGinty* was a great success, both artistically and financially. And that was the start of the writer-director 'trend' in Hollywood.

As a result of the acclaim won by *McGinty* and other films written and directed by Mr Sturges, such as *The Lady Eve, Sullivan's Travels, The Miracle of Morgan's Creek* and *Hail the Conquering Hero*, other screen-writers were given the opportunity to direct or produce their own scripts: John Huston, Clifford Odets, George Seaton, Dudley Nichols, Ben Hecht, Delmer Daves, Billy Wilder, Charles Brackett, Robert Rossen, Joseph Mankiewicz, Norman Krasna, Lamar Trotti, Nunnally Johnson, Harry Kurnitz, Sidney Buchman, Orson Welles and others. From this 'trend' emerged such superior writing-directing achievements as *The Maltese Falcon, None but the Lonely Heart, Citizen Kane, Double Indemnity, Lost Week-end* and *Miracle on 34th Street*.

What happened to this trend through the years? It faded almost as rapidly as it had developed. Film studio after film studio made the saddening discovery that if the writer they elevated to writer-director or writer-producer possessed mediocre talent, he continued to direct or produce mediocre films. Therefore, notwithstanding the excellent films created by a John Huston, a George Seaton and a Preston Sturges, the contributions of the lesser talents outweighed the worthy efforts in the eyes of the studio heads.

Another factor that helped reverse this trend towards combined operations was the tendency of many writer-directors to drop the writing chore in favour of straight directing. Delmer Daves, after writing and directing *The Red House,* co-wrote and directed *Destination Tokyo,* and then did a straight direction job on *To the Victor* and *Task Force.* Joseph Mankiewicz wrote and directed several films, but after *The Ghost and Mrs Muir,* he confined himself to the direction of screen-writer Philip Dunne's versions of *The Late George Apley* and *Escape.* Men who became writer-producers also tended to hire others to do the writing while they concentrated on production.

Now, unexpectedly, there has been a resurgence of the writer-director and writer-producer trend in Hollywood. However, where previously the trend was based on the artistic assumption that a film would be better if the writer could direct or produce his own material, the present trend seems to be largely based on economics.

The new argument is that when one man combines the functions of writer and director or writer and producer, he is less expensive to a studio than two men. This sort of reasoning, of course, makes much more sense to the film studios than a thousand appeals to their artistic natures. Films like Noel Coward's *In Which We Serve,* Marcel Pagnol's *The Baker's Wife,* Roberto Rossellini's *Open City* and *Paisa,* George Seaton's *Apartment for Peggy* are held up as examples, not of Art, but of Economy.

The response to such an appeal to the budget has been enthusiastic. Now, Abraham Polonsky directs as well as writes *Force of Evil*; Maxwell Shane writes, directs and produces *The Amboy Dukes*; Chester Erskine writes and directs *The Egg and I*; Claude Binyon writes and directs *Family Honeymoon*; Karl Tunberg writes and produces *You Gotta Stay Happy*; F. Hugh Herbert writes and directs *Scudda Hoo Scudda Hay*; Robert Buckner writes and produces *Rogues' Regiment*, to mention only a few of the new talents who are part of this trend.

All of these films have in common the fact that they are so-called 'box-office' pictures, with no pretence of artistry about them. Perhaps a trend which starts on such a practical economic basis has more chance of evolving artistically than the other way round, as was the case with the earlier trend towards combined operations. Certainly there would seem to be less danger of its collapse. Its current resurgence is a heartening proof that even in corporate Hollywood the urge for individual film creation, as opposed to the run-of-the-mill, assembly-line product, still flourishes, even though it sometimes has to wear the mask of Economy to accomplish its purpose.

As is the custom in Hollywood, whenever a 'trend' seems discernible, the publicity trumpets start blaring relentlessly. The new hero of the Hollywood scene is the two-for-one writer and director or writer and producer. An impression has even been created in some quarters that writers by the score are assuming the additional authority of directors and producers, and soon all inadequate creatures who can function only as writers will disappear from the sound stage.

Well, all fanfare to the contrary, an analysis of the situation reveals that the writer-director or writer-producer is still the exception rather than the rule in Hollywood. Even if the present trend should swell far beyond predictions, the regular set-up of separate writer, director and producer will continue for the majority of films.

There is a saying, the greater the art the greater the economy. This new Hollywood economy trend may yet develop film creators whose efforts may make previous accomplishments pale by comparison.

THE RETURN OF
ROMANTICISM

H. H. WOLLENBERG

*

PICTURE production as an art form, it seems to me, has once again entered a transitionary stage.

The signs of change and development may not yet be very conspicuous to cinema audiences generally. They may not be perceptible yet even in the studios, to those who actually make the films. In fact, the trends they foreshadow cannot yet be very clearly defined. Yet there are some indications of a change to come, and one of the symptoms confirming my opinion is the remarkable growth of the Film Society movement, both in numbers and intensity. Another symptom, no doubt, was the outcome of the last major international film competition, the Venice *Biennale* of 1948. While in preceding years the French and Italian cinema was well in the lead, last year it was the turn of British productions, such as *Hamlet, Oliver Twist, The Red Shoes* and *Fallen Idol*, to steal the show. Incidentally, this deserves all the more attention, as critical opinion in this country is only too inclined to underrate the native achievement.

Anyway, what at this stage seems possible is an appraisal, even if in rather general terms, of the implications of those portents for the future.

First we have to agree that in screen-craft industrial and æsthetic elements – the artistic, the technical and the business aspects – are indissolubly integrated. This, whether we like it or not, is probably the most significant characteristic of the cinema, this offspring of our industrial age. However, *L'art est la vie vue par un tempérament*, and this applies to cinematic art too, with its unlimited technical opportunity for 'portraying' life in the artist's own image.

Right through the relatively short history of the cinema we find two fundamentally and distinctively different types of film: those whose makers are content to reflect the fashion of the day and the whims of the public (as they see them); and those whose makers try to project their own thoughts, feelings and visions – in a word, their personality – on to their contemporaries. The former we may call craftsmen; *commercial* artists if you like. The latter are artists in the true traditional meaning of the term: *creative* artists. Even their failures are of infinitely greater value than any accomplished and polished piece of mere workmanship.

One remarkable thing about the creative screen artist is that by influencing the taste of the public he invariably influences the commercial film-maker who strives at catching up with and cashing in on what he calls 'audience reaction'. It is instructive no less than amusing to trace back this chain of cause and effect through the last thirty-odd years. In point of fact, we can watch it now.

I am, of course, alluding to the so-called 'New Realism'. It sprang up in various countries, large and small, at much the same time: in Britain, under the influence of Grierson and the Documentary School; in Switzerland, where Leopold Lindtberg (*Marie Louise* and *The Last Chance*); and in Italy, where Roberto Rossellini, Vittorio de Sica, Luigi Zampa, Aldo Vergano and others employed the style of *Neo-Verismo* as the creative means of expressing themselves, as the medium for showing us 'Life as seen through their temperament'.

The impact upon the public of an original idiom, so different from the conventional tongue of the commercial screen, could not be overlooked ; certainly not by those who, in the American Trade Press, are sometimes described as 'tycoons'. Trade statistics speak their own unmistakable language. They indicated a markedly expanding interest, since the end of the war, in British and Italian films in many markets, such as Latin America, where, until recently, they had never been shown to any appreciable extent.

The inescapable result was a noticeable turn to 'Realism'. Almost every major studio hastened to include in its production schedule at least one subject or another pretending to be 'real' and to be set in the world we actually live in. All of a sudden, production units set out on location for various corners of the globe, preferably places distinguished by some genuine war debris, thus to try to secure 'sincere' atmosphere and 'realistic' background. Unfortunately, the unreality of artificial characters and plots is stressed by realistic surroundings.

Integrity, alas, cannot be replaced by imitation. What matters is genuine inspiration rather than superficial trimmings.

I repeat, we have watched the same process more than once. What started as an original and fascinating movement, a genuinely artistic manifestation, inevitably fades away as soon as it changes hands from the creative to the commercial artist. It will soon be diluted by the slick methods of conveyor-belt routine; it quickly becomes its own substitute.

This is precisely what is about to be repeated in the style of New Realism. And this is what makes me feel that, so far as creative film art is concerned, we are at the threshold of new things to come. For this is the very moment when, as we are taught by experience, we may soon expect a new seed to spring up in the fertile soil of the film world.

The difference between the two terms Reality and Realism needs no explaining to the readers of this *Review*. Realism is one form of interpreting reality as a creative individual sees it. Naturalism, as it was then called, in dramatic art (as names like Ibsen or Shaw recall) reached its climax around the beginning of this century. Other forms, of course, are Classicism, Romanticism, Surrealism and so forth. A Sophocles, a Shakespeare, present us reality, or life, in the most truthful and convincing manner by means of dramatic styles very different from Realism.

Returning to the cinema, we acknowledge, by using the word 'Neo'-Realism, that the first great epoch of realism as an accomplished style of film-craft dates back to the 'silent' era: to the middle twenties, when creative geniuses like S. M. Eisenstein and V. I. Pudovkin devised and used it, as naturally as they breathed, in order to impose with the greatest degree of actuality their personalities upon a startled world.

All the more remarkable is the fact that, roughly twenty years later, the same Eisenstein in his last work should provide a striking example of symbolic Romanticism at a time when the cinematic potentialities of this 'mood' are almost completely unused. *Potemkin* and *Ivan* are obviously poles apart, but both radiate the same personality.

The recent death of Paul Wegener reminds us that Romanticism had its classical phase long before Soviet realism entered the scene. In fact, its origins can easily be traced back to those earliest days of cinematography when George Méliès was the first to discover the potentialities of the film trick, the first to introduce fantasy and imagination in the cinema. However, the great German actor, Paul Wegener, whose decease passed almost unnoticed, played the decisive historical part in lifting these primitive efforts of the pioneers to the level of a new development in screen art. It was his influence and vision which, in 1913, inspired the first version of *The Student of Prague*, followed by a number of distinguished films of a similar character. They brought to the screen the poetry of the ballad, the folk legend, the fairy tale, with all the magic of the supernatural. Some talented German directors of the 'twenties, including Fritz Lang (*Destiny*), F. W. Murnau (*Faust*) and Ludwig Berger (*Cinderella*), were to follow his lead.

Romanticism, as we may describe this peculiar form of cinematic expression, has (with a few rare exceptions) almost disappeared from international film production since the advent of sound. We may trace its influence in certain Walt Disney creations or in that fine Russian screen poem, *The Stone*

Flower. In the French cinema, it is Jean Cocteau who shows a distinct affinity with this approach.

A striking example of the romantic cinema was recently seen in Britain. This film, the Swedish *Himlaspelet* (*Way to Heaven*), can very well be compared with *Monsieur Vincent*, the outstanding French film, also treating a religious theme. Here we have two instructive examples of Romanticism and Classicism respectively. And is not the steady increase during recent years in religious film subjects in itself an indication of the gradual turn away from Realism? A French film journal has already coined its own phrase for this development: *Hagio-cinématographie* (hagios, ἅγιος – the Greek for 'holy'). Significantly, Roberto Rossellini, the initiator of the New Realism in Italy, is reported to have turned to St Francis as his subject.

Is the revival of Romanticism foreshadowed? Is this the meaning of the signs mentioned at the beginning of our survey? If so, they offer great promise.

There are, however, certain adverse factors which cannot be overlooked. First of all, a style of screen dialogue has still to be achieved to match organically the pictorial idiom of Romanticism. There is also the present trend towards the use of colour; the type of film we have in mind seems to call for black-and-white technique to suggest the specific poetry and the excitement of the miraculous, the supernatural.

However, in the last resort it will depend on whether film-makers of vision appear who will once again grasp this artistic opportunity, neglected for so long.

Not for a moment do I suggest that the return of Romanticism would imply the end of Realism. The latter, in point of fact, has not yet reached its final accomplishment; as an autonomous style it is an indispensable form of screen art. But so also is Romanticism. Will it once again make us see life through the temperament and the imagination of the poet?

EXPERIMENTS WITH CELLULOID

HANS RICHTER

★

THIS account of the origin and history of the German Avantgarde film is not written by a scholar of history. I wish to tell what I know about it; but as I am involved in it myself, it necessarily represents, besides dates and facts, also my personal viewpoint and experience.

My approach may be unorthodox, but it will nevertheless describe my experience, and might stimulate others who want to follow ideas of their own.

The Avantgarde film (the film as an art experiment) originated in Germany after the First World War in 1921. It became, nevertheless, not a real 'movement' in Germany itself, as it did in France. There might be several reasons. One of them certainly is that its roots were in the international art movement called modern art, which had its centre in Paris rather than in Berlin. Another reason might be that even before 1914 Delluc and Canudo in France had visualised the film as a plastic art form (*valeur plastique*), i.e. the film without story, and had formulated a new standard of form and expression in film, which Delluc called 'Photogénie'.

Whatever the reasons were, the fact is that it is *modern art* and its impulse upon which we must focus if we wish to understand the beginnings and aims of the first Avantgarde film (or, as they were called in those days, 'absolute films').

FIRST ACT

I spent two years, 1916–18, groping for the principles of what made for rhythm in painting. I studied the principles of counter-

108

point in music, and finally found valuable clues in the 'negative-positive' relationship, with which I experimented in painting and lino-cuts.

In 1918 I met a Swedish painter, Viking Eggeling. His drawings stunned me with their extraordinary logic and beauty. He used *contrasting* elements to *dramatise* two (or more) complexes of forms, and used *analogies* in these same complexes to *relate* them again. In varying proportions, number, intensity, position, etc., new contrasts and new analogies were born in perfect order, until there grew a kind of rhythm, continuity … as clear as in Bach.

We decided to work together, and Eggeling came with me to Germany. We composed 'variations' on one theme or another, usually on small sheets of paper which we arranged on the floor in order to study their relationship and to find out their most logical and convincing continuity. One day we decided to establish a definite form of continuity in a definite way: on scrolls. This step saved us first of all the pain of creeping over the floor, but it gave us something else: a new form of expression: scrolls (used 4000 B.C. already). Eggeling's first scroll was a 'Horizontal-Vertical Mass' early in 1919. Mine, at the same time, a 'Prelude'. Despite the fact that the scroll did not contain more than ten to twelve characteristic transformations of a theme, it became evident to us that these scrolls, as a whole, implied *movement* … and movement implied film! We had to try to realise this implication.

Not many had ever come into the film so unexpectedly. We did not know more about cameras than we had seen in shop windows, and the mechanised technique of photography frightened us.

One day in 1920 UFA allowed us to use their animation tables. We made a try-out with one figure of my scroll, 'Prelude'. It took the UFA technician more than a week to animate the complicated drawing (about 30 feet long).

This first arduous experiment taught me that it would be too difficult for us to translate our drawings into film. I discontinued, therefore, the realisation of 'Prelude', and animated instead a set of paper squares in all sizes, from grey to white. In the square I had a simple form which established, by its nature, a *rapport* with the square of the movie-screen. I made them grow and disappear, jump and slide in well-controlled tempi and in a planned rhythm. Rhythm had inspired my making the scrolls, and it seemed essential to follow it up even if it hurt me to drop the well-shaped drawings of my scrolls on which I had worked for two years. My first film became technically monstrously imperfect; but I was unprejudiced enough to discover that even the negative was usable.

Eggeling was more obstinate than I. He stuck to his original plan and filmed (his second scroll) *Diagonal Symphony*. He was even upset about my 'treason', as he called it, and we did not see each other for a certain time. He filmed his *Symphony* together with his girl friend, who learned animation technique especially for this purpose. She was not less obstinate than he, and finished the film under the most incredible conditions.

It was at this time that we heard of a painter, Walther Ruttman, who was said also to experiment with abstract forms on film.

SECOND ACT

When we saw the first screening of Ruttman's *Opera* at the Marmor-Haus in Berlin (end of 1921 or beginning of 1922), we felt deeply depressed. Our forms and rhythms had 'meaning', Ruttman's had none. What we saw were improvisations with forms united by an accidental rhythm. There was nothing of an articulate language (which was for us, as I have shown above, the one and only reason to use this suspicious medium, film). It seemed to us *vieux jeu*, pure impressionism! Yes! But on the other hand, we had to admit that Ruttman's films were technically better than ours, that he understood more of the camera and used it.

Ruttman used a small structure with turning, horizontal sticks on which Plasticine forms were easily changed during the shooting. If I remember rightly, his first films were hand-coloured. They made quite a sensation in Berlin. Neither Eggeling's nor my films were yet shown in Berlin. We had such big things in mind that we could not imagine showing our films publicly before a perfect stage had been reached. It was half by trick that my friend Theo van Doesburg had gotten my first film. He showed it at the beginning of 1921 in Paris at the Théâtre Michel. There an old gentleman, as Doesburg described it, looked at the title *Film is Rhythm* with interest, then started to clean his pince-nez, put it on his nose, just when the film was over (length 100 feet).

Eggeling's *Diagonal Symphony* was shown in his studio to friends at about the same time. As he was never satisfied, it was remade three times and publicly shown only in 1922, at the v.d.i. in Berlin, with fragments of Beethoven's symphonies as a musical background. It was a *succès d'estime*, but neither Eggeling nor I got anything out of these showings, and Eggeling died in 1925 embittered, without having found the possibility of making a second film (which would have revealed better than the first, with its thin drawings, the powerful artistic personality he was).

My *Rhythm 21*, in its original form, was never shown publicly in Berlin. Parts of it were incorporated in *Rhythm 23*, which was shown at the first International Avantgarde film show, together with Eggeling's, Ruttman's and French Avantgarde films, at the UFA theatre Kurfürstendamm, Berlin, 1925. *Rhythm 23* was distinguished from *Rhythm 21* by the use of lines in addition to squares.

THIRD ACT

If we felt before this International Avantgarde film show more or less as an 'Avant' without a 'Garde' behind us, we did not feel so any more after it. The existence of *Entr'acte* and *Ballet Mécanique* proved to us that we 'belonged' to something. The audience reacted violently pro and con.

That same year appeared already in Berlin a 'variation' of Léger's film by Guido Seeber, an old hand of a cameraman, who knew all the tricks. It was a commercial film for the Kino and Foto Exhibition in Berlin ('Kifo'). Another year or two later, Paul Leni, together with Seeber, produced one or two Léger-influenced crossword-puzzle films, in which the audience had to solve the puzzle. It was given up after one or two try-outs.

In the meantime, Ruttman, who had abandoned painting altogether, had made his first contact with the film industry in *Niebelungen*, by Fritz Lang, for whom he made the dream of Kriemhild (of Siegfried's death) symbolised by a hawk, for which Ruttman's birdlike abstract forms were well suited. In 1926 he convinced Karl Freund (now in Hollywood), then chief of production of Fox Film, Berlin, to tackle a documentary about Berlin – a city seen as an individual, as a big many-sided personality. Ruttman came out of this task on top. *Berlin, die Symphonie einer Grossstadt* ('Berlin, the Symphony of a City') showed imagination and musical rhythm. The awakening of the big city, the empty streets, alive only with a wind-blown piece of newspaper, the arriving of the workers, the starting of the machines, is pure poetry and will remain. Whatever there is to say against 'Berlin', this film was a work of art ... impressionistic art! That is where the critics caught up with Ruttman. Impressionism was a vision of yesterday, was dead as philosophy. 'Berlin, vue à travers un tempérament' was unsatisfactory and revolting to people who had grown up to understand more about the soul and problems of the big city than Ruttman showed. The splendid musical rhythm of the pictures seemed abused, and ran suddenly in a vacuum.

Edmund Meisel's music, the first score written for a film, at least in Germany, was an additional fact that made the première an outstanding event at the Tauentzien Palast. Since the days of *Potemkin*, in 1925, no other film had attracted as much public participation. The 'Berliner' participated in *Berlin*.

FOURTH ACT

In comparison with Ruttman, my success as film-maker was microscopic. My *Rhythm 25* was hand-painted, and used colour as another contrast to strengthen the expression of the movements of squares and lines. But from then on I got stuck with the film and quit painting for fourteen years. An American lady asked me to film 100 feet of 'abstract waves', which were later cut out anyhow (for a film called *Hands*). Albertini, an acrobat actor, a kind of early superman, asked for a tricky, half-abstract trade-mark in motion. To do these and other small jobs, I had to have an animation table and a camera. (The exposure at this animation table was regulated by a bicycle pump.) After having the equipment, it invited me to use it. In 1926 I filmed *Filmstudy*, one of the first 'surrealistic' studies developing from one sequence to the other by associations and analogies. It was a dream with rhythm as the lifeline. Its meaning I don't know. It ran approximately half a reel.

The next was *Inflation*, an introduction to a UFA film, *The Lady with the Mask*, a rhythm of inflation pictures with the rising \$ sign in opposition to the multitude of zeros (of the Mark) as a kind of leitmotiv. It was more an essay on inflation than a documentary. 'Here facts, abstract forms, symbols, comic effects, etc., were used to interpret happenings. *Inflation* set the pattern for Richter's later essay-films (semi-documentaries to express ideas)'. (Herman Weinberg in *Sight and Sound*.)

In 1927–28 I made a little film, *Vormittagsspuk* ('Ghosts before Breakfast'). It was produced for the International Music Festival at Baden-Baden, with a score by Paul Hindemith. It was conducted from a rolling score, an invention of a Mr Blum, in front of the conductor's nose. It did not sound synchronous at all, but it was. The little film (about a reel) was the very rhythmical story of the rebellion of some objects (hats, neckties, coffee cups, etc.) against their daily routine. It might represent a personal view of mine that things are also people, because such a theme pops up here and there in some of my films, even in documentaries. (Why not?) Tobis later bought the film, and recorded Hindemith's score on the early two-inch sound-film, but somehow it never was released and 'got lost' under the Nazis.

Because *Inflation* had been a success, other companies contacted me to make 'Introductions' for their films, to put 'a flower in the buttonhole', to pep up a poor film. I made *Renn-symphonie* ('Racetrack Symphony') (1 reel) for the feature *Ariadne in Hoppegarten*, and dozens of little films for publicity companies (Epoche, Kölner Illustrierte Zeitung, etc.). In each of them I was obstinately trying out some new problems. *Zweigroschenzauber* ('Twopenny Magic') was composed exclusively of related movements of diverse objects, one movement going over into the other, telling the 'story' of the contents of an illustrated magazine. It translated the poetry of 'Filmstudy' into the commercial film.

FIFTH ACT

When Vogt, Massoll and Engel, the three inventors of the 'Triergon' sound patents (on which the big Tobis company was based), decided they were ready to have their invention used, Ruttman was the first to have access to it. He recorded a sound montage of about 300 feet, *Wochenende* ('Week-end'), which is, in my opinion, among the outstanding experiments in sound ever made, and showed Ruttman as a true lyrical poet. There was no picture, just sound (which was broadcast). It was the story of a week-end, from the moment the train leaves the city until the whispering lovers are separated by the approaching, home-struggling crowd. It was a symphony of sound, speech-fragments and silence woven into a poem. If I had to choose between all of Ruttman's works, I would give this one the prize as the most inspired. It re-created with perfect ease in sound the principles of picture poetry which was the characteristic of the 'absolute film'.

That was in 1928. The same year, Ruttman started *Tönende*

Welle ('Sounding Wave'), a short-feature film and a survey of the world of sound offered by radio. The fact that it was commercial did not show. I remember the firemen's band (or whatever it was) that marched through the city with big drums and trumpets, and appeared off and on in the film as the place of action changed, giving it the epic flow that is so essential to a good movie and which is always a reliable way to give unity. One year later, in 1930, Ruttman produced *Die Melodie der Welt* ('The Melody of the World'). It was, technically speaking, also a commercial (one day somebody should figure out how much valuable 'experimental' work has been done in commercials that would not have been done otherwise). It was sponsored by the Hamburg–America Line to encourage travel by sea. I don't know whether more people travelled by sea because of this film, but it certainly was a success. Besides being a success, it had some unforgettable scenes. The nearly abstract symphony of ship sirens at the beginning of the film: deep and high, long and short in different rhythms in the harbour of Hamburg, became soon a standard device for any film which could manage somehow to get into the neighbourhood of a port. The film stimulated an audience, that, after a lost war, a lost revolution, a lost inflation, isolated amongst the nations, longed for a contact with the 'world'. The film had the same faults as *Berlin*. It got lost in a meaningless kind of picture postcard flow, which even Ruttman's musical montage technique could not overcome.

Just before Ruttman started *Melodie der Welt*, I began my first sound film also for Tobis, the three-reeler *Alles dreht sich, alles bewegt sich* ('Everything revolves, Everything moves'), a fantastic documentary of a fair after a script by Werner Gräff, who also played the leading rôle. The fun-machines and popular melodies of a fair attracted me for their folklore as well as for the richness of visual material and movements. Walter Gronostay, twenty years old, was the most understanding film composer, or should I say 'sound dramatist', I ever met. He gave the film the tumbling rhythm of the merry-go-round. The boy-meets-girl story in the film was not very seriously followed through, but it did not interfere with the success of the film at the opening in Baden-Baden, and brought me:

1. A contract-offer from Tobis (which was never realised).
2. A collision with two Nazis, who disliked 'degenerate art' on the screen and beat me up. This accident came into the papers, and was two years later one of the reasons why Prometheus-Film in Berlin hired me to direct an Anti-Nazi film, *Metal*.

Gronostay composed later the music for many successful films, and became, under the Nazis, one of the top film composers – a 'Cousin Pons', who loved good food and drink so much that he died at the age of thirty-one.

Ruttman and I were the only Avantgarde people up to approximately 1928. There were the charming silhouette films by Lotte Reiniger, who began already in 1921 as far as I remember. She certainly belonged to the Avantgarde as far as independent production and courage were concerned. But the spirit of her lovable creatures, 'Prince Achmed' and 'Doctor Dolittle', seemed always to me to belong rather to the Victorian period than to the one which gave birth to the Avantgarde in Germany and France.

And, of course, there had been, already in 1919, *Caligari*, one of the masterpieces of cinematography. Avantgarde? No! But the Avantgarde of the Avantgarde. It grew by a number of happy accidents. Two painters had designed and built expressionistic sets in which no normal actor could play, to whom, therefore, a special make-up had to be applied. The genius of Carl Mayer found a style of acting for these deformed actors, but the film was finally made only because the budget was too low, anyhow, for a 'good commercial' production and therefore the risk was taken after the money for the sets was spent already.

Caligari was the sign that something was preparing, but it was unrelated to and without influence upon the Avantgarde proper.

From 1928 to 1929 a new generation started to move.

SIXTH ACT

Where Ruttman had left off with his abstract work, Fischinger, a pupil of Ruttman, took over in 1929. A sensitive understanding of pictorial movement helped Fischinger to synchronise Ruttman-like forms to musical melodies. With the help of sound, the abstract film became fulfilled. I remember with delight his Brahms' *Hungarian Dance*. His films were unique because of the solid unity of sound and picture. The forms in themselves were quite 'meaningless'. It was obviously Ruttman's influence that shaped Fischinger's films. At the beginning of his career he made some excellent publicity films. Muratti's cigarette soldiers was one of the best, in the rather highly developed film publicity production in Germany. Fischinger marked the end of the Avantgarde as far as Germany was concerned. But as Ruttman has transplanted his artistic experience into the documentary field, so have others.

Wilfred Basse's *Markt am Wittenbergplatz*, 1929, was a solid documentary film, remarkable mainly because of his respect for the factual. No enacted scenes but real people. It was not exactly a critical film, but with some humour and less romantic than Ruttman's films. The documentary film was in those days still so far out of the normal production scene that an honest documentary was considered Avantgarde (as Ivens, Lacombe and Grierson).

More spectacular was another, semi-documentary, mostly re-enacted film, *Menschen am Sonntag* ('People on Sunday'), about 1929. It was realised by a collective of young professionals and non-professionals, Eugen Shuftan, Robert Siodmak, Edgar Ullmer and Billy Wilder. It was non-cliché, full of fresh observation and experiment. It pictures the Sunday excursion to the beaches and forests of the Wannsee (a lake near

Berlin) with a love-story and all the 'trimmings'. It had the charm of an art work whose creators are not yet conscious of what they were doing. It was concerned with ordinary people and a rather collective life. Its lack of pompousness and its documentary quality classified it as Avantgarde, a name which was at that time a kind of an 'Oscar'.

Überfall ('Accident'), one reel, 1929, by Ernö Metzner, a painter, was more Avantgarde in its true sense. It was a sort of mystery story, told with the devices and experiences of the Avantgarde film (distorting lenses, tricks, etc.), plus the montage technique of the Russians. It was the first time that a thriller was made that way, and its technique was readily taken over into the conventional production.

The three previously mentioned films had, each in a different way, developed a new tradition: to show the ordinary man on the screen. In *So ist das Leben* ('Such is Life'), by Karl Junghans, the ordinary man and woman were shown in a grim realistic style which was deeply influenced by the Russians but well translated into the German scene. It had none of the shortcomings which made the many 'poor people' films of that period such a painful experience. The funeral and the funeral party, with the dance of the drunk (Valeska Gert) to the music of a mechanical piano, had a macabre quality that reflected better than anything else in any German film the desperation of that time. It was a co-operative enterprise, and dragged, because of lack of money, over years. It was the work of an artist.

Not only the work of an artist, but a work about art itself, and a very remarkable one, was Oertel's film about Michelangelo. It was the first movie which used art objects as 'actors' by putting them in motion. Oertel continued a tradition which Eisenstein had started in his famous 'moving' stone lions in *Potemkin*, a tradition which has in my opinion a very great future indeed.

The time of Hitler was approaching, and the tension in Europe was so unbearable, especially in Germany, that there was, also in film, no way out but to deal with it directly. It was at this time that I started (for Prometheus Film, Berlin) *Metal*, a feature anti-Nazi-Stahlhelm film, about the metal-workers' strike in Henningsdorf, near Berlin. It was an ill-starred venture, because it tried to follow the political problem of the morning, which had changed already in the evening. The script was re-written seven times during the production, and was shot partly in Henningsdorf, partly in Russia. It was finally shelved altogether when Hitler came into power in 1933. *Kuhle-Wampe* (the name of a colony of barracks near Berlin inhabited by unemployed) just made the deadline before Hitler, in 1932. Produced by Bert Brecht and Slatan Dudow, it was not a 'poor people' film any more, but a full-fledged political film with a definite communistic line. There were others of that kind in Germany, but what distinguished this film was the direction and dialogue of Bert Brecht, which gave the whole film an explosive quality. The discussion in the overcrowded train about the use of coffee, whether coffee should be sold *under* world market prices or given to the poor or thrown into the sea, sounded then (and still sounds to-day) a foreshadowing of the world's end. Dudow, a Bulgarian writer, influenced by Pabst and the Russians and most of all by Brecht, did not muster as much visual imagination as Junghans and Metzner, and was far away from those problems which had motivated the Avantgarde.

The original artistic direction which gave the Avantgarde its meaning had evaporated. In exchange a human and social angle had come to the surface, which could certainly not be found in Eggeling's nor in Ruttman's nor in my earlier films.

FINIS

With the Nazis, the name 'Avantgarde' got, like 'Degenerate art', its honourable place beside modern art (where it belonged).

Ruttman made a film, *Stahl* ('Steel'), for Mussolini; later, Cityfilms (à la 'Berlin') for Stuttgart and for Hamburg ('Small film of a big city'). His co-operation with the obnoxious Leni Riefenstahl in the latter's *Olympiade* gave her glory and him 'a pain in the neck'. He was a poet, but obviously not a good judge of people and circumstances. He was killed on the German-Russian front in 1941.

Fischinger continues to produce 'non-objective' films in colour amidst a large family in Hollywood. He co-operated with Walt Disney on the Bach sequence of *Fantasia*.

Robert Siodmak is one of the top directors of mystery films in Hollywood, so is Billy Wilder.

Junghans is supposed to be in Hollywood too.

Also Metzner is in Hollywood, though not connected with film.

Brecht is in Zürich, writing plays and films. Dudow is in the Russian Zone of Berlin, connected with some film production. Basse died early in the war years.

I myself have produced, between 1930 and 1940, straight documentaries, essay films and commercials, mostly in Holland and Switzerland. I have written some books and lectured at universities, and become director of the Institute of Film Techniques at the City College of New York. I have just finished a colour-feature film, *Dreams That Money Can Buy*, using ideas and objects of five modern artist friends for a venture that took me three years to complete. It is an Avantgarde film.

(*Reprinted by the courtesy of the Grey Walls Press from their volume*, Experiment in the Film, *edited by Roger Manvell.*)

BOOKS ABOUT FILMS

EDITED BY R. K. NEILSON BAXTER

*

FOR the general public, there are only two of the recent appearances likely to be eye-catching – likely, that is, to pass away a train journey or get themselves thumbed through on a rainy afternoon in the bookshop. These two provide my main reviews.

BRITISH CINEMAS AND THEIR AUDIENCES
By J. P. Mayer
Reviewed by Eric Goldschmidt

In every theatre curtain there is a hole; every B.B.C. programme is sampled by 'Listener Survey'; every publisher employs 'readers' to test manuscripts; every West End play is shunted round the provinces for a try-out. It's as costly to launch an entertainment as a battleship. Promoters take good care that their forthcoming smasher shall have a more-than-bookie's chance. What happens in films? The favourite Wardour Street method is either sneak previews or hustling a dozen women into a private theatre together with a few experts. Women, film producers say, are the fulcrum of every film's success. Statisticians have produced figures showing that women, in British audiences, preponderate by a mere 7 per cent. No matter. The legend flourishes that British cinemas are matriarchic, that average tastes are trite and turgid, and that weepies, epics and whodunnits roll 'em in. 'My favourite critic,' says Paddy Carstairs the producer, 'is the box office.'

Mr J. P. Mayer is the latest challenger of such slipshod generalisations. In British Cinemas and their Audiences (Den-

121

nis Dobson, 15s.) he sets out to probe audience reaction. He does this more comprehensively than anybody before him. In effect, he produces a Domesday Book of British film-goers.

To do his job, Mayer has asked readers of a threepenny fan magazine to write letters which are here reprinted. About a quarter of the original 400 entries are arranged under two main headings: 'Films and the Pattern of Life' and 'A Study of Film Preferences'. These are perhaps the most vital topics on which we need information. How much glamour is taken out of the one-and-ninepennies to distort the humdrum lives of schoolgirls, joiners, clerks, nurses and soldiers? What, apart from rapturous abandon, do people get out of their weekly flick? Can we gauge the extent of a film-producer's power in, say, politics or fashions? Can we state to what extent films are habit-forming, and how much strife exists between schooling, for citizenship and drumming for gullible box-office suckers?

On specific topics we get a good deal of illumination. Readers of Mr Kracauer's From Caligari to Hitler may be interested to compare post-war Germany with post-war Britain. How much fear and masochism do films induce? Two-thirds of the replies show some trace of it. A typist aged twenty-one reports fairly typically: 'I went to see a "H" film called Vampire Bat when I was fifteen. ... That night I never slept at all. I remember screaming, which brought my mother hurrying in to see what the matter was. She found me in a cold sweat. I shiver now.' she adds, 'when I come to think of it.'

Before putting this down as 'the kind of thing that happens when you will flaunt the censor', consider a medical student who had seen a Laurel and Hardy comedy, 'where a gipsy girl was dragged out to be whipped'. Her reaction was to 'enact that and similar scenes over and over again in the privacy of my bedroom, with me playing the heroine'. In the ensuing seven years 'this effect of being excited by a scene faded a bit, but can be reactivated occasionally'.

This kind of thing would be important and disturbing if Mayer's book was a foolproof record and not a sociologist's puppet theatre. But – despite the explicit warning in his Foreword – I doubt the reliability of it all.

This is only confirmed by the COI survey which is given in the appendix. This survey, 'the most complete and detailed of its kind',* puts down the replies here represented as 71 per cent of the total audience. And 29 per cent seems a sizeable fraction to neglect when it comes to reaching 'purely quantitative conclusions' as Mayer intends.

Two further criticisms should be mentioned; one is important and the other æsthetic.

It seems to me that the prime function of a book is to be readable, and Mayer's is not. That may be a niggardly dart to throw out when considering a work of scholarship and enlightenment. Yet, of the 280 pages of this tome, 240 consist of nothing but unedited 1,000-word quotes from readers' letters. Relentlessly this parade of ill-sorted impressions is strung together without any attempt at presentation. The remaining fifteen pages consist of a high-flown, trilingual, impressionistic commentary. To drain the full value out of film fans' confidences, Mayer is obliged to draw on the diverse opinions of Marx, Mumford, Malraux, McIver and Molière – to name only those beginning with 'M'.

This, however, is not the important point. It's probably the publisher's fault or the paper controller's. The important criticism to be levelled against the author is the use of the royal 'We' and its implications.

Even among sociologists the dispassionate nostalgia which Mayer uses here may seem a little jaded. This back-seat condescension and old-world cafard is sorely out of tune with the allegretto enthusiasms which burble out of the film-goers' 'documents'.

My query concern ; the old schism between faith and works.

* Cf. *Penguin Film Review*, No. 7.

A fledgling business such as films lends itself to a lot of interpretation. Nobody knows a great deal about the game, and anybody's guess is as good as anybody else's. The contact between inmates of the celluloid empire and academic observers is slight. A little preaching on both sides can only improve matters of public health.

So far so good. The real scrap begins when both preachers and practitioners cloak their mutual labours and pose as experts. You can be an expert on Tiepolo's and French liqueurs; on mediæval spires and Dufaycolor. But an expert on films at large? An expert on that nascent and strapping off-shoot of the circus?

That seems a poor stance to adopt. It seems incongruous that people who discuss the most potent and popular entertainment of our day should be devoid of fun, and high-jacking their sense of dignity as furiously as all this.

DRAWN AND QUARTERED

By Richard Winnington

Reviewed by Roger Manvell

No one should belittle the importance of Richard Winnington's drawings. Every week they accompany his reviews of the three or four films shown to the Press and are by far his most telling comment. He seldom makes drawings from the films he likes. Winnington is an artist first and a critic second. He very seldom analyses a film. He plunges into it, artist fashion, and comes up warmed or writhing, spitting the words which express his feelings. Then he goes away and draws. He is a brilliant and highly individual artist, one of the great cartoonists of our time, maintaining an astonishingly high level in portraying the danse macabre of the star system.

There are at least two kinds of serious critics—those who analyse and those who quite simply react. Winnington is of the latter kind. He carries a temperamental thermometer around with him, and knows at once what he likes and hates. I would say he is seldom wrong. He makes no allowances, and is sometimes unjust if a film falls short of high endeavour. A lesser man could condemn the obviously bad films, and it seems a waste of an artist of Winnington's calibre for him to review them, except, of course, for the drawings which emerge afterwards. Winnington's importance as a critic lies in the sharpness of his personal values, which enable him to pick out at once films which touch life either with poetry or with an acid realism.

Winnington hates the smug sub-emotions which are the commonplace of British films just as he hates the crass, tasteless sentiments of too many Hollywood pictures. He likes actors and hates stars who cannot or do not act. He hates the average, the mediocre, the conventional. Therefore he hits the pretentious middle-brow moral film harder than the obviously bad low-brow product. The sentences come stinging out:

> 'Wherever strong men pioneered in the West, not far behind were the Harvey girls, winning the cowboys and miners from their hotsy-totsies, closing down the joints and opening up the churches. They were waitresses in a chain of restaurants, chosen for goodness, good looks, perfect make-up and coiffure, and the ability to out-dance and out-croon any honky-tonk queen.'   The Harvey Girls.

These are, like all Winnington's writings, personal statements, the direct thoughts of the man as he writes. He seldom has the space, and I would guess the inclination, to analyse at length.

In this selection of his reviews written from 1943 to 1948, called appropriately enough Drawn and Quartered (Saturn Press 12s. 6d.) it is interesting to observe some of the chief reasons for his blame and for his praise: they reveal a great deal of his personal romanticism and idealism.

Blame:

'The whole litany of that middle-class synthetic emotionalism meticulously annotated over a decade by tough and
sentimental studio experts has thus been procured for us.'

Since You Went Away.

'There surely was no need to be so naïve in characterisation or in telling the dear little refined love story. If we had
to have this, it might have been a little violent or a little
poetic or a little real.'   The Overlanders.

'In fact, Powell and Pressburger seem to have reached
their haven at last – in the OtherWorld, which is just like all
the Other Worlds film producers have cooked up for us – an
illimitable Wembley Stadium surrounded by tinkling music
and mists, from which all men of taste, if they were ever
careless enough to get there, would quickly blaspheme
their way out.'   A Matter of Life and Death.

Praise:

'The idiom is harsh and salty, the deliberately vulgar
atmosphere primed with the sultry, cruel passion of shoddy,
selfish, violent characters. There is a minimum of cliché'.

Double Indemnity.

'You will detect in this film the stuff of life. If you ever
felt them, the naked terrors of the classroom and the
examination will grope at you again. You will salute the
integrity that informs the scenes between the boy and shop-
girl – the first sordid, beautiful, shattering impact of sex on
the adolescent.'   Frenzy.

'... Nothing can tarnish the intense lyrical simplicity
underlaid with an aching irony and made almost unbearable
by the yearning musical score of Kosma. This is everybody's lost love.'   Partie de Campagne.

'And the lovers, sensual, jealous, cruel, like any one of us,
have, without recourse to petrified endearments, more love
in their little fingers than the whole content of the last

five years of British pictures, specifically dedicated to sacred and profane variations on the theme.'
Quai des Orfèvres.

'But it is revealed to us by an artist who filches the essential detail out of each small scene and thereby gives the film tempo.'
Farrebique.

'I estimate that I've spent sixty hours of my life looking at Marx Brothers' films, cosseting thereby a deep-seated anarchism.'
A Night in Casablanca.

Winnington should become a screen-writer, in spite of his avowed intention to continue 'the strange life' of the film critic as long as enthusiasm and eyesight hold out. He says:

'I think we can say that film technique has nearly advanced to the point at which the artist could control his medium wholly and thus bring it into the category of an art. The missing element is the artist himself, and we will find him, not as a director or producer, but as a writer who inscribes on paper, with a completely visual power of writing, the thing that will be put down into celluloid by craftsmen. He will at all points control these craftsmen to the extent that in their individual spheres they are subservient to the film as a whole.'

I reply to this, go ahead and try. Publish your scripts if they will not first make them into films. This next half-century has got to see the emergence of the film artist and the film addict from the present economic prison-house. Creative battles such as these can be fought on paper as well as on celluloid by those with the film instinct in their pens. It will be the only way so long as entertainment films go on costing at least forty pounds a second to produce.

OTHER BOOKS RECEIVED

Friese-Greene – Close-up of an Inventor, Ray Allister (Marsland Publications, 12s. 6d.).

I have seldom read a sadder book than this. The author, in an easily read narrative style, has brought vividly to life one of the gayest, most exuberant, and most tragic figures of British film history.

Art and Design in the British Film, Edward Carrick (Dennis Dobson, 18s.).

A beautifully produced book, of which Dobson's can be proud. A valuable work of reference for a very limited public, with one or two puzzling omissions.

Soviet Cinema, Thorold Dickinson and Catherine de la Roche, and *Fifty Years of German Film*, H. H. Wollenberg (Falcon Press, 12s. 6d. each).

Two in the series initiated with *Twenty Years of British Film*. These are better produced and well illustrated. The text is in the main good, the illustrations excellent. The German volume appears to suffer somewhat from compression.

Les Pionniers du Cinéma, 1897–1909, Georges Sadoul (Editions Denoël, Paris, 900 frs.).

This is the second volume of Sadoul's four-decker *Histoire Générale du Cinéma*. As far as it has gone, this work must rank as the most comprehensive and erudite (in the best sense) of film histories. Vol. I dealt with the development of the technique of producing moving images, leading up to 1897. Vol. II carries us a stage farther by introducing the early technicians who adopted the baby and brought it up. If the scope and authoritative examination of detail is maintained in the two volumes to come, it is to be hoped that an English translation will be published.

INDEX

This index refers to principal entries. Bold indicates a part number, normal type the page number within that part. Contributors are indicated by an asterisk.

A Nous la Liberté, **1** 36, **3** 22
Actors' Laboratory, **2** 61
Adamah, **5** 39–40
Addinsell, Richard, **6** 94
Admiral Nakhimov, **1** 52, 84, **4** 25
Adrievsky, Alexander, **1** 85
Affaire Jakob Blum, **8** 49
Afsporet, **3** 64
Agfacolor, **1** 39, **3** 18, **4** 114–17, **9** 78–80
Akselrod, Nathan, **5** 38–39
Alexander Nevsky, **1** 37, **7** 13, 15
Alexandrov, G. V., **1** 84, **3** 37, **4** 80, **7** 10–16
Alma Ata Studios, **1** 85–86, **2** 66
Alwyn, William, **1** 35, **2** 23, **3** 15–16, 41, **5** 15
Ambler, Eric, **9** 22–25
Anchors Aweigh, **1** 27
Andriot, Lucien, **1** 38
Anges du Péché, Les, **8** 66
Animal Crackers, **7** 72
Annensky, Isidor, **1** 85
Anscolor, **9** 81
*Anstey, Edgar, **4** 114–17, 126, **9** 17–21
Applause, **1** 20
Arias, Pepe, **4** 102
*Arletty **7**, 17–24
Armendariz, Pedro, **6** 78–79
Army General, The, **1** 85, **2** 69
Arnstam, L., **1** 84, **2** 52, 66, **3** 36
Arsenic and Old Lace, **7** 32
Artamonov and Sons, **1** 29
*Asquith, Anthony, **1** 10–26, 120, **5** 34
Associated British Picture Corporation, **7** 84–85
Association of Cine Technicians (ACT), **3** 42–48, **4** 8, **7** 89
L'Atalante, **1** 78, **6** 122

Atlantis, **7** 59
Aurenche, Jean, **1** 75, **8** 51–70
Auric, Georges, **1** 35, **8** 56
*Auriol, Jean Georges, **5** 94, **8** 51
Autant-Lara, Claude, **1** 75, 77, 78, **3** 83, **5** 73, **8** 64–65

Babochkin, Boris, **6** 107
*Batchelor, Joy, **8** 9–14
Bächlin, Peter, **4** 123–24
*Balcon, Sir Michael, **1** 66–73, 121, **2** 20, **7** 59, **9** 10
Barandov Studios, **1** 54
Baron Fantôme, **8** 55
Barrault, Jean-Louis, **2** 52, **8** 23
Basse, Wilfred, **9** 117
Bataille du Rail, La, **1** 75, **2** 53
Bath, Hubert, **6** 94
Battleship Potemkin, The, **6** 116, **7** 10–11, 15, 67, 92, **8** 123–26
Bax, Sir Arnold, **4** 17, 42, **8** 110–116
*Baxter, R. K. Neilson (Molyneux), **1** 37–39, 117–19, 120, **2** 25–28, 91–92, **3** 18–20, 68–71, 92–93, **5** 19–21, 92–95, **7** 83–90, 125–28, **9** 82–87
Beauty and the Beast (La Belle et la Bête), **1** 75, **2** 70–72, **4** 106, **8** 9, 55
Beaver, Jack, **6** 94
Bech, Lily, **2** 78
Becker, Jacques, **1** 77, **2** 47–49, **8** 52, 66
*Benoit-Lévy, Jean, **1** 117–19, **2** 39, **4** 126
Bérard, Christian, **2** 72
Berlioz, Hector, **1** 32
Berners, Lord, **5** 17
Bessy, Maurice, **5** 93
Best Years of our Lives, The, **5** 28

Bête Humaine, La, **6** 123, **8** 58
Bezhin Meadow, **7** 13
Blackmail, **1** 23–24
Blakeston, Oswell, **8** 175, **9** 32
Bliss, Sir Arthur, **1** 36, **2** 15, 21, 23, **4** 17, 41, **6** 91, 94
Blue Angel, The, **6** 11
Blue Dahlia, The, **1** 33
Bond, Jack, **4** 120–122, 126
Boomerang, **3** 12, 14
Border Street (Poland), **8** 50
Borneman, Ernest, **7** 96–106
Borrodaile, Osmond, **9** 12
Bost, Pierre, **1** 75
Boulting, Davide, **7** 125–28
Box, Sydney, **3** 49–52, 95
Bracho, Julio, **6** 75
Brasseur, Pierre, **2** 49, 52
Brecht, Bert, **9** 119–20
Breen, Joseph, **7** 128
Bresson, Robert, **1** 75, 77, **8** 66
*Brichta, Jindrich, **3** 53–58, 95
Brief Encounter, **1** 34, 36, 37–38, **3** 11, 32, **4** 14, 27–35, 108, **7** 91 **8** 75, **9** 95–96
British Board of Film Censors, **9** 61–66
British Kinematograph Society, **4** 7
Britten, Sir Benjamin, **1** 35, **4** 17, 41, **6** 96
Brumes d'Automne, **6** 118
*Brunius, Jacques, **5** 53–63, 96
Buñuel, Luis, **1** 79, **5** 61–62, **8** 59
Burgess, George, **1** 3–8
Burov, Semyon, **4** 76–82, 126
Buttolph, David, **1** 37

Cabinet of Dr Caligari, The, **1** 24, **3** 29, **6** 54, 117, **9** 116
Cabrera, Pancho, **6** 75
Caesar and Cleopatra, **1** 33, 35, **6** 13
Cameron, Ken, **8** 123
Cantinflas (Mario Moreno), **6** 76–77
Canudo, Ricciotto, **5** 55
Capra, Frank, **1** 33, **7** 25–34
Captain Boycott, **7** 91
Captive Heart, The, **1** 33

Caravan, **1** 33
Carmen, **1** 78, 104
Carné, Marcel, **1** 75–79, **2** 47, 52–53, 70–73, **3** 81–82, **4** 106, **8** 53–54
*Carter, Everett, **4** 52–68, 126
Casarès, Maria, **1** 75
*Castillo, Raymond del, **4** 100–104, 126
Cavalcanti, Alberto, **1** 69, 79, **5** 59–62
*Cave, G. Clement, **7** 50–54
Celos (Jealousy), **4** 23
Central Office of Information (COI), **7** 88, 103, **9** 17
Chalais, François, **1** 79
Chapaev, **4** 76–77, **6** 107
Chaplin, Charles, **1** 12–15, 28, 108, **3** 22, **6** 14, **7** 77–82, 94–5, **9** 40–42
Chauvel, Charles, **9** 10
Chavance, Louis, **2** 46, 50, **8** 43–44, 54, 65–66
Cherkassov, Nikolai, **6** 107–108
Chevalier, Maurice, **4** 14
Chiaurelli, Mikhail, **1** 85, **3** 36, **4** 76
Chienne, La, **1** 78
Childhood of Maxim Gorki, The, **1** 29, 65
Children of the Earth, **4** 72–73
Chirkov, Boris, **6** 108
Chirskov, B., **2** 69
Christensen, Benjamin, **2** 76–77, **3** 63
Christian-Jaque (Christian Maudet), **1** 78, **8** 67
Ciel est à Vous, Le, **1** 76, **2** 51, **3** 13, **8** 67
Cinecitta Studios, **1** 81
Cinecolor, **9** 78
Cinémathèque Française, **5** 52
Citizen Kane, **4** 30
Clair, René, **1** 20–21, 79, 104, **3** 22, 82, **4** 14, 107, **5** 54–62, 73, **6** 42, 119, 127–28, **8** 68
Clements, John, **4** 39

Clouzot, H. G., **1** 75, **2** 50–51, **8** 65
Cocteau, Jean, **1** 36, 75, **2** 49–50,
 70–72, **3** 82, **4** 106, **5** 62, **8** 9,
 54–56
Cohen-Séat, Gilbert, **5** 92
Cole, Emile, **8** 13
Comandon, Jean, **7** 118–19
Consitt, Frances, **1** 119
Cooper, Gary, **3** 73
Coote, J. H., **9** 73–81
Corbeau, Le, **2** 51–52, **8** 65
Cordova, Arturo de, **6** 95
Cory, Hans, **2** 10–13
Cousteau, J., **7** 124
Coward, Sir Noel, **4** 27–35, **8** 75
Craigie, Jill, **8** 28–29
*Cranston, Maurice, **9** 26–31
*Crichton, Charles, **7** 44–49
Crime et Châtiment, **6** 123
Crossfire, **5** 82–85, **8** 47
Crown Film Unit, **1** 67
Czech Film Archives, **5** 52

Daquin, Louis, **1** 86–90
Dames des Bois de Boulogne, Les,
 1 75, **8** 52
Damien, Father, **1** 33, **2** 31
*Daniels, F. E., **1** 112, 122
*Danischewsky, Monia, **5** 86–89,
 96
Dartington Hall Film Unit, **7** 123
Daves, Delmer, **9** 101
Davidson, Paul, **7** 57
Day of Wrath, **3** 67
Days and Nights of Stalingrad, The,
 1 52, 87
Dead of Night, **1** 34
Dearden, Basil, **4** 39
*Dekeukeleire, Charles, **8** 77–85
Delannoy, Jean, **1** 78, **2** 49, **8** 67
Delluc, Louis, **5** 55–62
DeMille, Cecil B., **1** 19, **3** 73, **7** 116
Dernier Atout, **2** 47
Dernières Vacances, Les, **8** 63
Desert Victory, **1** 35, 71, **3** 33
Deserter, **6** 120
Desire, **7** 66
Desnos, Robert, **5** 55–62

Dew, Desmond, **1** 35
Diable au Corps, **3** 83, **5** 73–76, **8** 64
*Dickinson, Thorold, **1** 36, **2** 9–15,
 93, **6** 62–72
Dietrich, Marlene, **2** 56, **7** 66
Dieudonné, Robert, **7** 20
Dillon, Carmen, **8** 21
Disney, Walt, **1** 110, **3** 22, **4** 30,
 8 12–13
Dmytryk, Edward, **5** 85
Dolin, Boris, **5** 78–79
Dolly Sisters, The, **1** 32
Donde mueren las palabras, **4** 102–3
Donskoi, Mark, **1** 85, **2** 69, **3** 37,
 4 110
Dorsey, Tommy, **1** 31
Double Indemnity, **1** 32–33
Dovzhenko, Alexander, **5** 81
Dreyer, Carl Theodore, **2** 77, **3** 62,
 67, **6** 118
Drifters, **7** 15
Druzhnikov, Vladimir, 110
Dryden, John, **6** 97
Duca, Lo, **5** 93
Duchamp, Marcel, **5** 59–62
Duck Soup, **7** 69–70
Dudoff (Dudow), Slaten, **5** 44,
 9 119
Dulac, Germaine, **5** 58–62, **6** 118
Dumont, Margaret, **7** 71–73
Durbin, Deanna, **1** 31
Dyke, W. S. van, **1** 108–9, **8** 96,
 98

Edge of the World, The, **1** 109, **4** 17
Eggeling, Viking, **9** 109
Egorov, Vladimir, **3** 76
*Eisenstein, Sergei M., **1** 13, 37,
 52, 84, **2** 65, **3** 79–80, **5** 34,
 6 101, 116, **7** 10–16, **8** 35–45
*Eisner, Lotte H., **6** 53–61
Ekman, Hasse, **3** 65
*Elvin, George H., **3** 42–48, 95
Emmer, Luciano, **1** 81
Enamorada, **6** 79
Enfants du Paradis, Les, **1** 75, 76,
 2 52–53, 71, **7** 23, **8** 62
Engel, Erich, **8** 49

Enough to East, **1** 60
Entr'acte, **6** 127
Epstein, Jean, **5** 94, **6** 119
Ermler, Friedrich, **1** 85, **4** 76
Escape to Danger, **1** 35
Eskimo, **1** 109
Espoir, **1** 78, **6** 122
L'Eternel Retour, **1** 70, 78, **2** 49, **4** 91, **8** 55
Eureka Stockade, **9** 13–16

Fadeev, Alexander, **4** 111
Fairbanks, Douglas, Sen., **4** 29
Falbalas, **1** 75, **8** 52
Falconnetti, **6** 118
Farrebique, **8** 63
Faure, Renée, **1** 75
Faustman, Hampe, **3** 65
Félix, Maria, **6** 75
Femme du Boulanger, La, **3** 33
Fernandez, Emilio, **6** 75–79
Ferno, John, **8** 96, 99
*Field, Martin, **6** 29–32, **9** 100–102
Fighting Lady, **4** 115
Figueroa, Gabriel, **6** 75–79
Film Actors' Theatre (USSR), **6** 106
Film and Reality, **1** 69
Film Polski, **4** 21
Film Societies, **8** 86–91
Fin du Jour, **3** 33
First of the Few, The, **1** 71, **3** 13
Fischinger, Oscar, **8** 12–13, **9** 117, 120
Flaherty, Robert, **1** 65, **8** 96, 100–101
Flanagan, Bob, **1** 34
Flor Silvestre, **6** 78
Fönss, Olaf, **2** 75
For Whom the Bell Tolls, **1** 106, **6** 19
Ford, Charles, **5** 94
Ford, John, **1** 33
Foreman went to France, The, **1** 71, **6** 91–92
Forgotten Village, The, **6** 81, 121
49th Parallel, **1** 71
Fowler, Harry, **7** 49
Freddi, Luigi, **1** 83

Fregonese, Hugo, **4** 103
Front Page, The, **6** 126
Furse, Roger, **8** 21

Gabrilovich, E., **2** 69
Gad, Urban, **7** 54, 57
Gabaldon, Roberto, **6** 75
Gallant Journey, **3** 13
Gance, Abel, **5** 56–62
Garbo, Greta, **1** 19, **2** 79, **7** 66, **8** 63–64
Garces, Delia, **4** 101
*Gassner, John, **3** 21–30, 95
Gelovani, Michael, **6** 109
General Line, The (The Old and the New), **6** 116, **7** 11, 15
General Post Office Film Unit (GPO Film Unit), **1** 69
Gentleman's Agreement, **1** 46–47, **9** 96
Gerassimov, Sergei, **2** 67, **4** 76, 111–12, **6** 106
Gertler, Victor, **3** 38
Gessner, Robert, **2** 60–61
Ghost that Never Returns, The, **6** 117–18
Gilliat, Sidney, **1** 35
Giudice, Filippo Del, **4** 33
Glenn, Jack, **9** 20–21
Goebbels, Josef, **8** 48
Gold Rush, The, **1** 108
Golden Star, **1** 84
Goldschmidt, Eric, **9** 121–124
Goldwyn, Sam, **1** 103, 107
*Gollings, O. F. A., **4** 83–88, 126
Goodman, Benny, **1** 31
Gottschalk, Joachim, **8** 49
Goupi Mains Rouges, **1** 76, **2** 48, **8** 66
Granger, Stewart, **1** 32
Grapes of Wrath, The, **1** 30, **3** 23, **6** 121
Gray, Allen, **4** 19
Great Dictator, The, **8** 49
Great Expectations, **2** 16–19, **3** 17
Green, Abel, **5** 64, 68
Grémillon, Jean, **1** 77–79, **2** 49, 51, **3** 81, **8** 54, 67

Grierson, John, **1** 60, 64–65, **2** 91–92, **3** 84–85, **7** 96, **8** 92, 95–97, 101, **9** 17, 40
Griffith, D. W., **1** 11–17, 28, **4** 29, **6** 114–15, **7** 15
*Griffith, Richard, 92–102
Grimault, Paul, **8** 14
*Grinde, Nick, **1** 40–51
Gronostay, Walter, **9** 115
Guitry, Sacha, **3** 82, **5** 74, **7** 20

*Halas, John, **8** 9–15
Halfway House, The, **1** 71
Hall, Ken, **9** 11
Hallelujah, **6** 120
Hamlet, **8** 16–24, 110–116
Hangmen also Die, **5** 27
Hanson, Lars, **2** 78–79
Harbou, Thea von, **6** 61
*Hardy, Forsyth, **8** 86–91
*Harris, Elizabeth M., **6** 80–86
*Harris, E., **5** 36–41, 96
Harris, Jack, **1** 38
Harrison, Rex, **3** 33
Havelock-Allen, Anthony, **2** 16
Hawes, Stanley, **9** 16
Hays, Office, **7** 125–28
Hellman, Lillian, **8** 29
Henry V, **3** 29, **6** 92–94, 101, **9** 30
*Hepworth, Cecil, **6** 33–39
Heredia, Saenz de, **2** 35
Herlie, Eileen, **8** 22
Herrand, Marcel, **1** 75, **2** 52
Hersholt, Jean, **2** 74
Hitchcock, Alfred, **1** 20, 23–24, **3** 26, **6** 119
Hitler, Adolf, **8** 48
L'Homme, **1** 75
Honnegger, Arthur, **6** 122
L'Honorable Catherine, **1** 76
Hope, Bob, **9** 45
Hôtel du Nord, **7** 20–22
House on 92nd Street, The, **1** 36, **3** 29
Housing Problems, **1** 60
Howard, Trevor, **4** 27–35, **8** 75
Hubert, Roger, **2** 50 **3** 16
Hue and Cry, **1** 13, **7** 44–49
*Huntley, John, **1** 33–37, 121,

2 21–24, **3** 15–17, **5** 14–18, **6** 91–96, **8** 110–16

*Ickes, Paul, **4** 95–99, 127
I Want to Live (Norway), **5** 43
I Know Where I'm Going, **1** 34, 64, **6** 12, **7** 41
In Which We Serve, **1** 64, **4** 33
Informer, The, **3** 28
Inglis, Ruth, **7** 126–28
Intolerance, **6** 114
Ipsen, Bodil, **3** 64
Ireland, John, **4** 17
Irving, Ernest, **5** 17
It Always Rains on Sunday, **7** 41, 92
It Happened One Night, **7** 29
Italian Army in the Liberation of the Country, The, **1** 81
It's a Long Way (W. Germany), **8** 49
It's a Wonderful Life, **7** 33
Ivan the Terrible, **1** 37, 52, **3** 79–80, **7** 13, 15, **8** 40
Ivanov, Sergei, **2** 29, **3** 71
Ivanovsky, Alexander, **4** 80
Ivens, Joris, **6** 127

Jacob, Gordon, **4** 18
Jacobsen, Johan, **3** 64
Jacoby, Irving, **8** 96, 98
*Jackson, Pat, **3** 84–87, 195
*Jackson, Ragna, **2** 74, 94, **3** 62–66
Jannings, Emil, **6** 116–17
Jarrel, Stig, **3** 65
Jaubert, Maurice, **1** 35
Jeanson, Henri, **1** 75
Jenkins, Jackie, **1** 30
Jennings, Humphrey, **1** 77
Jewish Agency, **5** 38
Johnson, Celia, **1** 36, **4** 15, 27–35, 38, **8** 75
Jour se lève, Le, **1** 78, **3** 11, **7** 22
Journey Together, **1** 34, 64
Jouvet, Louis, **4** 100, 104
Joyce, Eileen, **1** 36, 38, **2** 23
Junghans, Karl, **9** 118

Kanin, Garson, **1** 33, **3** 59

Kaplunovsky, Vladimir, **3** 78–79
Kaufmann, Michael, **5** 79–80
Käutner, Helmut, **2** 36, **3** 40,
  4 25, **7** 93
Kazan, Elia, **8** 46–47
*Keene, Ralph, **4** 47–51, 127
*Keir, Gertrude, **9** 67–72
Kelly, Gene, **1** 27
Kiev Studios, **1** 85
Kinematograph Renters Society
  (KRS), **7** 85
King, Henry, **1** 105
Kitty, **1** 27, 34
Kline, Herbert, **5** 39
Knef, Hildegard, **3** 40
*Knepper, Max, **7** 113–16
*Knight, Arthur, **9** 39–46
Knowles, Bernard, **1** 36
Kodachrome, **1** 97
Koppel, Walter, **4** 25
Korda, Alexander, **1** 26, **4** 7
Korngold, Erich Wolfgang,
  6 94–95
Kozintsev, Grigori, **5** 81
Kozlovsky, Sergei, **3** 78
*Kracauer, S., **9** 68–69, 95–99, 122
Kraly, Hans, **7** 63–65
Krasker, Bob, **1** 36, 38
Kuzmina, Elena, **6** 105–07

Lacombe, Georges, **8** 65
Lady for a Day, **7** 29
Lady Imp, **4** 102
Lady in the Lake, **3** 13
Laine, Elizabeth, **1** 119
Lallier, Etienne, **8** 61
Lamprecht, Gerhard, **2** 36, **5** 44
*Lang, Fritz, **1** 33, **5** 22–29, 96,
  6 53–61, 117, **7** 26
Langdon, Harry, **7** 27–28
Last Chance, The, **1** 29, 34–35, 55,
  4 23
Last Stage, The, **8** 50
Lattuada, Alberto, **1** 81, **3** 41
*Launder, Frank, **2** 80–82, 94
Laura, **1** 33
Laurentzsch, Curt A., **8** 117–122
Lauritzen, Lau, **2** 76, **3** 64

Laver, James, **1** 69
*Lean, David, **1** 36, 38, **2** 16–19,
  4 27–35, 127, **7** 91, **8** 75
Leaves from Satan's Book, **2** 77
Ledoux, Fernand, **1** 75
*Leech, Clifford, **6** 97–103
Leenhardt, Roger, **1** 79, **8** 63
Legion of Decency, **8** 29
Léger, Fernand, **5** 59–62
Legg, Stuart, **8** 95–98, **9** 17–21
L'Herbier, Marcel, **2** 46, **5** 58–62,
  94, **8** 54
Leigh, Vivien, **8** 31
Leningrad Studios, **1** 85
Leprohon, Pierre, **5** 93
Lermontov, **1** 29
Lerner, Irving, **8** 96
Lersky, Helmer, **5** 38, 40
Lévy, Jean Benoit, **1** 65
Levy, Louis, **1** 16
Liedtke, Harry, **7** 63
Life of Emile Zola, The, **8** 48
Linder, Max, **9** 40
Lindfors, Viveca, **1** 53
*Lindgren, Ernest, **5** 47–52, **8** 127
Lindtberg, Leopold, **1** 34
London Symphony Orchestra,
  5 15–16
Lorentz, Pare, **8** 92
Losey, Joseph, **8** 96
Losey, Mary, **8** 93, 95–97
Lost Horizon, **7** 30
Lost Weekend, The, **1** 27, 33, 36,
  38–39, **3** 12–13, 23, 33, 60
Louisiana Story, **9** 86–87
Love Parade, The, **7** 76
Love Story, **1** 31
*Low, Rachael, **7** 107–112
Lubitsch, Ernst, **4** 29, **7** 57, 61–67
*Ludwig, Emil, **1** 90–95
Lukhov, Leonid, **1** 87
Lumière d'Eté, **8** 66
Luna, Norman, **5** 39

M, **6** 58–60
Mackey, Percival, **5** 14
*Maddison, John, **7** 117–124
Madonna of the Seven Moons, **1** 33

Maetzig, Kurt, **7** 94, **8** 49
Magic Bow, The, **1** 36
Mains du Diable, Les, **2** 48
Major Barbara, **3** 22, **6** 91
Makarova, Tamara, **6** 105–106
Malraux, André, **1** 78, **6** 122
Malta G.C., **4** 17
Mamoulian, Reuben, **1** 20, **7** 26
*Mander, Kay, **3** 92–94
Mankiewicz, Joseph, **9** 101
*Manvell, Roger, **1** 102–110, 120,
  2 56, **3** 10–14, 67, **4** 12–16,
  5 9–13, 92–95, **6** 111–124,
  7 77–82, **8** 16–24, **9** 124–27
Marais, Jean, **2** 70
March of Time, The, **8** 93, **9** 17–21,
  44
Marey, Etienne, **7** 117
Margaritis, Gilles, **1** 75
*Margolis, Herbert F. (Fredric
  Marlowe), **2** 54–63, 93, **3** 72–75,
  96, **4** 7, **5** 82–85
Maria Candelaria (Portrait of Maria),
  3 39, 61, **6** 76
Marie Louise, **1** 29, 35
Marriage du Chiffon, Le, **1** 76
Marriage in the Shadow, **8** 49
Marshall, Herbert, **2** 56
Marshall, Nini, **4** 101, 104
Marx Brothers, **7** 68–76
Matter of Life and Death, A, **3** 18–19
*Mathieson, Muir, **1** 35–36,
  2 23–24, **3** 16, **4** 18–19, 41–46,
  127
*Mauerhofer, Hugo, **8** 103–109
Mayer, J. P., **3** 92–93, **9** 121–144
Mayer, Carl, **9** 116
McCarey, Leo, **2** 33
Meerson, Lazare, **1** 79
Meet John Doe, **7** 30–31
Meisel, Edmund, **9** 112
Méliès, Georges, **3** 22, **6** 117, **8** 9
Men of Two Worlds, **1** 36, **2** 9–15,
  4 17
Menuhin, Yehudi, **1** 36
Metropolis, **6** 56–59
Metzner, Ernö, **9** 118
Milestone, Lewis, **1** 20

Milhaud, Darius, **5** 41
*Miller-Jones, Andrew, **6** 42–52
Million, Le, **1** 20
Millions like Us, **1** 64
Mine Own Executioner, **6** 12
Minnelli, Vincente, **1** 33
Misr Studios, **5** 42
Molander, Gustav, **3** 64–66
Moley, Raymond, **7** 125–128
Molyneux, *see* Baxter, R. K.
  Neilson
Monopack, **9** 74
*Montagu, Ivor, **2** 86–90, 94,
  7 10–16
Moore, Kieron, **6** 14
Moreno, Zully, **4** 104
*Morgan, Guy, **6** 15–28
Mort du Silence, La, **1** 36
Moscow Arts Theatre, **6** 105
Moscow Studios, **1** 84
Motion Picture Production Code,
  7 126–8
Mr Deeds goes to Town, **7** 29–30
Mr Smith goes to Washington,
  7 25–31
Murderers are amongst Us, The,
  3 40
Museum of Modern Art Film
  Library (New York), **5** 51
Musical Story, The, **4** 80
My Father's House, **5** 39–41

National Film Board of Canada,
  9 17
National Film Library (Archive),
  5 51
Neagle, Anna, **8** 31
Neame, Ronald, **2** 16
Negrete, Jorge, **6** 75
Negri, Pola, **7** 63
Nekrasov, B., **5** 81
Neveux, Georges, **1** 79
New Entertainment Workshop
  (USA), **5** 71–72
New Teacher, The, **2** 67
Next of Kin, **1** 71
Nibelung Saga, The, **6** 57–61
Nielsen, Asta, **2** 76, **8** 54, 57

Night at Casablanca, A, **7** 73–74
Night at the Opera, A, **7** 70–71
Nine Men, **1** 54, 71
Nissen, Helge, **2** 77
*Northgate, Matthew, **6** 11–14
Notorious, **3** 26
*Novik, William, **2** 43–53, 56, 94
Now Voyager, **8** 27
Nuit Fantastique, La, **8** 54

O'Brien, Margaret, **1** 30–31
October (Ten Days that Shook the World), **7** 11, 15
Oetel, Kurt, **5** 44, **9** 118
Odd Man Out, **3** 11–12, **6** 19, **7** 41
O'Fredericks, Alice, **3** 63
*Oliver, Maria Rosa, **6** 73–79
Oliver Twist, **8** 110–116
Olivier, Laurence (Sir; later Lord), **4** 32, **7** 95, **8** 16–24, 110–16
Olsen, Ole, **2** 74–75, 76, **7** 56
On Approval, **1** 35
Orlova, Lyubov, **6** 109–10
Our Country, **1** 35
Our Vines have Tender Grapes, **1** 30
Overlanders, The, **4** 17, 37, **8** 10–16
Oxbow Incident, The (Strange Incident), **1** 70, **6** 81, 121

Pabst, G. W., **6** 119, **7** 94, **8** 49
Pagnol, Marcel, **3** 82, **5** 74
*Painlevé, Jean, **1** 78, **3** 69–70, **7** 123–24, **9** 47–52
Paisa, **9** 53–60
Parker, Clifton, **1** 15
Part de l'Ombre, La, **1** 78
Pascal, Gabriel, **1** 35
Passion (Madame Dubarry), **7** 58–59, 63–64
Passion of Joan of Arc, The, **3** 67, **6** 118
Paul, R. W., **6** 36–37
Périer, François, **1** 75
Philharmonia Orchestra, **5** 16–17
Philippe, Gérard, **1** 75, **5** 75
Pigaud, Roger, **1** 75

Polytechnic (Regent Street, London) Film Department, **4** 7
Pommer, Erich, **3** 40
Pontcarral, **1** 75, **8** 52
Popov, I. F., **2** 67–68
Poppe, Nils, **4** 22
Portes de la Nuit, Les, **1** 75, **2** 70–73, **4** 106
Portrait of Maria (see *Maria Candalaria*)
*Powell, Dilys, **3** 59–61, 96
*Powell, Michael, **1** 102–110, 122, **4** 18, 34
Presles, Micheline, **1** 75, **5** 75
Pressburger, Emeric, **4** 34
Prévert, Jacques, **1** 75, **2** 47, 52–53, 71, **5** 63, **8** 54, 61–62
Production Code (USA), **5** 71–72
Professor Mamlock, **8** 48
Prokoviev, Sergei, **1** 37, **6** 96
Protossanov, Y., **2** 29
Proud City, The, **1** 35
Prudhommeau, Germaine, **7** 121
Prozess, Der, **8** 49
Psilander, Valdemar, **2** 75, 76, **7** 56
Ptushko, A., **4** 81
Pudovkin, V. I., **1** 13, 52, 84, **3** 37, **6** 116, 120, **7** 11
Pyriev, I., **1** 84, **2** 66

Quai des Orfèvres, **8** 65
Queen of Spades, The, **1** 85
Quo Vadis?, **7** 56
Quota Act, The (British), **5** 9–11, **7** 86

Rafferty, Chips, **9** 13
Rahiba, **4** 22
*Rahim, N. K., **4** 69–75, 127
Raimu, **3** 33
Raizman, Yuli, **4** 76
Rake's Progress, The, **1** 35, **3** 33
Rank, J. A. (later Lord), **1** 33, 71, 107, 113–14, **2** 19, **4** 31–35, **5** 66, **6** 13, **7** 83–85, **9** 30
*Rawnsley, David, **9** 32–38
Ray, Man, **1** 79, **5** 59–62
Razor's Edge, The, **3** 14

*Read, Jan, 5 64–72, 96
Red Meadows, The, 3 64
Reggianni, Serge, 1 75
Règle du Jeu, La, 8 59
Reiniger, Lotte, 9 116
Rembrandt, 1 28
Remy, Jacques, 4 100
Renaud, Madeleine, 2 51
Renoir, Jean, 1 30, 33, 38, 78, 79,
    5 61–62, 8 58–60, 9 96
*Richter, Hans, 9 108–120
Rio, Dolores del, 6 75–79
*Road, Sinclair, 1 57–65, 121
Road to Life, The, 6 120
*Robertson, E. Arnott, 3 31–35,
    96
Robin Hood, 4 29
Robinson Crusoe (stereoscopy), 1 85,
    2 29, 3 71, 8 35
*Roche, Catherine de la, 1 84–89,
    122, 2 64–69, 3 76–80, 4 109–13,
    5 77–81, 6 104–10, 7 35–43,
    8 25–34, 9 86–94
Rochemont, Louis de, 5 70,
    8 96–102, 9 18–19
Rome Open City, 1 81, 4 106, 5 27,
    9 96–97
Romm, Mikhail, 2 66, 3 37
Room, A., 3 36
Room Service, 7 74
Rosa de Lima, 4 103
Roshal, Grigori, 5 81
Rosten, Leo, 2 56
Rosza, Miklos, 1 36, 6 94
Rotha, Paul, 1 77, 119, 7 122
Rouquier, Georges, 8 63
*Rowland, Richard, 7 68–76
Ruttmann, Walter, 9 110

Sadoul, Georges, 1 79, 5 92–93
Saga of Gosta Berling, The, 2 79
*Salemson, Harold J., 7 25–34
Salou, Louis 1 75
San Demetrio, London, 1 64, 71
Sang d'un Poète, Le, 1 36, 8 55–56
Sartre, Jean-Paul, 1 75
Saslavsky, Luis, 4 102
Savchenko, Igor, 1 88

Scarlet Street, 1 33, 5 28, 6 60
*Scherk, Alfred, 1 80–83, 121
Schneiderov, V., 5 80
Seashell and the Clergyman, The, 6 118
Sennett, Mack, 9 40
Seventh Veil, The, 1 31, 33, 36, 38,
    4 23, 102
Shchukin, Boris, 6 189
*Sheerman, John, 6 87–90, 8 124
Shklovsky, V., 2 69
Shuftan, Eugen, 9 117
Silence est d'Or, Le, 4 14, 5 73
Silone, Ignazio, 1 81
Sim, Alastair, 7 46
Simon, Michel, 7 21
Simonov, K., 2 66
Simmons, Jean, 6 14, 23
Sinclair, Upton, 7 12
Siodmak, Robert, 1 33, 9 117, 120
Six Juin à l'Aube, Le, 8 68
Sjöberg, Alf, 4 22
Sjöström, Victor, 2 78–79, 4 65–66
Smart, Ralph, 9 12
Smith, Percy 7 119–20
Smith, Sam, 4 34
Soffici, Mario, 4 23, 101, 104
Soldati, Mario, 3 41
Soler, Roberto, 6 75
Somewhere in Berlin, 2 36
*Somlo, Josef, 7 55–60
Song of Abai, 1 86
Song of Bernadette, 1 105–6
Song of Russia, 1 36
Song to Remember, A, 1 31
Southerner, The, 1 29–30, 38
Sovcolor, 1 87–89
Soviet Film Academy, 4 7
Spaak, Charles, 1 75
Squadron Leader X, 1 35
Speakman, W. J., 8 27
Spottiswoode, Raymond, 8 95–98
Spy, The, 6 58–59
Stafford, John, 1 81
State of the Union, 7 33
Staudte, Wolfgang, 2 36, 3 40,
    5 44, 7 93
Steiner, Ralph, 8 96
Stereoscopic film, 3 68–70, 8 35–45

Stevens, George, 2 56
Stiller, Mauritz, 2 78–79
Stokowski, Leopold, 1 31
Stolper, A., 1 52, 87, 3 37, 4 78,
    9 100
Story of G.I. Joe, The, 3 29
Story of Jesus Christ, 1 81
Strange Incident (see The Oxbow
    Incident)
Strange Interlude, 6 101, 8 23
Strike, 7 15
Stroheim, Erich von, 4 29
Sturges, Preston, 1 33, 9 97
Sullivan's Travels, 9 97
Sunday Dinner for a Soldier, 1 31
Suvorov, Nikolai, 3 76, 78
Sydney, Basil, 8 22–3
Sylvie et le Fantôme, 1 75, 77
Symphonie Fantastique, 1 32

Takhir and Zukhra, 1 86
Tarcai, Mary, 2 62
Target for Tonight, 1 54, 64, 69, 71
*Taig, Thomas, 5 30–35, 96
Tbilisi Studios, 1 85
Technichrome, 9 97–98
Technicolor, 4 114–17, 9 74–78
Tedesco, Jean 5 57
Tharnäs, Charles, 3 64
Theirs is the Glory, 4 20
They Came to a City, 4 39
They Knew What They Wanted, 6 59
They Made Me a Fugitive, 7 37
Thief of Bagdad, The, 1 39
Things to Come, 1 36
This Happened in Donbas, 1 87
This Modern Age, 5 21, 9 17–21
Thorp, Margaret Farrand, 3 92–94
Tidblad, Inga, 3 65
Tinaye, Daniel, 4 104
Tiomkin, Dmitri, 6 96
Tisse, Eduard, 7 10–16
Today and Tomorrow, 1 64
Tolnaes, Gunnar, 7 56
Tourneur, Maurice, 2 48
Trinka, Jiri, 8 14
True Glory, The, 1 35, 64
Tselikovskaya, Lyudmila, 6 110

Turning Point, The, 4 79
Tyler, Parker, 9 70

The Unconquerable, The, 1 85
UNESCO, 4 9, 7 96–106
Ustinov, Peter, 4 14

Vanel, Charles, 2 51
*Vargas, A. L., 8 71–76
Vassiliev, Bros., 1 85, 2 67
Vassiliev, G. N., 2 29
Vavra, O., 1 34
*Vedrès, Nicole, 1 74–79, 121,
    2 70–73, 3 81–83, 4 105–108,
    5 73–76, 93
Vergano, Aldo, 3 34
Vidor, King, 4 3
Vigo, Jean, 1 78, 6 119–20
Vilar, Jean, 1 75, 2 71,
Vinnitsky, Andrei, 5 78
Viot, Jacques, 1 75
Visiteurs du Soir, Les, 1 76, 2 47,
    4 91, 7 23, 8 62
Viva Villa, 4 77
Vivere in Pace, 4 14
Vodyanitskaya, Galina, 6 110
Volga-Volga, 4 80
Voyage dans le Ciel, 1 78
Vow, The, 1 85

Waiting-room of Death, 1 53
Walton, Sir William, 2 9, 24,
    4 17, 19, 41, 6 91–94, 8 22,
    110–116
Ward, Edward, 6 94
Warner, Jack, 7 46
Warrack, Guy, 3 16, 4 20
*Watkins, A. T. L., 9 61–66
*Watt, Harry, 2 19–20, 4 37,
    9 10–16
Watt, Watson, 7 121
Way Ahead, The, 1 71
Way to the Stars, The, 1 34, 71, 3 33
Wegener, Paul, 9 106
Weiss, Jiri, 4 12
Welcome to Britain, 1 35
Wellman, William, 1 33, 3 13
Welles, Orson, 1 38, 6 121

Western Approaches, **1** 71, **3** 34
White Shadows on the South Seas, **1** 108–9
Why We Fight, series, **8** 94
Wicked Lady, The, **1** 33–34
Wieth, Clara, **2** 77
Wilder, Billy, **1** 32–33, 36, 39, **9** 117
Williams, Charles, **6** 94
Williams, Sir Francis, **1** 63
Williams, Vaughan, **2** 23, **4** 42–46 **6** 96
Williamson, W. L., **4** 18
*Winnington, Richard, **1** 27–34, 111, 121, **2** 16–20, **9** 124–127
*Withers, Googie, **4** 36–40, 127
Wolf, Friedrich, **2** 36
Wolf, Julia, **4** 89–94, 128
*Wollenberg, H. H., **1** 32–34, 115–16, 120, **2** 29–36, **3** 90–91, **4** 118–19, 123–24, **5** 42–46, **6** 40–44, 125, **7** 61–67, 91–95, **8** 46–50, 127, **9** 103–107
Wolpert, Moura, **6** 128–30

Woman in the Window, **2** 28, **6** 55–56
Woman of Paris, A, **1** 12
Woolf, C. M., **7** 59
World in Action series, **5** 20, **9** 19–20
World of Plenty, **1** 35, 64
*Wratten, I. D., **1** 96–101, 122
*Wright, Basil, **1** 65, 77 **2** 37–44, 93, **8** 45
Wyer, Reg, **1** 38
Wyler, William, **9** 99

Yankee Doodle Dandy, **1** 32
You Can't Take It With You, **7** 31
You Only Live Once, **6** 61
Yurenov, V., **5** 80
Yutkevitch, Sergei, **1** 52

Zarchi, N., **2** 56–66
Zéro de Conduite, **6** 122
Zguridi, Alexander, **5** 77–78
Zhakov, Oleg, **6** 105–106
Zhelyabuzhsky, Y., **5** 80
Zinnemann, Fred, **1** 33, **7** 93, **9** 99
Zuiderzee, **6** 127